Comparative Arawakan Histories

Comparative Arawakan Histories

*Rethinking Language Family
and Culture Area in Amazonia*

EDITED BY
JONATHAN D. HILL AND
FERNANDO SANTOS-GRANERO

University of Illinois Press

URBANA AND CHICAGO

∞ This book is printed on acid-free paper.

The Library of Congress cataloged the cloth edition as follows:
Comparative Arawakan histories : rethinking language family
and culture area in Amazonia / edited by Jonathan D. Hill and
Fernando Santos-Granero.
p.   cm.
Includes bibliographical references.
ISBN 0-252-02758-2 (cloth : acid-free paper)
1. Arawakan Indians—Congresses.
2. Arawakan languages—Congresses.
I. Hill, Jonathan David, 1954– .
II. Santos-Granero, Fernando, 1955– .
F2230.2.A7C63   2002
972.9′004979—dc21   2001007537

PAPERBACK ISBN 978-0-252-07384-7

Contents

Acknowledgments

THE CHAPTERS in this book were written in 1999 and 2000 in preparation for the international conference "Comparative Arawakan Histories: Rethinking Language Family and Culture Area in Amazonia," organized by Fernando Santos-Granero and Jonathan D. Hill. The conference took place May 24–26, 2000, at the Smithsonian Tropical Research Institute (STRI) in Panama City, Panama, and was sponsored by the Smithsonian Tropical Research Institute and the Wenner-Gren Foundation for Anthropological Research. Fifteen specialists on Arawak-speaking peoples—twelve ethnologists, two archaeologists, and one linguist—attended the conference. Aside from the two organizers, participants included Peter Gow, Michael Heckenberger, Søren Hvalkof, Olga Linares, Alan Passes, Donald Pollock, France-Marie Renard-Casevitz, Dan Rosengren, Sidney da Silva Facundes, Hanne Veber, Silvia Vidal, Neil Whitehead, Robin Wright, and Alberta Zucchi. Two other specialists, Alexandra Aikhenvald and Nicolas Journet, were invited to attend the conference but unfortunately had to withdraw during the planning stages.

STRI provided funds allowing Jonathan Hill to return to Panama City in late September 2000, where he and Fernando Santos-Granero completed initial stages of editing the revised conference papers and completed a draft of the introductory essay. We are very grateful to the Wenner-Gren Foundation, STRI, and all the individuals named above for their support and effort, without which neither the conference nor this book would have been possible. However, the information and interpretations contained in this book are those of the editors and individual authors and not those of the organizations acknowledged above.

Comparative Arawakan Histories

Introduction

JONATHAN D. HILL AND
FERNANDO SANTOS-GRANERO

COMPARATIVE ARAWAKAN HISTORIES is the first attempt to bring together
the writings of ethnologists and historians who have specialized in the study
of the Arawak-speaking peoples of South America and the adjacent Caribbean basin. Speakers of Arawakan languages are best known to the general public
as the first indigenous Americans contacted by Columbus in 1492. Evidence
of the influence of Arawak-speaking peoples on European understandings of
the "new" world they had "discovered" can be found in the persistence of such
common words as *canoe, cacique, hammock, hurricane, barbecue, maize, cas-
sava,* and *tobacco* (Arrom 1999, xii, xviii, xxvii; Rouse 1992, 12). The phenomenon of cannibalism—a term originated in the Arawak word *caniba*—continues to intrigue and stimulate Western imagination and imaginary.

Arawak-speaking peoples spread far and wide across the landscapes of
South America and the Caribbean, more so than any other language family
before the great population declines that accompanied European colonization (see map 1). Archaeology, linguistics, and history point to the existence
of a dynamic, expanding diaspora of Arawak-speaking societies occupying
vast stretches of land along the Amazon and Orinoco rivers and their tributaries. The diversity and numbers of Arawakan peoples living in South America today have been greatly diminished, but they continue to live in large
concentrations in eastern Peru, southern Venezuela, central Brazil, northeastern Brazil, and southwestern Brazil.

The fact that contemporary Arawakan peoples are widely dispersed geographically bears witness to the grand scale of their movements and the far-
flung settlements they established across pre-Columbian South America and
the Caribbean. It also reveals the terrible loss of population and land that they

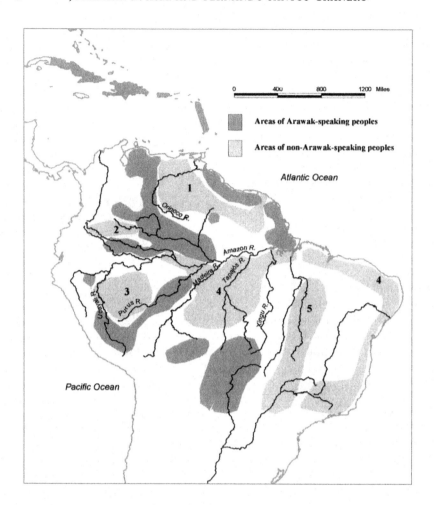

Map 1. Location of Major Arawakan Groupings at the Time of European Contact.
The non-Arawakan groups occupying main areas are (1) Carib, (2) Tukano, (3) Pano, (4) Tupi-Guaraní, and (5) Gê.

have suffered over the past five centuries. Their current spatial distribution spans wide distances across the continent, attesting to the continuous flow of trade and migration that had unfolded before European colonization of South America.

The first European to comprehend the immense geographic expanse underlying the Arawakan diaspora in South America was probably the Jesuit missionary and linguist Father Filippo Salvatore Gilij (1780–84). Working in the Middle Orinoco region during the late colonial period, Gilij was the first scholar to propose an underlying unity for the Arawak language family. He did so by associating a large number of languages spoken among peoples of the Orinoco basin with those spoken by peoples living as far away as the Llanos de Mojos in eastern Bolivia. Modern linguists continue to recognize Gilij's work as the first systematic linguistic study of a South American language family and as the point of departure for American linguistics (Noble 1965, 1–2; Durbin 1977). Historical linguistics continues to play a major part in current understandings of the Arawakan diaspora. It provides clear empirical evidence that the contemporary pattern of dispersal into distant regions was preceded by a pattern of continuous interactions across the span of South America.

The Arawakan diaspora has stimulated twentieth-century anthropologists to formulate a variety of theories about the peopling of Lowland South America.[1] Interpretations of the role of Arawakan peoples in the settling of South America can be found in volume 5 of Steward's *Handbook of South American Indians* (1949), Meggers and Evans's *Archeological Investigations at the Mouth of the Amazon* (1957), and Lathrap's *The Upper Amazon* (1970a, 70–79). Both Lothrop (1940) and Radin (1946) advocated the idea that Arawakan peoples served as bearers of "high-culture" traits introduced to other indigenous American peoples. In an article titled "South America as Seen from Middle America," Lothrop advanced the hypothesis that the Arawaks influenced the higher cultures of Central America and the Andes rather than the other way around:

> The present writer is of the opinion that the key to understanding of the higher cultures in the New World may lie in the expansion of the Arawak tribes, whose original home seems to have been in the Orinoco basin. . . . Did the Arawak expansion penetrate Central America in times early enough to influence the building of the higher cultures? We think it quite possible. We suggest that the Arawak afford a logical explanation in part for the existence of the "common Middle American material" recognized by Kroeber (q.v. Kroeber, 1930), that they offer a possible mechanism for the spread northward in early times of such typically South American traits as manioc, coca, the blow gun and the rubber ball game. Furthermore, Arawak art is essentially curvilinear and, as known in isolated areas, for instance the Antilles, it affords a common base from which specialized styles, such as Maya, Cocle, Marajo and Chavin might alike have sprung. (Lothrop 1940, 425)

In Paul Radin's *Indians of South America* (1946, 24), Arawak-speaking peoples were portrayed as having a highly developed culture based on the use of "the dugout, the bow and arrow, and the war club; an agricultural mode of life, with maize and manioc as staples; and, finally, a closely knit social structure with matrilineal clans, stratified classes, and a highly centralized chieftainship." They moved across South America, overwhelming or enslaving other indigenous peoples who were "more simple" (Radin 1946, 25, 45). The latter included their old enemies, the Carib, who "culturally . . . were to become almost entirely dependent upon" the Arawak and in some cases "were to be completely absorbed" (Radin 1946, 32).

Radin (1946, 32) argued that the Arawak were "the pioneers of a new type of civilization." They not only imposed their culture on previous, simpler populations but also adopted many traits from the peoples they conquered, whether forcibly or peaceably. When they came into contact with peoples who had a more complex culture, such as the Chiriguano, they lost most of their cultural traits. Radin (1946, 45) concluded that "in spite of all these weaknesses, their role of culture-bringers to an area of tremendous extent in South America is in no way diminished, nor can their cultural virility be questioned." From a current anthropological perspective, much of Radin's theory is flawed by an essentialized notion of Arawakan peoples as "peaceful culture-bringers" and by speculative chronologies that have little archaeological or historical backing. Nevertheless, Radin's early formulation did identify, or at least hint at, such cultural features as hierarchical social organization and transethnic identities. These features have been more fully documented and studied by subsequent generations of anthropological researchers.

The concept of language family has served as a major organizing principle in lowland South American ethnology for many years (Loukotka 1968; Mason 1950; Nimuendajú and Guérios 1948; Greenberg 1957, 1987). Studies focusing on societies with common linguistic affiliation have emerged from time to time (Basso 1977; Maybury-Lewis 1979; Butt-Colson and Heinen 1984; Brown 1984). On the other hand, the idea that linguistic affiliation has broad sociocultural significance has been undermined by approaches emphasizing culture areas consisting of complex mosaics of language use and cultural interactions (Murdock 1951; Steward and Faron 1959).

Our goal in this volume is not to reject this older, descriptive and relativistic approach to comparison but to revisit the twin concepts of language family and culture area in light of recent ethnographic, historical, and theoretical developments. The increasing attention ethnologists have given to long-term historical processes of change (Wolf 1982; Price 1983; Comaroff and Comaroff 1992; Schneider and Rapp 1995; Sahlins 1995) clearly demonstrates that there is no simple one-to-one relationship between linguistic affiliation and cultural pattern. Recent attention paid to the problem of essentialism in anthropology has added a further reason to maintain a healthy skepticism toward deterministic theories of language-culture interrelations.

The term *Arawak* is itself a complex category having problematic historical origins and meanings that have often been absorbed into mainstream anthropology without sufficient questioning (see chapter 2). Challenging, questioning, and critiquing the ethnological, historical, linguistic, and archaeological realities behind the term *Arawak* is crucial to any exercise in comparative history, including this one. As important as critical reflexivity may be, we intend it to foster rather than dampen the search for new comparative insights, retheorizings of earlier theory and method, and novel generalizations or hypotheses. In the process of critiquing the term *Arawak* and in questioning the concepts of language family and culture area, can we articulate new understandings of such terms and concepts, allowing for the emergence of new generalizations that avoid ahistorical essentialism? Are there cultural practices that can be said to be characteristic of geographically dispersed Arawak-speaking peoples? Regardless of how such questions may be answered eventually, it is important to raise them. The development of new comparative theoretical understandings in South American ethnology and in general anthropology greatly depends on asking the right questions. In a broader sense, reopening these older comparative questions in light of new theory and knowledge moves us beyond the sterility and defeatism of hyperrelativism and postmodernist doubt, ills that have afflicted anthropology in recent decades (Knauft 1996).

Thinking along these lines led us to organize an international conference focused on explicitly comparative goals that brought together specialists in Arawak ethnology, history, linguistics, and archaeology. In the initial proposal we encouraged all participants to emphasize interethnic processes such as the emergence of new religious movements, the consolidation of interethnic confederations, and the establishment of alliances with colonial powers against other indigenous groups. Although these specific topics have remained centrally important, we have seen the list of historical themes expand to include such topics as identity politics, ritual and political hierarchies, gender relations, cultural landscapes, and linguistic variations.

The immediate goal of the conference was to bring together specialists who had done fieldwork or archival research on Arawakan peoples living in the Upper Rio Negro region of Brazil, Venezuela, and Colombia, as well as those living in the sub-Andean lowlands at the headwaters of the Madeira and Ucayali rivers in southwestern Brazil and eastern Peru. We chose those two areas as the anchor points for our comparative project because the largest concentrations of Arawak-speaking peoples live there today. Linguistic reconstructions (Key 1979) show that these two geographically separate areas were formerly connected by a vast network of Arawak-speaking peoples who occupied large territories in the central Amazon floodplain as well as contiguous riverine territories extending up the Rio Negro into the Orinoco basin and Llanos to the north, up the mainstream of the Amazon/Marañon River, and along the Madeira River up to its source (see map 1).

During the colonial period, epidemics, warfare, missionization, and forced relocations decimated the Arawakan peoples of Lowland South America. Entire societies living in accessible coastal, riverine, or savanna territories either disappeared or were reduced to a handful of survivors. Huge losses of population and other major changes also unfolded in more remote interior regions such as the Upper Rio Negro and the lowlands of eastern Peru. In part because of their location at the margins of expanding, competing colonial empires, Arawakan and other indigenous peoples survived in greater numbers in these headwater regions than anywhere else in the Amazon basin. Nevertheless, even in the more remote areas of the Upper Rio Negro and eastern Peruvian lowlands, Arawak-speaking peoples suffered major population declines and loss of autonomy in campaigns to recruit forced labor during the Rubber Boom (ca. 1860–1920). Contemporary ethnopolitical arrangements in these two headwater regions reflect a series of profound adjustments, losses, recoveries, and transformations that unfolded along centuries of colonialism, rubber gathering, and other long-term interethnic processes.

Because our priority has always been to understand long-term historical processes of change that have produced contemporary ethnolinguistic geographies, we extended our original focus on eastern Peru and northwestern Amazonia to include specialists who have worked with Arawak-speaking peoples in areas of the Orinoco basin, the circum-Caribbean region, eastern Bolivia, and southern Brazil. Coverage of the latter areas was necessary to fill in some of the immense spatial and temporal discontinuities that have developed over centuries of western state expansion in Lowland South America (see maps 2–6). Comparison across widely dispersed geographic areas was informed by a rigorously historical approach to ethnogenesis and cultural differentiation. These processes have unfolded through the replacement or transformation of ancient trading networks by or into specific regional patterns of alliance.

Extreme geographic dispersal poses particular opportunities and challenges for a comparative study. In terms of opportunities, the contemporary distribution of Arawak-speaking peoples into widely separate geographic regions provides an ideal context to assess problems having to do with the relationships between linguistic affiliation and cultural practices. The Arawak language family is unique in the extent to which its member groups have expanded into a variety of physical and social environments. Arawak-speaking

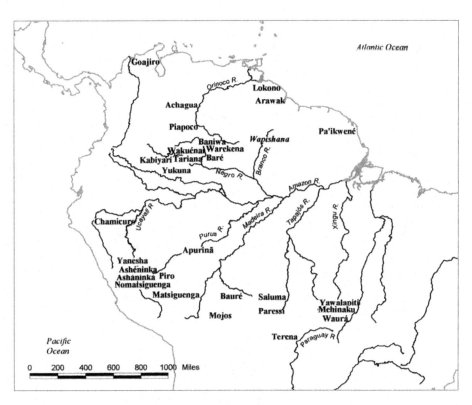

Map 2. Location of Contemporary Arawak-Speaking Peoples

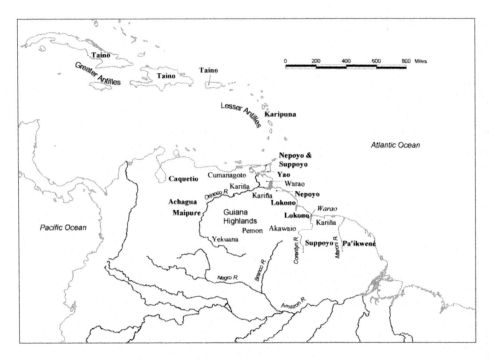

Map 3. Location of Caribbean and Northeastern South American Arawakan Peoples and Their Neighbors, Sixteenth Century

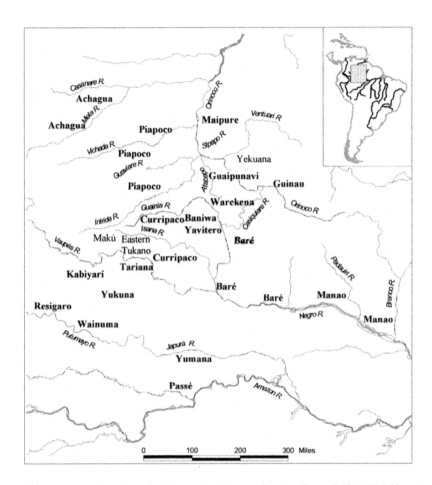

Map 4. Location of Orinoco–Rio Negro Basin Arawakan Peoples and Their Neighbors, Eighteenth Century

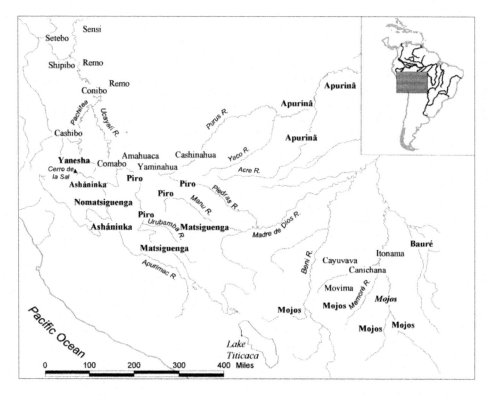

Map 5. Location of Eastern Peru and Eastern Bolivia Arawakan Peoples and Their Neighbors, Early Eighteenth Century

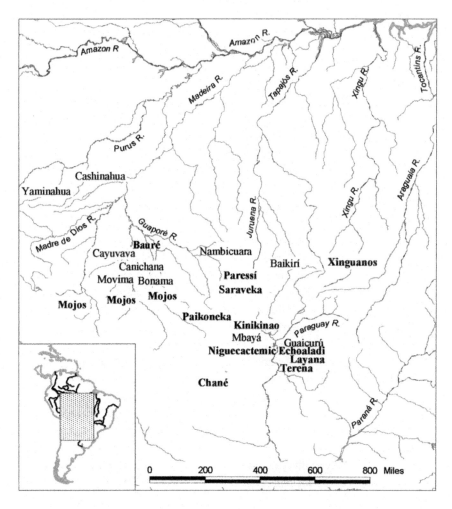

Map 6. Location of Southern Brazil Arawakan Peoples and Their Neighbors, Eighteenth Century

peoples entered into historical relationships with groups belonging to most of the major language families of Lowland South America: Carib, Tukano, Pano, and Tupi. In addition, archaeological and historical evidence suggests that they had developed exchange relationships with the large-scale societies of Mesoamerica, southeastern United States, and the Andes. In contrast to this immensely expansive cultural geography, most of the other large language families in Lowland South America are concentrated in more circumscribed areas, making it difficult, if not impossible, to sort out which common traits are a product of linguistic affiliation and which are the result of shared geographic and historical space.

At the same time, the wide spatial distribution that characterizes the movements of Arawak-speaking peoples and the different historical trajectories they have experienced have brought about starkly divergent patterns of ecological adaptation, social organization, and political structure. Perceiving underlying similarities when these are vastly overshadowed by apparent differences can be a daunting task. With increased emphasis on particular aspects of Amazonianist anthropology and the development of new research communities around Latin America, it has become increasingly difficult for individual scholars to gain extensive knowledge of all the different areas where Arawak-speaking peoples are found (see chapter 9, this volume; Knauft 1999). The sheer size and complexity of the historical and cultural processes that have marked and been marked by the Arawakan diaspora have eluded a comprehensive understanding by ethnologists and historians.

The comparative theoretical perspective we are seeking to develop in this volume is intrinsically historical. Previous applications of the comparative method to the ethnological study of particular language families have included a historical component, but scholars have not centrally concerned themselves with long-term historical processes. Along with this synchronic method of comparison came a tendency to reduce cultures to lists of traits or to limit them to normative structures. In contrast, the authors represented in *Comparative Arawakan Histories* make a concerted effort to draw illuminating comparisons between diverse historical processes and historically produced cultural practices. By focusing on cultural practices rather than on traits we hope to move beyond a routine discussion of the myriad details of social structure, ecological adaptation, and material culture. Our overriding aim is to identify and elucidate the underlying elements shared by most Arawak-speaking societies (see chapters 1 and 4). We cannot always assert that phratric organization, sibs, or clans are found widely among contemporary Arawakan peoples, for example, but we can point out that notions of descent, genealogy, and consanguinity are crucial to Arawakan conceptualizations and organizations of social life.

There is another important aspect of the comparative historical approach that we seek to develop in this volume: grounding the project in studies of culturally specific modes of historical consciousness. Similar processes of inscribing historic knowledge into cultural landscapes have provided a particularly fruitful point of comparison across separate regions. These indigenous ways of constructing history had already stimulated authors to undertake comparative studies before the conference (Hill 1989, 1993; Santos-Granero 1998; Zucchi et al. 2001; Vidal 2000). The importance of toponymy, topography, and related ways of imbuing landscapes with historical meaning has emerged as a major comparative theme in this volume (see chapters 7–10). Anchoring comparison to these local constructions of history complements rather than excludes the concern with macrolevel processes of migration and interregional trade in pre-Columbian times. It also helps to elucidate processes of postcontact expansion of colonial and national states.[2]

The underlying theoretical orientation of *Comparative Arawakan Histories* is twofold. First, we are concerned with reconstructing the long-term processes of interethnic change that transformed a continuous, flowing diasporic pattern characteristic of riverine Arawakan societies in the past into the dispersed pockets and clusters of Arawak-speaking peoples found in contemporary times. Second, we focus on the twin concepts of language family and culture area to explore the complex relationships between language and culture. Neither of these two emphases is more fundamental than the other. Rather, as the title *Comparative Arawakan Histories* suggests, the authors' intentions are to document, interpret, and compare sociocultural diversity within a single language family as specific language groups have become transformed across centuries of colonial and more recent history. The general effort to document cultural and linguistic diversity along a historical gradient is complemented by an interest in exploring the multitude of ways in which Arawak-speaking peoples have incorporated and engaged the effects of long-term processes of change, both precontact and postcontact, into narrative discourses, ritual performances, and topographic practices.

We seek to develop a long-term historical perspective that acknowledges important transformations and traumatic losses while refusing to reduce contemporary Arawakan societies to mere remnants of the past. These long-term processes of change are still evolving. In Peru, for example, the Asháninka (Campa) and Yanesha (Amuesha) struggled—successfully—to free themselves from political subjugation by the Shining Path and the Tupac Amaru

Revolutionary Movement during the 1980s and 1990s. In northwestern Amazonia, the Wakuénai (including the Curripaco) continue a centuries-old pattern of migrations to areas of safety, today in response to demands placed on them by the insurgent Revolutionary Armed Forces of Colombia. Despite centuries of intensive, extremely disruptive pressures that still continue, Arawak-speaking peoples have not simply survived; in some regions they have thrived and prospered.

For a number of empirical and theoretical reasons, a more global comparative study of Arawak-speaking peoples is only now becoming feasible. In-depth ethnographic and historical studies of Arawakan societies have lagged behind research conducted on groups affiliated with other language families in Lowland South America. This neglect results partly from the fact that most Arawakan peoples long ago adopted Western clothes and material culture through missionaries and trade with national societies. They simply did not conform (at least outwardly) to the exoticized image of "Indians" that implicitly colored most ethnographic studies written during the era when ahistorical modes of theory were in vogue. In addition, the vast geographies covered by the Arawakan diaspora, together with the tendency to focus research on specific indigenous localities, hindered the development of a critical number of ethnographers and historians working in close proximity. However, the theoretical turn toward critical, historical approaches to culture and power developed over the last two decades has had the effect of bringing Arawak-speaking peoples into the forefront of ethnological and historical research. Arawakan studies have greatly increased our understanding of complex, long-term, macrolevel historical processes in Lowland South America. *Comparative Arawakan Histories* bears testimony to the emergence of a new cohort of interactive scholars whose work amply compensates for the previous absence of detailed, reliable ethnographic and historical information.

Recovering vital knowledge about Arawak-speaking peoples is important not only because it gives expression to voices that have been silenced before but also because it helps us to understand more general historical trends affecting Amazonian indigenous societies. Clearly, the diaspora of Arawakan peoples has deep roots in the pre-Columbian past. Consequently, the comparative study of Arawakan histories necessarily sheds light on the kinds of social processes that probably generated long-distance migrations, interregional trade networks, and supraregional macropolities (see chapters 4–6, 8, and 10). We hope that the comparative perspective on long-term histories developed in this volume will give Amazonianist archaeologists a more solid foundation on which to construct models and hypotheses than the narrowly synchronic localized approaches that informed earlier ethnographic studies. As intermediaries in relationships taking place across regions of Lowland South America and with Andean and Mesoamerican state polities, Arawakan societies are extremely important for efforts to recover the pre-Columbian connectedness that existed among macroregions now severed by centuries of colonial demographic and political history. Moreover, Arawakan peoples were among the first indigenous societies to enter into direct contact with Europeans. Interactions between them have been ambiguous and complex, ranging from hostility and open resistance to peaceful relationships and even formal alliances.

Despite, or perhaps because of, the historical processes underpinning interethnic relations—both pre- and post-Columbian—we are able to identify cultural practices that are widely shared by contemporary Arawakan peoples. The persistence of these practices suggests that language-culture relationships are not purely arbitrary, that linguistic affiliation can remain connected with a set of particular cultural practices over long periods of time. In asserting that such a linkage is possible we do not intend to perpetuate the historical tendency of previous anthropologists and historians to essentialize Arawak-speaking peoples into exotic images of "friendly" and "peaceful" Indians, in opposition to "hostile" and "bellicose" native peoples such as the Carib (see Radin 1946). This polarization is a projection of early colonial political agendas and strategic positionings. It is not an accurate reflection of linguistically based cultural differences (see chapters 1 and 2). Be that as it may, the manipulation of linguistic classifications for purposes of domination during the early colonial period does not negate the long-term connections between linguistic affiliation and specific sets of cultural practices.

This point was brought home to us at the conference in discussions generated over Don Pollock's paper on the Culina and Sidney Facundes's overview of Arawakan linguistic classifications. When exploring issues raised in Pollock's work and relating them to broader contexts of Arawak-speaking peoples, many of us felt that the Culina differed so profoundly from the Arawaks that it was difficult to conceive of them as part of their overall diaspora. For example, the Culina practiced endo-warfare, and they did not form regional alliances with neighboring peoples. Our gut feeling was confirmed by Sidney Facundes's presentation, in which we learned that linguists had only recently determined that Culina does not belong in the Arawak language family (see chapter 3).

Initially, none of us had departed from the premise that there was a discernible set of cultural practices that could be considered distinctively Arawakan. We became aware of these practices only as the writing of the conference papers unfolded and as we read each other's work before the conference and commented on it at the gathering. The conference culminated in panel discussions summarizing emergent topics; this led to the articulation of a final statement. Here, we provide a brief overview of these comparative topics to suggest possible future lines of inquiry in anticipation of the specific ethnographic and historical cases covered by the particular chapters.

The broadest and clearest general feature to emerge from the conference papers is a distinctive pattern of sociogeographic flow, connectedness, openness, and expansiveness of Arawak-speaking peoples living along the major rivers of Lowland South America. This feature is most directly conveyed by ethnohistorical maps that attempt to reconstruct how Arawak-speaking peoples were distributed before the colonial period (e.g., Nimuendajú 1981; Key 1979; see also map 1). A pattern of continuous expansion is also evident from comparative linguistics (see chapter 3), ethnographic accounts of indigenous myths and rituals (see chapters 7, 9, and 10), and the archaeological record (see chapter 8). The far-flung expansion of Arawak-speaking peoples may have responded to demographic and ecological conditions, but our comparative project indicates that internal social and political dynamics are equally important (see chapters 4 and 8). Continuous, flowing, diasporic movement is not exclusively or distinctly Arawakan, yet it can be seen as characteristically so when taken together with a range of other practices.

Closely related to the flow, or connectedness, is the widespread occurrence of regional and even interregional or macroregional social formations organized around common sacred places. This feature may be superficially similar to the ceremonial central plazas of Gê-speaking and other indigenous peoples of Amazonia. But many Arawak-speaking groups have a much more strongly developed sense of intercommunity linkage in the organization of numerous local communities in relation to a shared central place. Together with a clear orientation around regional centers we find a variety of practices having to do with the appropriation of landscape. These include elaborate ritual performances naming places and movements across large areas, imbuing natural landmarks with historical significance, and imprinting landscapes with cultural designs (see chapters 8–11). Processes of landscape construction, including regional orientation to a shared central place, are not fixed in time and place. Instead, they are often replicated in newly settled areas, whether these are a result of internal sociopolitical dynamics or colonial processes of displacement (see chapter 7). Iterative toponymies, sacred cartographies, and enchanted landscapes are found among widely dispersed Arawakan peoples. Once established, these ethnoscapes become central to processes of appropriation of new territories, social reproduction, and indigenous historical consciousness.

A central feature of Arawakan sociopolitical formations is their open and inclusive character, which often expresses itself in the establishment of broad alliances between local and regional groups at both intraethnic and interethnic levels (see chapters 1, 5, 6, and 10). This feature is not found among other indigenous peoples of Lowland South America, among whom social and political relations tend to fragment, resulting in community-based political orderings that detract from the ability to coalesce into broader regional social formations.[3] An important social mechanism underlying Arawakan alliances is the existence of widespread networks of ceremonial exchange linked to sacred sites, temple-like structures, and hierarchies of ritual specialists. These exchange networks facilitated processes of political aggregation of like peoples and alliances across ethnolinguistic boundaries. The propensity to form cross-ethnic alliances was (and is) also manifested in the ability of Arawak-speaking peoples to rapidly create new regional confederacies in the context of colonial and national state expansion (see chapter 10).

Related to the openness and inclusivity of Arawakan social and political formations is the frequency and intensity of multilingualism, cross-linguistic ties, and the development of transethnic identities (see chapter 1). In eastern Peru we find "Panoization" of Arawakan peoples and "Arawakized" Pano-speakers. Similar processes of "Tukanoization" and "Arawakization" are at work in northwestern Amazonia (see chapter 11). In the Caribbean basin we find the so-called Island Caribs—Karipuna—speaking an Arawakan language during the early colonial period while simultaneously displaying Carib-derived forms of social and political organization (see chapters 1 and 2). That these linguistic processes have taken place in such diverse situations of interethnic contact strongly suggests they are intrinsic to Arawakan constructions of social identity.

The comparative study of Arawakan histories demonstrates with striking clarity that warfare was suppressed within Arawakan ethnolinguistic groups and within the larger regional formations in which they were embedded. Although exo-warfare between Arawakan groups and other, non-Arawakan groups is common in the historical and ethnographic record, there is overwhelming evidence of the suppression of endo-warfare. Organized raiding and slaving, institutionalized cycles of vendettas, and forms of collective violence linked to ritual practices are almost entirely absent from the historical and ethnographic records on Arawakan societies (see chapters 1 and 5). The relative absence of endo-warfare does not mean that Arawak-speaking peoples did not wage warfare against other non-Arawakan peoples or that they were more peaceful than their neighbors. There is plenty of evidence that Arawakan peoples did indeed practice raiding and enslaving of others; they had powerful war leaders, and in some cases they were known to engage in cannibalism (see chapters 2 and 10). Having said this, it is important to emphasize that warfare and its ritualization are not constitutive of Arawakan social identities, as is the case among the Jivaro, Carib, Pano, and Tupi. This striking contrast suggests the existence of a deeply seated Arawakan ontology in which ritual power and relations of trade and ceremonial exchange predominate over predation and conflict as basic principles for ordering social life and constructing sociality. The relative absence of endo-warfare may well be linked to the ability of Arawakan groups to form regional macropolities in the northwest Amazon, the Llanos, the southern Amazon periphery, and other areas where hierarchy is most clearly expressed. Alternatively, suppression of endo-warfare in eastern Peru and Bolivia may respond to the threat posed by expanding imperialistic pre-Incan, Incan, and Spanish states in the neighboring Andean highlands for nearly a thousand years.

Ethnographic accounts often characterize Arawakan "region-centrism" as primarily egalitarian, with intercommunal exchange patterns emphasizing balanced reciprocity between local groups of roughly equal strength and status (see chapter 5). However, we know from the historical and archaeological data that in the past Arawak-speaking regional formations developed into larger, more hierarchical polities (see chapters 2, 4, 7, 8, and 10). In both contemporary and historical contexts we find clearly articulated ideologies of social and ritual hierarchy based on notions of descent, ancestry, and consanguinity. These ideologies took the form of ranked social and political organization in some areas where inherited status was linked to marriage practices that ensured the reproduction of hierarchies (see chapters 1, 2, 4, 9, and 10). Awareness and enactment of genealogical knowledge, social histories, and mythic ancestries were much more pronounced among people of higher status than among lower-rank individuals, or "commoners."

Common expressions of hierarchy are heightened reckoning of genealogies, primogeniture, patrivirilocal residence, polygyny, rank endogamy, and other social practices that result in the overdetermination of descent relations among people of high status. Elaborate male and female initiation rituals involving sacred musical instruments, specialized ritual speech genres, and chiefly elite languages often accompany these social practices. At one end of the spectrum were groups such as the Taíno and Lokono, among whom, according to early colonial sources, were found chiefly elite lineages, rituals supporting hierarchical orderings, and ideas of divine ancestry. Hierarchy is also strongly present in Arawakan groups of northwestern Amazonia (Baniwa, Wakuénai [Curripaco], Warekena, Baré, Piapoco), the Llanos (Achagua, Caquetio), Lower Rio Negro (Açutuba), southern Amazon periphery (Bauré, Paressí, Terena, Upper Xingu), and eastern Peru (Yanesha [Amuesha]). Hierarchy is less clearly expressed among the Pa'ikwené (Palikur) of northeastern Brazil and among the cluster of Arawakan groups in eastern Peru and southwestern Brazil (Asháninka [Campa], Yine [Piro], Apurinã, Mojos). At the other end of the spectrum, we find groups such as the Matsiguenga, among whom social and ritual hierarchy is but weakly represented.

Variations among Arawak-speaking peoples living in different areas of Lowland South America are better understood as an outcome of differences in the degree to which ideologies of hierarchy are enacted in specific historical and ecological conditions rather than as a simple dichotomy between the presence and absence of hierarchy. The same variability has been well documented to exist within specific Arawak-speaking societies that construct hierarchy situationally so that hierarchical structures can alternate with or give way to more egalitarian modes of organization (Hill 1984, 1989; Santos-Granero 1986a, 1993a). Expressions of social hierarchy are almost invariably tied directly to ritual power, often manifested in exclusive rights to ritual performances, languages, chants, and paraphernalia (see chapters 9 and 11). Moreover, secular political leadership generally is associated with the power exercised by ritual specialists; sometimes it is even subsumed by the latter (see chapters 1 and 10).

The salience of ritual power as a central feature of political organization and its historical transformations is another theme that cuts across the entire Arawakan diaspora. The importance of ritual power manifests itself most dramatically in the emergence of powerful shamans, priestly leaders, or prophets in millenarian movements. Ritual power is equally crucial in understanding the ways in which Arawakan peoples have attributed sacred mythic and historical meanings to landscapes and, in particular, to the tendency to form regional polities based on shared notions of a sacred central place of origin.

The chapters in *Comparative Arawakan Histories* are organized into three sections, reflecting the theoretical approaches and substantive topics discussed here. Part 1, "Languages, Cultures, and Local Histories," contains three chapters that probe the comparative and theoretical issues of language family and culture area in long-term historical perspective. Fernando Santos-Granero's chapter, "The Arawakan Matrix: Ethos, Language, and History in Native South America," explores the diversity of cultural practices and social institutions encompassed within the Arawak language family by focusing on three important Arawakan clusters—eastern Peru, northwestern Amazonia, and northeastern South America—at the time of contact and in later colonial times. Although expressing skepticism about the use of the term

Arawak, Santos-Granero's research affirms the existence of an "Arawakan ethos," a set of sociocultural practices that taken together are characteristic of Arawak-speaking peoples. Neil L. Whitehead's chapter, "Arawak Linguistic and Cultural Identity through Time: Contact, Colonialism, and Creolization," examines the history and genesis of the term *Arawak.* It argues for a critical understanding of the notion of language family as a historical construct. Sidney da Silva Facundes's chapter, "Historical Linguistics and Its Contribution to Improving the Knowledge of Arawak," analyzes three languages that constitute a subgroup within Arawakan and reconstructs their protolanguage. He shows that even scientific classifications are historically circumscribed and open to error. Facundes's ability to demonstrate how the Apurinã language belongs in the Arawak family whereas that of the nearby Culina does not is a valuable example of how comparative linguistics can corroborate and enrich archaeological, historical, and ethnological knowledge. In short, the first section of this volume tackles the central theoretical task of rethinking the twin concepts of language family and culture area from three different angles: historical ethnology, critical historiography, and comparative linguistics.

Part 2, "Hierarchy, Diaspora, and New Identities," consists of four chapters that examine the topics of hierarchy and political organization from a historical point of view. In all regions of the Arawakan diaspora, hierarchy is accompanied by strongly centrifugal forces that encourage processes of fission, dissimilation, and genesis of horizontal trade relations. Michael J. Heckenberger's chapter, "Rethinking the Arawakan Diaspora: Hierarchy, Regionality, and the Amazonian Formative," assembles archaeological, historical, and ethnographic evidence from the Caribbean, northwestern Amazonian, and southern Amazonian Arawak-speaking peoples of the Maipuran branch to suggest that political hierarchy, sedentism in circular settlement patterns, and regionality are found in all these areas. France-Marie Renard-Casevitz's chapter, "Social Forms and Regressive History: From the Campa Cluster to the Mojos and from the Mojos to the Landscaping Terrace-Builders of the Bolivian Savanna," looks at an alternative form of political organization among the diverse "Campa" groups (Asháninka, Ashéninka, Matsiguenga, and Nomatsiguenga) and the Mojos people of eastern Peru and eastern Bolivia, respectively. Among them hierarchical elements such as rank endogamy and chiefly polygyny are present but are overshadowed by fairly egalitarian and horizontal intraethnic and interethnic trade relations extending across long distances. Peter Gow's chapter, "Piro, Apurinã, and Campa: Social Dissimilation and Assimilation as Historical Processes in Southwestern Amazonia," explores processes of assimilation and dissimilation among the Piro, Apurinã, and

Campa-Matsiguenga to suggest—in an exercise of "conjectural history"—how these patterns of interethnic relations might have arisen in eastern Peru. Alan Passes's chapter, "Both Omphalos and Margin: On How the Pa'ikwené (Palikur) See Themselves to Be at the Center and on the Edge at One and the Same Time," analyzes the spatial metaphors that accompany the appropriation of new territorial space and reproduction of identity among the Pa'ikwené of northeastern Brazil. The author uses historical and ethnographic evidence to demonstrate how the Pa'ikwené have transported and reconstituted their notion of a sacred central place in the aftermath of migrating from previous locations to the south of their present territory.

Part 3, "Power, Cultism, and Sacred Landscapes," explores the different ways in which ritual power manifests itself in the construction of landscapes, gender relations, political confederacies, and millenarian movements. Alberta Zucchi's chapter, "A New Model of the Northern Arawakan Expansion," marshals linguistic, archaeological, historical, ethnographic, and ecological data to build a new model for understanding the expansion of the northern Maipuran branch of Arawakan peoples in the Upper Negro and Orinoco rivers. Jonathan D. Hill's chapter, "Shamanism, Colonialism, and the Wild Woman: Fertility Cultism and Historical Dynamics in the Upper Rio Negro Region," demonstrates the mythic and ritual dimensions of landscape construction among the Wakuénai (Curripaco) and shows how local definitions of gender enter into these imagined geographies. Hill also develops a model of how Arawakan peoples of northwestern Amazonia construct an understanding of their own history as a series of movements, or expansions, away from and back to a central place of ancestral emergence. Silvia M. Vidal's chapter, "Secret Religious Cults and Political Leadership: Multiethnic Confederacies from Northwestern Amazonia," documents the emergence and transformations of large multiethnic confederacies along the Rio Negro and Upper Orinoco in the eighteenth century. Vidal argues for the central importance of sacred landscapes, mythic knowledge, and male-controlled ritual hierarchies in the making of powerful regional leaders and confederacies. Robin M. Wright's chapter, "Prophetic Traditions among the Baniwa and Other Arawakan Peoples of the Northwest Amazon," also examines ritual power and mythic knowledge in the construction of indigenous leaderships. But he focuses instead on their role in supporting millenarian movements and shamanic leaders in northwestern Amazonia.

The cultural practices explored in this volume are found in various combinations and patterns among specific Arawak-speaking groups of Lowland South America. We do not claim that any one of these practices, taken in isolation, can be considered to be unique to or distinctive of the Arawak language family. However, when most or all of these cultural practices are taken together, they outline a model of social and historical dynamics that is specifically Arawakan. The volume on *Comparative Arawakan Histories* is only a first attempt to identify and compare such cultural practices. We both expect and encourage future research projects that will test, refine, challenge, or extend the generalizations and interpretations made in this volume. Focusing on a single language family dispersed into widely different culture areas and ecological zones of South America has been extremely productive. By accounting for rather than ignoring macrolevel political history, we hope to fill in some of the middle ranges of comparative social history that lie between the global and the local.

Notes

1. For our purposes, the term *Lowland South America* includes the Amazon basin, the Orinoco basin, the Guiana Highlands, and other tropical and subtropical regions of the Caribbean and South America east of the Andes.

2. By using the term *post-contact,* we do not want to imply that the time of contact was uniform for all Arawakan peoples. On the contrary, the time of first contact with European peoples varied widely across different regions, ranging from the fifteenth to the eighteenth centuries. The term *post-contact* is thus a relative and multivocal term.

3. By calling attention to this contrast, we do not mean to deny the capability of many non-Arawakan indigenous peoples of Lowland South America to aggregate into larger multiethnic groupings in the face of a common outside threat. The Shuar Federation of eastern Ecuador and the Kayapo-led resistance to the building of a hydroelectric dam in Brazil are among the most visible expressions of this capacity in recent years.

PART 1

Languages, Cultures, and Local Histories

1 The Arawakan Matrix: Ethos, Language, and History in Native South America

FERNANDO SANTOS-GRANERO

THE RELATIONSHIP between language and culture has been the subject of much speculation in Western philosophy and social sciences. In the recent past, the tendency has been to contest the one language–one culture hypothesis implicit in the writings of eighteenth-century German philosopher Johann G. Herder, an idea that, under several guises, dominated early anthropology and linguistics. In his 1769 essay "On the Origin of Language," Herder asserted that polities are unified neither by the acceptance of a common sovereign power, as proposed by Hobbes, nor by a social contract based on the general will, as advocated by Rousseau (Barnard 1969). Instead, he indicated, first, that the basis for the sense of collective political identity was the sharing of a common culture and, second, that the emergence and reproduction of a group's culture are based on the use of a common language. Herder referred to units possessing a common culture and language by the term *Volk,* or nationality. Members of such communities are united by the collective consciousness of a common cultural heritage. This consciousness, which distinguishes members of a collective from those of similar communities, is what Herder calls "national character."

Herder's propositions found their way into historical linguistics and through it to modernist ethnology. The detection of connections between Sanskrit, Persian, and European languages by Sir William Jones in 1786 and the discovery by Jacob Grimm of the existence of regularities of sound change between different but related languages established the framework for the emergence of comparative linguistics. The Neogrammarians, a group of scholars working in Leipzig, formulated the principles and methods of the new discipline in the late nineteenth century. Its basic premise is that languages that have a large number of cognate words descend from a common ancestral language and thus belong to the same family. Implicit in this proposition is the assumption that speakers of the protolanguage constituted a culturally unified community and that its descendants share at least some aspects of that culture.

This was Brinton's (1891) approach in *The American Race,* which provides the first modern linguistic classification of Native South American languages. In addition to associating language and culture—in Herder's tradition—the author posited a linkage between language and race. Brinton (1891, 57) suggested, "Similarity of idioms proves to some extent similarity of descent and similarity of psychic endowments." In an intellectual environment in which evolutionism was becoming a dominant mode of thought, it was only a short step from here to assert that certain combinations of language, culture, and race were superior or inferior to others. Anthropology was quick to reject this argument by refuting the assumption that there existed an immanent connection between language and culture or race and culture.

In *The American Indian,* Wissler (1917) asserted that there are "no correlations between culture and linguistic type." According to him, the fact that speakers of the same language stock are represented in several cultural areas demonstrates that "language can travel independently of culture" (Wissler 1917, 332). Edward Sapir (1921/1931, 143) went a step further, declaring that "races, languages and cultures are not distributed in parallel fashion, that their areas of distribution intercross in the most bewildering fashion, and that the history of each is apt to follow a distinctive course." Franz Boas (1928) was equally definitive. From then on it became almost anathema in anthropology to propose a connection between language and culture, except as formulated in the milder versions of the Sapir-Whorf hypothesis, which postulate that language influences but does not determine the way we think and perceive the world (see Sherzer 1992, 274).

The notion of language family, seen by Brinton (1891, 57) "as the only one of any scientific value," became outdated among anthropologists and was replaced in subsequent classifications of South American indigenous peoples by that of culture area. Julian H. Steward's (1946–59) *Handbook of South American Indians* is the most outstanding example of this new approach. He and Louis C. Faron (1959, 26) argued that although linguistic affiliation and distribution have certain implications for the cultural history of South American Indians, "there is no direct relationship between language groups and culture." The principal value of linguistic classifications and the comparative method was to supply, through the method known as glottochronology, information on the dates of divergence of languages belonging to the same family and thereby on possible migration routes.

However, even the scholars who most firmly opposed the idea that people belonging to the same language family shared a common cultural tradition had trouble accounting for the numerous ethnographic cases that did not fit their model (e.g., Wissler 1917, 333). In fact, to explain the relative cultural homogeneity that characterizes members of the most important Amazonian language stocks, despite their widespread geographic distribution, Steward and Faron (1959, 26) suggested that they must have separated quite recently and in fairly rapid waves of migration.

A certain ambiguity with respect to the sociological value of the notion of language family is also found in two collections devoted to the study of Carib-speaking societies. In the first, Ellen B. Basso (1977, 17) identifies eight material and nonmaterial cultural traits of what she considers to be a typical Carib complex. However, Basso warns the reader that these traits are not uniquely Carib and concludes that most Amazonian indigenous societies fall "into general social and cultural units that often encompass local groups of different language affiliation and history." In short, after a painstaking reconstruction of Carib culture, we are advised that it is more productive to think in terms of culture area than of language family.

This same stance is defended by Audrey Butt-Colson (1984a, 11) and, even more strongly, by Simone Dreyfus (1983–84, 39–40), who argues that what is perceived as "Carib unity" appears to be based more on the characteristics of culture areas—geographic, ecological, historical, and sociological—than on linguistic affiliation. From a slightly different perspective, it is also supported by Whitehead (1994, 34; chapter 2), and by Urban and Sherzer (1988, 297), who assert that to have a better understanding of the history of Amerindian cultures, researchers should pay more attention to cases of actual multilingualism and to the more-than-one-language-per-culture hypothesis.

In this chapter I assess the sociological significance of the notion of language family by analyzing "Arawak unity," which has been the object of little attention from specialists. Based on the premise that ethnohistorical studies can be meaningful only if one adopts an interethnic perspective (Santos-Granero 1995), I examine the issue of "Arawakanness" by comparing Arawakan cultural and social organization with that of their most meaningful counterparts in three tropical regions: eastern Peru (Panos), northwestern Amazonia (Tukanos), and northeastern South America (Caribs). I argue that there is a connection between language and culture expressed in the fact that peoples belonging to the same language family share a common cultural matrix and a certain ethos.

In so doing, it is not my intention to perpetuate early colonial stereotypes or subsequent ethnographic accounts depicting the Arawak as "gentle, hospitable and cultured" pioneers, in contrast with other peoples, such as the Carib, characterized as bellicose "adventurers, cannibals and colonists" (Radin 1946, 23, 25, 49). It is not my intention to uphold the notion that such a connection is in any way immanent or essential. The dialectical relationship between language and culture is historical and can be understood only through history. Thus, together with determining what are the central features of the Arawakan ethos, I examine situations of interethnic cultural influence and exchange. I pay particular attention to the emergence of what I call transethnic identities, that is, groups that adopt the cultural ethos of another language stock but retain their language or, conversely, groups that adopt a different language but retain their ethos. It is in the boundaries between peoples of different linguistic affiliation that we may observe the intricate ways in which ethos, language, and history combine in the negotiation of ethnic identity, sometimes reinforcing existing ones and sometimes promoting the formation of new identities.

The Arawak-Pano Cluster of Eastern Peru

When the Spanish entered into the tropical forest region east of the Peruvian central Andes in the second half of the sixteenth century, they encountered two different types of indigenous societies. Along the Upper Ucayali and Lower Urubamba rivers they found two bellicose peoples—probably the Pano-speaking Conibo and the Arawak-speaking Piro—living in large settlements under the rule of powerful war leaders (Alès 1981, 93, 95). In contrast, the Arawak-speaking peoples living along the eastern slopes of the Andes lived in small, scattered settlements led by headmen with little political power (Santos-Granero 1980, 29; Renard-Casevitz 1981, 130). Because of the high uniformity of their cultural practices, these hinterland peoples came to be known collectively as Chunchos or Antis in the sixteenth century and as Campa in the seventeenth century. In the early 1900s, linguists began to refer to them as the pre-Andine Arawak (Rivet and Tastevin 1919–24).

In the second half of the seventeenth century, when Franciscan and Jesuit missionaries started working in the area, the Conibo and Piro monopolized trade along the Ucayali-Urubamba axis by means of large armed fluvial expeditions. These two dominant peoples are described as engaged in constant war with each other and with their weaker semiriverine or interfluvial neighbors: the Pano-speaking Shipibo, Setebo, Cashibo, Amahuaca, Mochobo, Comabo, Remo, and Sensi, who lived along the tributaries of the Lower Urubamba and the Ucayali River, and the Arawak-speaking peoples who inhabited the vast area along the Andean piedmont (see map 5, p. 10). The

Spanish divided these latter peoples into two large nations: the Campa (the present-day Asháninka, Ashéninka, Matsiguenga, and Nomatsiguenga) and the Amage (the Amuesha, known at present as Yanesha). For reasons of simplicity, from here onward I shall refer to all of these peoples as Campa, except when it is necessary to distinguish them from the Yanesha.

Pano warfare against the Arawak had a long tradition. Archaeological evidence and oral tradition suggest that the Arawak were gradually pushed against the Andean range by successive waves of Pano-speaking peoples who settled in the Ucayali River (Lathrap 1970a; Santos-Granero 1998). The Piro (Yine), who had reached the Urubamba River from the east (see chapter 6), also pushed the Arawak in a westward direction.

In addition, Pano-speaking groups were in constant war with each other. In general terms, the Conibo raided the semiriverine Pano groups, while all of them assailed the more interior, headwater groups; these, in turn, were continually raiding each other (Frank 1994; Erikson 1994; Townsley 1994; Dole 2000; Morin 2000). Pano endo-warfare, under the guise of blood feuds, slave raids, and pillaging, increased in colonial times as each group attempted to monopolize trade in tools with the Spanish (Frank 1994, 148).

Conibo raiders killed adult men and elderly people who could not work as servants and took with them their women and children (Biedma 1981, 95; Huerta 1983, 123–24). They also plundered their villages, stealing all valuable goods, such as spun cotton, cotton textiles, feather ornaments, and salt. Enemies were beheaded, their heads ritually insulted, and their blood drunk, mixed with manioc beer (Amich 1975, 108). As a sign of their courage, victorious warriors hung the heads and dried hearts of their enemies from the rafters of their houses (Biedma 1981, 95). Captive women were taken as cowives or servants. As a result, most Conibo men had two or more wives (Beraún 1981, 181). Captured children had to work for their captors but were raised as Conibo and eventually married into the group (Amich 1975, 93). The Conibo came to depend so much on pillage that their women no longer spun or wove cotton. Conibo pillaging and raiding created many enemies for them. To enhance their capacity for defense, allied Conibo groups gathered in large settlements of up to 2,000 people under the joint rule of their respective leaders (Amich 1975, 93).

The interfluvial Arawak presented a stark contrast with their Pano neighbors. As France-Marie Renard-Casevitz (1985, 1993) has pointed out, one of the outstanding features of pre-Andine Arawak social organization was the absence of endo-warfare. The only exceptions were the Piro, described in more detail later in this chapter. This in no way means that conflicts, hostility, and violence had been eradicated from Campa society but, rather, that aggression was canalized through intrafamily or intracommunity individual violence or through exo-warfare (Renard-Casevitz 1985, 90). When conflicts at the local level could not be resolved peacefully, they usually led to sorcery accusations and even to murder. However, these killings involved individuals rather than the social groups to which they belonged and never gave rise to intratribal cycles of vendetta. The only context in which intratribal attacks were admitted was in case of betrayal of common "tribal" interests, such as support of foreign invaders when this was not a collectively approved political strategy (see Biedma 1981, 162; Amich 1975, 73).

The rejection of endo-warfare among the Campa must not be taken as an expression of pacifism or a peaceful disposition. With the exceptions of the Yanesha and the Matsiguenga (Rosengren 1987), Arawak leaders derived much of their authority from their capacity as warriors. This was especially true of the Campa peoples of the Apurimac, Ene, Tambo, Ucayali, and Gran Pajonal areas, whose territories bordered on those of the Piro and Conibo. Although weaker in military capacity than their riverine enemies, Campa leaders not only defended their communities from enemy attacks but also waged an active war against them (Steward 1946–59, 3:537). However, the Campa shared none of the ritual war practices characteristic of the endo-warring Pano, and there is no evidence that they took war captives to transform them into wives or servants. This took place much later on, during the late nineteenth century, as a result of the demands of powerful rubber extractors.

Renard-Casevitz (1993, 32) explains Arawak suppression of endo-warfare as resulting from the need to present a common front vis-à-vis constant attempts by Andean state societies to subjugate them. However, the fact that other peoples facing similar threats—such as the Jivaro of eastern Peru and Ecuador—did not follow the same strategy suggests that the suppression of endo-warfare must be attributed to other factors. Risk of revenge feuding and slave raids was avoided among Campa groups by promoting regular dialogue between local leaders, intersettlement quarantine in case of conflicts, or, in extreme cases, geographic distancing (Renard-Casevitz 1993, 33). A concentric model of social organization, based on ever-increasing spheres of solidarity in which each local settlement created its own social network through marriage ties, residence rules, ritual gatherings, commerce, and political alliances, generated a dense web of relations of exchange, stimulating greater social cohesion.

Particularly important in this context were salt extraction and trade centered on the Cerro de la Sal, which each year, during the dry season, promoted the peaceful communication of hundreds of peoples belonging to the diverse groups that composed the Arawakan cluster (Tibesar 1950, 108). Central features of this kind of trade were formal trading friendships, which could be established only between Arawak speakers and were based on deferred exchange (Bodley 1984, 49; Schäfer 1991). After the expulsion of the Spanish in 1742, trade between Arawak-speaking groups was further enhanced by the emergence of numerous temples that functioned simultaneously as forges in the Upper Perené region (Santos-Granero 1987). Yanesha and Campa ironworks became the center of an active trade in iron tools that overlapped with the more traditional salt trading network.

Equally relevant for intra-Arawak cohesion were the pilgrimages and religious celebrations that took place regularly in places of panethnic mythological significance. The most important landmarks in the Campa sacred landscape were two hills in the Cerro de la Sal, where the Arawak venerated the sun (Salgado de Araujo 1986, 153; Ordinaire 1988); three stone divinities adored at Palmaso (Navarro 1924, 16); a site in the Gran Pajonal, where people gathered for an annual sun festival (Ordinaire 1988, 71); and, later on, the tomb of the messianic leader Juan Santos Atahuallpa in Metraro, a place that at least the Yanesha came to consider the "center of the world" (Carranza 1894, 23). Intratribal cohesion was further reinforced by what Ordinaire (1988, 91–92) called the Campa "moral decalogue," a ritual litany recited when two unrelated Arawak men met, in which the speaker lists all the moral duties owed to his interlocutor for the mere reason of being a fellow Arawak.

Despite the lack of centralized political structures, this intricate web of relationships and the values that sustained it allowed the rapid establishment of military alliances against indigenous or foreign enemies whenever necessary. Alliances could be regional and brief (Amich 1975, 73), or they could involve several regions and persist for a longer time (Biedma 1981, 181). More importantly, under special circumstances, the Arawak could confederate with non-Arawakan groups to undertake particularly ambitious military enterprises. The best known of these multiethnic military alliances was the one inspired in 1742 by the messianic and anticolonial leader Juan Santos Atahuallpa, who was able to persuade ancestral enemies such as the Campa, Piro, and Conibo to put their differences temporarily aside to join forces against the Spanish (Santos-Granero 1992). Whites were not able to reenter the region until 1847, allowing the native population to recover from the impact of colonial subjection.

The Piro occupied a singular place within the Arawakan cluster, for despite an undeniable Arawak linguistic affiliation they shared many traits with the riverine Pano, a fact that was noticed by early colonial chroniclers. This has prompted Peter Gow (1991, 31; chapter 6) to assert, quite justifiably, that "there is little justification for lumping the Campa, Matsiguenga, and Piro together on linguistic grounds alone." Like the Conibo, the Piro were great warriors and pirates, navigating in large flotillas of canoes along the Urubamba, Tambo, and Ucayali, to trade with or steal from their Panoan and Arawakan inhabitants. They took war captives and lived in big riverine settlements under the rule of influential war-trading leaders. According to at least one source, Piro warriors drank the blood and ate the flesh of enemies killed in war, much like their Pano neighbors and sometimes allies, the Comabo (Maroni 1988, 180; Huerta 1983, 121; Amich 1975, 107, 114; Vital 1985, 159, 164). Like most riverine Pano, they also practiced female circumcision (Amich 1975, 298). Piro clothing combined Panoan and Arawakan traits (Steward 1946–59, 3:544); whereas Piro pottery, although of a lesser quality, was very similar in design to that of the Conibo.

This evidence would be more than enough to assert that at the time of contact the Piro had undergone an intense process of Panoization. However, the most conclusive piece of evidence of the Panoization of the Piro is the fact that they did not reject endo-warfare as their Arawakan neighbors did, constantly raiding the Matsiguenga for slaves (Camino 1977) and combining trade, pillage, and slave raids in relation to the Campa (Zarzar 1983).

The Piro were not the only example of an Arawakan group that practiced endo-warfare, regularly organizing slave raids against other Arawak-speaking groups. In the context of the late-nineteenth-century rubber boom, large rubber extractors engaged the Ucayali Campa into this kind of slave trade through a combination of force and persuasion. The most famous Campa slaver was Venancio Amaringo, the leader of a large village of 500 people located at the mouth of the Unini River (Santos-Granero and Barclay 2000, 42–43). In the 1880s and 1890s, Venancio's followers attacked the Campa of the Gran Pajonal (Sala 1905–09, 12:85, 91, 64, 114; Hvalkof 1986, 24). Not surprisingly, however, like the Piro, the Ucayali Campa are described by contemporary sources as being very different from the Campa but quite similar to the riverine Pano (Samanez y Ocampo 1980, 83). Thus, we may conclude that the only Arawakan groups that practiced endo-warfare were those that had undergone significant processes of transethnic change.

The Arawak-Tukano Cluster of Northwestern Amazonia

Whereas in Peru most Arawak-speaking peoples were sandwiched between powerful riverine Amazonians and imperialistic highland Andeans, in northwestern Amazonia they had a dominant position, occupying both margins of the Rio Negro. In the late sixteenth century, these riverine Arawakan groups were the center of a vast network of indigenous peoples, which Silvia Vidal and Alberta Zucchi (1996, 113–15) call the "Manoa political macrosystem." This polity was divided into three confederated "provinces": Yumaguaris, Epuremei, and Manao. It was a multiethnic, plurilingual, and hierarchical political formation based on economic specialization, increasing levels of alliances between chiefs, and the subordination of weaker by stronger groups (Vidal and Zucchi 1996, 116). The polity involved peoples belonging to three linguistic families: the dominant riverine Arawak and the subordinate interfluvial eastern Tukano and Makú (see map 4, p. 9).

In the late seventeenth century, European competition for control of lands, resources, and Indians led to armed confrontation, slave raids, and rapid dissemination of epidemics. In turn, Amerindian competition for control over trade in European goods led to the rupture of old allegiances and to intratribal and intertribal warfare. All of these elements caused the breakdown of the Manoa macropolity by the early eighteenth century (Vidal and Zucchi 1996, 117). Its constituting provinces separated, and the groups that composed them regrouped (by revamping old alliances or establishing new ones) into three multiethnic confederations. These were composed of several allied chiefs under a powerful shaman-warrior leader who presided over large settlements and was in charge of complex religious ceremonies (Vidal 1999, 519; chapter 10). The new confederations comprised almost the same areas as the old provinces and were controlled by the two most powerful riverine Arawakan groups, the Manao and Baré (Vidal 1997, 120).

Beginning in 1720, the Portuguese increased slave raiding along the Lower Rio Negro. The Manao fiercely opposed their attempts to achieve control of the slave trade, which until then they had monopolized (Wright 1992b, 211). To counter their resistance, the Portuguese enrolled two Baré groups belonging to the Manao confederation (Vidal 1997, 32). This promoted hostilities between the dominant Manao war chiefs and their respective allies, leading to the defeat of the Manao in 1727 and to the subsequent "pacification" of the Lower and Middle Rio Negro. In 1731, the groups that had not been enslaved or exterminated were reduced to mission posts. Portuguese pressure eroded the power of the Manao and forced the riverine Arawak who had escaped colonial domination to move into the Upper Rio Negro.

Between 1725 and 1755, the Arawak reorganized themselves into three significantly smaller military confederations led mostly by the Baré, who replaced the Manao as the dominant Arawakan group (Vidal and Zucchi 1996, 119). Beginning in 1731, the Portuguese started raiding the Indian peoples of the Upper Rio Negro and Upper Orinoco region, where they clashed with the Spanish. To better confront the Spanish, the Portuguese recruited the paramount chiefs of the three Baré-led confederations as allies and commercial partners (Vidal 1997, 34). This enhanced intertribal competition for control of commercial routes. Between 1740 and 1755, the Portuguese enslaved and removed around 20,000 Indians from the region (Wright 1992b, 211). It is not clear who were the victims of Arawakan slave raids, but the evidence points to hinterland peoples, who were mostly eastern Tukano, at least on the right bank of the Upper Rio Negro.

Around 1755, competition between the Spanish and the Portuguese, attacks by Caribs along the Orinoco River, and intertribal warfare led to the fragmentation of the existing confederations into six much smaller and weaker ones (Vidal 1997, 38). Although these confederations were still multiethnic, comprising Tukano-, Makú-, and Carib-speaking groups, they were composed mostly of Arawakan groups, including the ancestors of the present day Baré, Baniwa, Wakuénai (Curripaco), Tariana, Warekena, and Piapoco. They consisted of groups of allied settlements or "tribes" united under paramount military chiefs whose office was hereditary (Chernela 1993, 20).

In the 1750s, these confederations were engaged in fierce warfare against Carib- and Arawak-speaking groups of the Orinoco River. The two most important groups, who vied for control over the region, were the Guaipunavi and Warekena, allied with the Spanish, and the Baré and Manao, allied with the Portuguese (Vidal 1997, 37; Chernela 1993, 19). With Spanish support, the Guaipunavi were able to vanquish their Arawak rivals in the Upper Rio Negro and displace the Carib from the Orinoco River. However, by 1759 the Spanish and Portuguese forced their former allies to accept subjection to their respective crowns.

During the second half of the eighteenth century, the Manao and other large riverine Arawak-speaking groups were exterminated, and large tracts of the Lower and Middle Rio Negro became depopulated (Wright 1992b, 211). To escape enslavement, the ancestors of the Baniwa and Wakuénai (Curripaco), who until the 1750s had been able to avoid direct European control, had to flee upriver, to the headwaters of the Isana/Guainía drainage area (Hill 1993, 46). In the 1780s, severe epidemics decimated the indigenous population of the Upper Rio Negro, leaving vast areas largely uninhabited. By the end of the eighteenth century, most of the riverine Arawak had been exterminated, reduced, or forced to flee into interfluvial areas. However, the collapse of the Portuguese colonial government of Manaus at the end of the century, and the inability of the Spanish to settle permanently in the region, created the conditions for the demographic recovery of the region's native peoples (Hill 1993, 46).

During this period, the Arawakan groups that migrated upriver along the Isana and Guainía rivers came into close contact with the eastern Tukano of the Vaupés basin (Hill 1993, 47). Some of these groups merged with the Cubeo (Nimuendajú 1927/1950, 165; Goldman 1963, 26). From this region, the Baniwa moved southward and westward into the Middle Vaupés River, where they clashed with the native Tukano-speaking population (Chernela 1993, 25). At about the same time, the Tariana expanded northward, from the Rio Negro into the Lower and Middle Vaupés River, displacing or absorbing the Tukano-speaking Arapaço, Pira-Tapuya, Mirití-Tapuya, and Tukano that they met on their way (Chernela 1993, 24). Finally, the Baré, who had disintegrated as the result of colonial domination, reconstituted through the fusion of Arawak, Tukano, and Makú groups and the adoption of Tukano or Nheengatú (*lingua geral*, "common language" or "trade language") as their common language (Vidal 1997, 41–42; Sorensen 1967, 682).

All of these events gave rise to an intensive process of ethnic and cultural exchange that led to the Tukanoization of Arawakan groups and the Arawakization of Tukano groups. This has prompted much discussion as to whether what are considered to be typical northwest Amazon traits—social organization based on exogamous patrilineal sibs, association of sibs into exogamous patrilineal phratries, origin myths depicting the emergence of hierarchically ranked sibs, and rites involving the use of sacred trumpets—are Tukano or Arawak in origin. Goldman (1963, 14) and Jackson (1983, 19) propose that the eastern Tukano preceded the Arawak; Wright (1992c, 257) and Hill (1996b, 159) suggest instead that the Arawak were the original inhabitants, whereas the Tukano were latecomers. Be that as it may, most specialists agree that at present northwestern Amazonia is composed of a variety of societies displaying Arawakan and Tukanoan cultural traits in different combinations. The center of the region, comprising the Vaupés river basin, is occupied by the eastern Tukano, who form what Jean Jackson (1983, 101) calls the "Central Northwest Amazon multilingual system." What distinguishes this cluster is language group exogamy, a practice that has led to multilingualism at the social level and polylingualism at the level of individuals (Sorensen 1967, 671).

The eastern Tukano are surrounded by Arawak-speaking groups to the north (Curripaco and Baniwa), east (Tariana and Baré), and southwest (Kabiyarí and Yukuna). These groups have a similar social organization but do not practice language exogamy. Additionally, they distinguish themselves from their eastern Tukano neighbors, among whom phratries are epiphenomenal, by the fact that their phratries are territorially localized and often function as political units composed of allied sibs under the leadership of phratric chiefs (Hill 1996b, 143). In between these two clusters are a series of Tukano-speaking groups that display what Stephen Hugh-Jones (1979, 19) has called "transitional features," that is, Arawakized Tukano traits or Tukanoized Arawak features. These groups include the Cubeo to the north, the Wanano to the east, and the Barasana to the south. The Cubeo do not comply with the rule of linguistic exogamy and for this reason are sometimes excluded by the Tukano from the category of "real people" (Jackson 1983, 97). They and the Wanano are closer to the Arawak than to the eastern Tukano in that they are divided into territorially localized phratries and link marriage preferences to inherited rank (Wright 1992c, 260; Hill 1996b, 146; chapter 9). Finally, the Barasana and other Tukano-speaking peoples of the Pirá-Paraná and Apaporís river basins reveal Arawakan influence in such cultural features as the masked dances associated with pupunha palm fruit (Hugh-Jones 1979, 19).

Jonathan Hill (1996b, 158–59) has put forward the provocative hypothesis that the two main features that characterize the Arawak and eastern Tukano— ranked localized phratries and linguistic exogamy, respectively—emerged in the postcolonial period of recovery. According to this view, to create social distance between the Arawak and themselves, the Tukano inverted the Arawakan practice of dividing the language group into ranked, exogamous phratries, promoting instead the emergence of ranked phratries through language group exogamy. In this sense, Tukano language group exogamy and Arawak ranked phratric organization would be mirror-image institutions.

Whether or not this distinction took place at such a late stage, it would explain why endo-warfare was more prevalent among the eastern Tukano than among the Arawak. Whereas phratric organization within language groups promotes intraphratric and interphratric alliances and therefore the formation of large political conglomerates, phratric organization involving various language groups seems to inhibit political aggregation. One of the most remarkable features of the northwest Amazon Arawak was their extraordinary capacity to build alliances between a variety of Arawak-speaking peoples under strong military leadership and for prolonged periods of time. Such alliances, which could be extended to include linguistically different peoples, prevented the eruption of internal warfare within vast regions. In this context, the instances of Arawakan endo-warfare reported in late colonial times seem to have been a response to increasing European demand for Indian slaves rather than an integral feature of Arawakan social organization.

This is confirmed by what we know of northwest Amazon Arawakan warfare through oral tradition. Robin Wright (1990, 222) argues that there is no evidence of intraphratric hostilities among the postcolonial Baniwa and that the few cases of interphratric warfare reported ended with the formation of alliances through marriage exchange. He concludes that Baniwa warfare was waged mainly against "other peoples," linguistically different or geographically distant, and was therefore "situated at the periphery of their society" (Wright 1990, 219, 222). Vidal (personal communication, 2000) confirms this view and adds that interphratric warfare generally occurred when one of the phratries did not comply with the Kúwai rituals. In contrast, there is plenty of evidence that in the not so remote past the eastern Tukano were in permanent war with each other (Goldman 1963, 162; C. Hugh-Jones 1979, 11, 63; Jackson 1983, 97, 133; Chernela 1993, 23–24). Except for this difference, Arawakan and Tukanoan war practices were very similar. Peoples belonging to both language families practiced feuding and raiding, took women and children as spouses and servants, and practiced war cannibalism (Wright 1990, 222–25; Goldman 1963, 162–64). In addition, the Baniwa decapitated their vanquished enemies to prevent mystical attacks from the dead (Wright 1990, 231), whereas the Cubeo wore the smoked genitals of killed warriors over their own as a war trophy (Goldman 1963, 164).

The Arawak-Carib Cluster of Northeastern South America

By the end of the fifteenth century, Arawak- and Carib-speaking peoples occupied most of northeastern South America and the Caribbean. The region's ethnic configuration suggests that the Carib had expanded as a wedge north from the Amazon River into the Lower Orinoco (Durbin 1977, 34). As a result, Carib-speaking peoples composed a solid mass, occupying the Guiana Highlands, the Gran Sabana, part of the Lower Orinoco, and large tracts of the coast of present-day Venezuela and Guiana, surrounded by Arawak-speaking peoples to the west, east, south, and north (see map 3, p. 8). Arawak-speaking peoples also occupied the Lesser and Greater Antilles, and there is evidence that by then they were also experiencing the pressures of the expanding Carib.

The Spanish recognized two large groups in the Caribbean region: a number of highly sophisticated hierarchical chiefdoms sharing many cultural traits, which occupied most of the Greater Antilles, the Bahamas, the Virgin Islands, and the northern portion of the Lesser Antilles (Leeward Islands), which generally but not always welcomed the Spanish peacefully; and a number of smaller and less complex groups, which occupied the southern portion of the Lesser Antilles (Windward Islands), who shunned contact with the foreigners or opposed firmly their presence. The sociological differences between these two clusters have been confirmed by archaeological information (Sued Badillo 1995, 17).

The diverse peoples belonging to the first category—the Boriqua, Lucayos, and other islanders—came to be known collectively as Taíno in 1836 (Whitehead 1995a, 92). In 1871 Daniel G. Brinton demonstrated that theirs was an Arawakan language—similar to that of the Lokono or mainland Arawak—and for this reason decided to call them Island Arawak (Rouse 1992, 5). The Taíno referred to peoples in the second category, the inhabitants of the Windward Islands, as *caniba* or *caribe* and portrayed them as bellicose, cannibalistic savages who constantly waged war against them. This label was later applied to mainland indigenous peoples who had similar cultural traits and, more particularly, to the Kariña of the Lower Orinoco. In time, the Kariña came to be referred to by Europeans as Caribe, Carib, or Caraïbe, whereas the inhabitants of the Windward Islands came to be known as Island Carib, which, as we will see, was an unfortunate denomination.

The Taíno were divided into three subgroups that differed slightly from each other in terms of language, social organization, and cultural practices (Rouse 1992, 5–7). The classic Taíno lived in Puerto Rico, Hispaniola, and the eastern tip of Cuba. The western Taíno inhabited Jamaica, the Bahamian archipelago, and Cuba, except for its western tip, which was occupied by the Guanahatabey, the remainder of the island's original population. The eastern Taíno lived in the Virgin Islands and the Leeward Islands.

Classic Taíno lived in large villages of several hundred houses, each inhabited by an extended family, ruled by village chiefs (Dreyfus 1980–81, 240). The houses of village chiefs were always associated with ball courts, a trait that might have been adopted through contact with Mesoamerican societies. Independent villages were loosely organized into district chiefdoms, which in turn were grouped into regional or provincial chiefdoms, each headed by the most prominent district chief (Rouse 1992, 9; Sued Badillo 1995, 78). Although these chiefdoms were not integrated into larger polities under unified leadership, there is evidence that under external threat they were able to confederate.

Chieftainships were divided into three ranked groups. At the top was the *casik,* or provincial chief, who could be a man or a woman. Paramount chiefs were transported in litters, sat in ceremonial seats, and were surrounded by servants, councillors, and wives. These external signs of power led the Spanish to call them "kings." Beneath chiefs and their families there was a class of nobles, who under the chief's orders commanded the rest of the people. At the bottom were the commoners, who had a low status and did most of the work but were not slaves taken in war (Dreyfus 1980–81, 241; Rouse 1992, 9).

The Taíno had priests, temples, and shamans, but life, reproduction, and the welfare of the people were guaranteed by chiefs who owned the mystical stones used to ensure fertility of the gardens, control of the weather, and safe childbirth (Dreyfus 1980–81, 242). Succession to chiefly office was matrilineal and avuncular, from chief to eldest sister's son. The notion of noble descent was central to Taíno chieftainships, as expressed in ancestor worship, ritual narration of chiefly genealogies, and endogamy among high-rank lineages (Dreyfus 1980–81, 243).

Endo-warfare, in the sense of cyclical blood feuds and regular slave raiding between settlements, was absent among the Taíno. Armed confrontation was limited to avenging murders, resolving disputes over hunting and fishing rights, or forcing a chief who had received a bride price to deliver the promised woman (Rouse 1992, 17). In none of these cases did warfare include the taking of women as wives or servants or of men and children as slaves. According to Taíno sources, the only other cause of war was defense against attacks by the Island Carib. Although the reliability of these reports has been questioned (Sued Badillo 1995), it seems to be confirmed by the fact that the eastern Taíno, who were closer to the Windward Islands, territory of the Island Carib, are portrayed as being much more militaristic than the western Taíno, who were farther away and buffered from their attacks by the classic Taíno (Rouse 1992, 18–19). Ritual war cannibalism, which was so prominent in depictions of the Island Carib, seems to have been absent among most Taíno groups (Rouse 1992, 146). However, it has been recently asserted that the Taíno of Puerto Rico and Hispaniola also practiced it (Sued Badillo 1995, 79; Whitehead 1995a, 96).

The Island Carib have been the subject of much discussion in anthropology. They were originally thought to speak a Cariban language. Later on, it was acknowledged that they spoke two languages: an Arawakan language that differed from Taíno (Island Arawak) and Lokono (mainland Arawak) and was everybody's mother tongue; and a Cariban language or Cariban-based pidgin that was spoken only by men among themselves or during their trading expeditions with Carib-speaking mainland groups. On the basis of oral traditions gathered in Dominica in the seventeenth century, it became accepted that this patterned bilingualism or gender dimorphism originated in the invasion of the Windward Islands by the Carib-speaking Kariña of the Lower Orinoco River, who killed most of the male inhabitants and took their wives and children. The Kariña were unable to impose their language but retained it as a prestige men's language and as trading language with their mainland relatives. In their Arawakan mother tongue these people referred to themselves as Karipuna—the term I will use to designate them from now onward—and in the Cariban men's language as Kalinago.

This traditional view has recently come under heavy attack by Neil Whitehead (1995a, 1995b; chapter 2) and some of his colleagues in an edited volume on the so-called Island Carib. They argue that the oral tradition on which this view is based is suspect and that Karipuna bilingualism could also be explained as the result of peaceful immigration of Kariña-speaking peoples into the islands (Boomert 1995, 32) or of a political and economic alliance with the mainland Kariña to confront sixteenth-century European colonial pressures (Whitehead 1995a, 93).

Be that as it may, what seems clear is that the Karipuna are an outstanding example of transethnic identity. Although their mother tongue was Arawakan, their social organization and cultural practices were closer to those of the Carib-speaking Kariña than those of the Arawak-speaking Taíno or Lokono. The Karipuna lived in small villages composed of a single uxorilocal extended family led by a headman and a men's assembly (Dreyfus 1983–84, 43). Village headmen who had a reputation for being courageous warriors were able to gather around them a large following through polygyny, a larger number of children, and the practice of exceptional virilocality for them and their sons. Old men's councils led groups of villages interconnected by marriages and other exchanges. Karipuna political institutions were based on frequent war and trading parties. Chiefs chosen for courage displayed in war led these expeditions, whose main objective was the taking of slave-wives and captives, some of whom were consumed in anthropophagous ritual performances (Dreyfus 1983–84, 43–44). The Karipuna waged war against their northern Arawakan neighbors, the eastern Taíno, from whom they took women and children, whereas they alternated war with trade with the Lokono, or mainland Arawak (Dreyfus 1983–84, 45).

The Taíno disappeared as a distinct ethnic group early on, in 1524, as a result of bad labor conditions, failed rebellions, and foreign epidemics (Rouse 1992, 158). During the remainder of the sixteenth century, the Spanish were not able to subject any of the other major groups of the region: the Caribized Karipuna, the Kariña, or the Lokono. However, as a result of preexisting conflicts and European pressures, by the early seventeenth century the Lokono allied with the Spanish. To counter their power, the Kariña allied with the Dutch and British. What began as an Amerindian conflict entailing warfare and a multiplicity of commercial, ritual, and marriage exchanges was elevated to the rank of "ethnic vendetta" (Whitehead 1990a, 360). It was in this context that the Lokono and Kariña, designated misleadingly as True Arawak and True Carib, respectively, became the models on which the stereotypes of the peaceful and civilized Arawak versus the warlike and savage Carib took shape.

They did not differ so much, however. The Lokono were not the peaceful victims of the Kariña and Karipuna, as they were depicted in colonial chronicles. They were organized in powerful chiefdoms interlocked in a large polity, which extended from the coast of Guiana to the Amazon, and linked the Essequibo and Corentyn with the Paru and Trombetas (Whitehead 1994, 38). Lokono settlements were also found in the right bank of the Lower Orinoco River and on the island of Trinidad (Whitehead 1988, 18). Early chronicles mention the existence of large Lokono settlements of up to 200 houses under numerous chiefs led by a priestly leader (Whitehead 1988, 12). There is also evidence of segmentary lineage and matriclan organization (Whitehead 1994, 39). Lokono chiefdoms were ruled by elite lineages in which transmission of chiefly status was, as among the Taíno, avuncular. The Lokono were also brave warriors who regularly organized and conducted long-term war and trading expeditions. In their raids against the Kariña and Karipuna they took goods, women, and slaves (Dreyfus 1983–84, 45). However, there is no evidence that they practiced endo-warfare; on the contrary, Lokono groups tended to establish extensive alliances. Some authors assert that, unlike their Carib neighbors, the Lokono did not practice exocannibalism (Dreyfus 1983–84, 45); others say they did (Whitehead 1995a, 99).

Strategically located along the lower course of the Orinoco River, the Kariña were at the center of a vast polity comprising the Orinoco River basin, the Venezuelan Llanos, the Venezuelan Guiana, and the Lesser Antilles (Biord-Castillo 1985; Arvelo-Jiménez and Biord 1994). This vast network was to a large extent a horizontal system composed of culturally and linguistically distinct units of similar category, integrated by relations of warfare and exchange. It was a decentralized polity in which no group dominated or oppressed the others.

Kariña social organization at the local level—very similar to that of the Karipuna—was based on numerous independent communities, each under the leadership of a war chief and an elders' council (Biord-Castillo 1985, 86). Village chiefs built their followings through control and manipulation of marriage alliances involving members of their extended family and through exogamous polygamy, mostly through capture of slave-wives (Biord-Castillo 1985, 95; Whitehead 1994, 41, 1995a, 96). In times of war several communities could ally to form a "province" led by a war chief elected from among the diverse village leaders, who composed his advising council. However, the authority of provincial war chiefs was temporary, and the position was that of *primus inter pares* rather than paramount chief.

The Kariña practiced both exo- and endo-warfare. The scope of warfare increased in the early seventeenth century, after the Kariña allied with the British and Dutch against the Lokono and their Spanish friends. Because of their access to European firearms and in response to European demand for slaves, the Kariña intensified slave raiding (Biord-Castillo 1985, 86). Alone, or in alliance with the Karipuna, they regularly attacked coastal peoples such as the Carib-speaking Yao of Trinidad and the Arawak-speaking Lokono and Palikur (Pa'ikwené) (Dreyfus 1983–84, 50). They also navigated up the Orinoco River and its tributaries, raiding Carib groups such as the Akawaio, Ye'kuana, and Cabré, as well as the numerous Arawakan peoples living along the Middle and Upper Orinoco (Whitehead 1990a, 365; Dreyfus 1983–84, 48; Biord-Castillo 1985, 87). Carib endo-warfare continued in postcolonial times (Farabee 1967; Butt-Colson 1984b, 114; Hoff 1995, 40–43).

The Arawakan Ethos

This quick overview of the Arawak and their neighbors at the time of European contact shows that there was no single Arawakan type of social organization and culture. On the contrary, Arawakan social and cultural patterns varied significantly. Nonetheless, beneath the important differences in form and structure there are a number of elements that keep reemerging and suggest the existence of a common Arawakan matrix, which, in turn, finds expression in a particular Arawakan ethos. I understand the notion of "cultural matrix" in the traditional senses of "womb" and "mold" but also in the newer, cybernetic sense of "network" (*womb* because it refers to the original Arawakan culture, the historically produced set of cultural perceptions, appreciations, and actions of which the Proto-Arawak were bearers; *mold* because, as in type-founding, the cultural matrix of a given language family leaves a certain imprint—which, I shall argue, is its ethos—in all its members). However, as a historical product, a cultural matrix is not a closed, integrated, coherent, and fixed whole but rather a loosely organized network that, very much like the Internet, constitutes simultaneously the background, framework, and source of information that informs the sociocultural practices of the members of a given language family. Thus, the imprint it leaves and the ethoses of its members have common elements without being identical.

In Aristotle's original usage, *ethos* referred to the prevalent tone of sentiment of a people or community. Anthropology has appropriated this Greek notion for similar purposes—the description of a certain dimension of a people's culture—but with widely varying meanings. In *Naven*, arguably the first attempt at reflexive anthropology, Gregory Bateson (1936/1980) uses the terms *ethos* and *eidos* to refer to two different but complementary dimensions of cultural "configurations." Bateson (1936/1980, 33) argues that the pervading and recurrent characteristics of a given culture not only express but also promote the standardization of individuals. In his view, *ethos* alludes to the "emotional tone" of a culture, the expression of the "culturally standardized system of organization of the instincts and emotions of the individuals." In contrast, *eidos* refers to the corresponding expression of their standardized cognitive aspects (Bateson 1936/1980, 33, 118). Thus, whereas *ethos* alludes to the tone, behavior, and system of emotional attitudes of the culture of a given group, *eidos* refers to its logic, ways of thought, and system of classification (Bateson 1936/1980, 265). Bateson does not state whether the ethos and eidos of a culture operate in conscious or unconscious ways but seems to suggest that they relate to the notion of "tradition" as unconscious to conscious aspects of culture (Bateson 1936/1980, 121).

Clifford Geertz proposed a similar dualistic conception of culture in a 1957 essay in which he contrasts the notion of ethos to that of worldview. In his use, however, the term *ethos* refers not only to the tone, character, and quality of a people's life (in accordance with the original Greek notion) but also to the evaluative elements of a given culture, that is, to its moral and aesthetic aspects (Geertz 1993, 127). In turn, the worldview consists of a people's ideas of order, their concepts of nature, self, and society—in brief, the cognitive, existential aspects of culture. Like Bateson, Geertz (1993, 130) argues that, considered separately, the ethos and the worldview, the normative and metaphysical aspects of a given culture, are arbitrary, but taken together they form a gestalt, a whole or configuration. He contends that ethos and worldview are related in such a way that each acts upon the other to render it meaningful and thus legitimate (Geertz 1993, 127). Unlike Bateson, however, Geertz (1993, 129) implies that both ethos and worldview are conscious aspects of culture in that they explicitly establish "the approved style of life and the assumed structure of reality."

In his *Outline of a Theory of Practice,* Pierre Bourdieu (1972/1993) sets about to explain social regularities—Bateson's systematic aspects of culture—without resorting to the concept of "culture," which he believes has been extremely reified. Central to his theory is the notion of "habitus," or "ethos," a term that he sometimes uses as a synonym (Bourdieu 1972/1993, 77, 82, 85). The notion of habitus dispenses with the dualistic perspectives of culture characteristic of previous analysis, integrating the emotional with the cognitive, the normative with the metaphysical, and the perceptual with the factual. In his view, habitus is a system of dispositions—schemes of perception, thought, and action—characteristic of a social group or class, which is the historical product of a given set of objective conditions of existence (Bourdieu 1972/1993, 85, 90). Among these objective conditions or structures, Bourdieu places particular emphasis on language and economy. The habitus acts as "structured structures predisposed to function as structuring structures, that is, as principles of the generation and structuring of practices and representations"

(Bourdieu 1972/1993, 72). The practices—and the dispositions of which they are the product—are the result of the internalization of the same objective structures while being indispensable for the reproduction of those objective conditions. They are normative without responding to explicit rules and are well adapted to their goals without being the product of conscious aiming (Bourdieu 1972/1993, 72). Moreover, although they are well orchestrated they do not respond to the action of a conductor; in other words, they do not function as ideological constructs.

My use of the term *ethos* is consonant with Bourdieu's rather than with that of Bateson or Geertz, for I conceive of the ethos of a people as express-ing not only one particular facet of their culture, whether standardized af-fective aspects of behavior or moral and aesthetic prescriptions, but as a set of perceptions, values, and practices, which are unconscious but inform the more conscious aspects of culture. The ethos of a people is made up not of rules, strategies, or ideological constructs but of unconscious dispositions, inclinations, and practices, which shape those rules, strategies, and ideolo-gies while being shaped by them.

However, because I am not dealing with the ethos of a group (or of a so-cial class within a group) but with that of the several groups that compose a language family, some allowances must be made. First, given that a certain ethos is the historical product of a particular set of objective conditions and given that the objective conditions of the several Arawak-speaking peoples have changed through time as a result of diasporic movements, occupation of different ecosystems, and interaction with different peoples, the Arawa-kan ethos should not be expected to be as dense and rich as the ethoses of particular Arawak-speaking peoples. In other words, given that the objective conditions that gave rise to the Arawakan cultural matrix have changed, the ethos shared by Arawak-speaking peoples today is more abridged and gen-eral. Second, although Arawak-speaking peoples share a common ethos or set of dispositions, the actual practices that result from them in particular settings can differ substantially in form and structure. In other words, what persist are the organizing principles rather than the organized practices or, in Bourdieu's terminology, the structuring structures rather than the struc-tured structures. Third, given that the different groups belonging to the Arawak language family have undergone different historical processes since their separation, the elements that define their common ethos are in some cases manifested as unconscious general dispositions, whereas in others they might assume a more conscious normative nature.

Bearing these caveats in mind, I suggest that five elements define the Arawakan ethos. First and foremost is an implicit or explicit repudiation of endo-warfare, that is, of war against peoples speaking one's own or related languages, people who share one's own ethos. Second is an inclination to establish increasing levels of sociopolitical alliance between linguistically related peoples. Third is an emphasis on descent, consanguinity, and commensality as the foundation of ideal social life. Fourth is a predilection for ancestry, genealogy, and inherited rank as the basis for political leadership. Last but not least is a tendency to assign religion a central place in personal, social, and political life. None of these elements can be said to be exclusively characteristic of Arawak-speaking peoples. Each can be found among members of other language families. What makes them meaningful is that all of them are present in the Arawakan clusters examined here.

The avoidance of endo-warfare seems to be one of the most outstanding pan-Arawak characteristics. Even in the case of northwestern Amazonia, where the evidence is not conclusive, we know that endo-warfare was not practiced, at least not within the boundaries of the large military confederacies that prevailed during much of the seventeenth and eighteenth centuries. This in no way implies that internal conflict or violence had been eliminated or that the Arawak were less aggressive than their neighbors. It indicates only that for the Arawak the "other," or enemy, is not to be found within the boundaries of one's own macrosociety but beyond, among those speaking different, unrelated languages. It does not mean that the Arawak were less fierce, either. Although the Campa, western Taíno, and classic Taíno did not take slaves, accumulate human war trophies, or practice war cannibalism, other Arawak-speaking peoples, such as the Manao, Baré, Baniwa, eastern Taíno, and Lokono, did. Therefore, the distinction is not one between "peaceful" and "bellicose" peoples or between "civilized" and "savage" but rather one between endo-warring and exo-warring societies. This distinction, I believe, is particularly relevant for our understanding of tropical forest native societies and introduces a much-needed historical perspective into the present debate between defenders of the "predation" and "morality" models of Amerindian sociality (see Taylor 1996; Viveiros de Castro 1996; Overing and Passes 2000; Santos-Granero 2000).

Intimately linked with the abstention of endo-warfare is the Arawakan propensity to establish political alliances with linguistically related peoples. These alliances were not aleatory or temporary military confederacies with specific narrow aims but an integral part of Arawakan sociopolitical systems. They were more developed and enduring in the Caribbean and northwestern Amazonia, where they involved hundreds of villages under the rule of powerful paramount chiefs, than in eastern Peru. But even in this latter region, where alliances tended to be established only in response to external threats, there is also evidence of more permanent coalitions (Renard-Casevitz 1993, 37; chapter 5). It should be noted that these political alliances did not necessarily coincide with ethnic or linguistic boundaries. The Baré and Taíno were divided into different confederacies. In turn, the Manao, Baré, and Campa coalitions could be extended to incorporate peoples of different linguistic affiliation—the endo-warring eastern Tukano and Pano—if the latter complied with the inhibition of endo-warfare.

The importance attributed by the Arawak to descent, consanguinity, and commensality as the proper basis for a "good" social life acquires a more visible expression in northwestern Amazonia and northeastern South America. The patrilineal sibs and phratries of the Baniwa and Wakuénai (Curripaco), the patrilineages and patriclans of the Palikur (see chapter 7), and the matrilineages and matriclans of the Taíno and Lokono constitute the social expression of this kind of ideology. The ideal of consanguinity was further reinforced by concomitant postmarital residence rules: virilocality in northwestern Amazonia, uxorilocality in northeastern South America. Although the Arawak of eastern Peru are cognatic, named descent groups are mentioned frequently in Yanesha and Piro oral tradition (Santos-Granero 1991, 48–54). This has led Gow (personal communication, 2000) to talk of a Piro and Yanesha "ghost clan organization." Although in an earlier work I have argued that reference to the existence of descent groups in past times is a mythico-philosophical device to stress the contrast with and desirability of present-day social organization (Santos-Granero 1991, 48), I am now inclined to concur with Smith (1985, 13–14) that they may be reminiscences of actual past social structure.

Hereditary leadership has been reported for all Arawakan clusters. In northwestern Amazonia and northeastern South America this trait was associated with a hierarchical social organization and an emphasis on high rank ancestry. Chiefly lineages, clans, or sibs have been reported among the Taíno, Lokono, and Wakuénai. The noble or divine ancestry of these groups was periodically reinforced through mythical narratives, genealogical recitals, and ritual performances. It was also marked through chiefly elite languages or specialized ritual languages. High status was maintained through "royal marriages" between chiefly families (Taíno), endogamous polygamy of chiefs, priests, and warriors (Lokono), or marriages between highly ranked patrisibs belonging to different phratries (Wakuénai) (Dreyfus 1980–81, 243; Whitehead 1994, 41; Hill 1996b, 144). A similar phenomenon was taking shape among the Yanesha, where descendants of priestly leaders composed a high-status, named descent group (Santos-Granero 1991, 309–10). Affiliation into this group was not indispensable to become a priest, but its members tended to intermarry, and priestly leaders tended to pass on their office to their actual or classificatory sons.

The tendency to assign religion a central place in personal, social, and political life is manifested in several forms. Unlike other Amazonian peoples, the Arawak have elaborate mythologies, often organized sequentially in temporal terms, in which creator deities or cultural heroes play leading roles. These mythologies were associated with complex ritual ceremonies. Among the Taíno, the Yanesha, and the Upper Perené Campa such celebrations were held in temples and conducted by specialists who combined the functions of shaman and priest (Rouse 1992, 14; Santos-Granero 1991, 126; Weiss 1973, 46). Similar specialists are reported among the Lokono and Baniwa (Whitehead 1994, 41; Wright 1992b, 196) and among the Mojos (see chapter 5). Arawak-speaking peoples imbue their environment with religious significance, writing history into the landscape through origin myths, the sagas of creator gods, the journeys of the ancestors, petroglyphs, musicalized naming of places, and an iterative toponymy (Santos-Granero 1998; Hill 1989, 1993; Renard-Casevitz 1993; see also chapters 8 and 10). Some of these sites were the object of pilgrimages and periodic ceremonial celebrations.

Among the Arawak, political power was often linked with religious authority. Sometimes this took the form of an association between secular and religious leaders, as was the case among the Taíno, Lokono, and Baniwa. In other contexts, secular and mystical power was vested in a single person, as was the case of Yanesha priestly leaders or Manao shaman-warrior chiefs (see chapter 10). This connection, together with millenarian conceptions, often gave rise to messianic movements in response to situations of internal or external crisis (Wright and Hill 1986; Brown and Fernández 1991, 1992; see chapter 11). Above all, however, religious ideologies promoting generosity, hospitality, and fraternity—even with strangers—contributed to inhibit endo-warfare and generate broader spheres of intraethnic and interethnic exchange and solidarity.

Ethos, History, and Transethnic Identities

The Arawakan ethos differed sharply from that of their neighbors. In contrast with the exo-warring Arawak, the Pano, eastern Tukano, and Carib placed great importance on endo-warfare and wife-taking raids not only as means of building society but as constitutive elements of their identity. Rather than encouraging social integration through descent, consanguinity, and increasingly broader spheres of solidarity between like peoples, the Pano, eastern Tukano, and Carib favored affinity, exogamy, and the constant incorporation through warfare of differentiated others—whether or not linguistically related—to enhance their demographic base. The Arawak privileged what Whitehead (1994, 39) calls a theocratic-genealogical mode of leadership based on notions of noble ancestry, social rank, and priestly attributes. In contrast, the Pano, the Carib, and, to a lesser extent, the eastern Tukano favored a trading-military mode grounded on martial prowess, control of people through military subjection, and the constant conversion of trading partners into political supporters and military allies. In fact, one could affirm that the Arawak-speaking peoples were able to maintain their distinctive ethos despite the spatial and temporal distance that separated them because of the constant interaction with peoples who had antithetical social practices.

However, such clear-cut contrasts are too tidy and do not reflect the complexity of identity affiliations and political arrangements over time. Although it is possible to recognize a distinctive Arawakan ethos, there is clearly no essential, straightforward connection between speaking an Arawakan language and behaving in a certain "Arawakan way." On the contrary, the historical data suggest that there was a continuous flow of exchange between the Arawak and their neighbors. Ideas, values, know-how, practices, and objects moved freely between the different groups involved in the vast political macrosystems of pre-Columbian times. In fact, there are probably more outer cultural similarities between the Arawak and their non-Arawakan neighbors in each of the clusters mentioned earlier than between Arawakan groups pertaining to different clusters. This would support the relevance of the notion of culture area. However, this does not negate the existence of an Arawakan ethos that likewise is a historical product and, as a constitutive element of one's identity, is generally reinforced by historical interaction with peoples bearing other, contrasting ethoses.

However, the permeability of ethnic boundaries and the ease with which ethnic groups could shift language, identity, and political affiliation are well illustrated by the numerous cases of transethnic transformation reported in pre- and post-Columbian times. Such cases present us with a great variety of situations. The Piro and Ucayali Campa retained their Arawakan languages but assumed the ethos of the riverine Pano, with whom they continued to be bitter enemies, however. Karipuna men adopted a Kariña-related Cariban language in addition to the Arawakan language everybody spoke, but along with it they adopted a Cariban cultural ethos and shifted political allegiance from their Arawakan to their Cariban neighbors. The Tariana, having vanquished and absorbed several Tukano-speaking groups of the Lower and Middle Vaupés River, adopted the language of their subjects while retaining most of their Arawakan ethos, particularly the propensity to forge alliances under powerful chiefs. This situation suggests that adopting the language of another group is not necessarily proof of a weaker political or military position.

Transethnic changes were neither gradual nor irreversible affairs. Koch-Grünberg (quoted in Goldman 1963, 14–15) reported the case of a northwest Amazon Arawak-speaking group whose members adopted a Tukanoan language but who in less than a generation switched back to Arawakan. As a result, in 1903, by the time he met them, the elders of the group were speaking Arawakan again, whereas the young could speak only Tukanoan. The Tariana shift to a Tukanoan language and the Ucayali Campa adoption and subsequent suppression of a Panoan ethos were equally quick. This suggests that shifts in identity and language cannot be conceived of as mere cultural phenomena or as passive responses to external events (acculturation) but above all are conscious political strategies. In such cases, the innovators adopt the cultural elements, expressive of their neighbors' ethos, that they consider more adequate for their survival and that eventually they may internalize as part of their own ethos.

It should also be stressed that transethnic changes do not necessarily involve whole ethnic groups, whatever the notion of ethnic group means in contexts of such fluid and rapid interethnic flows. For instance, there is evidence that the Piro did not experience a uniform process of Panoization. Subgroups that were in closer contact with the Pano-speaking Conibo, Comabo, and Mochobo, such as the Chontaquiro (Urubamba River between the Sepahua and Yavero), the Simirinche (confluence of the Urubamba and Tambo rivers), and the Cusitinavo (left margin of Upper Ucayali), underwent a more complete process of Panoization. In contrast, subgroups such as the Upatarinavo (Upper Tambo and Ene rivers), which settled in areas closer to the Campa cluster, shared with members of this cluster many of the basic features of the Arawakan ethos (Maroni 1988, 294; see chapter 6).

In short, language and culture are connected. This connection is not genetic but historical and thus dependent on geographic contiguity and social vicinity. In other words, the notion of culture area could be more adequate than that of language family if the aim is to understand interethnic similarities and dissimilarities. However, if we agree that there is something like an Arawakan ethos, we must conclude that the ethos of a particular language family can persist long after the societies that belong to it have separated. In the case of the Maipuran branch of the Arawak language family—to which most of the above-mentioned Arawak-speaking peoples belong—this would mean more than 3,000 years (Noble 1965, 111). This is remarkable considering that the Arawak of eastern Peru, northwestern Amazonia, and northeastern South America have been heavily influenced by their Pano, eastern Tukano, and Carib neighbors, as well as by other quite different peoples from the Andean highlands, Central America, and even the southeastern United States. However, the constant emergence of transethnic Arawakan groups demonstrates that despite this remarkable persistence, the link between language and culture is indeed historical and therefore subject to the broad fluctuations of political and economic interests.

2 Arawak Linguistic and Cultural Identity through Time: Contact, Colonialism, and Creolization

NEIL L. WHITEHEAD

> To imagine a language is to imagine a form of life.
> —Ludwig Wittgenstein, *Philosophical Investigations*

THIS CHAPTER is concerned with the basis of linguistic classifications, the particular history of how the linguistic classification "Arawakan" worked culturally in the region of northeastern South America during the colonial period, and the pitfalls that process presents to the uncritical identification of sociocultural relatedness on the basis of such categories. The essays collected here show convincingly that such pitfalls can be negotiated and that there are many reasons for seeking to identify the long-term historical trajectories of linguistically related groups. This issue has been particularly sensitive within the study of indigenous South America because models of historical evolution have tended to take a dehistoricized view of linguistic relatedness, assuming that such relatedness was itself suprahistorical and therefore a given rather than a matter to be investigated (Greenberg 1987; Loukotka 1968; Rouse 1948a, 1948b, 1992). The essays collected here depart from such models by demonstrating the meaning of linguistic relatedness through attention to the archaeology, history, and ethnography of Arawak speakers. In this way they have broken the mold of glottochronological approaches to historical linguistic relatedness by emphasizing social and cultural historical trajectories over rates of linguistic change. The two phenomena are closely related, but the ground-breaking aspect of these studies lies in their attention to processes that produce glottochronological change rather than seeing that change as evidence of historical relatedness in itself.

The emphasis on linguistic over historical relatedness really begins with the classification of languages by the colonial regimes throughout South

America, the Caribbean, and beyond. This was a powerful political tool because to identify a language was to simultaneously "invent" a new culture. Thus, it was thought that the intellectual capacities and cultural proclivities of a culture stemmed from the workings and complexities of that language (Kroskrity 2000). As a matter of intellectual history it must be noted that the concept of language precedes that of culture and that to a large degree the pre–nineteenth-century notion of a language was equivalent to the modern notion of culture. Therefore, it should come as no surprise that the identification of indigenous languages in South America and the Caribbean was a highly political process. Moreover, because communication with colonial subjects was key to the success of the colonial project, gaining competency in native languages was a principal concern for colonial regimes. In this context missionary evangelism, centered on verbal communication of the gospel and textual ordering of indigenous speech, was pragmatically relevant to the colonial project as a whole. Nowhere is this more evident than in the initial contacts with indigenous American cultures in South America and the Caribbean (Whitehead 1999a, 1999b), and it is the purpose of this chapter to examine how that moment came to exercise an influence on the subsequent linguistic ethnology of the whole region and beyond.

The Columbian Encounter and the Politics of Language

It was Columbus himself who made the first and fundamental politicolinguistic distinctions with regard to the native population of the Americas, and our subsequent failure to understand our own cultural prejudices with regard to ideas of culture and language has perpetuated those distinctions and allowed them to become encrusted with glottochronological and historical linguistic theory (Whitehead 1995b). This has resulted in a confusing picture of the ethnic identities and cultural relations that once pertained to the native peoples of Amazonia and the Caribbean.

Most obvious among these confusions is the question of the ethnic and cultural nature of so-called Island Carib society because it appears that these people were neither Cariban (linguistically)—their natal language being Arawakan—nor islanders (exclusively), as there is evidence that they were also settled extensively on the mainland, in the coastal area between the Orinoco and Amazon rivers (Whitehead 1995a). This paradoxical situation directly results from the initial ethnographic judgment made by Columbus and confirmed by other contemporaries that there were two principal groupings of native peoples, one "tractable" (*guatiao, aruaca*) and the other "savage" (*caribe, caniba*). Although not a linguistic classification, this ethnological scheme came to directly inform colonial policy and so was also self-fulfilling (Sued Badillo 1995). Consequently, subsequent ethnolinguistic studies, as with the missionaries discussed in this chapter, reflected precisely these changes in native society, induced by the consequences of colonial policy, reconfirming the initial discriminations and definitions of the colonizers. Also contributing to the perpetuation of this dualism was the ethnological substitution of the mainland *aruacas* (Lokono), for the *guatiao* of the islands, as the latter were destroyed or dispersed in the occupation of the islands in the sixteenth century.[1] This dualism was not simply a colonial projection nor a purely linguistic judgment but reflected real divisions in the native population. How such divisions functioned politically, linguistically, and culturally is still a matter of controversy as new historical and archaeological evidence continues to emerge.

Modern anthropological approaches to the archaeology, history, linguistics, and ethnography of the northern region of the South American continent and the Caribbean islands took these colonial schema as their starting point, especially as seventeenth-century native testimony on their own cultural origins was already partly expressive of these dualistic cultural schema, as a direct result of Spanish colonial policies of ethnic discrimination and slavery of those designated *caribes*.

The analysis resulting from this set of assumptions was given its classic statement by Irving Rouse (1948a, 1948b) in his essays on "Arawak" and "Carib" for the *Handbook of South American Indians*, and even in more recent publications (Rouse 1986, 1992) it is still maintained that "Island Carib" origins are linguistically and historically extraneous to the islands themselves. Thus the character of their society, as well as its political and military conflicts with other peoples in the Caribbean, is held to have resulted from a pre-Columbian military invasion and occupation of the Lesser Antilles by the "mainland Carib" (i.e., Kariña), as a result of which the Arawakan (i.e., Igneri, *guatiao*) men of these islands were killed and cannibalized, whereas the women were taken as concubines by the Kariña war-parties.

Linguist Douglas Taylor (1977) also maintained that the explanation of the different speech modes of the "Island Carib" (i.e., a natal language, Igneri, and several jargons or pidgins used exclusively by men) were the result of this pre-Columbian conquest by a group of Kariña speakers of the Igneri, using the example of Norman French supplanting Saxon English as his model for linguistic replacement. Certainly autodenominations within these gendered speech modes differed, Karipuna being used within the natal language and Kalinago in the male jargons. Taylor further argued that the natal language of the Kariña fell into disuse as the offspring of the Kariña conquerors and their captive Karipuna wives evolved a new society, although the "fact" of this past conquest continued to be expressed in the gender polarity of the "female" Karipuna and "male" Kalinago speech modes.

Luridly attractive though this tale may be, other explanations of these speech patterns are equally possible and more plausible. For example, given both the frequent communication between the islands and mainland, which presumably facilitated this "conquest" in the first place, and the fact that Kariña lived alongside Karipuna on the islands as well as the mainland, the pidgin-Kariña used by the Karipuna men could have easily had other origins (Whitehead 1988), not least because that pidgin was used with an Arawakan syntax (Hoff 1995, 49–50). Most probably, as historian Sued Badillo (1978) has also suggested, a political and economic adaptation and alliance to the emergent Kariña polity of the sixteenth century (Whitehead 1990b) resulted in the name *Carib* often being applied, by indigenes and colonial alike, without regard to strictly linguistic or cultural considerations, just as the Spanish used the term *caribe* to denote all wild or fierce Amerindians (Whitehead 1988). French usage of the terms *Galibi* and *Caraïbe* to designate the difference between island and mainland ethnic groups therefore was more precise than the English *Carib* or Spanish *Caribe,* and it is significant to note that Jesuit linguist Raymond Breton (1665, 105) also refers to "Caraïbes insulaires" ("Island Caribs"), implying that they were present on the continent as well because he does not confuse them with the Galibi.

Further evidence of these close social and political relationships was the use of a Kariña pidgin, or even Kariña itself, by other Amerindian groups as a *lingua geral* (common language) in the Antillean-Amazonian corridor (Barrère 1743; Biet 1664; Boyer 1654; Pelleprat 1655).[2] Moreover, gender polarity in speech, as well as the use of special male jargons, is noted both from Kariña itself (Chrétien 1725) and from Arawakan languages such as Palikur (Grenand 1987) and Lokono (Stæhelin 1913, 112, 170), as well as from the Tupian (Magalhães 1576, 33), whose speakers had further notable cultural homologies with the native peoples of the islands. Given this complexity and variety in indigenous linguistic practice, the burden of explanation seems to fall on those who insist that there was a "conquest" by Kariña speakers because if this was indeed the case, why didn't the natal Karipuna (or Igneri) language die out, given the facility with which contacts with Kariña speakers could be maintained?

In any case, the first modern efforts to give the conquest theory a scientific footing—by attempting to correlate the data of archaeology with those of linguistics (Rouse and Taylor 1956)—produced contradictory results as to the time-depth of a Karipuna (or Igneri) presence in the Lesser Antilles, which remain unresolved. Accordingly, it is necessary to examine the theo-

retical origins of this situation by appraising the ethnological and anthropological judgments of Columbus and his contemporaries, discussing the
linguistic theories that informed later missionary accounts of Arawakan and
Cariban languages, and assessing how that has affected current anthropological thinking.[3]

Most recent work on Columbus's interpretations and inferences about the
native Caribbean emphasizes the extent to which the ethnological categories
he uses derive from his own cultural expectations (Greenblatt 1991). The
expectation of encountering Asia led Columbus to construct the *caniba* as
soldiers of the "Great Khan," the expectation of encountering human mon-
strosity led him to note the existence of people with tails or without hair, and,
most notoriously, by the second voyage, the expectation of anthropophagy,
deriving from Columbus, led Chanca (1907) to interpret funerary customs
on Guadeloupe as evidence of anthropophagy.

Nonetheless, whatever the intellectual origins of these categorical antici-
pations, it is legitimate to ask what elements in the resulting interpretations
derive from the unique experience of the Caribbean encounter. In particular, the contradictory and confusing way in which the term *caribe* and similar terms such as *caniba, canima,* and *canibales* are used in the texts generally is held to express Columbus's own confusion and inability to understand
what was being told to him. However, this does not mean that this uncertainty may not also reflect the complex and contradictory nature of native
sociopolitical reality, although the manner of its refraction through the Columbian lens is certainly difficult to reconstruct.

Equally, the Columbian presentation of the *caribe* as fierce and warlike,
wild and man-eating, although most often thought to derive from the need
to justify the colonial ambitions of the Spanish—which it certainly later came
to do—in the first instance may be seen as reflecting the opinions of the ruling elite of Bohío (Hispaniola). Columbus's adoption of their viewpoint
manifestly led him and others into a number of contradictory propositions
within their texts, especially as regards the timidity, civility, and lack of anthropophagy of those who are not *caribe.*

For Irving Rouse (1948a, 1948b, 1986) these confusions result from the
unreliability of the historical data in general, and the scheme of "fierce Carib" and "timid Arawak" is chosen from a number of possibilities that the
ethnographic observations of Columbus actually permit. The reasons for this
choice are many and are not properly part of this chapter, but the fact that
the idea of a group of men advancing through the islands eating enemy men
and copulating with their women is so powerfully resonant for our own
culture may be the most relevant consideration here, rather than native Ca-

ribbean behavior in 1492. In any case, as indicated earlier, both native testimony as to conflict between the "Island Carib" and the "Arawak" (Lokono) in the seventeenth century and the work of seventeenth-century missionaries in the field of linguistics have been misunderstood as directly verifying the conquest theory.

However, the extent to which the conquest theory also relies on a misreading of Columbian texts is nicely illustrated in the well-known *Journal* entry for November 23, 1492. At this point Columbus was sailing off Colba (Cuba) toward Bohío in the company of some Amerindian captives: "Those Indians he was carrying with him . . . said . . . that on it [Bohío] there were people . . . called *canibales*, of whom they showed great fear. And when they saw that he was taking this course, he says they could not speak, because these people would eat them, and are well armed. The admiral says that he well believes there was something in this, but that since they were well armed they must be people with reason; and he believed that they must have captured some of them and because they did not return to their lands they would say that they ate them. They believed the same thing about the Christians and about the admiral the first time some of them saw them" (Hulme and Whitehead 1992, 18).

A number of features in this passage could well stand as an example of how the Columbian texts have been poorly analyzed in anthropological readings. First, the identification of the Spanish, as rapacious conquerors, with the *canibales* is most striking and often commented upon, as is the empathetic treatment of the political consumption of those captured (see also Whitehead 1990a). Second, the link between military capability and being "people with reason" is an explicit anthropological principle found throughout the Columbian texts. Its significance is illumined by this identity of Carib and Spaniard, the Spanish having just completed their own *Reconquista*, overthrowing Muslim rule. However, because these observations and interpretations relate to the heartland of "non-Carib" settlement—Bohío—they have been ignored or suppressed in the analyses of subsequent commentators, as in the later Columbian texts, rather than being treated as evidence of the inadequacy of the resulting dualistic ethnographic schema. Similar contrasts in the ethnographic observations of the *Letter* and *Journal* emerge concerning the diversity of language and custom present in the islands, material culture, and the identification of cannibalism with the *caribes* (Hulme and Whitehead 1992, 12, 13, 15, 21, 26). Indeed, Columbus is quite explicit in his *Letter*: "In all the islands I saw no great diversity in the appearance of the people or in their manners or language; on the contrary they all understand one another, which is a very curious thing" (Hulme and Whitehead 1992, 13).

Nevertheless, by the second voyage we find that Columbus is making greater discriminations and notices some lexical differences between those he suspects of being *caribes* and others in the islands, although this is a long way from being the profound cultural difference implied by the conquest theory because we are told that his native interpreters "understood more, although they found differences between the languages because of the great distances between the lands" (Hulme and Whitehead 1992, 25).[4] Las Casas (1992, chapter 197) also tells us that there were three languages spoken on Bohío that were not mutually intelligible, thus further emphasizing how deceptive an appearance of linguistic homogeneity may have been.

However, such ambiguities were not an idle question of scholarly dispute but intimately connected to the pragmatics of conquest. Consequently, subsequent accounts attempt to resolve issues of variation in dialect as well as appearance, for the *caribes* are described by Columbus in the *Journal* as wearing black body dye and long hair tied with parrot feathers (Hulme and Whitehead 1992, 25). Chanca's "official" anthropology, incorporating Columbus's first ethnography, achieves this by the consistent application of a political decision to use the *caciques* of Bohío, not the soldiers of the *el Gran Can,* as a bridgehead into the regional native polity. Accordingly, the ambiguities and uncertainties surrounding the identity of *caribes* within the ethnoscape of the sixteenth-century Caribbean are resolved by casting *caribes* in the role of ferocious human-eaters and *guatiao* or *aruacas* as tractable and pliant. Thus, for Chanca, the recovery of human longbones on Turuqueira (Guadeloupe) is linked to cannibalism (Hulme and Whitehead 1992, 32), but on Bohío the recovery of human heads is linked to funerary rites (Gil and Varela 1984, 1689). More generally, the *caribe* cannibalism of the natives of Burequen (Puerto Rico) and the other islands is given continual emphasis, although it is also briefly noted, "If by chance they [of Burequen] are able to capture those who come to raid them they also eat them, just as those of Caribe do to them" (Hulme and Whitehead 1992, 36).

This residual ambivalence as to the nature of the *caribes,* as well as its manner of resolution within Chanca's text, is fully revealed in his closing remarks on Turuqueira. Chanca writes first, "These people seemed to us more polished than those who live in the other islands. . . . They had much cotton . . . and many cotton cloths, so well made that they lose nothing by comparison with those of our own country. . . . [But] the way of life of these *caribe* people is bestial" (Hulme and Whitehead 1992, 33). Such an analytical distinction, if not an actual contradiction, must clearly derive from the political purposes of the text.

The political factors that had informed Chanca's anthropology changed over the next twenty years or so, not least because of the extinction of the native elites of Bohío and Burequen. As a result, and because Chanca's anthropology had been given legal force through Queen Isabella's proclamation of 1503, which rendered all *canibales* who resisted the Spanish liable to enslavement, it was necessary to conduct a second ethnographic exercise, in one sense precisely because of the ambiguity between the status of *canibal* (i.e., eater of human flesh) and that of *caribe* (i.e., native resistant to the Spanish) that the proclamation itself implied.

To this end, in 1518 Charles V dispatched the Licenciado Rodrigo Figueroa to determine the exact locations where *caribes* were to be found. However, the ethnographic criteria for their identification had simplified under the political necessities of colonial establishment, as foreshadowed in the proclamation of Isabella, and mere opposition or intractability toward the Spanish, rather than anthropophagic customs, was deemed sufficient to consider a given population *caribe*. However, at no time was any kind of dialect or other linguistic feature suggested as a way of achieving this discrimination. It should thus be very evident that it was the politics of colonialism that determined the ethnological agenda and thus the creation of the ethnographic observations and linguistic descriptions that were thought to verify it.

However, these colonial linguistic and ethnological texts were not composed of seamless arguments and perfect data sets but often were mere accumulations of unsorted observation and secondary testimony. As a result, such texts also contain many indications for other kinds of interpretations of the native Caribbean and, when combined with later sources and the data from archaeology, may be used to provide a more complete interpretation of the situation encountered by Columbus, particularly the significance of the terms *caribe/caniba* and *aruaca/guatiao*.

In short, the social interdependency and cultural similarity of *caribe* and *aruaca* is a possibility that was still ignored in earlier anthropological schema, which relied on the assumption that the *caribe* were invasive or external to a primordial "Arawakan" or "Taíno" cultural context. Yet evidence of social continuity underlying an ethnic and cultural interchange between *caribe* and *aruaca* is present, as we have seen, in the early Columbian documentation, particularly in regard to behavior considered definitional of the *caribe*: anthropophagy. Thus, aside from the ambivalence of Columbus and Chanca we learn that the natives of Bohío "les pagan [los caribes] en la misma moneda, pues descuartizan a un canibal ante los ojos de la demas, lo asan, lo desgarran a rabiosas dentelladas y lo devoran" ("pay them in the same coin, dismembering a *canibal* before the eyes of the rest, they roast him, tear him up with a rabid gnashing of teeth, and eat him" [my translation]; Anghiera 1530, 2:912).

Fernando Colón (1947) stated that Caonabo, one of the principal chiefs of Bohío, was himself a *caribe* and a stranger. Traces of such cultural homology also seem to be reflected in the way in which the much-abused term *taino* has registered in the speech of the Karipuna. Thus, Taylor (1946) gives the orthographic form *ni'tinao* (formal friend [ws] or progenitor [ms/ws]); Raymond Breton (1665, 454; 1666, 19, 315) giving the form *ne'tegnon* and *nitino/neteno* (husband's father, husband's mother, or daughter's husband [ws]).[5]

Mutuality in the ethnic definition of *carihe* and *aruaca* is also clearly implied by evidence from the myth cycles of native Bohío, as recorded by Pané (1496/1999) and Oviedo (1535). Thus, Guayahona, their mythical progenitor, in search of the mystic alloy *guanin* traveled to the lands south and east of Bohío—that is, the Lesser Antilles and the mainland—taking with him their women and children. At the *isla de guanin* golden objects were collected, but the women and children were lost, providing a symbolic alternative to the gastronomic context in which most commentators, from Chanca onward, have evaluated the claims by the ruling caciques as to their "consumption" by the *caribes*. Also, by initiating the exchange cycle of women for *guanin*, Guayahona may also be said to represent the first *cacique caribe* of Bohío, an ideological model for the authority of Caonabo and thus providing a myth-charter for the chieftains of Bohío and legitimizing their marriage exchanges, or marriages by capture, with the *caribes* who controlled access to *guanin* (Whitehead 1996b, 1998b).

It is thus evident that European fascination with the consumption of human flesh, as in the case of Columbus, led to a total identification between "caribism" and "cannibalism," but as argued earlier, it is evident from the Columbian texts that there were a variety of orthographically related terms (i.e. *caniba, caribe, canima, caribal*) in usage in the Antilles, which arguably had two referents, not just one. One pole of reference among these terms, deriving from the politics of the ruling elite of Bohío, was the meaning of "mainlanders/enemy people from the South," as Goeje (1939) suggests, and is indeed the contextual sense because the form *caniba* occurs alongside, not just as an alternative to, the term *caribe* in the Columbian sources. Taylor (1946) in particular gave much attention to the derivation of such terms, but only as ethnic designations, and did not consider the second, supraethnic pole of reference, orthographically represented by *caribe* (or *caraïbe* in the later French sources) and for which there is a wealth of evidence from the mainland through the widespread use of the terms *caraybe, caraïbe,* and *karai* as Tupian spiritual honorifics or Cariban designations of a martial prowess, associated with the possession of related anthropophagic rituals.

Missionary Linguists and the Cultural Inscription of Language

If the earliest reports belie later interpretations, it remains to examine how explicit consideration of native language by the missionaries of the seventeenth and eighteenth centuries consolidated an erroneous ethnological dualism in the Caribbean and northern South America, in which the Arawakan "Island Carib" came to stand as an icon of "caribness" (Whitehead 1995b; Trouillot 1991). The missionaries brought a variety of different ideas to the task of conversion, and the evaluation and recording of the speech practices of linguistic communities effectively set the agenda for evangelism. Thus, those with the capacity for rational understanding and spiritual enlightenment were separated from those whose primitive and undeveloped speech warranted military chastisement rather than spiritual suasion. In the words of one Jesuit missionary, "They do not hear the Voice of the Gospel where they have not first heard the echo of gunfire" (Whitehead 1988, 147).

For instance, Raymond Breton, a Jesuit missionary to Dominica, states that the Caraïbe "have no words to express the power of the soul, such as the will, the understanding, nor that which concerns religion, [or] civility. They have no honorific terms like Our Lord. They express however some acts of the understanding and of the will, such as to remember, to wish" (Hulme and Whitehead 1992, 110).

However, a later account, written by a lay Protestant traveler, Charles Cesar de Rochefort, notes that the Caraïbe word for rainbow is "God's plume of feathers" (Hulme and Whitehead 1992, 122) and emphasizes the complexity and creativity of the Karipuna language. In short, the cultural positioning of the reporter had a fundamental influence on the nature of linguistic representation. Accordingly, I briefly discuss Cesar de Rochefort, Raymond Breton, and the accounts of two other Catholics, missionary Jean Baptiste du Tertre and layman Sieur de la Borde, who wrote from a Jesuit mission, in terms of both the influence of the French Enlightenment on their analyses of native language and the way in which their analyses further influenced French Enlightenment thought. The contrast between Catholicism and Protestantism in their approaches to language is also relevant and reminds us that linguistic description was not the simple recording of "natural" facts but a complex argument about "moral" capacities.

For seventeenth-century thinkers language was an important indication of the capacity for "civility," "polity," and "religion" which set human beings above animals and corresponded to the historical level of development of society as a whole. In this way analysis of native languages was integral to the development of colonial and missionary policies.[6] Breton asserted that the Caraïbe did not have words that would enable or reveal cultural development and so by implication provided justification for the French colonial project in Dominica.

In religious debates of the era concerning the evolution of human society and the role of divine creation, understanding the origin of language was as relevant for the doctrine of natural law as it was for biblical criticism.[7] In turn, many Enlightenment philosophers were profoundly influenced by the work of the missionaries. Indeed, Jean-Jacques Rousseau used du Tertre's characterization of the Caribs as "noble savages" as a point of departure in his writings on human nature and society (Hulme and Whitehead 1992, 128), and the influence of both missionary linguistic judgments and the philosophical assumptions of Enlightenment thinkers are still very much present in modern anthropology, as we have seen.

Raymond Breton

By contrast with Rousseau, the views of Raymond Breton (Hulme and Whitehead 1992, 107–16) on the origins of Karipuna society were consistent with his negative views of their language. Breton concedes that the Karipuna are not monstrous cannibals, as was the Columbian representation, but he does see them as truly *sauvage,* lacking strict marital laws, and so apt to practice incestuous relations. They lack the capacity for human affection and merely mate out of instinct and a desire to reproduce. Crucially, he claims that there is a separate language for men and women, and this is reflected in his two-volume *Dictionnaire* (Breton 1665, 1666), which paradoxically expresses a supposed absence of linguistic complexity via an excess of lexical notation and cultural explanation. The *Dictionnaire* also systematically favors male speech forms over female in the representation of the Karipuna speech community. Breton thus firmly but incorrectly inscribes the notion that male speech forms, referred to as Kalinago, constituted a distinct language.[8] Breton's account of the Karipuna language reflects European colonial thought and the cultural construction of the colonized. Indeed, even as the "Island Caribs" provide Rousseau with an icon of noble savagery, they function as the "wild man" of the European imaginary. Bartra (1994, 124) neatly summarizes the attitudes encapsulated in this icon of the colonized and its connection to theories of language and civilization: "The wild man did not have language, but took words by storm in order to express the murmurings of another world, the signals that nature gave to society. The wild man spoke words that did not have literal meaning, but were eloquent in communicating sensations that civilized language could not express. His words were devoid of sense, but expressed feelings."

In just the same way Caliban, in Shakespeare's *The Tempest*, is a ghostly reminder of the reality of Karipuna survival in a colonized Caribbean and the notions of linguistic superiority that underpinned that colonization:

> . . . I pitied thee,
> Took pains to make thee speak, taught thee each hour
> One thing or other. When thou didst not, savage,
> Know thine own meaning, but wouldst gabble like
> A thing most brutish, I endow'd thy purposes
> With words that made them known.
>
> (act 1, scene 2, lines 353–58)

Jean Baptiste du Tertre

A similar depiction, consonant with the same general linguistic analysis, emerges in the account of fellow Jesuit Jean Baptiste du Tertre (Hulme and Whitehead 1992, 128–37), who wistfully stresses the rude superiority of the Karipuna over the civilized nature of the Europeans, which isolates them from their simpler and gentler natures: "So, at the very word Savage, most people imagine in their mind's eye the kind of men who are barbarous, cruel, inhuman, without reason, deformed, as big as giants, as hairy as bears: in a word, monsters rather than reasonable men; although in truth our Savages are Savages in name only, just like the plants and fruits which nature produces without cultivation in the forests and wildernesses, which, although we call them wild, still possess the true virtues in their properties of strength and complete vigor, which we often corrupt by our artifice, and change so much when we plant in our gardens" (Hulme and Whitehead 1992, 129).

Thus, du Tertre, while accepting Breton's ideas about the origins of Karipuna culture and language, sees the "Caraïbes" as exemplifying a noble simplicity, and he stresses the difficulty in learning their language, that it is "impoverished and imperfect" (Hulme and Whitehead 1992, 137). Breton is accordingly congratulated for having made their conversion more possible through his notation of their speech, and the main obstacle to evangelism becomes the poor treatment they have learned to expect from the Europeans. This contrast between Breton's and du Tertre's account is interesting for the way in which it highlights shifting missionary attitudes, but notice that the ethnology, captured in the linguistic judgments of Breton, goes unchallenged. Du Tertre writes, "They have good reasoning, and a mind as subtle as could be found among people who have no smattering of letters at all, and who have never been refined and polished by the human sciences, which often, while refining our minds, fill them for us with malice; and I can say in all truth that if our Savages are more ignorant than us, so they are much less vicious, even indeed that almost all the malice they do know is taught them by us French" (Hulme and Whitehead 1992, 130). A linguistic incapacity, whatever its origins, thus still remains the key trait of "primitive" society.

Sieur de la Borde

Although de la Borde was not a missionary, the Jesuit missionaries with whom he worked, especially Father Simon, influenced him. He was either part of the French military and naval presence or a functionary of the local administration. De la Borde shares with Breton the idea that the Caraïbes are savages, with no trace of the nostalgia for simplicity that du Tertre shows. Nonetheless, de la Borde provides an important description of the myths and spiritual beliefs of the Caraïbes, although he treats most of these beliefs as primitive superstitions; he acknowledges that the Caraïbes are capable of forming ideas of spirituality and divinity, albeit regarding the devil and evil spirits. He writes, "Their language is very destitute: they can only express what is obvious. They are so materialist that they do not have a term to designate the workings of the spirit, and if the beasts were able to speak I would want to give them no other language than that of the Caraïbes. They have not one word to explain matters of religion, of justice, and of what pertains to the virtues, the sciences, and a great number of other things about which they have no notion. They are not able to converse, as I have said elsewhere" (Hulme and Whitehead 1992, 153).

However, it is again a contradiction and irony that de la Borde provides detailed descriptions of the complex spiritual beliefs of the Caraïbes, only to suggest that they are linguistically impoverished. Nonetheless, he precedes this passage with the following comments: "Although there is some difference between the language of the men and that of the women, as I have said in the chapter on their origin, nevertheless they understand one another. The old men [also] have a jargon when they are dealing with some plan of war, which the young do not understand at all" (Hulme and Whitehead 1992, 153).

De la Borde also refers to a copious linguistic study made by one Father Simon that "will be useful to those who might plan to acquire some awards in the conversion of these infidel peoples," and one wonders whether this lost work might have given a very different view of gender, age, and the linguistic practices of the Caraïbes given these few tantalizing remarks.

Charles de Rochefort

Charles de Rochefort provides an account of the Caraïbes, which differs notably from those of Breton, du Tertre, and de la Borde. This contrast is certainly connected to the fact that he was a Protestant in the service of a particularly anticlerical governor in Dominica, and his discussion of the Caraïbe speech practice therefore is revealing. He immediately stresses the unity of human speech practices, noting, "The Caribbians have an ancient and natural language, such as is wholly peculiar to them, as every nation hath that which is proper to it" (Hulme and Whitehead 1992, 118), and emphasizes that "what advantage soever the Europeans may imagine they have over the Caribbians, either as to the natural faculties of the mind, or the easiness of the pronunciation of their own language, in order to the more easie attainment of theirs, yet hath it been found by experience, that the Caribbians do sooner learn ours than we do theirs" (Hulme and Whitehead 1992, 119).

Rochefort actually offers a detailed account of the Karipuna language and, consonant with the idea that attitudes toward language are part of a wider cultural interpretation, also challenges the established theory, so often advanced to explain gender differences in speech, of a Carib invasion from the mainland. Certainly his work was controversial in its own day because of the explicit challenge it made to Jesuit views of the Karipuna, and he was accused of having plagiarized the work of du Tertre. Subsequent commentators, no doubt because of the ethnographic authority of du Tertre's work resulting from its association with that of Raymond Breton, have also largely accepted du Tertre's published accusation against Rochefort. Nevertheless, Rochefort's account is accurate and intelligent for the way in which it recognizes a plurality of influences in the linguistic repertoire of the Caraïbes. He also illustrates the complexities and idiomatic uses of Karipuna speech, noting that besides their "ancient and natural language" "they have fram'd another bastard-speech, which is intermixt with several words taken out of foreign languages by the commerce they have had with the Europeans . . . among themselves they always make use of their ancient and natural language" (Hulme and Whitehead 1992, 118).

In short, we have here clear testimony as to both the propensity for forming creolized or pidgin languages by the Karipuna, influenced by the presence of the Europeans, and gender and age differences in the use of similar jargons formulated via interactions with other indigenous peoples. None of these complexities have been adequately recognized in the missionary or later accounts.

The Enlightenment and Linguistic Representation

As is anticipated in the account of Rochefort, Enlightenment philosophies increasingly emphasized the idea that language was not a preordained product of divine intervention but the result of human experience and custom and therefore open to human manipulation (see Ricken 1994; Bono 1995). Principal among the proponents of this view were John Locke in *An Essay Concerning Human Understanding* (1690) and Etienne Condillac's *Essai sur l'origine des connaissances humaines* (1793). For Locke there were no innate ideas, and all human thought and classification had their origin in sensory experience, understood as both sensation and reflection, or memory. In short, God did not invent language but placed humanity in the world with a capacity for such, and in this way modern theory, supplanting God by the inheritable cognitive and motor abilities that support speech behavior, remains embedded in Enlightenment analysis. This line of reasoning was a radical departure from the Cartesian and pre-Cartesian traditions of seeing humans differing from animals through the possession of a faculty of *raison*, of which language was the prime symptom. For Descartes animals were mere automatons, lacking *raison* and thus the ability to use or learn language. For Locke, however, both humans and animals show cognitive activities that develop on the basis of sense perception, yet only for humans do these reach such a level of abstraction that they become expressed in words.

Condillac (Ricken 1994, 80) further developed this sensualist philosophy, placing the origins of language and thought in a phylogenetic, or evolutionary and historical, perspective rather than the ontogenetic relationship pictured by Locke. Again this debate is still current in modern linguistics, as the resurgent interest in the materialist theories of Vygotsky (1986, 1994) illustrates.

The entanglement of linguistic philosophy and ethnological observation is extensively and overtly developed in the writings of Jean-Jacques Rousseau (1959), who broadly adopted Condillac's sensualist philosophy but added to that a distinct historical sense of the conflicts and differences that arise as a result of the contradiction between the social nature of human beings and the inequalities of their social existence. Rousseau therefore explicitly links language theory and anthropological theory through sensualist philosophy. The result is the rediscovery of the primitive as a subject free from the constraints and inequalities of the civilized and expressing a unique, untranslatable, and even impenetrable cultural outlook. It is arguable that we have yet to divest ourselves of such notions, as recent debates on cultural commensurability and comparability suggest (Obeyesekere 1992; Sahlins 1995). Moreover, such ideas are still relevant to anthropological theory because advocates of linguistic relativity in cognition supplant the Lockean notion of "innate ideas" with the Whorfian argument that anthropological linguistics would be another way through which the culture and mentality of a particular linguistic community could be uniquely revealed, as in the well-known example of the supposed absence of recognizable temporal terms in the Hopi language (Whorf 1962, 58).

However, for these reasons ideas about the origins and development of language are not just matters for linguistic description and analysis but reverberate in current anthropological theory in a number of ways. In archaeology the assumption of a close fit between language and culture is necessary for the idea that linguistic groups represent historical (archaeological) cultures (Lathrap 1970a). This is not to suggest that there are never continuities and historical equivalences between a speech community and a sociocultural group (Loukotka 1968), but it does mean that these must be demonstrated before glottochronology can be used to substitute for history or other kinds of temporal sequencing (Renfrew 1987; Whitehead 1993a). This much is clearly shown by the divergence between linguistics and archaeology over the time depth of "Island Carib" occupation in the Caribbean discussed earlier and in the utter failure of attempts to distinguish the "Carib conquest" as a discrete style emerging in the ceramic sequence for the Lesser Antilles (Boomert 1995, 30–33). Moreover, the wider implications of the overidentification of language with a cultural worldview become evident in the work of Greenberg (1966, 1987) who, with geneticist Cavalli-Sforza et al. (1996), has recently grouped most of the world's languages into just eighteen primal groupings. On the basis of genetic similarities between modern speakers from these groupings, these language distributions are also held to be expressive of a "race" history.

Certainly, the idea of a close integration of language and culture often has been contested and has led repeatedly to the formation of theories about the role of language in the development of specific representational and cognitive modes within a given linguistic community. However, what should have become very clear from a consideration of the case of the "Island Carib" is that although a language is a Wittgensteinian "form of life," a cultural phenomenon, it is also a historical one, and this fundamentally affects the character of its development and thus the relevance and validity of any comparative exercise.

This history of the Karipuna and the way it is reflected in linguistic usage through time makes the search for an Arawakan cultural-linguistic substrate that might identify "Arawakan" peoples in the historical past appear pointless. The Arawakan Karipuna have been "caribe" for so long that even today ethnologists are unable to let go of the idea that they are Caribs in some sense, for indeed that is the opinion of their modern descendants, the Garifuna, themselves. The story of the Garifuna of Belize therefore is instructive as to the meaning and colonial origins of the categories of "Arawak" and "Carib," the creolization of an Arawakan language, and the confusion this causes to an anthropology still dependent on the dualism of the colonial past and wedded to the idea of language as a cultural substrate that produces social continuity through time.

The Garifuna are the descendants of African slaves who fled to St. Vincent from the sugar plantations of Barbados. The wreck of a slave ship off St. Vincent in 1635 greatly augmented the black population, who were integrated into Karipuna society as they had been throughout the previous century (see Hulme and Whitehead 1992, 38–44). Over the next 150 years the "Black Caribs," as they were known, grew in political significance within the colonial rivalries of the French and British for control of the Lesser Antilles. The Carib War by the British against these Karipuna communities in 1795 lasted three years, with the result that the British deported the entire "Black Carib" community to an island off Honduras from where they gradually migrated to the mainland of Honduras and Belize. Their communities have survived to the present day and still speak the Garifuna language, unlike their fellow "Amerindian" or "Red" Caribs in St. Vincent and Dominica, who retain only a few words and phrases of Karipuna.

For the eighteenth- and nineteenth-century colonial regimes of this region, however, these *caribes* were quite different from the *aruacas* who were retroactively identified with the lost populations of the Greater Antilles. In fact, the term *aruacas* historically referred to the Lokono, settled from the Amazon north to the Essequibo along the Atlantic coast and into the uplands at the head of the Demerara, Berbice, and Corentyn rivers.[9] The Lokono quickly allied with the Spanish who were attempting to settle the Orinoco and Guyana coast in the sixteenth century because they received Spanish military assistance in occupying rivers north of the Essequibo, including the Pomeroon and Orinoco and parts of the Caribbean coast of Venezuela. Here the Lokono drove out the existing population of Kariña, Warao, Yao, Nepoyo, and Suppoyo. The Lokono were also given black slaves by the Spanish to work the tobacco plantations they had pioneered in the Lower Orinoco. These events were the origin of a lasting military exchange between the Lokono and the Kariña, who in turn made use of Dutch and French allies in opposition to the *aruaca* occupation of the Essequibo and Orinoco regions (Whitehead 1988).

The Karipuna played into this situation as allies of the Kariña (hence their honorific in the men's jargon Kalinago) and as war and trade partners of the

Lokono. The tradition of raid for women and *guanin* (gold work) between the Karipuna and Lokono was thus expressive of their basic cultural similarities; Loquo was the first man in both Karipuna and Lokono myths of origin, and the sources of the magic metal *guanin* lay in an exchange of women for this substance with the mythical ancestor Guahayona. In this way Lokono and Karipuna conflicts and exchanges in the seventeenth and eighteenth centuries reproduced the military and ritual exchanges in the fifteenth and sixteenth century that were described by Columbus. However, none of this was understood (or at least it was ignored) by earlier commentators, who saw in the tales and practices of Karipuna and Lokono raiding another aspect of a supposed Manichean struggle between Arawak and Carib across northern South America. In this way, as the ethnologists of the eighteenth and nineteenth centuries moved to classify and delineate major cultural and linguistic relationships, the scheme of "Arawak versus Carib" seemed a ready-made heuristic device. This model then attracted further confirmation as a specifically linguistic style of comparison deriving from the work of missionary evangelists encrusted this distinction with further evidence, notwithstanding the gross anomalies this created in describing and interpreting perhaps the best-documented and most-studied Arawakan population in the whole of the Americas, the Island Caribs. It thus transpires that the category "Arawak" is no less historically and culturally complex than its twin "Carib," and the Karipuna transgress such ethnic, cultural, and linguistic boundaries.

The urge to group such cultural complexity and variety into finite categories has its intellectual roots in the Western scientific project as a whole, but the immediate historical impulse to such an approach to cultural and linguistic typology was the colonial conquest itself. As we have seen, the role of missionary evangelists in constructing languages from the speech behavior of the native population and in providing ethnological context for colonial policy resulted in a perfect identification of linguistic and ethnic identity. Of course such keen observers were aware of the anomalies this produced in practice, and the Jesuit missionaries of Orinoco were fully aware, and utterly frustrated, at the tendency of non-Cariban-speaking groups to become *caribe* for the same political and economic reasons that the Karipuna did (Whitehead 1998a). Nonetheless, they pursued policies of settling evangelized populations in villages that were monolingual, thus directly acting to produce the fit of culture, society, and language that was a theoretical desideratum of linguistic theories of the time.

In the absence of this missionary infrastructure, as in the Dutch, French, and British Guianas, an implicit system of ethnic ranking achieved the same effect. "Carib" groups were treated as wild but fierce mercenaries and were used to hunt down escaped black slaves and to provide a buffer against Spanish expansion beyond the Orinoco basin. "Arawaks" were used to guard the immediate plantation and to provide servants in the planter's household. They were also courted and co-opted by the missionaries as evangelical agents among the hinterland peoples, just as they had acted as military intelligence for the Spanish of the sixteenth century.[10] By underwriting and promoting a strong identification of language and political attitude, the permeability of ethnic boundaries, clearly evident from the history of the Karipuna, was curtailed. Well-defined ethnolinguistic groups—something that was no less the object of "nationalist" policies in Europe of the nineteenth century— enabled better administrative control of the native population. As a result, by the end of the nineteenth century European national political loyalties also spread among the Amerindians, producing indigenous groups calling themselves "Spanish Arawaks" and "British Arawaks," who then acted as the slavers and evangelists of their own and neighboring peoples (Whitehead 1990a, 1990b). It therefore appears that the correlation between linguistic groups and sociocultural ones is uncertain at best, for speech communities may be riven by political, economic, and ideological divisions that in practice outweigh the notional ties of sentiment and cultural similarity that common speech modes seem to imply.

This created many problems for the linguists of the nineteenth century, who, working from the missionary materials gathered in the widespread evangelization of native populations in the eighteenth century, were unable to classify the Karipuna population properly. Im Thurn (1883) was the first to attempt to resolve this situation by designating the Kariña as "True Caribs" and the Karipuna as "Island Caribs." This was partly done not just from the linguistic evidence but also via a general identification of cannibalism with the presence of "Caribs." William Brett (1868), having overseen the opening of some shell mounds in the Pomeroon Barima River in northwestern Guyana, interpreted the skeletal material uncovered to be the detritus of cannibal feasts. Given the estuarine position of the site, he further inferred that these feasts must have been conducted by the local Kariña in conjunction with their "Carib" allies from the islands. In fact, such skeletal evidence is related to a much more ancient occupation of the region and is funerary in origin (Williams 1981). In this way Brett and Im Thurn perfectly recapitulate the false ethnological inferences made by Chanca in his fifteenth-century account of Guadeloupe (discussed earlier) and so provided a revitalized basis for the persistence of the old Arawak-Carib dualism.

Other attempts to classify Arawakan languages moved to a new level with the work of Daniel Brinton (1871, 1891). Brinton (1871) demonstrated the stability of the Lokono lexicon through comparison with sixteenth-century materials and made reference to the work done on the Lokono language by missionaries in Surinam (see Crevaux et al. 1882; Quandt 1807; Stæhelin 1913). In his search for linguistic affiliates to the Lokono language and with the aim of identifying an Arawak family of languages, Brinton considered historical sources mentioning the term *Arawak,* which suggested connections with western Venezuela and the Amazon north bank. However, it was in the Caribbean that he felt the closest connection would lie, so he attempted to reconstruct elements of the Igneri or "Island Arawak" language as well as that of the Greater Antilles, although he chose not to call this language "Taíno." Again, with regard to the story of "Carib conquest," Brinton (1871, 1) wrote, "From the earliest times they [Arawaks] have borne an excellent character. Hospitable, peace-loving, quick to accept the humbler arts of civilization and the simpler precepts of Christianity, they have ever offered a strong contrast to their neighbor, the cruel and warlike Caribs." Precisely because of his credulity with regard to this colonial scheme, Brinton never attempted a comparison between Karipuna and Lokono lexicons and so did not even consider including the Karipuna in an "Arawakan" language grouping.

Unfortunately, Goeje (1939), who had already done much to expand the recording of Lokono (Goeje 1928), adopted this same framework of historical and linguistic interpretation. Still considering a ghost language, Igneri, to have been the aboriginal language of the Karipuna (before the supposed "Carib conquest"), he convincingly demonstrated continuities and relationships between Lokono, female word forms from Karipuna, and the "language" of the Greater Antilles that he called "Taíno." However, he did take the suggestion made by Adam (1878), who had noticed that the male speech forms in Karipuna were close to Kariña, and those of the women were close to Lokono. He also realized that the still extant Garifuna were a source of further information on these linguistic relationships and included materials from the "Caribe du Honduras" for comparative purposes and as an example of "Maipuran Arawak." However, although gender difference in lexical items was apparent from these comparisons, his tables (1939, 3) actually show that in all but four out of the nine categories of lexical comparison, word forms in common between men and women exceed those that were distinct.

Therefore, it is not surprising that when linguist Douglas Taylor and archaeologist Irving Rouse published a joint article (Rouse and Taylor 1956) on the peopling of the Caribbean, "We found ourselves in complete disagreement" (Rouse 1985, 18). On one hand, Rouse thought that the ceramic evidence showed that there had indeed been a movement from the mainland to the islands in late prehistory, which he assigned to the "Carib conquest."

However, Taylor had already recognized the inconsistencies in this position, especially the identification of "Taíno" with "Igneri": "This seems to imply that the Antilles were peopled by two distinct migrations of different Arawakan tribes. . . . In this case, it seems unnecessary to assume that any 'conquest' or fighting took place" (1956, 108–9).

Taylor also suggested that Karipuna was part of a "Nu-Arawak" family, which, following Mason's suggestion that this grouping be so named for the invariable presence of *nu* as first-person pronoun, included the Campa and Amuesha.[11] Thus Karipuna origins were still seen as extraneous to the islands, but their linguistic affiliations and the fallacy of a "Carib conquest" theory was beginning to be recognized. In conjunction with linguist Berend Hoff, Taylor finally realized that the Kariña elements in the men's speech actually were assimilated using an Arawakan syntax (Taylor and Hoff 1980). However, this important finding was not integrated in archaeological understanding, and Irving Rouse (1985), though now recognizing the Arawakan nature of "Island Carib," prefers to classify it along with "Taíno" as a separate "West Indian" branch of "Northern" Arawak. Rouse (1985, 1986) also now accepts that "immigration" into the islands best explains the nature of the ceramic evidence, but the idea of a conquest to explain gendered speech modes remains despite the many cogent archaeological reasons for rejecting it (Boomert 1995).

In short, the Karipuna have continued to challenge conventional forms of linguistic and cultural classification. This suggests that our categories of classification are inadequate to the complexity and dynamism of indigenous linguistic practices, just as the linguistic exogamy of Tukanoan groups in the western Amazon confounded historical linguists into suggesting a compression of previously dispersed populations instead of appreciating the way in which language was manipulated as a cultural and ethnic marker by native people, themselves rarely monolingual anyway (Reichel-Dolmatoff 1996). As Sorensen (1972, 91) realized in his analysis of multilingualism in northwestern Amazonia, "a linguistic theory limited to one language–one group situations is [itself] inadequate to explain . . . actual linguistic competence." This point is strongly reiterated by Butt-Colson as regards groups of northeastern Amazonia (1984a, 11; 1984b).

Conclusion

I have tried to show how the category "Arawak/*aruaca*," originally political as well as linguistic in its meaning, subtly evolved into a colonial cultural classification that in turn constrained the development of both historical and ethnographic understanding of the indigenous people in the Caribbean and northeastern South America. This suggests that a linguistic connection or relatedness by itself does not translate directly into social and cultural propinquity but is produced by processes of historical transculturation, as occurred in the case of the "Island Caribs." This implies that the relationship between language and the rest of culture is a matter for historical investigation through archaeology, linguistics, and historiography, as is carried out in the essays collected here. The evidence of the comparative Arawakan histories presented through the case studies in this volume show many such relationships. The substantive comparisons that emerge from this volume proceed by reference not to the mere presence of linguistic similarity but also to the cultural products of shared historical circumstance, such as ritual discourse. For example, the Karipuna *areyto,* a ritual forum for male and female oratory about the past and its continued presence in a landscape of mythic significance (see discussion of *guanin* and Guayahona above), is clearly analogous to the ways in which musicality, enchanted landscapes, and supraethnic sodalities have produced and defined ethnic consciousness in multiple contexts, both "Arawakan" and otherwise, as in Reichel-Dolmatoff's (1996) discussion of the Yuruparí myth of the Tukano.

This may not uniquely define "Arawakans" as opposed to others, but such long-term cultural features do demonstrate a substantive historical aspect to Arawakan identity. Similarly, a wide range of evidence presented in other chapters in this volume strongly indicates long-term continuities and similarities in the local sociocultural practices of Arawakan speakers. This is particularly important where the archaeology and history (see chapters 4, 8, and 10) produce striking analogies with contemporary or recent ethnographic description of the ritual use of landscape and the practice of social hierarchy (see Santos-Granero 1998; and chapters 6, 7, and 11). However, very distinct kinds of historical and sociocultural experience are also present among Arawakan speakers, as shown by the contrasting social and military orientations of, say, the Matsiguenga and Piro (see chapters 5 and 6) to the Palikur or Karipuna (see chapters 2 and 7). This suggests that we can already demonstrate strong local or regional historical and cultural relatedness among Arawakan groups and that an even broader relatedness is to be expected.

Moreover, notions of "Arawakanness" do not emerge only from contemplation of the peoples discussed in this volume but take shape from the similar relatedness of other language families, such as the Tupi-Guaraní. However, five hundred years of colonial conquest has badly damaged our ability to reconstruct the historical and cultural interactions of many peoples, and that process itself has marked modern indigenous consciousness of history and cultural identity (Hill 1996a). It has been the aim of this chapter to show

how that process must be thought through carefully, as in the case of the "Island Caribs" in all the local and regional contexts where we encounter Arawak speakers. However, what the essays here clearly indicate is that despite these obstacles, Arawaks share a substantive cultural repertoire that has proved highly resilient to such external intrusions, producing a distinct historical trajectory that is still being played out. In this way, the identification of the nature of that Arawakan historicity has become integral to all future archaeological, historical, and ethnographic understanding not just of Arawaks but of indigenous South America overall.

Notes

1. The *guatiao* came to be known as the Taíno in the nineteenth century, following the terminology coined by antiquarian C. S. Rafinesque (1836, 1:215–59). Today this term is still used to suggest a profound cultural cleavage in the aboriginal population.

2. Comparison with the formation and usages of *neêhengatú*, a Tupi-based pidgin, seems to be particularly appropriate.

3. In a brief presentation such as this it is necessary to concentrate on a few key texts: the *Journal* and *Letter* of Columbus, the *Letter* of Chanca, and the *Life of the Admiral* by Fernando Colón. For a more extensive discussion see Whitehead (1995a).

4. It should also be emphasized that the use of the term *lenguaje* did not necessarily carry the sole meaning of "language" in its modern linguistic sense but would have meant a manner of speech, or dialect.

5. ws = woman speaking, ms = man speaking.

6. During the fifteenth-century evangelization of Brazil, French missionaries likewise formulaically judged many indigenous groups to be "sin loi, sin foi, sin roi" ("without law, without faith, without king") and therefore more difficult to convert (Whitehead 1993b; see also Bono 1995).

7. Ricken (1994, 140) notes, "Every . . . theory of the origin of language also contains considerations of the origins of society . . . but also as it pertained to the nature of the human species at the beginning of human history."

8. Lexically this jargon was based on Cariban Kariña but used an Arawakan syntax, consistent with the natal language, Karipuna, of its male users (Hoff 1995).

9. *Aruaca* derives from the Lokono word for manioc flour, *aru*, which was their principal item of trade to the Spanish, just as the name *Pomeroon* derives from *baurooma*, a ball of such flour (Bennett 1989), reflecting the strategic nature of that river in the trade with the Spanish.

10. In particular, native evangelist Jeptha, a Lokono from the Berbice River, provided the Moravians in Surinam with a continentwide digest of the location of various ethnic groups and their associated political relationships with each other (Stæhelin 1913, II-2, 174–75)

11. Taylor noted that Karipuna was such a language and so unlike Lokono, Goajiro, or reconstructed Taíno, which have a prefixed marker of first person singular with apical stop ("T-dA," "L-dA," "G-tA") not nasal as for "Island Carib, Campa and probably the majority of Arawakan languages" (1954, 154).

3 Historical Linguistics and Its Contribution to Improving Knowledge of Arawak

SIDNEY DA SILVA FACUNDES

THE PURPOSE of this chapter is to discuss the method of historical linguistics that can be used to improve our knowledge of Arawakan languages, Proto-Arawakan, its subgroupings, and relationships with other language groups. *Arawak* is introduced in the second half of this chapter as the term used to refer to the genetically related languages that are sometimes called Maipure or Maipuran languages, which exclude, for example, Arauán (or Arawan/Arawá) languages. The terms *Arawakan, Maipure,* and *Maipuran* are used in the first half of the chapter until the reasons are presented later for the preference for the term *Arawak* rather than *Arawakan,* or *Maipure,* or *Maipuran.*

This chapter is organized as follows. The first section reviews the concepts, motivations, and methods used in historical linguistics for studying linguistic prehistory. The second section presents a historical overview of the linguistic studies of Arawakan languages, the linguistic reconstruction and internal classification of Proto-Arawakan, and an illustrative and preliminary reconstruction of Proto-Apurinã-Piro-Iñapari. The final section presents some conclusions about the past, present, and future contributions of linguistics to the study of the history of the Arawakan peoples, languages, and cultures.

In writing this chapter, I have assumed almost no knowledge of the principles and methods of historical linguistics. Therefore, those with a good background on the history and methods of historical linguistics, especially about the comparative method, can skip the second section of the chapter.

Establishing Language Relationships and Doing Linguistic Reconstruction

In the first of the two subsections that follow I review the historical facts that led to the development of historical linguistics, providing linguistics with a scientific method for studying language change and language relatedness. In the second subsection I briefly describe the methods for investigating linguistic history and language relatedness and discuss the status of the methods in present-day historical linguistics.

Historical Overview

It is a fact about natural languages that what were once mutually intelligible varieties of the same language may, over the course of time, diverge to the point where they become mutually incomprehensible, giving rise to two or more distinct languages. Natural language must include as part of its definition the fact that it is not static. Therefore, if varieties of the same language can change to the point where they become different languages, it follows that some of the world's languages may have originated in a common source, which may no longer be spoken.

Before scientific methods were developed for the study of language change, "divine intervention" or "barbarous corruption of speech" was given as explanation for changes in the language (Hock 1991, 1; Lehmann 1992, 23–24). However, systematic studies taking place in the last two hundred years have revealed that "language change is not completely random, unprincipled deviation from a state of pristine perfection, but proceeds in large measure in a remarkably regular and systematic fashion, without any profound effects on our ability to communicate" (Hock 1991, 2). It is among the tasks of linguists to describe how language changes come about, explain why they happen, and provide the means to describe and explain such changes. The subfield of linguistics whose primary tasks are to describe, explain, and provide the techniques or methods for studying language change is known as historical (or diachronic) linguistics (Fox 1995, 1; Campbell 1999, 5). "Historical linguists study these developments, documenting the changes that have taken place, and are still taking place, in the pronunciation, grammar, and vocabulary of the languages of the world, and relating them to the historical and cultural context in which they occur. They examine the characteristics of related languages, and try to determine the scope and nature of their relationships, and the historical connections between them. And, finally, they attempt to go beyond the history of individual languages, to an understanding of the general principles which underlie *all* language change" (Fox 1995, 1).

In 1786 an English jurist in India, Sir William Jones, made the observation that Sanskrit (an ancient language from India) bore some systematic similarities to Greek, Latin, and English. The often-quoted observation states that "The Sanskrit language, whatever be its antiquity is of wonderful structure; more perfect than the Greek, more copious than the Latin, and more exquisitely refined than either, yet bearing to both of them a stronger affinity, both in the roots of verbs and in the forms of grammar, than could possibly have been produced by accident; so strong indeed, that no philologer could examine them all three, without believing them to have sprung from some common source, which, perhaps, no longer exists: there is a similar reason, though not quite so forcible, for supposing that both the Gothic and the Celtic, though blended with a very different idiom, had the same origin with Sanskrit; and the old Persian might be added to the same family" (from "The Third Anniversary Discourse on the Indus," delivered in February 2, 1786, and more recently published in Lehmann 1967, 15).

Based on this observation, European scholars later began to compare older forms of English and German with Latin, Greek, Sanskrit, and other languages. As a result of these comparisons, in the nineteenth century these languages were classified as belonging to the Indo-European family, giving rise to the development of historical linguistics as a discipline (Lehmann 1992, 8).

The data used as evidence for language changes can be from various sources. In practicing historical linguistics, one can distinguish between historical data, that is, data based on texts, inscriptions, and other documentary evidence, and prehistorical data, that is, data whose existence precedes historical data. In most cases prehistorical data are the only source of evidence that can be constructed to acquire some knowledge of earlier stages of a language or group of languages (Fox 1995, 2). Both historical and prehistorical data can be used in studying language changes that can be identified through the comparison of related languages. Studies involving comparison of languages generally are called comparative linguistics (Campbell 1999, 4). The part of historical linguistics that focuses specifically on the investigation of prehistoric linguistic data is linguistic reconstruction. "This term refers to the practice of creating, on the basis of extant historical evidence, hypothetical language forms from which the actually occurring forms of one or more languages may be systematically derived" (Fox 1995, 3). Depending on the assumptions of individual linguists about the status of the hypothetical language forms, these reconstructed language forms can be equated with earlier forms of the language or groups of languages compared, or they can be considered to have methodological value in the process of establishing historical relationships between languages.

Methods for Investigating Language Change and Language Relatedness

For more than a century historical linguists have been trying to refine the goals, techniques, and assumptions used in recovering the linguistic past. Most of the current work on linguistic reconstruction is based on principles, methods, and assumptions developed in the nineteenth century in the research of Indo-European and Finno-Ugric languages. There are two main methods that are more widely accepted and used in linguistic reconstruction: the comparative method and internal reconstruction. The development of cross-language studies and in-depth research of individual languages in the twentieth century has led to great advances in our knowledge of the ways in which languages are structured. As a result, language universals and linguistic typology have been more recently incorporated as ancillary tools of much research using the comparative method and the internal reconstruction method. Other, more quantitatively based methods have also been used in reconstructing language relationships: lexicostatistics (or glottochronology) and mass comparison. However, these two quantitative methods, especially the second, are highly controversial.

The comparative method makes use of comparison between linguistic properties in two or more languages to determine whether these languages share a common ancestry and to reconstruct as much as possible of the linguistic properties of such an ancestral language. This method was the earliest developed for establishing language relationships and doing language reconstruction. Comparison as a way to determine language relationships can be traced back to what is sometimes cited as the origins of historical linguistics, that is, the observation made by Sir William Jones (quoted earlier) about some of the languages that have Proto-Indo-European as common source. However, despite the attempt of nineteenth-century linguists to develop scientific methods for making language comparisons, it was only in the twentieth century that linguists tried to make as explicit as possible the techniques that are part of the comparative method (Fox 1995, 57).

The comparative method starts with the assumption that "if two or more languages share a feature which is unlikely to have arisen by accident, borrowing, or as the result of some typological tendency or language universal, then it is assumed to have arisen only once and to have been transmitted to the two or more languages from a common source" (Baldi 1990, 6). To claim that two or more languages are genetically related means that they share common ancestry. However, it is generally easier to demonstrate that two or more languages are related than to recover the linguistic properties of the ancestral language. The difficulties in establishing well-motivated intermediate and ancestral forms involve answers to the following questions: "Which features in which of the languages being compared are older? Which are innovations? Which are borrowed? How many shared similarities are enough to prove relatedness conclusively, and what sort of similarities must they be? How are these weighted for significance? What assumptions do we make about the relative importance of lexical, morphological, syntactic and phonological characteristics, and about directions of language change?" (Baldi 1990, 5–6).

Internal reconstruction applies to a single language to determine systematic regularities within this language so that a hypothetical source (i.e., properties of an ancestral language) can be reconstructed. The first use of the internal reconstruction method (though still unsystematic) can be traced back to Saussure in 1872 (see Fox 1995, 146). In this method the assumption is that the regular changes that occur in a language will produce systematic alternations between the forms involved and that a careful examination of these alternations will allow us to recover the original state of the language that produced such alternations. To recover earlier stages of the language, the distribution of related linguistic forms is examined in different contexts; if an abstract linguistic unit can be reconstructed on the basis of these related linguistic forms, then the identity of the related forms is established. However, because internal reconstruction does not rely on comparison of languages but on investigation of forms within a single language, its results sometimes are considered by some comparative linguists to be less reliable than those provided by the application of the comparative method.

Lexicostatistics, or glottochronology, is a quantitative method for reconstructing genealogical relationships between languages on the basis of a comparison of the vocabularies of these languages or establishing the time scale of genealogical relationships between languages. Lexicostatistics has been used to establish degrees of linguistic similarities on the basis of a quantitative study of the vocabularies of languages. According to this method, the degree of similarity between the vocabularies of the languages being compared determines how closely related two or more languages are. The originator of this method was anthropological linguist Morris Swadesh (1950, 1951, 1952). It has generally been anthropological linguists who have attempted to apply this method most consistently. Archaeologists such as Lathrap (1975, 75–81) have also used this method to corroborate hypotheses originally based on archaeological evidence.

When the method is used to establish the time scale of genealogical relationships between languages, the method generally is called glottochronology. The general assumption in glottochronology is that "the rate of vocabulary loss in languages is constant" (Fox 1995, 282). In this method a core
vocabulary is selected for comparison. The core or basic vocabulary is assumed to consist of the concepts that are more resistant to change and replacement, unlike the "peripheral" or "cultural" vocabulary. Swadesh's original list of core vocabulary consisted of 200 items, which was later reduced
to a list of 100 items to eliminate culture-dependent items. Lexicostatistics
or glottochronology attracted various criticisms from historical linguists
about its assumptions and techniques. The first potential problem with the
method is that it relies on the vocabulary of the language, which is generally
regarded as "an unreliable basis for determining language relationships;
phonological and grammatical correspondences are held to be more trust-
worthy" (Fox 1995, 287). Also, it is difficult, if not impossible, to separate
"basic" from "cultural" vocabulary in some languages, so sometimes the list
of vocabulary suggested by Swadesh is not properly translatable into other
languages. Criticisms were also directed toward the standard rate of change
assumed in the method and its statistical basis. However, the most common
criticism was about the assumption that there is a uniform rate of vocabulary loss and that such a rate is universal for all languages at all times. As Fox
(1995, 287) states, "Apart from the fact that such an assumption is a priori
unlikely—every language is subject to different influences and pressures, to
which its vocabulary will respond in different ways—many instances have
been adduced where the results of applying the method of glottochronology do not tally with the time-scale known from other sources."

There is another quantitative method, mass comparison, which has been
used in linguistics to determine language relationships. Joseph Greenberg
(1987) has recently applied this method to the study of American languages.
Various linguists have extensively reviewed Greenberg's work (see Goddard
1987; Golla 1987, 1988; and Campbell 1988). The most general conclusion
about it is that he "has expounded a very good method for forming hypotheses about genetic relatedness, but has included some practices and excluded some others that have the overall effect of hampering its effectiveness"
(Kaufman 1990, 15–16). That is, the validity of Greenberg's method is can-
celed by the fact that much of the data he used are just plain wrong, as stated by several specialists in the relevant languages. Furthermore, the effectiveness of the method will be verifiable only when sufficient (and correct) data
are used. Because one of the major problems for studying the languages of
the Americas (especially those from South America) is precisely the lack of

good-quality data, Greenberg's method was bound to fail, as in fact it did. As more descriptive works on these languages become available, Greenberg's method might then become testable.

The linguistic method most often used and considered by most historical linguists as the most reliable to establish genetic relationships and to reconstruct earlier stages of languages still is the comparative method. Although the internal reconstruction method is also used, it is used in addition to the comparative method or where the latter cannot be applied (that is, when data from only one language are available for investigation). However, lexicostatistics or glottochronology is still used as a preliminary tool before the other, more rigorous methods are applied or as a method to corroborate hypotheses formulated on the basis of language-external evidence. In fact, based on his experience in Mesoamerica, Kaufman states, "If the method is applied properly, the glottochronological rate of retention on the 100-word list is 86% ±3% over 100 years and is applicable to 95% of all languages" (1990, 27). He also concludes that part of the "widespread aversion to glottochronology" is motivated by specific misapplications of the method by various linguists, including Swadesh himself. However, other historical linguists (e.g., Dixon 1997, 35–35) are not so optimistic about the potential of this method. Other uses of lexicostatistics or glottochronology constitute modifications of the original assumptions or techniques that were part of Swadesh's original proposal (see brief overview in Klein 1994, 349–50).

Comparative Linguistics Applied to Arawakan Languages

In this section I review the most important comparative pieces of work done by linguists on Arawakan languages, its history, current status, and prospects for the future. I start with an overview of the research on Arawakan languages, then I discuss the current status of the reconstruction of Proto-Arawak and its internal classification. Finally, I present an illustrative and preliminary comparative study of three Arawakan languages.

History of Linguistic Studies of Arawakan Languages

Although a genetic group of Maipuran (named after the Maipure language) languages was first suggested in 1782 by Italian missionary Filippo Salvatore Gilij while working in Venezuela (Noble 1965, 1; Payne 1991, 363), the number of languages that belong to such a group has varied to a great extent depending on the author of the classification. There were 67 languages included in Goeje (1928), 122 in Mason (1950), 89 in Noble (1965), and 154 in Loukotka

(1968). According to Aikhenvald (1999a, 73), it was Brinton (1891) and Steinen (1886) who renamed the linguistic group as Arawak, after the Arawak (or Lokono) language spoken in the Guianas. Later some linguists started using the name *Maipuran* to refer uniquely to the group of languages that were undoubtedly genetically related. The term *Arawak* or *Arawakan* was reserved to refer to a supposed higher genetic group of languages that would include the groups Maipuran, Arauán, Guahibo, Puquina, and Harakmbet (see Payne 1991, 365; discussion in Aikhenvald 1999a, 73–75; and references cited in this latter work).

Most recently, as descriptions of more languages have become available, it has become more and more clear that there is no tenable linguistic evidence to postulate a higher genetic group that would include Maipuran, Arauán, Guahibo, Puquina, and Harakmbet. The classifications by Goeje (1928), Mason (1950), and Loukotka (1968) were based primarily on geographic distribution of languages rather than in any linguistic method (see Taylor 1961; Valenti 1986; Payne 1991; Dixon 1995, Appendix A; Dixon and Aikhenvald 1999, Introduction; Aikhenvald 1999a; and Dixon 1999). As has been pointed out by Tovar and Tovar (1984), Rodrigues (1986, 65–72), and, more recently, by Dixon (1995, 89) and Aikhenvald (1999a, 73–74), there is no linguistic ground to postulate that Maipuran (i.e., Arawakan) languages form a genetic group with the Arauán (i.e., Arawá). Earlier attempts to reconstruct the protolanguage that would comprise Proto-Maipuran and Proto-Arauán, such as Matteson (1972b), did not use the comparative method that is accepted by historical linguists (briefly described in the previous section).

Payne (1991) carried out the first comparative linguistic study of Maipuran languages following the comparative method. He reconstructed 203 items for Proto-Maipuran, using twenty-four Maipuran languages from all the putative main branches of the family. Only very recently was a detailed comparative study done for the Arauán languages by Dixon (1995, Appendix A; 1999). Dixon reconstructed 370 lexemes for Proto-Arauán and, by comparing the reconstructed forms for Proto-Arauán and Proto-Maipure, reached the following conclusion: "Three possible cognates can be recognized between these lists, none of them fully convincing. The grammatical morphemes of Proto-Arawá [i.e., Proto-Arauán] are also quite different. It must be concluded that there is no evidence whatsoever that (despite their similar names and geographical proximity) the Arawá and Arawak language families are genetically related" (Dixon 1995, 290). The most recent classification of the Arawá family is given in Dixon (1999, 294) and is reproduced in simplified form in table 3.1.

Unfortunately, as noted by Tovar and Tovar (1984), Dixon (1995, 289) and

Table 3.1. Composition of the Arawá Language Family

Paumarí
Madi (with three dialects: Jarawara, Jamamadi, and Banawá)
Sorowahá
DENI-KULINA
Deni
Kulina (or Madiha or Madija)
Arawá[a]

a. Arawá is extinct. DENI-KULINA is a subgroup of the Arawá family.

Aikhenvald (1999a, 73–74), it is unsubstantiated classifications such as Noble (1965) and Matteson (1972b) that have been generally adopted by scholars outside the field of linguistics, including anthropologists, archaeologists, and geneticists. Moreover, as Aikhenvald (1999a, 73–74) notes, the "deeply flawed" studies of "Arawakan" languages influence "ideas on putative proto-home and migration routes for Proto-Arawakan."

Therefore, to the extent that linguistic evidence is used in investigating the prehistory and culture of the so-called Arawakan peoples, Maipuran and Arauán groups are better treated as genetically unrelated language groups. Moreover, following Dixon (1995) and Dixon and Aikhenvald (1999), I hereafter refer to the linguistically attested Maipuran genetic group as Arawak and to the unrelated group of Arauán languages as Arawá. In this manner, I will also be following the tradition in South America, where the two linguistic groups have been generally distinguished as unrelated language families, called Aruák (or Arawak or Arahuaca) and Arawá (Tovar 1986, 2; Rodrigues 1986, 65; Aikhenvald 1999a, 73). Furthermore, following Tovar (1986, 10) and based on the results presented by Payne (1991) and, more recently, by Aikhenvald (1999a), I do not include Guahibo, Puquina, and Harakmbet in the Arawak language family.

The conclusion that the languages of the Arawak and Arawá families and the languages Guahibo, Puquina, and Harakmbet are not related genetically does not mean that the histories of these groups and their cultures may not be interrelated and that they cannot be studied together; it means only that there is no linguistic evidence that these groups ever spoke the same (ancient) language. Also, their linguistic genetic unrelatedness does not mean that the speakers of those languages are not related racially. A poor dialogue between linguists and anthropologists has led to some confusion about the implications of linguistic classification for anthropological studies and vice versa. Linguistic changes, reconstruction, and classification (when the proper methods are used) have long ago been proved to be of great importance for the understanding of how languages evolve and the understanding of the prehistory of various social groups, and they have greatly contributed to our understanding of how human languages work, regardless of their cultural correlates. However, although linguistic classification can also be used as an important initial heuristic procedure in doing comparative studies of various social groups, one should always keep in mind that the relationship between language and culture is conditioned by the historical factors that maintain individuals closely bound together in systematic contact or that set them apart. The problem in trying to correlate language and culture is that despite the undeniable fact that they are always in close and dynamic interaction, as noted long ago by Edward Sapir, culture changes faster than language, and "the forms of language will in course of time cease to symbolize those of culture" (1949, 102). Therefore, the linguistic genetic classification should never be equated with ethnological classification.

Linguistic Reconstruction and Internal Classification of Proto-Arawak

As confirmed by two of the most recently published detailed works on the classification of Arawakan languages (Payne 1991; Aikhenvald 1999a), there is general agreement about which languages belong to the Arawak family. However, as Aikhenvald (1999a, 73) points out, the internal genetic relationships within Arawak still are problematic. A quick glance at Payne's and Aikhenvald's internal classification, for example, will reveal precisely how much work still is needed in this area.

In his phonological reconstruction of Proto-Arawak, Payne uses twenty-four languages, whereas Aikhenvald includes all the languages known as Arawak in her preliminary classification. Differences between the languages common to Payne's and Aikhenvald's classifications can be seen in various places. Payne posits four levels of subgroupings within Arawak (respectively highlighted here with capitals, double quotes, italics, and single quotes, in decreasing order), whereas Aikhenvald posits only three levels of subgroupings. More specifically, whereas Paressí and Waurá are grouped together within one major branch (i.e., CENTRAL) in Payne's classification, these two languages are placed in two separate branches (i.e., *Xingu* and *Pareci-Saraveca*) of the "Pareci-Xingu" subgroup (which itself is a branch of South and South-Western Arawak) in Aikhenvald's classification. The same is true of Amuesha and Chamicuro, grouped immediately under WESTERN by Payne and, separately, under *Amuesha* and *Chamicuro* (both also branches of South and South-Western Arawak), respectively. Whereas Payne places Resígaro immediately under *North-Amazon* (which itself is under "Inland," which is under the NORTHERN major branch of Arawak), and Achagua, Cabiyari, Curripa-co, Piapoko, Tariana, and Yukuna together under 'Rio Negro' (also a branch of *North-Amazon*), Aikhenvald groups Resígaro together with Yukuna, Piapo-co, Cabiyari, and Maipure under *Colombian* (a branch of North-Amazonian under NORTH-ARAWAK). Finally, another difference between the languages shared by both classifications is Yavitero, which Payne places immediately under the "Inland" group of the NORTHERN major branch of Arawak, whereas Aikhenvald groups it together with Baré, Baniwa of Guainía, Man-dawaka, and Yabaana, under the *Orinoco* (a branch of North-Amazonian).

Various factors underlie the lack of agreement about the internal classifi-cation within the Arawak family. One factor is that Payne bases his internal classification on shared lexical retentions found among the languages he used in his comparison, whereas Aikhenvald bases hers partly on an "areal-geo-graphic principle" (Aikhenvald 1999a, 75). To some extent, differences in subgrouping may also reflect the appearance of newer data and descriptions of Arawakan languages (e.g., Aikhenvald 1995, 1998; Parker 1995). After all, as already anticipated by Tovar, among the linguistic families of South Amer-ica "es la arahuaka la más antiguamente difundida, y en una extensión mayor, y, por lo mismo, en la que han de esperarse divergencias mayores, tanto en el léxico como en los rasgos tipológicos" ("it is Arawak that spread the earli-est and over the greatest expanse, and for this reason it is the family in which one would expect the greatest divergence, both in lexicons and typological features" [my translation]; 1986, 2). Aikhenvald (1999a, 74) also notes that the difficulties in doing comparative analyses of Arawakan languages and of determining its internal classification come from the lack of adequate data for many languages, in addition to their geographic expansion and linguis-tic diversity within the family. However, the problems with the subgroupings of Arawakan languages also reveal a general trend that, until recently, was present among Arawak linguists, namely to attempt to reconstruct and clas-sify Arawakan languages only in relation to the general Arawak family (or in relation to the putative larger group that would include Arawá languages) rather than in relation to how these languages related to one another inside the family. This trend is likely to derive historically from the fact that "research on American Indian languages has been dominated from the beginning by a desire to determine the origin and relationships of the languages of the New World. This has tended to put an emphasis on distant relationships before the details of the closer relationships were worked out" (Campbell and God-dard, 1990, 18). A notable exception to this trend (as acknowledged by Payne 1991, 371) among earlier Arawak scholars was the work of Douglas Taylor (e.g., Taylor 1977).

More recently, however, serious attempts to resolve some of the problems with or disprove earlier suggestions about Arawakan subgroupings have started to appear (see Aikhenvald 2001). Another attempt to resolve an Arawakan subgrouping is briefly illustrated in the next section, where I provide a preliminary phonological reconstruction involving the languages Apurinã, Piro, and Iñapari.

In her short discussion about subgroupings within the Arawak language family, Aikhenvald (1999a, 73–75) notes that scientific arguments in favor of North Arawak as a separate group have been given by Taylor and that some low-level reconstructions have been made for Proto-Lokono-Guajiro, as well as for Proto-Xingu, but she concludes, "Though there are a few comparative studies of various subgroups . . . further investigation is needed to decide whether this division is genetic, or is due to different patterns of areal diffusion, and exactly what the subgrouping is. For the time being we can only be certain of subgroupings of Arawakan languages on a very low taxonomic level (e.g. Xinguan languages, South Arawak of Brazil, Pi[ro]-Ap[purinã])" (Aikhenvald 1999a; see also references therein).

No solid glottochronological study has been made yet on the basis of the most recent classifications of Arawakan languages. Although Tovar (1986) uses the lexicostatistical method in suggesting subgroupings within the Arawak family, his view of the glottochronological method was that "las bases matemáticas de la glotocronología, que podían hacer de ella algo como un método comparable al del carbono 14, se han desvanecido" ("the mathematical bases of glottochronology that make it a method comparable to carbon-14 have vanished" [my translation]; 1986, 11).

The Apurinã-Piro-Iñapari Subgroup

The purpose of this section is to summarize the results of a partial comparison between Apurinã, Piro, and Iñapari, presenting the preliminary reconstruction of the segmental inventory (i.e., consonants and vowels) that was arrived at through a historical comparative analysis. The results presented here are still preliminary because the focus of the reconstruction was based primarily on lexical items (such as nouns and verbs), because the reconstruction did not include morphological or syntactic properties, and because nasalization, vowel lengthening, and suprasegments (i.e., stress and tone) were left out of this preliminary reconstruction. Therefore, the comparative analysis sketched here is only a partial illustration of the application of the comparative method in investigating a putative subgroup of Arawak, the Apurinã-Piro-Iñapari (API).

Apurinã is the language I have been working on for the last ten years, having recently concluded a preliminary (still unpublished) descriptive grammar of the language (Facundes 2000b). The Apurinã data used here come exclusively from the various field trips I have made to eleven Apurinã communities in the State of Acre and along the Purus River in the State of Amazonas in Brazil, between 1990 and 1997. The data from Piro come from Matteson (1965, 1972b). The data from Iñapari come from Parker (1995). The clustering of Apurinã, Piro, and Iñapari as members of a branch of Arawak has already been implied by the classification given in Payne (1991, 364). The attempt at a reconstruction presented here provides some preliminary information on which basis a branch within Arawak can be verified later on, as the information brought about by the partial phonemic reconstruction of Proto-Apurinã-Piro-Iñapari (P-API) is compared with the reconstructions available for Proto-Arawak and its subgroups. Furthermore, the fact that API are all Arawakan languages has already been demonstrated by previous comparative works (see Valenzuela 1991; Payne 1991; and Aikhenvald 1999a).

The method used in analyzing the data of the three languages is the comparative method briefly described earlier. The proper presentation of the comparative analysis, including a detailed presentation of the data used and the various steps of the investigation, would require a separate essay; therefore, I focus on the results of the comparison and refer to Facundes (2000a) for the details of the analysis and the data, where the reader will find the information necessary to verify the plausibility of every set of correspondences and the cognates themselves.

Before presenting the results of the analysis, I must introduce a few terms that are part of the linguistic jargon (following, in general, the wording by Campbell 1999, 111–12). A protolanguage is the ancestral language from which daughter languages descend and can be reconstructed if the application of the comparative method is successful. Sister languages are languages that are related to one another as daughter languages that descend from the same ancestor (protolanguage). A cognate is a word or morpheme that is related to another word or morpheme of a sister language insofar as both derive from the same word or morpheme of the protolanguage. A cognate set is the group of words or morphemes that are related to one another because they descend, or have been inherited, from the same word or morpheme of the protolanguage. A sound correspondence is the set of sounds that are found to correspond to one another in the cognate set by virtue of having descended from a common ancestral sound. The reflex is each sound that descends from a common ancestral sound in the protolanguage and is found in the sound correspondences of the daughter languages. Shared retention is the linguistic property that "different daughter languages inherit unchanged from the proto-language regardless of whether the daughters belong to the same subgroup [of languages] or not" (Campbell 1999, 173). Shared innovation "is a linguistic change which shows a departure (innovation) from some trait of the proto-language and is shared by a subset of the daughter languages" (Campbell 1999, 170).

In the preliminary reconstruction, a total of 327 words were examined, including body parts, kinship terms, various animal and plant names, and descriptive and grammatical words. There were a total of 122 cognate sets shared by API, 56 shared by Apurinã and Piro (but not by Iñapari), 28 shared only by Apurinã and Iñapari (but not by Piro), and 12 shared by Piro and Iñapari (but not by Apurinã). The 122 cognate sets represent 39% of shared lexical (i.e., vocabulary) retention in API. Although such a vocabulary similarity confirms earlier suspicion that API are closely related and may descend from a protolanguage (i.e., API as part of an intermediary branch of Arawak), these shared lexical similarities cannot be used to show how closely related to one another these three languages are, nor can they be used to prove that API indeed form a subgroup of Arawak. Shared lexical retentions alone cannot be used to show whether languages group together within a genetic group. The reason for this follows from a general principle in genetic linguistic classification, namely that only shared innovations can be used as reliable evidence of subgrouping. The assumption is that shared innovations constitute linguistic changes that happened in the protolanguage and were preserved in the daughter languages. Only the languages (that have also been shown to have shared retentions) exhibiting linguistic changes that happen in some but not in other languages within the larger group (i.e., only the ones showing shared innovations) can be grouped together in subbranches of their larger family. Therefore, although Apurinã and Piro share 178 cognates (122 + 56), Apurinã and Iñapari share 150 cognates (122 + 28), and Piro and Iñapari share 134 cognates (122 + 12), it does not necessarily follow, for example, that Apurinã and Piro (but not Iñapari) descend from a common protolanguage (i.e., Proto-Apurinã-Piro, or P-AP). Only if shared innovations can be shown for Apurinã and Piro but not for Iñapari and if P-AP can be reconstructed can the subgrouping within P-API be confirmed.

Table 3.2 gives a partial list of the cognate sets illustrating the most obvious sound correspondences that were used to reconstruct a preliminary segmental inventory for P-API. The first column of table 3.2 provides the English gloss of the cognate sets given in the second, third, and fourth columns for Apurinã, Piro, and Iñapari, respectively; the fifth column gives the reconstructed proto-sounds for P-API (starred to indicate their status as reconstructed forms). These reconstructed forms are easily arrived at when their reflexes remain the same in all sister languages, as shown by most of the sound correspondences given in the table. For example, in the cognate set *pekiri:pexØri:pehirí* "agouti," because the word initial sound *p* remains constant in the same environment across the three items being compared, **p* can be posited as the ancient (proto-sound) from which the reflexes *p:p:p* descend. Where the reflexes found in the sound correspondences do not coincide, principles of sound changes (i.e., from phonetics and phonology) and universal principles of languages and typological generalizations must be applied to determine which proto-sound will be reconstructed. For example, in the cognate set *kotʃi:katʃi:Øutʃi* "rat," the word initial phoneme *k* is found both in Apurinã and in Piro, respectively, but the same phoneme is absent in the word initial position in Iñapari in pretty much the same environment (where the absence of the phoneme is represented by Ø).

Table 3.2. Preliminary Reconstruction of the Proto-Phonemes of Apurinã-Piro-Iñapari

Gloss	Apurinã	Piro	Iñapari	Proto-Phoneme
	*p > p	**p > p*	**p > p*	**p*
agouti	pekiri	pexØri	pehirí	
	*t > t	**t > t*	**t > t*	**t*
butterfly	katato	katato	Øatʃatú	
	*ts > ts	**ts > ts*	**ts > t*	**ts*
urine	tsɨna-ka	tsɨná-ka	tɨni- ʔa	
	*tx > ts	**tx > t*	**tx > tʃ*	(**tx*)
breast	-tenɨ	tØnɨ	tʃini-	
	*tʃ > tʃ	**tʃ > tʃ*	**tʃ > tʃ*	**tʃ*
sand, beach	kɨpatʃi	xØpatʃi	hipɨtʃi	
	*k > k	**k > k*	**k > Ø / #_{*a,*u}*	**k*
rat	kotʃi	katʃi	Øutʃi	
	*s > s	**s > s*	**s > Ø / _{*a,*e,*o,*u}*	**s*
moon	kasɨrɨ	kØsɨrɨ	Øa Øɨrɨ	
	*ʃ > ʃ	**ʃ > ʃ*	**ʃ > h*	**ʃ*
fish	ima-	ima	himá	
	*x > ʃ / _i	**x > x*	**x > Ø / i_i*	(**x*)
earth, land, soil	tiʃi	tʃØxi	tʃiØi	
	*h > h	**h > h*	**h > h*	**h*
piranha fish	homa	homa	huma	
	*r > r	**r > r*	**r > r*	**r*
nose	kiri	xØri	hirí-	
	*l > r	**l > l*	**l > r*	(**l*)
buzzard	mayorɨ	mayØli	mayúri	
	*m > m	**m > m*	**m > m*	**m*
piranha	homa	homa	huma	
	*n > n	**n > n*	**n > n*	**n*
tongue	nɨnɨ	nØnɨ	není(pa-)	

Table 3.2. Con't.

Gloss	Apurinã	Piro	Iñapari	Proto-Phoneme
	*y > y	**y > y*	**y > y*	**y*
squirrel	*yōpɨtɨrɨ*	*yopitxri*	*yupítʃiri*	
	*w > w	**w > w*	**w > w*	**w*
canoe	*kanawa*	*kanawa*	*Øanawá*	
	a	*a*	*a*	**a*
canoe	*kanawa*	*kanawa*	*anawá*	
	e	*e*	*e*	**e*
younger brother	*epɨrɨ*	*hepɨrɨ*	*epɨri-*	
	i	*i*	*i*	**i*
earth, land	*tiʃi*	*tʃixi*	*tʃiØɨ*	
	*I > ɨ	**I > ɨ*	**I > i*	(**I*)
breast	*-tenɨ*	*tØnɨ*	*tʃini-*	
	ɨ	*ɨ*	*-ɨ*	**ɨ*
younger brother	*epɨrɨ*	*hepɨrɨ*	*epɨri-*	
	o	*o*	*o*	**o*
eye, face	*okɨ*	*hoxi*	*oxɨ-*	
	o	*o*	*u*	**u*
arrive	*apo-ka*	*hapoka*	*apúʔa-*	

Note: Ø represents cases in which the reflex of the proto-sound is phonologically null (i.e. phonetically absent) in the vocabulary item in question. Formulas such as **p > p* read as "the proto-phoneme **p** changes to/realizes as the phoneme **p**," where an asterisk (*) marks the status of the phoneme as a reconstructed (therefore hypothetical) form. More complex formulas such as **k > Ø / #_{*a,*u}* read as "the proto-phoneme **k** changes to/realizes as zero (i.e., the null set) in the word initial environment, preceding the proto-phoneme **a** or **u**," where a number symbol (#) indicates a word boundary and an underscore (_) replaces the phoneme undergoing change (i.e., **k**). Such formulas are part of the linguistic convention, and its general template is *X > Y / Z* (i.e., *X* changes to/realizes as *Y* in the environment *Z*). When no environment is specified (i.e., when "/ *Z*" is not mentioned), it means that the sound change took place in all environments in the language. Other special symbols include *ts* = alveolar fricative consonant; *tʃ* = alveopalatal affricate consonant; *tx* = palatal affricate consonant; *ʃ* = alveopalatal fricative consonant; *x* = palatal fricative consonant; *h* = laryngeal fricative consonant; *I* = semi-high front unrounded vowel; *ɨ* = high central unrounded vowel. Proto-forms given in parentheses must be verified further before the status of their reconstruction can be confirmed. **Boldface italic** is used to indicate that specific phonemes are undergoing transformation from prototype to contemporary languages.

Because it is more likely that one language alone changed and the other two did not, rather than the reverse (there being no evidence to the contrary), and because the dropping of a consonant is quite common as a historical phonological process (i.e., more common than the addition of it) across languages, we can posit that in the correspondence set *k:k:Ø,* **k* was originally found in P-API and that this original sound was preserved in Apurinã and in Piro, but **k* was dropped in word initial environment in Iñapari. In fact, to give a more complete picture, **k* was preserved (as *k*) in all environments in Apurinã (as in *katʃtitɨ* "type of ant," *katato* "butterfly," *nakɨ* "egg of," *hākipa* "heart of," etc.); in Piro, **k* was preserved only when preceding the proto-API vowels *a and *o (as in kat/iti "type of ant," katato "butterfly," etc., but not in naxi "egg," haxi "heart," etc.); finally, in Iñapari, *k changed into Ø also preceding the proto-API vowels *a and *o (as in Øatítli "type of ant," Øat/ato "butterfly," etc., but not in (a)nahi(rɨ) "egg," hãhipa- "heart," etc.). That the historical sound change posited here is real is confirmed by its regularity in the cognate sets attested, and that it was *k that changed into Ø in Iñapari and not, for example, that the absence of k (i.e., *Ø) changed into k in Apurinã and Piro, can be confirmed by the fact that words that started with *a and *o in P-API can be found without an initial k in both Apurinã (as in apɨ "bone of," okɨ "eye of," etc.) and Piro (as in hapɨ "bone," hoxi "eye"— where the presence of h in Piro is independently required by an obligatory insertion rule in words that otherwise would start with a vowel).

The additional examples in the languages being compared, which corroborate the linguistic analysis, indicate that the processes needed to posit the reconstruction given in table 3.2 occur regularly enough in these languages, suggesting that such a reconstruction is at least plausible. The cognate sets given in table 3.2 are obviously incomplete and constitute a group of some of the most obvious cognates (selected here for ease of illustration) that were actually used in the reconstruction of the segmental inventory of P-API listed in the rightmost columns of table 3.2.

Finally, as seen in table 3.3, a higher number of shared innovations is attested for Apurinã and Piro. Thus, this partial segmental phonological reconstruction suggests that Iñapari might have split earlier from Proto-Apurinã-Piro, thus allowing Proto-Apurinã-Piro to develop some innovations that were preserved by Apurinã and Piro after their (later) split from one another. Obviously, to verify such a chronological sequencing of splits we need not only to develop a separate phonological reconstruction for Proto-Apurinã-Piro but also to reconstruct elements of the grammars of these languages, aside from reconstructing some vocabulary.

How can information from historical linguistics, such as the reconstruction presented here, tell us anything about the prehistory of the speakers of Apurinã, Piro, and Iñapari? I should first note that until the reconstruction is confirmed by executing the next steps of the analysis (i.e., reconstructing other aspects of the phonology, such as nasalization and suprasegments, and reconstructing vocabulary and elements of the grammar), the inferences made on the basis of the linguistic reconstruction must be verified later. These inferences will be reliable only after the next steps of the reconstruction have been completed. On the other hand, if such additional steps were successfully completed, the preliminary segmental reconstruction already allows us to reconstruct some vocabulary for P-API. For example, one important item that is reconstructable is the word for "hammock," which is *ke* in Apurinã, *xe* in Piro, and *he* in Iñapari. The sound correspondence *k:x:h* is one that occurs regularly in API and can be motivated by positing that the proto-phoneme in P-API was **k*, changing into *x* in Piro (before **e, *i, *I,* and **ɨ*) and into *h* in Iñapari (also before **e, *i, *I,* and **ɨ*). Based on this alternation rule, "hammock" can then be reconstructed for P-API as **ke*.

Gow (chapter 6) says that the word for "hammock" is found in Piro only in a myth. From this, Gow suggests that Piro abandoned hammocks as they moved toward Campa and Matsiguenga, a claim that becomes more plausible when the word for "hammock" is independently shown to have been found in the putative protolanguage from which Piro descends (directly or indirectly). Also, further inquiry would reveal that the word for "bed" cannot be reconstructed for P-API (at least, not with the meaning "bed"), again making Gow's claim more plausible. Thus, Gow's suggestion that Piro abandoned hammocks to use beds by influence of Campa and Matsiguenga finds some independent support in the linguistic reconstruction of P-API. Finally, once the reconstruction of P-API is completed successfully, as its possible internal relationships are determined, other comparisons can be made between the three language groups to verify, for example, the extent to which this internal subgrouping within Arawak correlates in any way with ethnographical features or whether there are any traces of shared identity properties common to these groups despite the obvious historical and geographic gaps setting them apart.

Other Contributions from Linguistics to the Study of Arawak

Two important areas of historical linguistics that I have not discussed yet but are extremely relevant for discovering more of the history of Arawakan people are areal or contact linguistics and paleolinguistics. Areal or contact linguistics deals with linguistic phenomena that arise from contact between different (not necessarily genetically related) languages and cannot be investigated using the comparative method because, put in simple terms, they involve nongenetic relationships. However, only after the application of the comparative method can languages be convincingly shown *not* to be genetically related (at least within the time depth that can be assessed through the linguistic methods); therefore, the study in the field of areal or contact linguistics, in theory, necessarily follows studies that use the comparative method.

Very little published material in this area is applied to Arawakan languages. A recent contribution in this field is the work of Aikhenvald (2001), where she examines contact-induced language changes in various sociolinguistic

Table 3.3. Preliminary Set of Shared Phonological Innovations in Apurinã-Piro-Iñapari

Apurinã and Piro Innovations		Apurinã and Iñapari Innovations		Piro and Iñapari Innovations	
*tx > t		*l > r		*I > e / {*k}_	
Apurinã	*káikti* ("non-Indian person")	Apurinã	*mayori* ("buzzard")	Piro	*xexi* ("man")
Piro	*kaxit* ("non-Indian person")	Iñapari	*mayúri* ("buzzard")	Iñapari	*Øeli* ("man")
cf. Iñapari	*Øahitʃi* ("non-Indian person")	cf. Piro	*mayØli* ("buzzard")	cf. Apurinã	*kiki* ("man")
*ts > t / _*i					
Apurinã	*natʃi-* ("hunger")				
Piro	*natʃi-* ("hunger")				
cf. Iñapari	*nati* ("hunger")				
* > i / h_{*r,*t}					
Apurinã	*hito* ("body of")				
Piro	*hito* ("flesh")				
cf. Iñapari	*Øitʃi-* ("flesh")				

		u > o	
Apurinã	apoka	("arrive")	
Piro	hapoka	("arrive")	
cf. Iñapari	apúka	("arrive")	

		I > i	
Apurinã	teni	("breasts of")	
Piro	tɵni	("breasts")	
cf. Iñapari	tʃini-	("breasts")	

Total of innovations = 5   Total of innovations = 1   Total of innovations = 1

Total of innovations = 1

Note: ∅ represents cases in which the reflex of the proto-sound is phonologically null (i.e., phonetically absent) in the vocabular item in question. Formulas such as **p > p* read as "the proto-phoneme *p* changes to/realizes as the phoneme *p*," where an asterisk (*) marks the status of the phoneme as a reconstructed (therefore hypothetical) form. More complex formulas such as **k > ∅ / # _{*a,*u}* read as "the proto-phoneme *k* changes to/realizes as zero (i.e., the null set) in the word initial environment, preceding the proto-phoneme *a* or *u*," where a number symbol (#) indicates a word boundary and an underscore (_) replaces the phoneme undergoing change (i.e., *k*). Such formulas are part of the linguistic convention, and its general template is *X > Y / Z* (i.e., *X* changes to/realizes as *Y* in the environment *Z*). When no environment is specified (i.e., when "/ *Z*" is not mentioned), it means that the sound change took place in all environments in the language. Other special symbols include *ts* = alveolar fricative consonant; *tʃ* = alveopalatal affricate consonant; *tx* = palatal affricate consonant; *ʃ* = alveopalatal fricative consonant; *x* = palatal fricative consonant; *h* = laryngeal fricative consonant; *I* = semi-high front unrounded vowel; *i* = high central unrounded vowel. Proto-forms given in parentheses must be verified further before the status of their reconstruction can be confirmed. *Boldface italic* is used to indicate that specific phonemes are undergoing transformation from prototype to contemporary languages.

contexts of North Arawak languages and the problems they pose to internal classification of the Arawak family. In another publication, Aikhenvald (1999b) also examines three unrelated groups of languages—North Arawak, East Tucano, and Makú—all spoken in the Vaupés area. Aikhenvald observes that Tariana (the only Arawakan language in the area), Makú languages, and East Tucano languages share a number of phonological, grammatical, and semantic features despite the fact that they are unrelated genetically. She concludes that the region is marked by areal diffusions that may originate in the East Tucano languages because "the majority of the features shared by the languages in the Vaupés are found in Tucano languages outside the Vaupés, and are not attested in languages of the Arawak and Makú families spoken outside this area" (Aikhenvald 1999b, 411). Therefore, in the Vaupés region, certain shared linguistic similarities between Tariana, East Tucano, and Makú languages can be explained in terms of historical, social, and cultural factors shared by those people, which appear to have led to the diffusion of linguistic features from East Tucano languages into Tariana and Makú. In such a situation, the methods of contact linguistics are more useful in helping to disentangle the various factors involved in determining the characteristics of the languages in question, whereas the comparative method does not apply or applies only to a very limited extent.

The work of Thomason and Kaufman (1988) is an excellent source of information on the types of contact-induced language changes found around the world. They also present a well-constructed framework for distinguishing and investigating the various types of contact-induced language change. In this work they distinguish "normal" from "imperfect" language transmission, where the type of language transmission is determined by the sociolinguistic history of the speakers and where only "normal" transmission entails genetic relationship. More recently, Dixon (1997) proposed a different way of approaching the study of language relationships: the punctuated equilibrium model. Basically, Dixon claims that the situations in which the model of language change behind the comparative method (based on the methods used to reconstruct Proto-Indo-European) works constitute the minority of the cases in human history, and that, most often, language change results from the diffusion of linguistic features "across the languages of a given area so that—over a very long period—they converge on a common prototype" (Dixon 1997, 4). According to Dixon, periods during which languages expand and split into new languages descending from a common protolanguage are brief. Dixon and Aikhenvald (1999, 17) cite the adoption of agriculture as one factor that could have caused expansion and split in South America, thus explaining "the readily provable genetic unity of the Arawak, Carib and Tupí families" (1999, 17). It is too early to know how well Dixon's model will help us to understand better the prehistory of the Arawakan people and their language. The more recent works by Aikhenvald (1999a, 1999b) on Arawakan languages seem to use the punctuated equilibrium model. The fact is that the field of linguistic investigation on contacts between Arawakan languages still is full of unanswered questions, and a detailed discussion of it is beyond the scope of this chapter.

Paleolinguistics deals with the reconstruction of culture and environment by means of linguistic comparison; it is perhaps the area that can provide the most direct contribution to anthropological and archaeological studies of Arawak and therefore is also one of the areas in which linguists, anthropologists, and archaeologists would naturally be expected to interact the most. No discussion of it was included earlier in this chapter because very little has been done in this area with respect to Arawakan languages, although some relevant data are available. For example, Payne (1991) has already reconstructed 203 items for Proto-Arawak; whether such items can tell us anything interesting about Arawakan proto-culture and prehistory remains to be seen. The example given earlier for "hammock" is one instance in which both linguistic and anthropological information may combine to produce a better understanding of various issues involving Arawakan groups and languages. With the aid of anthropologists and archaeologists, it is possible to attempt to reconstruct items in the vocabulary of various protolanguages for cultural or environmental concepts that may help establish migration patterns, homelands, and other features for various of the Arawakan groups and, ultimately, for Proto-Arawak as well.

Prospects for Arawak Language Studies

The purpose of this chapter was to review critically the sort of contribution that the linguistic method can provide (or has provided) to improve our knowledge of the prehistory of the Arawakan people, their language, and their culture. Particular attention was given to the methods (and their history) in historical linguistics for investigating language prehistory, especially by means of the comparative method. The emphasis on history and methods was chosen because there is a good degree of mismatch between what is generally accepted by historical linguists as scientific methods for investigating language prehistory and methods that have traditionally been applied by linguists working on Arawakan languages and whose results have influenced researchers outside the field of linguistics. One of the conclusions arrived at was that although it is reasonably clear what languages can be shown today to be genetically related within the Arawak family, very little work has been done to determine how individual Arawakan languages relate to one another inside the Arawak family. Some of the attempts to start resolving this problem are the recent work of Aikhenvald (2001) and the brief and illustrative analysis presented earlier for the reconstruction of P-API.

Finally, when linguistic methods indicate that two or more languages are not genetically related, this does not mean that the linguistic histories of the people speaking these languages cannot or should not be studied together. On the contrary, if there were initial reasons to suspect that two or more languages shared a common ancestor, the linguistic history of the speakers of these languages should be compared even after the possibility of genetic linguistic relationship (i.e., "normal" transmission) has been eliminated. It is precisely the linguistic phenomena that occur in situations of contact between speakers of distinct languages that are the major subject of study of areal or contact linguistics. Therefore, some work remains to be done to explain the reasons that led scholars to believe that the Arawak and Arawá language families were derived from a common ancestor.

Note

This chapter was started while I was finishing the doctoral program in linguistics at SUNY-Buffalo, in the United States, and concluded while I was teaching in the graduate program of the Universidade Federal do Pará, supported by a fellowship from the Conselho Nacional de Desenvolvimento Científico e Tecnológico (CNPq), in Brazil.

PART 2

Hierarchy, Diaspora, and New Identities

4 Rethinking the Arawakan Diaspora: Hierarchy, Regionality, and the Amazonian Formative

MICHAEL J. HECKENBERGER

THE ARAWAK, or Maipuran, languages were the most widely distributed language family in South America—perhaps in all of the Americas—in 1492.[1] Arawakan peoples were spread from southern Brazil to as far north as Florida and from the sub-Andean Montaña of Peru and Bolivia to the mouth of the Amazon. It was one of the great diasporas of the ancient world. Not surprisingly, their distribution and cultural history have long interested lowland specialists.[2] Broad cultural comparisons within the family have languished in recent decades, however, and questions of origins, cultural and linguistic relationships within the family, and the processes that lie behind the Arawakan diaspora remain poorly resolved. This chapter considers these broad questions—history writ large—with the aim to agitate debate about the deep historical roots, the deep temporality, of Amazonian peoples. Recent broad comparative studies along linguistic lines in Amazonia (Basso 1977; Butt-Colson and Heinen 1984; Dixon and Aikhenvald 1999; Maybury-Lewis 1979; Viveiros de Castro 1984–85, 1992) and "phylogenetic" modeling of dispersal and divergence within large prehistoric diasporas elsewhere in the world, such as Europe (Indo-European), Africa (Bantu), and the Pacific (Austronesian) (Anthony 1990; Kirch 1984; Kirch and Green 1987; Renfrew 1987; Rouse 1986; Vansina 1990), gives us reason to feel optimistic about the results.

The specific themes in this chapter are as follows. First, I explore Arawak origins, which I take to be somewhere in northwestern Amazonia, and primary dispersal routes, c. 500 B.C. to A.D. 500, largely along rivers and littoral areas of northern South America, as reconstructed from linguistic, archaeological, and ethnological information. Second, I explore the general cultural schemas or deeply "sedimented" practices that characterize peoples within

the diaspora, including ancestral peoples; Arawakan peoples, though en-
meshed in unique pluriethnic, multilingual regional social systems, generally share three features: settled agricultural village life, social hierarchy, and
regional social organization (regionality). Third, the appearance of these
structural features or cultural schemas among the progenitors of Arawakan
peoples (Proto-Arawak) represents one of the earliest, if not the earliest chiefdom society in Amazonia; it represents a "rank revolution" (Flannery 1994)
after c. 1000 B.C. and heralds what we might call an Amazonian "Formative,"
following convention for similar instances of early sedentary (generally agricultural), hierarchical, and regional societies (i.e., early chiefdoms) elsewhere in tropical America (Ford 1969).[3]

The Root of the Matter

The 1970 publication of Donald Lathrap's *The Upper Amazon* and Robert
Carneiro's "A Theory of the Origin of the State" marked a major turning
point in regional anthropology: The standard model, the long-held view that
Amazonia was uniformly "the habitat of small, dispersed, isolated groups that
were autonomous and self-contained, egalitarian, and technologically aus-
tere," was on the wane (Viveiros de Castro 1996, 180–82). Just the year before, almost no mention was made of Amazonia among the ranks of early
chiefdoms, the Formative cultures, identified elsewhere throughout the neotropics (Ford 1969). Most Americanists denied that the early state—even in
its most initial stirrings, that fitful transition from autonomy to earliest state-
hood, the chiefdom—ever arose there. The areas where complexity seemed
undeniable, where the chiefs, temples, priests, idols, and the like were simply too big or too numerous to ignore, were seen as the decadent progeny of
Andean chiefdoms that could not sustain their past size or grandeur in the
tropical forests of Amazonia; they devolved into the ubiquitous "tropical
forest tribes" (see Roosevelt 1980, 1–30, for a fuller discussion). By 1970 such
a view could no longer stand unquestioned: "Only by comparing the flourishing sixteenth-century inhabitants of the Circum-Caribbean area with the
marginal and shattered tribes now surviving in the Amazon Basin does this
contrast [circum-Caribbean chiefdoms versus tropical forest tribes] become
evident" (Lathrap 1970b, 47). Cultural variance was more continuous.

   Far from being a cultural backwater—peopled with tradition-bound,
"primitive" tribes for whom change was an imported commodity—the
Amazon floodplain was increasingly seen as a locus of major cultural developments, including early agriculture, sedentism, and complex social formations. A new *várzea* model took shape that envisioned not one (the "tropical

forest tribe") but two social realities: floodplain chiefdoms and upland tribes. This new orthodoxy, which was widely held by the 1990s, assumed that within Amazonia, there was something extraordinary about the *várzea* and its people; they were very statelike, which for many meant very un-Amazon-like.[4] The reason was simple: Chiefdoms arose in select "circumscribed" ecological settings, namely the rich floodplains of the Amazon and, perhaps, some of its major "white-water" (Andean derived) tributaries, because of the specific ecological conditions for technological innovation, economic intensification, and population growth in these areas (Denevan 1976; Gross 1975; Meggers 1996; Roosevelt 1980). The productive superiority of major rivers over uplands was long recognized (Steward 1949; see also Meggers 1996), but "revisionists" made this ecological distinction—the *várzea–terra firme* dichotomy—the key independent variable in explanatory models of differential evolution in Amazonia.

Although divided on which happens first, most commentators agreed that techno-economic innovation and demographic growth were the motors of prehistoric cultural change; the specific causal lever was population pressure, defined in vague terms of scarcity, competition, and conflict over productive bottomland resources. In areas of high productivity, notably the Amazon floodplains, population grows rapidly, quickly outstripping the means of local communities to produce essential economic resources in quantities sufficient for their preferred lifestyles. People suddenly had to work harder, change what they ate, compete more aggressively, and, ultimately, develop into increasingly complex social formations, or move. In contrast, in areas of low productivity (e.g., interfluvial and some riverine settings), population growth was held in check by some control mechanisms. As the story went, complex societies emerged in *várzea* areas because these areas, and only these areas, had the right ecological conditions for demographic growth, economic intensification, and the inevitable competition and conflict that resulted in these areas of circumscribed floodplain resources.

The fundamental flaw with the model is not theoretical but empirical: There is simply no compelling evidence that populations were large enough to produce the assumed population pressure, at least coincident with the presumed Arawakan migrations, after c. 3,000 B.P. Indeed, one need not probe too deeply into questions of Amazonian cultural history before facing an inescapable and surely disheartening realization: We simply cannot stipulate, in any precise way, the ecological or demographic parameters of any past Amerindian societies. Moreover, even if these could be established, the historical, symbolic, and political aspects of ecology and demography loom large before us, particularly in light of the dimensions of post-1492 disruption and change.

The expansion of pioneering agricultural populations was constrained by ecology because emigrating populations tended to colonize riverine and, later, littoral settings conducive to the reproduction of their settled agricultural and fishing lifeways (just as upland peoples might be predisposed to maintain their nonriverine lifestyles). However, there is no direct evidence of what mechanisms actually *caused* prehistoric migrations at different times and places within the Arawakan diaspora. Certainly the processes were varied and caused more commonly by local and contingent social and political conditions rather than the general, presumably impersonal forces of, for instance, demographic growth, at least if ethnographic patterns are any guide. Furthermore, as commonly seems to be the case elsewhere, competition over valuable resources is as often the cause as the effect of changing demographic patterns, including rapid population growth. Scarcity and circumscription are important, but both involve a variety of valued resources, symbolic as well as economic, and all the cultural means by which they are put in play. Furthermore, different cultural groups, corresponding, at least in part, to macrocultural traditions (defined at least initially along linguistic lines, e.g., Arawak, Carib, Tupi), are predisposed to reproduce certain characteristic features, including, I argue in the case of Arawak speakers, sedentism, social hierarchy, and regional social organization.

Reconstructing the Arawakan Diaspora

Most contemporary anthropologists probably would reject out of hand any scenario that too narrowly demands like causes for like effects. If not already prejudiced against overdetermination, compelled by a common legacy of relativism, critical reflection, and cultural exegesis—the multiplicity of voice and scale—Amazonianists are faced with an additional challenge: finding order in the bewildering array of biodiversity and remarkable cultural variation and pluralism that has only recently come to light. In the place of cultural uniformity and ecological homogeneity, recent research provides unequivocal evidence of enormous diversity, rivaling that of any world region in 1492.

Ultimate causality and predictability aside—what should happen, predictably, based on rules (deduced probabilistic laws)—there remains the historical problem that so challenged hopeful "Arawak-ologists" from the start: what to make of the widespread distribution of the language family and apparent cultural patterning isomorphic with it. Not all cultural groups in South America were so inclined to move, and none more widely than the Arawak. Not all groups so visibly carried so much of their past, their cultural heritage, forward through time. The historical questions of continuity and change, of cultural transformation, are different—"what" and "how"—from the "why" questions of absolute origins, causality, and law; they focus on the performance of sociocultural entities, in this case Arawakan peoples or those directly interacting with them through time under changing ecological and historical conditions. Of course, this must be based on the reconstruction of actual sociohistorical trajectories (i.e., the patterns of reproduction and transformation of cultural entities through time): cultural phylogenies. It is hard to proceed with a phylogenetic approach before interest turns, by whim or necessity, toward questions of genetic relationships between languages. Mason (1950, 160) perhaps overstates it in proposing that the "classification of human groups according to their languages [is] the best system for reconstructing historical connections," but it does provide an excellent starting point.

Language Groupings

The recent publication of *The Amazonian Languages* (Dixon and Aikhenvald 1999), a compendium of overviews of all the major language groupings, provides a point of departure to discuss relations within the family. Several things particularly relevant here emerge from it. First, since the 1960s, the centers of dispersion can be more firmly established for Macro-Tupi (Rondônia, Brazil), Carib (Guiana uplands), Macro-Gê (central Brazilian uplands), and Pano and Arawá (western Brazil/eastern Peru). Most peoples within these large groupings (except Pano and Arawá) were concentrated in upland areas, and their movements are commonly overland rather than along rivers, contrary to Lathrap's general proposition.

The center of dispersion of Arawak is less certain, but most evidence today points to the northwest Amazon, that is, riverine areas between the Upper Amazon (Solimões) in Brazil and the Middle Orinoco in Venezuela (Aikhenvald 1999a; Lathrap 1970b; Oliver 1989; Rouse 1992; Zucchi 1991a; Urban 1992, 95–96) (see map 1, p. 2). Noble favored a point of origin in western Amazonia, in part based on a postulated link between Andean (Uru-Chipaya) and Arawakan languages. Max Schmidt (1917) had come to a similar conclusion, including a southwestern origin, based on a link he felt between "ancient Tiahuanaco culture" and "ancient Arawak culture," that is, an ancient South American "high culture." Today most linguists eschew suprafamilial connections, including various lowland families such as Arawá and Guahibo, now believed to be commonly a result of borrowing (Payne 1991).[5] Indeed, as Aikhenvald (1999a, 74) notes, not only is there a lack of adequate data from many languages, but "geographic expansion and considerable linguistic diversity within the family pose the problem of distinguishing areal from genetic phenomena."

Today it seems prudent to limit discussion to the demonstrably related languages within the family (Dixon and Aihkenvald 1999). Within the family, a northwest origin, broadly defined, probably would find more general acceptance by most commentators in terms of linguistic and archaeological plausibility (Aikhenvald 1999a; Lathrap 1970b; Oliver 1989; Rouse 1986, 1992; Zucchi 1991a; see also chapter 8), although differing on details of dating or specific affiliations. Following Aikhenvald (1999a, 66–71), the Arawak can be divided into ten major subfamilies: (1) South Arawak, (2) Paressí-Xingu, (3) South-Western Arawak, (4) Campa, (5) Amuesha, (6) Chamicuro, (7) Rio Branco, (8) Palikur, (9) Caribbean, and (10) North Amazonian (see map 4.1). These subfamilies can be grouped into three macrogroupings: South Arawak (e.g., Mojo, Bauré, Saluma, Paressí, Xinguano, Terena, and Chané), Southwest Arawak (e.g., Piro-Apurinã, Campa, Yanesha, and Chamicuro), and North Arawak (e.g., Taíno, Caquetio, Lokono, Achagua, Piapoco, Wakuénai, Manao, Baré, Wapishana).

These three groupings seem to make good historical and geographical sense, with one caveat. Considering history—that is, a history of European colonialism, including the massive cultural loss and fragmentation of pre-Columbian social systems in the aftermath of 1492—we might well recognize that large contiguous territories and dialect chains once were fragmented and included many groups decimated in the early centuries of European occupation. This is particularly true in areas of first contact in the sixteenth and seventeenth centuries, such as along the Amazon before c. 1750, so the distribution of Arawakan groups in these areas is poorly known.[6] Accepting this, at least for the sake of argument, there probably was a significant Arawak presence along the main axis of the Amazon River, linking the eastern and western Amazon, and perhaps along the Madeira and Purus (map 4.2).

The archaeology of much of this broad area is poorly known. Many of the Arawakan groups that traditionally occupied this area are also poorly known because, as settled riverine farmers, they were rapidly denuded and dislocated during the contact period (c. 1492–1750). Zucchi's (1991a; see also chapter 8) reconstruction of an Arawak cultural lineage extending back into truly ancient times, c. 3,000 or more years ago, in one early homeland of Arawakan peoples is particularly important, indeed remarkable. If true (and I find her arguments quite compelling; see also chapters 9 and 11), it represents a trajectory of symbolic transformations within a group of related cultural groups (Northwest Arawaks) that rivals some of the longer cultural continua known from the New and Old Worlds alike. Regardless of absolute origins, when considered historically, as Lathrap (1970b, 73–74) notes, echoing Schmidt's earlier synthesis (1917, 15), "the whole core of Maipuran-speakers is oriented

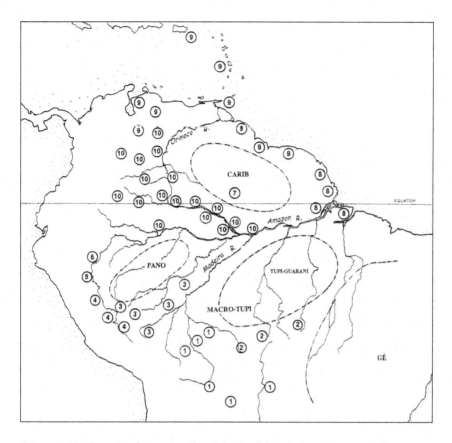

Map 4.1. Northern South America Showing Distribution of Major Historically Known
Arawak Groupings

The numbered circles mark the approximate locations of groupings following Aikhenvald ("The
Arawak Language Family," in *The Amazonian Languages,* ed. Robert M. W. Dixon and A. Y. Aikhenvald [Cambridge: Cambridge University Press, 1999], 65–106): (1) South Arawak, (2) Paressí-Xingu,
(3) South-Western Arawak, (4) Campa, (5) Amuesha, (6) Chamicuro, (7) Rio Branco, (8) Palikur,
(9) Caribbean, and (10) Northern Amazonian. Suggested areas of major concentrations of other
primary language groups at the height of Arawak expansion (c. 500 B.C.–A.D. 500), including Macro-
Tupi, Gê, Pano (and Arawá), and Carib, are also noted.

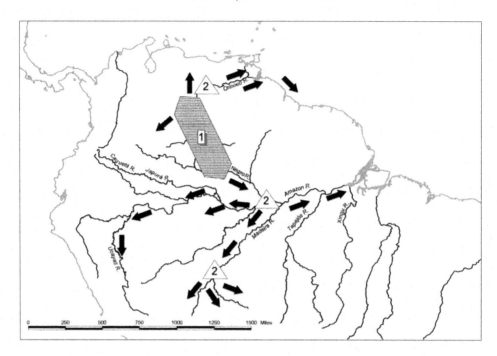

Map 4.2. Proposed Locations of Proto-Arawakan Languages in Northwestern Amazonia (Hatched Box); Secondary Centers of Dispersal in the Middle Orinoco, Central Amazon, and Upper Madeira (Triangles); and Major Routes of Expansion (Arrows)

along the network of waterways made up by the Upper Amazon, the Negro, the Casiquiare Canal, and the Orinoco, and it is clear that the Taíno did not reach their final home by walking on water," and "there is strong reason to believe that this [fishing and root crop agriculture] was the economic pattern of the speakers of the proto-language at the time that they started their outward migrations."

Limited lexical reconstructions of Proto-Arawak shed light on the cultural patterns of these early groups: Already in Proto-Arawak there are words for manioc, sweet potato, caiman, cooking pot, and, perhaps, domesticated (tended?) animals and an older versus younger brother distinction (Payne 1991). Linguistic reconstruction of Proto-Arawak leaves little doubt that they had the "developed tropical forest (root crop) agricultural" pattern that Lathrap (1977) envisioned and probably were focused on rivers (because caiman are largely limited to major waterways). Archaeology suggests that after the Arawak began to split up, probably sometime before 3,000 B.P. according to linguistics (Noble 1965; Payne 1991), early pioneer groups moved rapidly throughout floodplain areas of the Negro and Orinoco (by c. 1000–500 B.C.) and, from there, up and down the Amazon, into the Caribbean and Guiana coast, and along several major southern tributaries of the Amazon (e.g., the Madeira, Purus, and perhaps others) soon thereafter and from these areas even more broadly, reaching their maximal extent by c. A.D. 500.

If Pots Could Talk

Despite the obvious pitfalls of turning potsherds into people, it is perhaps overly pessimistic to suggest, taking the other extreme, that because "in Amazonia today native populations do not segregate cross-regionally by distinctive ceramic styles, lifeways, or languages," they may not have in the past (Roosevelt 1997, 173–74; Whitehead 1994). In point of fact, lifeways, including material culture, and languages do segregate cross-regionally, even today. Pots may not be people, but they are *of* people, just like language, and although material culture may not naturally or even commonly change in tandem with language, particularly over broad stretches of time and space, we are on solid empirical and theoretical ground to say that sometimes it does (see Petersen et al. 2001). Different institutions, like different people or different societies, follow their own trajectories of change, but these are not autonomous. Each articulates with and impinges on others, all of which are embedded in and informed by larger cultural systems; the point is that we cannot assume that it will or it won't.

The ability to pursue such questions of historical performance and comparison across time hinges on the issue of visibility: what can be visualized at different levels of analysis. This is why Lathrap placed so much emphasis on ceramics, one of the few nearly ubiquitous categories of prehistoric technology that preserves well in Amazonian archaeological sites. Lathrap (1970b) was the first to suggest a clear genetic correlation between ceramics—associated with one or another "Saladoid-Barrancoid" style—and Arawakan languages (see also Dole 1961–62; several earlier researchers also recognized affinities, including Bennett 1936; Nordenskiöld 1913, 1924; Schmidt 1917, but favored Andean connections). His view that most major ceramic discontinuities correlate with major linguistic diasporas (e.g., Arawak, Tupi-Guaraní, Carib, and Pano families) was flawed (Heckenberger et al. 1998), but as far as we know, he probably was right about a link, although not absolute, between Saladoid-Barrancoid ceramics and Arawaks; in other words, there was an expansion of early agricultural peoples, largely from c. 500 B.C.–A.D. 500, who spoke Arawakan languages and made Saladoid-Barrancoid ceramics, and both were reproduced (Brochado 1984; Oliver 1989; Rouse 1986; Zucchi

1991a).[7] Lathrap's error was not that he proposed a link between material culture, notably pottery, and language; he simply took it too far (every potsherd should have a name).

Noble's (1965) classification of Arawak and the stratigraphic and radiocarbon evidence from the Middle and Lower Orinoco, the Caribbean, and the Middle and Upper Amazon that appeared in the 1950s and 1960s gave Lathrap a solid empirical basis, at that time, for this correlation. This macroceramic tradition, called the "Incised-Rim" (Meggers and Evans 1961), "Modelled-Incised" (Lathrap 1970b, 113), "Parallel Line Incised" (chapter 8), or Amazonian Barrancoid tradition, is defined by diagnostic decorative features: incision and modeling including appliqué, adornos, and appendages (lugs and handles), and occasional painting (typically executed with a black or white pigment applied over a red slip). But although broad affinities are recognized within this long-lived continuum of ceramic arts, it underwent diverse permutations, including at least three major traditions: Orinocan Saladoid-Barrancoid, Caribbean Saladoid, and Amazonian Barrancoid, hereafter referred to generally as Saladoid-Barrancoid ceramics. More recent research (Heckenberger 2001) supports Lathrap's main conclusions that Arawakan peoples expanded from riverine areas of the north central Amazon and carried their unique economic pattern with them after c. 500 B.C. His recognition of a basic correlation between Saladoid-Barrancoid and Arawakan languages was a watershed for understanding phylogenetic relationships between Amazonian peoples. Certainly, as with the languages themselves, ceramic and other technologies (i.e., visible features of the archaeological record) have changed dramatically because of diverse cultural and historical factors, but tremendous continuity can be seen throughout the sequence.

The question is actually twofold: Do Saladoid-Barrancoid ceramics have anything to do with the dispersal of some culturally related group—a prehistoric diaspora? If so, is that group Arawak? Roosevelt (1997, 173) argues, as Lathrap did, that the Saladoid-Barrancoid styles have great integrity over time and space, and "seem linked by common origins [rather] than by contemporary communication." She believes that the "spatial-temporal patterning of the series [Saladoid/ Barrancoid] is consonant with . . . a slow migration," which seems to suggest some linguistic continuity, but nonetheless argues that "the theory [that the distribution of these ceramics is strongly correlated with Arawak-speaking peoples] has weak empirical grounds" because this style had "gone out of use by the time of conquest, and no group documented as speaking an Arawakan language has ever been shown to be using a style of the series." The real issue, however, is not whether such styles were made by historically known Arawakan peoples, because the style presumably had gone out of use prehistorically, but whether cultural continuity can be demonstrated between ancient groups, who did make such ceramics, and Arawak-speaking peoples of the recent past. (In fact, there is a case, the Upper Xingu, in which living peoples made ceramics best classified as Saladoid-Barrancoid, making the historical "slope" of the tradition even more impressive.) To qualify as a candidate for such a direct historical connection, any case must meet three conditions: There must be Saladoid-Barrancoid ceramics, there must be evidence of an Arawakan presence historically, and there must be evidence of cultural continuity between them. Four areas meet these general criteria: the Middle to Lower Orinoco, the central Amazon, the Caribbean, and the Upper Xingu (see Heckenberger 2001 for a fuller discussion of the evidence).

Recent research also demonstrates continuity in settlement patterns, as well as ceramic industries, because circular plaza (ring) villages are associated with Saladoid-Barrancoid ceramics in areas where village spatial organization can be reliably reconstructed, including the Lesser Antilles (Petersen 1996), the central Amazon (Heckenberger et al. 1999; Neves et al. 2001; Petersen et al. 2001), and the Middle Orinoco (chapter 8).[8] Most contemporary Arawakan peoples have a very clear settlement pattern, which also follows a pattern organized around a central plaza or other central sacred space. Mid- to late-first-millennium B.C. radiocarbon dates on circular villages encountered with Saladoid-Barrancoid ceramics in both the central Amazon and Lesser Antilles, in both cases retaining this basic form until well into the Christian era, indicate that Arawakan peoples carried both Saladoid-Barrancoid ceramics and circular plaza village patterns as they expanded across the lowlands. In fact, the central plaza configuration and Saladoid-Barrancoid ceramics, associated with Arawak-speaking populations, continues into historic times in the Upper Xingu (Heckenberger 1996, 2001). It also supports a suggested time length, 3,000 years, for separation of the Arawakan languages (Noble 1965; Urban 1992).

Toward a Cultural History of the Arawak

When Max Schmidt published his treatise on the Arawak in 1917, based on his field experiences among Southern Arawak and synthesis of the large body of earlier materials, several things stood out in his mind, things that also impressed his predecessors and contemporaries (Nordenskiöld 1913, 1924; Steinen 1894). First, and most obviously, was the widespread distribution of the family, which Schmidt defined reasonably accurately. Second, he recognized that "everywhere we find Arawakan tribes or their influence, they are agriculturalists, their life ways, while very diverse in form, are always found intimately linked with cultivation of the soil," also noting the critical importance of "their navigation arts," that is to say their riverine and coastal orientation (1917, 15). Third, he surmised that Arawakan cultures probably expanded through a variety of means, including peaceful expansion. For Schmidt, the notion of the "peaceful Arawak" was not a hollow reification to be accepted prima facie but something that he considered deeply.[9] Finally, he duly noted an Arawakan "high culture," a cultural pattern characterized by institutional social ranking based on birth order ranking, distinction of an elite rank, and hereditary succession. In fact, he related "ancient Arawak culture" to the "ancient Tiahuanaco culture" of the Antiplano, that is, Andean civilization: "It was above all economic-administrative factors that elevated the ancient Peruvian cultures, in a manner similar to that of the Arawaks, to the [high] level in which they were encountered by European culture" (Schmidt 1917, 68, 71–75). According to Schmidt (1917, 61), the cultural expansion itself involved not (or not only) the movement of communities but, specifically, the immigration of elite social groups that successfully grafted onto, and typically "Arawakized" (i.e., acculturated), autochthonous groups.

Lathrap (1977, 1985) was also struck by these similarities, including technology (e.g., ceramic industries), economic patterns (settled, riverine agricultural lifeways), social hierarchy, and regional social organization. Indeed, almost all commentators who have pondered the issue carefully have come to the same conclusion: There is something more than a common linguistic thread that links Arawakan peoples across time and space; they are permutations of an underlying symbolic structure, a structure already present in the ancestral Arawakan peoples of ancient Amazonia.[10] Arawak "high culture," as earlier diffusionists called it, though spread over a vast area, was unique in the lowlands. It stood out among lowland peoples in part because of its internal consistency, expressed in terms of shared cultural practices such as language and material culture, but also because of its civility, settledness, and developed economy and industry and the sophistication and elaboration of their arts and religion, things not typical of other lowland groups.

Outdated generic labels aside (the "peaceful" Arawak, Arawak "high culture," or the like), it is clear that something about the past, a past with ancient roots, has been reproduced over broad sweeps of time. It was not plaza villages, technology, and language as isolated (autonomous) cultural phenomena that were brought across the lowlands by pioneering Arawakan populations. The correspondences between various areas of known Arawak occupations in post-European times (at least in the four areas discussed earlier) and prehistoric evidence of certain types of ceramics (Saladoid-Barrancoid), manioc agriculture, and concentric plaza villages provide strong evidence of significant continuity in less directly visible aspects of social, political, ritual, and ideological processes, continuity in the broader cultural pattern—a system of cultural meanings—that was carried by the Arawakan colonists. Although it is difficult in some cases to elucidate common structural traits before the ethnographic period (i.e., the past 100 or so years) because of a lack of archaeological and historical data, and because Amerindian groups were radically altered by "contact," there usually is sufficient information to reconstruct basic features of what Santos-Granero (chapter 1) calls an Arawakan ethos: continuity in the key symbols, the root cultural categories, principles, and metaphors, carried by the ancient Arawaks who colonized much of the riverine and maritime lowlands and, although transformed, were present in many areas in historical times (see Heckenberger 1996). Such structural continuity, the resilience of the symbolic structures (what we might gloss as culture) underpinning ecological orientation and social logic, has strong cross-cultural support in other cultural groups in the lowlands and worldwide, such as Oceanic Austronesian, Bantu (Niger-Congo), and Indo-European (Basso 1977; Butt-Colson and Heinen 1984; Maybury-Lewis 1979; Renfrew 1987; Vansina 1990; Viveiros de Castro 1984–85, 1992).

A constellation of cultural features commonly distinguish Arawakan peoples from other Amazonian peoples, notwithstanding groups such as Eastern Tukanoan, Bakairi, Upper Xingu Carib, and others who have become "Arawakized" (and, conversely, some Arawakan groups that apparently underwent some intertribal acculturation as well, such as Chiriguano and Kokama; see chapter 1). These cultural features include large, permanent villages, densely distributed in discrete regions and interlinked through well-developed communication routes; concentric village plans, gravitating toward central public and sacred space; fairly intensive agricultural economies based on diverse crop plants but typically focused on manioc and aquatic resources; regionality, or sociopolitical integration based on formalized (institutionalized) patterns of exchange (e.g., exchange, intermarriage, visitation, and intercommunity ceremonialism) and regional sociality rooted in shared substance or heritage (kinship), geography (territory), and an ideology of "in-ness" in a regional moral community (i.e., generally shared cultural values); commonly "nonpredatory" ideologies, accommodating relations with neighboring groups, and defensive military strategies, sometimes including sophisticated defensive structures; and institutional social hierarchies and hereditary chiefly ascension. A variety of elements of material culture also seem to cluster around Arawaks, including ball games, hammocks, bull-roarers, atlatls, sacred flutes, wooden benches, masks, and idols—what we might

call a cultural aesthetic of heightened ritual. Many of these common material culture, ritual, political, and social categories provide fertile ground for
historical linguistics.

These traits vary widely between groups, and each, considered individu-
ally, is also shared by non-Arawakan groups (e.g., the circular villages of central Brazil), but considered in composite, these traits link Arawak-speaking
peoples and separate them from many other Amazonian peoples. Although
variably transformed over time by ecology, historical contingency, and personal and social choice, the broad cultural schema, glossed here as an ethos
of settled village life, regionality, and social hierarchy, is present in most of
historically known Arawak. When considered historically, it is clear that there
is nothing that prevents Arawakan peoples from developing into large, settled, regionally organized, and hierarchical societies (i.e., chiefdoms); in fact,
this was precisely what came to pass among many Arawakan peoples in a wide
variety of historical and ecological conditions. In 1492, the majority of Arawakan societies probably were organized into regional chiefdoms, but it is also
important to recognize that these societies were integrated in larger regional political economies, incorporating societies with a variety of ideologies,
including more egalitarian, "predatory," and autonomous societies.

Settled Village Life   Preliminary linguistic reconstruction (Payne 1991) of
Proto-Arawak demonstrates that these groups (c. 3,000–4,000 B.P.) already
had a developed agricultural technology, including ceramics, diverse domesticated plants (e.g., manioc, corn, sweet potato, pepper, urucu, and tobacco),
and possibly "domesticated" (managed?) animals (e.g., agouti, paca, coati,
and large fowl). Based on the suggested subsistence patterns of ancient
Arawakan populations in the Caribbean, the Lower Negro, and the Upper
Xingu, as well as ethnographic patterns, it seems likely that manioc was the
staple crop of the early Arawakan populations (Lathrap 1970b; Roosevelt
1997). Historically known Arawakan populations are also notable for their
settled village life, subsistence patterns dominated by manioc farming and
fishing, and ideologies that privilege not only settled ways but also development of highly constructed landscapes (see Santos-Granero 1998; and chapter 8). Likewise, settlement patterns from these three areas support the view
that early Arawakan populations preferred to live in settled plaza villages in
riverine areas. Their progeny tended to reproduce this pattern. Over time,
subsistence patterns changed because of local ecological and historical conditions (e.g., maize or some other crop replaced manioc as the staple, as may
be the case in the Middle Orinoco and some places along the Amazon
[Roosevelt 1980, 1997]; coastal replaced riverine resources in northern South

America and the Caribbean [Keegan 1992; Petersen 1997]). Likewise, we see changes in settlement patterns, including instances of abandonment of primary riverine areas, such as in the Upper Amazon, where some groups apparently were forced out of major floodplain areas (Lathrap 1970b); some villages became smaller, to the point in the Northwest Amazon, for instance, that villages became single houses (*malocas*).

Social Hierarchy   Hierarchy in Arawakan societies typically is manifest as a pyramidal social structure defined by two primary segments, elite and commoner, with diffuse boundaries and diverse secondary ranks (e.g., warriors, shaman, craft and ritual specialist, and slave statuses). Descent and rank ordering of individuals and social groups are based, as in other chiefdoms worldwide, on bloodline and birth order ranking. Preliminary linguistic reconstructions also suggest the possibility that an institutional contrast between older and younger brothers (i.e., primogeniture), the fundamental basis of social hierarchy in ethnographic Arawakan groups, was already present in Proto-Arawak as well (Payne 1991, 397).

Social hierarchy, although legitimized and naturalized by genealogy and history, does not require strong linear, particularly unilinear, principles of descent (i.e., corporate descent groups or lineages based on descent from a specified, apical ancestor). It is generally traced through an individual's immediate predecessors, including parents and, notably, grandparents (from whom chiefly names are commonly transferred) and a metaphorical connectedness with distant and mythological ancestors. In part, relative rank of social groups is tied to a founder principle, but this is tied to shallow conceptions of parentage, not necessarily deeply rooted lineages tied to some named distant ancestor but more generally tied to the collective memories, landscapes, and histories of local groups. Furthermore, personal and social identities operate differently for upper and lower segments of society. Genealogy is important, but it is more important for the powerful; in systems of hereditary status, it provides the basis of political legitimacy.

Such an organization shares much in common with "house societies," which, following Lévi-Strauss (1982, 174; see also 1987), can be defined roughly as "a corporate body holding an estate made up of both material and immaterial wealth, which perpetuates itself through the transmission of its name, its goods, and its titles down a real or imaginary line, considered legitimate as long as this continuity can express itself in the language of kinship or affinity and, most often both" (see also Carsten and Hugh-Jones 1995). In Amazonia, Arawak and culturally related peoples of the northwest Amazon, notable for their regional social organization and social hierarchies—"rank consciousness" (Goldman 1963)—have been described as both "house societies" (Hugh-Jones 1995) and "conical clans" (Chernela 1993).[11]

The hierarchical ordering of different social relations, based on symbolic transformations of basic social contrasts of senior and junior, inside and outside, superior and inferior, and sacred and profane, within a conceptual geography that similarly parses up space (upper and lower, center and periphery, public and domestic), as Lévi-Strauss (1963) noted long ago, pervades different levels of organization (e.g., family, household, village, and larger regional clusters; see Sahlins 1968, 24). In other words, social relations at all levels are organized by similar principles: husband (male):wife (female):: parent:child::older:younger sibling::chief:commoner::divine:human. The hierarchies of family and household are nested within broader hierarchies of kindreds, factions, and villages in a regional social arena. Where such hierarchical relations exist, we must therefore recognize difference between high-ranking, elite, or noble houses (the kindreds of primary chiefs), and lesser households; thus a village is made up of diverse households, each with its own head, but at another level these resolve into larger entities (what we might call chiefly or noble houses) that form the major factions or political coalitions in village political arenas. At the regional level, the village itself forms a house, or, put another way, the chief represents society: The village is a Great House interacting and contextually ranked against others like it, based on kinship and strategic control of resources.

Obviously, the distribution of power and struggles over it do not simply correspond to a hierarchy from highest chiefs to lowest commoners but to competing centers of power ranked in diverse ways along varied dimensions (e.g., male and female, chief and nonchief, ritual and secular), which is sometimes called "heterarchy" (Crumley 1987, 1991). But whereas the structure of power in society is always diverse and contextual (heterarchical), Arawakan groups are notable for the degree to which vertical hierarchies, based on hereditary ranking, are expressed in social, ritual, and political relations. In other words, the question is not how heterarchical systems are transformed into hierarchical systems but when does a hierarchy of bloodline and birth order come to be the dominant dimension of sociopolitical organization, or when does social organization come to be predetermined by an institutional social hierarchy that creates a pyramid of ranked individuals and kin groups.

Regionality   Arawakan peoples tend to form regional societies (i.e., moral communities sharing a common culture and ideology), reproduced through formal networks of interaction, including intermarriage, exchange, ceremonial interdependence, and diffuse patterns of sociality within and between communities. This pattern, called regionality here, has an essential regional dimension, and the symbolic reproduction of society depends on institution-alized intercommunity ritual and interaction. In other words, regional organization is based not simply on interaction within regional social systems, or interaction spheres (a ubiquitous condition of social life in Amazonia in 1492 and probably for a long time, perhaps millennia before), but specifical-ly on elite exchange organized around intercommunity chiefly rituals, includ-ing rites of passage (especially funerals) and rituals of intercommunity ex-change (the "trading game"). This pattern can be contrasted with the more atomistic pattern typical of most Carib, Tupian, and many other Amazonian groups that, while engaging in supralocal exchange and alliance, are largely autonomous symbolically, socially, and politically (i.e., alliances are common-ly impermanent and flexible). The latter amount to generalized regional spheres or systems of interaction and interdependence, almost ubiquitous in lowland neotropics, but do not constitute regional "moral communities."

An important dimension of regional social patterns relates to exchange and warfare, notably formalized trade and elite exchange networks (marriage alliance, prestation, and intercommunity rituals) between culturally related groups and warfare with neighboring cultural groups, with strong ideolog-ical and social prohibitions against endo-warfare (chapter 1). Arawakan peo-ples may make war as commonly as other peoples, but they generally do not engage in warfare with peoples whom they view as culturally related. Arawa-kan peoples were not always, or even commonly, peaceful in practice, but what distinguishes them from many Amazonian societies (e.g., Tupi-Guaraní, Jivaro, Carib, Gê) is the centrality of warfare in the construction of personal and collective identities. In other words, the identities are not constituted vis-à-vis an "ontology of predation." It is also important to recognize that the outside is contextual and permeable when we consider the incorporation (acculturation) of non-Arawakan peoples (e.g., Eastern Tukanoan, Bakairi, and Upper Xingu Carib), and in 1492 many regional Arawakan societies were tied into vast networks of sociality. There is no central symbolic function attached to predation; in fact, among many Arawakan peoples there were often elaborate ritual apparatus for tension reduction, both within and be-tween villages, through rituals of sexual antagonism, sporting events (wres-tling, ball games, running contests), and ritualized conflicts.

There is obviously no one-to-one relationship between hierarchy, region-ality, settledness, and "Arawakanness"; that is, not all Arawakan groups share these features equally, nor was social and symbolic reproduction structural-ly predetermined. The nature of specific social systems was determined through the dynamic and complex interplay of diverse forces of culture, ecology, and history. What does seem clear, however, is that Proto-Arawakan groups probably were characterized by these features and that they were variably reproduced over time: Many Arawak became much larger, more socially elaborated, in terms of local and regional social hierarchy, more intensive economies, and more diverse technologies (e.g., Manao, Taíno, Xinguano, and Caquetio), but others became smaller, less sedentary, less hierarchical, or less regional. Likewise, there is no reason to suggest that other Amazonian peoples did not follow similar social logics. What I do suggest, however, is that ancient Arawakan groups, the Proto-Arawak, were among the earliest peoples in Lowland South America to develop such a social structure—that the type of institutional social hierarchy and regional organization usually considered characteristic only of much later "chiefdom" populations (c. A.D. 1 or later) in Amazonia were present in Arawakan peoples before their expansion across the lowlands (by c. 1000–500 B.C.) and that this structure was an important catalyst for the expansion itself, as well as the course of cultural development in many riverine and coastal areas after that time.

The Arawakan Diaspora and the Amazonian Formative

Speaking of an Arawakan diaspora draws our attention to issues of culture, history, and geography. Using the term implies a systematic link between words, gestures, and ideas, an underlying (precedent) structure or system of meaning that inflects human actions of all kinds. The type of diaspora I have in mind is among a subset of major human movements that might be called linguistic diasporas, the dispersal and influence of a cultural pattern, with a common ancestor, identified first and most clearly by linguistic means: the widespread distribution of a language family. First and foremost, it is a *cultural dispersal*, as much a question of history as geography. Primary examples of other such distributions, great tropical diasporas of the ancient world, include the Austronesian speakers of Oceania, c. 3,500–2,500 B.P. (Kirch 1984); Bantu speakers of equatorial sub-Saharan Africa, c. 4,000–2,500 B.P. (Vansina 1990); and the Arawak and Tupi-Guaraní diasporas of the American neotropics.

In all cases, it is hard, if not impossible, to say what exactly caused specific migrations or generally prompted the initial expansive pulse c. 1000–500 B.C., but as Anthony (1990, 899) points out, "While it is often difficult to identify specific causes of particular migrations . . . it is somewhat easier to identify general structural conditions that favor the occurrence of migrations." Given the size of the communities apparently involved, during the primary period of expansion (c. 500 B.C.–A.D. 500), at least, it seems unlikely that population pressure related to subsistence resources was the root cause or common condition of the Arawakan diaspora: Populations were simply too small. Population pressure can also be measured in social and symbolic rather than strictly caloric terms, in terms of an individual's ability to pursue political aspirations. The pressure most likely to prompt large-scale residential movements (i.e., large portions of communities) was competition between the powerful, framed in terms of control over symbolic (history, knowledge, sacred space, ritual, prestige goods) and human (labor and loyalty) as well as economic resources. In other words, symbolic resources, prestige, and control over human labor were the circumscribed or scarce resources being competed over.

The powerful forces of intragroup and regional competition and the intrinsic urge of factional leaders to increase the production of symbolic (prestige) and economic (wealth) resources, within an inherently settled and highly productive economy, might result in population expansion. Thus, competition may have been as commonly the cause as the effect of demographic growth. As is well known ethnographically, people choose to move for a variety of reasons (e.g., witchcraft, natural disaster, better economic opportunities, easier work conditions, or even personal tastes), and there is no reason to assume that this is any less true of ancient migrations. However, there is a common tendency for schisms, divisive movements or expansions, to correlate with political tensions between rival chiefly factions. Patterns of fission and migration correlate, at least crudely, with ecological and demographic factors (Carneiro 1987), but "the recognition that factional competition is shaped by ecological variables does not imply that factional competition is always, at the base, caused by subsistence shortages" (Brumfiel 1994, 7).

Within diasporas of similar proportions (e.g., Austronesian, Bantu) relating to the fairly rapid expansion of early agriculturalists, factional competition within a hierarchical social structure was an important factor stimulating residential movements, including long-distance migration. This is considered a common feature of the social institution known as the chieftaincy (Kopytoff 1999), status lineage (Goldman 1955), conical clan (Kirch 1984; Sahlins 1968), or house (Hugh-Jones 1995), considered characteristic of chiefdoms (Chernela 1993; Earle 1997). The tendency among hierarchically organized societies to split was so common, in fact, that Firth (1936) defined such an institution in Polynesia as a "ramage," based on its tendency to "ramify," or split along lines of status rivalry between elite individuals.

Early root crop agriculturalists tended to reproduce integrated regional landscapes, including ties with ancestral areas and, commonly, with their new neighbors, potentially articulating large riverine and maritime regions; the rate of movement across regions (i.e., the degree to which Arawakan colonists "filled in" a region before a splinter group moved on) is uncertain. Also uncertain is the degree to which interregional interaction within large regional political economies characterized these early sedentary occupations, as was critical in later periods. Perhaps it was the settled lifestyles, food production, or demographic changes tied to them that provided the conditions for the emergence of institutional social hierarchy, which was a "structural contradiction" some 3,000 to 4,000 years ago but, after established, took on a life of its own, causing as often as being caused by changes in ecology, technology, or demography. Even the tangible economic elements of such a political economy were turned toward not accumulation of subsistence goods but wealth; their import in local social dynamics was as much symbolic as economic.

Minimally, we must recognize that, among the Proto-Arawak people (c. 3000–1500 B.C.), there is little to suggest that competition over scarce ecological resources and pursuant population pressure were the primary drivers of population expansion. The colonization of diverse riverine and coastal areas by expanding agricultural populations must be understood in the context of factors other than basic ecological orientation and technology, such as social hierarchy, regionality, and a cultural predisposition to exploration and symmetrical acculturation. It is clear that not only people and ideas but also things were moving: pots, minerals, feathers, woods, and other precious materials, plants, knowledge, and people as things (captives, slaves, or enemies)—that is, prestige goods, esoteric knowledge, and other symbolic valuables. The channeling of these, as much as that of any strategic economic resources, was the basis for control over human labor and support. Competition clearly took place in the realm of symbolic resources (authority) and human labor as well as in economic resources. The pathway to political power was as much symbolic as economic; that is, the economic relationship of exploitation must be preceded by the symbolic relationship of social difference (superiority). Conceived in these terms rather than in terms of technological innovations, agricultural intensification and surplus, or economic exploitation or centralization, might (following Southall 1999) be called the "ritual phase of political economy," based on symbolic, social, ritual, and political resources rather than merely economic resources (Heckenberger 1999, 2000).

Early floodplain sedentism, agriculture, and ceramics, the harbingers of the "formative period" elsewhere in the Americas, were not simply the result of some economic (Neolithic) revolution. The period of Neolithic experimentation was a long and gradual process (Lathrap 1977), as recent research regarding the antiquity of manioc, maize, and other domesticates in the neotropics (perhaps as early as 6,000–7,000 years ago) further demonstrates (Bush et al. 1989; Piperno et al. 2000). The tropical forest agricultural complex was established very early, and changes transpired not through innovation as much as intensified production and elaboration within the existing economic pattern, based on root crop agriculture and fishing. Technological changes in tropical forest agriculture (related, for instance, to forest clearing, processing, or cooking utensils) may have made these early agriculturalists adaptively advantaged over foraging populations they encountered during their expansion, but there is little evidence that it was population growth and stress on local resources or economic innovations that triggered population movements in the first place.

If there was little change in staple foods or technology (i.e., the economic pattern based on rich aquatic resources and stable agriculture of a wide diversity of domesticates and wild foods), we might ask what kind of extratechnological mutation prompted the Arawakan diaspora or subsequent cultural development in riverine and coastal areas (Descola 1996, 330; Viveiros de Castro 1996). In other words, demographic growth and the expansion of riverine groups were as much a result of changes in the political realm as the subsistence economy, what Flannery (1994, 104) calls a "rank revolution" for nuclear America: The rise of hierarchical social formations "involved changes in *ideology* and *social relationships* rather than the *means of production*," which may well have differed little from "the egalitarian societies that preceded them." It was control of labor and accumulations of symbolic resources, including titles, ritual control and prerogatives, knowledge, and prestige goods, not material surplus, that rulers and nobles concentrated (Flannery 1994, 107). As noted elsewhere in the Americas for the "theocratic formative," "the real driving forces of a cultural revolution are intangible ideas, particularly religious concepts," representing "the sudden appearance of a religio-political group of ideas" (Ford 1969, 180). The implication is that though culturally, historically, and ecologically unique and diverse (i.e., genuinely Amazonian), the region was not out of stride with happenings elsewhere. A condition of institutional social hierarchy, a structural contradiction defined by a vertical division of society and regional social organization, may be as ancient in Amazonia as in other areas of the New World, such as in western South America (c. 4,500–3,500 years ago), lowland Mesoamerica (c. 3,500–3,000), and the Southeast (c. 3,500–3,000).

Discussion

Since the 1970s, it has become harder and harder to escape the fact that, compared with many world areas, Amazonia was not ecologically handicapped, socially recalcitrant, or uninfluenced by the major ebbs and flows of other major areas of American civilization, notably the central and northern Andes. The question is no longer whether there were ancient civilizations in Amazonia, a question put to rest through recent research (Porro 1993, 1996; Roosevelt 1980, 1991, 1999; Whitehead 1994), but what was the nature of Amazonian social complexity and what was the distribution of complex societies in Amazonia (where and when did they arise). This social condition is still seen as unusual—a mutation, and a generally late mutation at that, of the "typical" Amazonian person or perspective. But if we were to travel back in time and encounter a native Amazonian person from the fifteenth century, would he or she be more like one of the many ethnographic peoples known from this century, or might he or she have been a member of a large, regional, and hierarchical society, a citizen of some form of Amazonian state?

It is beyond the scope of this chapter to describe the nature of these regional societies in Amazonia or the transformations they underwent on the path to complexity. In the Lower Negro, Middle Orinoco, and Caribbean, this political structure evolved from circular villages (c. 500–1 B.C.) to major central plazas, ball courts, and temple mounds, which ultimately became important centers in macropolitical entities (chapter 1). Ethnohistorical descriptions state quite clearly that many Arawakan groups were precisely the kind of society that is described elsewhere as the state, at least in the initial pulse of patrimonialism and sovereignty that is sometimes called the chiefdom. One is reminded of the numerous chiefdoms of northern South America (Lokono, Achagua, Caquetio) and the Caribbean, the Manao and others of the Rio Negro, those of the Lower Amazon (including Palikur and Arúa) and of the southern Amazon (e.g., Mojos, Bauré, Terena, Paressí, and perhaps the speakers of Kokama languages along the Upper Amazon), all of which were large, settled populations clearly organized into regional chiefdoms (Oliver 1989; Whitehead 1994).

What so often catches our eye, what seems to simultaneously hold the Arawak together as a group and distinguish them from so many lowland Amerindian groups, is precisely that they do not seem primitive or archaic at all unless we allow ourselves to be seduced into believing that ethnographic history is representative of the totality of Amerindian experience (Roosevelt 1989). Indeed, the unusually hierarchical nature of Arawakan peoples, within the broader universe of Amazonian societies, has been widely noted by comparativists; Schmidt, as noted earlier, was very clear on this point nearly a century ago, as was Pierre Clastres (1987, 28) in his seminal discussion of political power in Lowland South America: "Among the great number of tribes accounted for in [sub-Andean] South America, the authority of chieftaincy is explicitly documented only in the case of a few groups, such as the island Taíno, the Caquetio, the Jirajira, and the Otomac. But it should be pointed out that these groups, almost all of whom are Arawak, are located in the Northwestern part of South America and that their social organization presents a marked stratification into castes: this latter feature is found again only among the Guaycuru and Arawak (Guana) tribes of the Chaco."

Steward (1949; Steward and Faron 1959, 252–59) classified various ethnohistorically known Arawakan groups as theocratic chiefdoms, including the southern Amazonian Paressí, Bauré, and Mojos and the northern Amazonian Caquetio, Lokono, Achagua, and Taíno, but failed to recognize the underlying (Arawak) phylogenetic relationship. These and numerous other commentators viewed the emergence of chiefdoms in the Caribbean, northwestern South America, lowland Bolivia, or along the Amazon in the sixteenth century as a result of the unusually high productivity of these areas for human exploitation and population growth or, conversely, diffusion from the highlands—shopworn explanations for complex social formations everywhere in Lowland South America. Rather than recognizing these societies as permutations of an underlying hierarchical ideology common to Proto-Arawak and its cultural progeny, they saw the developments of complex societies as unique historical developments in each area where they occurred—either local evolution or particular migrations. Such a view fails to recognize the cultural relatedness of the southern and northern Arawakan chiefdoms.

Had these authors recognized the historical relationship between these groups, as did Schmidt, it might have led to a startling conclusion: Culture, as much as ecology or demography, plays a key role in differential cultural development in Amazonia. The distributional pattern—the correlation between language and culture—is unmistakable: Where we find Arawak speakers we typically also find social hierarchy, sedentism, and regionality. The intent is not to trade one dogma for another, cultural in place of ecological determinism; clearly origins are multicausal, the historical process is complicated and contingent, and the resulting trajectories of cultural development are diverse and multilinear (Yoffee 1993). Obviously, the historical processes are far more complicated than any simple correlation would suggest, and cultural diversity between regions and within language groups is considerable, but we should not overlook a valuable lesson: Hierarchy and egalitarianism not only represent stages of regional development (one always leading into the other) but also reflect different cultural solutions or logics with their own internal inertias (Dumont 1970).

Notes

1. Steinen (1886, 254–58) was the first to describe these broadly related languages, previously recognized by Gilij (1782), under the name *Nu-Arawak*.

2. See Lathrap 1970b; Oliver 1989; Schmidt 1917; also see Aikhenvald 1999a; Ehrenreich 1891; Greenberg 1960; Koch-Grünberg 1911; Mason 1950; Noble 1965; Nordenskiöld 1913, 1924; Payne 1991; Rouse 1986, 1992; Schmidt 1914; Steinen 1886, 1894; Zucchi 1991a.

3. I use the term *chiefdom* not as a precise analytical or theoretical concept but as a gloss for societies that are neither acephalous nor autocratic (see Heckenberger 2001 for a fuller discussion).

4. For Meggers (1996) and most others, *várzea,* meaning simply "floodplain" or "bottomlands" in Portuguese, is used to refer more specifically to the floodplains of the Andean-derived rivers of the Amazon basin, known to lowland specialists as whitewater rivers.

5. If the Proto-Arawá family was more closely related to Proto-Arawak than, say, Proto-Carib, Proto-Tupi, or Proto-Pano, then a central Amazon origin, as Lathrap (1970b) proposed, is likely, following the general rule that the area containing the most concentrated linguistic diversity within a grouping probably is the zone of origin (Urban 1992, 95). But, following this logic, the Middle Orinoco and northwest Amazon seem like logical candidates as well if other divergent languages, such as Guahibo, Harakmbet, or Puquina, are ultimately determined to be closely related to Arawak.

6. Rodrigues (1999), Cabral (1995), Jensen (1999), and Urban (1992) all recognize this reclassification. Although the root language onto which the Tupi-Guaraní (very close, in fact, to coastal Tupi) lexicon was grafted is uncertain, it seems as likely as not to be Arawak, based on geographic distribution of Arawak upstream and downstream from the Kokama languages and their riverine orientation, something at least not refuted by linguistic evidence (Cabral, personal communication, 1999; Rodrigues, personal communication, 1999). Therefore, the Kokama languages, including Kokama, Kokamilla, Omagua, and probably others, would be representatives of the riverine Arawaks who controlled much of the Amazon main branch.

7. Tupi-Guaraní languages may have a loosely fixed relationship to ceramics of the Tupi-Guaraní tradition (Prous 1991), but a direct genetic relationship between Amazonian Polychrome and Tupi-Guaraní languages is questionable (see Heckenberger et al. 1998; Brochado 1984; Lathrap 1972; Noelli 1996).

8. Santos-Granero (1991, 129–30) describes the ceremonial centers of the *cornesha',* or Yanesha priestly leaders, as circular plaza villages revolving around a circular, two- to three-storied temple with conical roof. Hugh-Jones (personal communication, 1999) has collected oral histories of groups from the Upper Rio Negro who recall a time when they lived in large circular plaza villages of multiple *malocas* before they were reduced to single *maloca* villages. Gow (personal communication, 1997) also mentions a myth among the Piro of large plaza villages with roads inhabited by peccaries.

9. Compare Schmidt's 1914 work, when he was less certain of "peaceful" expansion, and his major synthetic work of 1917.

10. *Structure* has various meanings in anthropology; in the current context the term is used loosely to define preexisting conceptual schemes that guide social life.

11. Goldman's (1963) work on the Eastern Tukanoan is notable considering that he studied hierarchical societies in Polynesia and the Northwest Coast, making his recognition of "rank consciousness" among the Cubeo and other northwest Amazon groups all the more compelling.

5 Social Forms and Regressive History: From the Campa Cluster to the Mojos and from the Mojos to the Landscaping Terrace-Builders of the Bolivian Savanna

FRANCE-MARIE RENARD-CASEVITZ

> Wherever property is an individual right and everything is
> measured through money, it will be impossible to organize justice
> and social prosperity, unless you consider it just for the worst sort
> of people to have the best living conditions, or unless you are
> prepared to call prosperous a state in which all the wealth is owned
> by a handful of individuals avid of pleasures, while the masses are
> devoured by misery. . . . The only means of organizing public
> happiness is the application of the principle of equality. . . . The
> only means of distributing goods with equality and justice . . . is
> the abolition of property.
> —Thomas More, *Utopia,* book 1 (my translation)

FOR A LONG TIME an old field note of mine referring to a Matsiguenga group that claimed the self-designation of Mojos has been demanding my consideration. Our reflection on the Arawakan diaspora gives me the opportunity to do it. After some preliminary clarification on the claim suggested by this self-designation, I will discuss diverse sociopolitical aspects of the pre-Andine Arawak cluster, of which the Matsiguenga of Peru are the southernmost province.[1] Then, through a comparative analysis of the Mojos of Bolivia, I will try to reconstitute their type of organization at the time of contact with Jesuit missionaries. This should allow me to determine the validity of the assertion of the above-mentioned Matsiguenga group, an astonishing assertion given the long distance between them and the Bolivian Mojos and the ethnic patchwork characteristic of the intermediate regions. Subsequently, and in light of the analysis of these Amazonian clusters, I will hypothesize as to the type of social formation of the predecessors of the Mojos, that is, those who modeled the landscape of the Sabana de los Mojos. To conclude, I will question epistemologically the models we use when we talk about ancient macropolity formations in the Amazon.

Links between the Pre-Andine Arawak and the Mojos

In the 1960s, while writing an ethnohistorical thesis on central and southern Peru, I was struck by the breadth of the alliances that, according to some chroniclers, had brought together several units of forests or savannas all along the Inca empire. Chronicles recounting the revolt of the Inca against the Spanish, as well as the history of the neo-empire of Vilcabamba (1536–72), mention negotiations between the Mojos of contemporary Bolivia and the Antis—an Inca name given to all the nonsubjugated pre-Andine Arawak living in the Antisuyu—to support Inca resistance.[2] After mentioning the old political alliances between the lowland peoples and the Inca, these sources evoke rumors in relation to preparations for the general rebellion planned by the Inca. The Antis, the Chunchos, the Mojos, and the Diaguitas from Tucuman and Chile took part in this uprising. Urged by these persistent rumors, Viceroy Toledo attacked and defeated the neo-Inca empire of Vilcabamba, putting an end to the projected uprising (Maúrtua 1906, 5:58–103).

It surprised me to see that those ancient alliances and rumors eventually found contemporary echo. Shortly after starting my first fieldwork in 1969–70 in the Upper Urubamba valley, I worked with these Mojos, a group of Southern Matsiguenga who insisted that they were related to their Bolivian homonyms. This self-designation accentuated their role as a double link. On one hand, according to a north-south axis and going up the Urubamba River—named Vilcanota in the sacred valley of the Inca—they bordered and were in contact with the Andean world and its main symbolic centers (Machu Picchu, Ollantay Tambo, and Cuzco).[3] On the other hand, along a northwest-southeast axis, they could communicate with the Matsiguenga from the Upper Madre de Dios River and vice versa. From there, they could have access to the lowland valleys of the Madre de Dios River, the Beni, and the faraway Mojos. Today these connections, as well as others further north between the valleys of the Urubamba-Ucayali and the Madre de Dios or the Jurúa-Purús (such as the Fitzcarrald Isthmus) are still known, and some are still used (see map 5, p. 10).

The Pre-Andine Arawak or Campa Cluster

In using the name *Mojos,* this group of Matsiguenga also emphasized its heroic origin as descendants of a couple of ancestors who founded their territory. Soon, their downstream neighbors, who claimed a similar prestigious origin, challenged the heroic origin of these so-called Mojos. In fact, the importance that the Matsiguenga-Mojos placed on their founders seemed to be replicated by members of each region and kin group with respect to their own founders. Presently, I discovered a founding myth whose regional versions reveal a common mode of construction: an Ego-centered perspective that renders every single territorial point of view relative. I think this myth is worth summarizing because it expresses the ideology of the whole society and because its versions are built according to schemes that organize, *mutatis mutandis,* the areas of social life.

Founding Myth: On the Campa Nation's Common Origin and on the Equality of Its Members

The founding myth starts with the alliance of four celestial siblings: two gods and two goddesses (Seripitontsi and Koyarikinti, Shaoreni and Shonkiaba).[4] Each couple gives birth to four children (two gods and two goddesses), and those eight divinities form four couples that are sent to Earth and assigned a wide territory each: the four provinces of the pre-Andine Arawak cluster (Asháninka, Matsiguenga, Nomatsiguenga, and Yanesha). It was they who were responsible for the divine, multiple, and egalitarian origin of the pre-Andine Arawak.[5]

Each of these couples gave birth to eight children, four demigods and four demigoddesses, whose marriages subdivide each province into four regions.[6] At this stage versions diverge: Only the more erudite myth-tellers list by name the eight siblings who founded a region. All the versions leave in the background the divinities born of the founding couples of the three other regions. Then, according to the same scheme (two by four), the leading couple of each region gives birth to eight siblings, whose alliances founded the four vast kindreds into which each region is supposed to be divided.[7] The so-called Mojos are one of these kindreds, together with the Antis (in the narrowest sense) of the southwest region.[8] Erudite or not, each version named the founders of the local kindred; this named couple directly engenders the grandparents (for a female Ego linked to the space of kinship) or, at best, the great-grandparents (for a male Ego linked to the time or dynamic dimension conferred on the structure by the patrilateral marriage formula) and their descendants, ending up in Ego at the end of the story. These heroic names can refer to important figures of the past through substitution of their nickname fallen into the public domain or by inclusion, under the name of a mythical hero, of facts attributable to these historic characters.[9]

As becomes apparent, the Ego-centered perspective of each version does not aim to construct a lineage. The purpose is neither to exhibit high-class nobility nor to remember a long lineage. What is actually intended is to link oneself to the common origin and thus to identify oneself as a member of a nation considered to be of divine origin. The adoption of a genealogy that links four generations of immortals to two or three ascending generations of mortals with respect to the narrator emphasizes the fragmented contribution of each version. These characteristics contribute to the elaboration of a founding myth in which every voice is only one element of a plural partition; it controls only a tiny portion of the immense network thought to be continually in expansion.[10] Each voice allows the others to insert their own contributions into the common and infinite updating of this narrative. At the heart of this system there are subjects founded on incompleteness and interdependence. In their dynamics, these voices interweave the infinite series of familial, regional, provincial, and national identifications, requiring everyone to participate in the collective production of both myth and society.

These myths do not construct a clanlike ontogenesis and a hierarchical social space. We are in a spatiotemporal foundation in which everyone is at the same distance from a divine origin so homogeneous that it becomes differentiated only after settling in an earthly place. Difference does not derive from birth order or from a superior or inferior corporeal organ, which becomes the matrix of a clan (as is the case in other Amazonian traditions such as the Tukano). Difference arises from the gods' territorialization, and through this spatial foundation it is asserted that everyone is equally close to their divine origin. The processes of hierarchization are depicted in other myths, notably in the heroic sagas, and thus are posterior to the equality established by the foundation and creation myths. If I have dwelled so long on this founding myth, it is because its versions reveal an ideology that operates at various levels of social organization and because its Ego-centered form and its fragmentary character are isomorphic to those of other narratives and to constructs in the fields of kinship and affinity.

Social Organization and Campa Geopolitics

Given the intricate complex of relationships that unite members of the Campa social formation (80,000 people inland, nearly 100,000 as a result of the rubber boom diaspora) I focus only on a few elements that will help clarify Campa social organization and facilitate comparison with the ancient Bolivian Mojos: settlement patterns, commerce, and war.[11]

Settlement Patterns   The Dominicans exploring the Matsiguenga territory at the beginning of the twentieth century and the Franciscans planning the conquest of the Campas in the mid-eighteenth century describe the same extreme dispersion of people and sites inhabited by five to sixty people. This first impression is not far from the description left by the Jesuits who penetrated in the Mantaro-Apurimac Montaña region at the end of the sixteenth century. In the report of their exploration, Fathers Juan Font and Antonio Bivar concluded "They are dispersed throughout the land; and the largest settlements are inhabited by no more than eight to ten Indians. . . . There is no subjugation to chiefs, although they call them chiefs, since they do not obey them and do not serve them. . . . Not being subjected, having no order, no headman, and not using punishments among them, they cannot be forced to pay obedience. . . . I believe that it would be better to abandon it [the project of mission]" (Font 1602, 270–71; see also Contreras 1651/1906, 64).[12] And they abandoned all projects of conquest and reduction, condemned in advance by the social chaos that the Spanish used to call *behetría.*

At the same time, other Jesuit missionaries and Spanish witnesses reporting on Anti delegations arriving in the highland region of Cuzco to establish an alliance with Viceroy Toledo as soon as Vilcabamba was conquered (1572) or, later on, with other Viceroys in Lima, attribute the leader of the delegation the title of King (Maúrtua 1906, 5:62–63; AGI Ind. Gene. 1240, fol. 62, 65–70; Renard-Casevitz et al. 1986, 159), a title that reappeared at the end of the eighteenth century. Such was the case of Mathaguari—which, actually, is still a family name—among others (Maúrtua 1906, 12:165, 168). This designation reflects the extremely hierarchical bias of Spanish perceptions of human societies, the political strategies that shaped the writing of chronicles and reports to the Crown, and the haughty or "sovereign" behavior that every Campa (man and woman) adopts when visiting.

In between the libertarian and quasianarchist society described in the texts and the certified presence of big chiefs, or even kings, where does the truth lie? Or, more precisely, what social form organizes the vast Campa cluster described, among others, as *behetrías* by the Spanish, who did not care much about the sociological paradox inherent in the conjunction of kings with the notion of *behetría*? In the case of the Campa, once "kings" disappear gradually from written testimonies, missionaries and travelers underscore the absence of a centralized decision-making organ and of an encompassing hierarchical order while recognizing the presence of a collective identity shared by people living in thousands of dispersed sites along the central and southern Montaña region of Peru.

The dispersion of sites is replicated in the type of dwelling, generally a single-family house, which never received the kind of attention paid to *malocas* ("long houses"). These uxorilocal residential units, occupied by a couple and their children, were made up of a house where people slept linked to a small kitchen house, or of a larger oval house with a fireplace on one side and a large sleeping quarter on the other. A settlement could be made up of several of these household units: one belonging to the eldest couple and others belonging to their married daughters. In cases in which a chief headed the settlement, it differed in that it contained a large social house, which most of the time was unoccupied. This social house sheltered the grinding stone that women used to grind the corn that was added to the manioc beer for special celebrations. It also served as a guesthouse (Biedma 1685/1906, 323; Renard-Casevitz 1972). Men and women gathered in this house to drink, sing, and start dancing before moving to the adjacent patio. Among the Mojos, the *bebederos* ("drinking houses," according to the Jesuits) had similar functions.

This residential pattern derives from two social practices: the departure of young men to settlements where they can find wives and the construction of a new house in the vicinity of that of her parents once a young woman gets married. But the smallest residential units formed by a biological family constitute the dispersed elements of a "house" comprising 80 to 400 people; all the women and some of the men belong to the same extended kindred. These kindreds are anchored by women to a given territory and are connected to similar kindreds within the region, the province, or the "nation" by the men who leave to get married. These alliances run through the whole system encompassed by and encompassing identification processes that go from the local to the global. It should be noted that this integrative alliance system did not stop at the level of the Campa "nation" and that peripheral groups or prestigious chiefs could unite with neighboring foreign groups. Thus, in each generation alliance creates strong centripetal ties with close and distant places and people (sometimes from 200 to 300 kilometers along the rivers), which counterbalanced the centrifugal divisions that affected residential units periodically (Renard-Casevitz 1977, 1998–99).

The habitat type, subjected to a regular process of matrimonial dispersion, raises frequent justifications or apologies. Some assert that this model allowed better exploitation of the resources of the Montaña's fragile ecosystem. It ensured individual freedom and harmonious human relationships by avoiding the frictions inherent in too much promiscuity. It intensified the taste for visiting and traveling frequently. Finally, and above all, it served important geopolitical purposes. For the Campas, the major argument in favor of dispersed dwelling and small-scale settlements was that it constituted the best deterrent to surprise attacks by potential conquerors who, chasing "preys" impossible to catch, eventually got lost in the forest.[13] This is an old strategy that uses one's apparent weakness to turn the visible strength of others against them. When the Jesuits first attempted to missionize the Mojos, the latter raised the same argument against reduction in mission posts, asserting that concentration offers easy prey to the predator: "They thought that concentration in missions was a way of preparing them to be handed in opportune time to the Spaniards and that reduction in larger towns was a way of gathering the prey so as to avoid the waste of dispersed dwellings" (Maúrtua 1906, 10:3).

Commerce and Warfare   The extreme dispersion and lability of settlements and the horizontality of a global reticular system deprived of a chief that could represent it are thus conceived of as guaranteeing their freedom and autonomy. "They are perfectly aware of their personal freedom and they die defending it," wrote Father Biedma as early as 1685 (p. 322). In the absence of political representatives to capture or control, the conquest of the Campa—or Mojos—nations could be achieved only by destroying every single site that has long been deserted to organize the resistance. Instead of making a show of strength through large fortified villages, this kind of social formation relies on the invisibility of relationships that link together its member groups into a cluster whose joint forces far exceed the capacity of the largest villages. Certainly, in the case of an enemy attack, the first settlements to be assailed might suffer important losses, but at the same time they constitute the safeguard of all the other settlements, which, having been rapidly alerted, can organize their defense and counterattack.

Here is a recent example of this kind of strategy. In mid-December 1989, after an attack and several killings, the Asháninka of the Selva Central region declared war on the Shining Path and Tupac Amaru Revolutionary Movement. In less than a month, around 15,000 Asháninka had confederated to wage war against the guerrillas. By mid-February 1990, 30,000 Asháninka, Yanesha and Nomatsiguenga had allied, expelling the Tupac Amaru guerrillas from the Pichis River and the Shining Path from the Tambo River. This example attests to the strength and extension of the relationships linking the Campa together and to the vitality of confederate processes that had not been put into action for such a long time that they were thought to have fallen into oblivion.

Given that Asháninka is used as a self-designation term by the inhabitants of the Selva Central region—as Matsiguenga is used by those living in the southern province—I use the term *Campa* to refer to the totality of sociopolitically united pre-Andine Arawak with the exception of the Yine, to wit, the Asháninka, Matsiguenga, Nomatsiguenga, and Yanesha.[14] All of these peoples share a common cultural trait rarely evoked in Amazonia and thus not often taken into account in sociopolitical analyses: the prohibition of raids and vendettas between them.[15] This prohibition is a corollary of the dispersed settlement pattern with a large network of relationships, the frequent traveling throughout the nation's territory, and the confederate model.

The interdiction of killing people like oneself, which myths link to the foundation of human social life (see Smith 1977 and Santos-Granero 1991 on the Yanesha), is one of the claims that Campa chiefs recite when they meet for the first time: "We are Asháninka (a-shaninka: a = inclusive we; shaninka = origin of humans) and the Asháninka do not kill each other." Coming out of the past, these were the same words pronounced by the Tambo Asháninka to address their brothers captured by the Shining Path and freed after the above-mentioned war (Renard-Casevitz 1991b, 1992a, 1993). This interdiction, already studied in its long history, is what distinguishes the Campa from other large clusters of the Andean piedmont, such as the nearby Panoans or the more distant Jivaroans, who practiced raids and vendettas among themselves. Such suppression of internal warfare is a trait that makes them sociologically similar to the Chané and the Mojos, both of whom are Arawak-speaking peoples. Even Tessmann (1930), whose work Varese (1968, 110ff.) considers to be "that of a zoologist who should have studied something else," noticed this remarkable Campa institution.

When taking into consideration this unwritten law, as well as the vast network of inter-Amazonian political alliances that prolonged the network of marriage alliances and commercial links based on the salt trade, it becomes clear why Inca historiography celebrates the relation of friendship and alliance that the Inca entertained with their lowland neighbors while enumerating Anti uprisings in the face of Inca attempts to conquer them.[16] Given that the Spanish were introduced to this historiography through the Quipucamayus, it also becomes clear why at the time of the Vilcabamba rebellion they took the rumors of alliance between Manco Inca and the Antis (Campas) and Chunchos seriously.

Confronted with the expansionist attempts of their Andean neighbors—the Huari empire, followed by bellicose highland kingdoms and fiefdoms, the Inca empire, and, finally, the Spanish Crown—since at least the Middle Horizon (seventh to tenth centuries), the Campa seem to have set up the strategy of those who, many centuries later, gave birth to the Iroquois league,[17] a strategy that, in the words of Lévi-Strauss (1943, 138), consisted in suppressing internal antagonism to allow external antagonisms to better express themselves. But in the face of Inca expansion, how was it possible to ensure respect for their frontiers without resorting to ever-increasing armies? And how was it possible to increase and maintain alliances on the vast scale necessitated by the extension of the border between the unified highlands and the multiethnic lowlands?

The military confederations that the Spanish discovered as early as the first expedition of Gomez Arias (1559) into the Selva Central region profited from previous economic and political relations (Maúrtua 1906, 5:83–176). There is a close correlation between the development of inter-Amazonian commercial networks and that of military associations. These increasingly larger networks comprised lowland societies whose material culture, standard of living, and political ideologies were globally homogeneous. With respect to war, this implied that internal struggles (private interests) were obliterated in the face of external threats (general interest). As soon as neighboring hegemonic societies threatened to conquer them, the potential "pan-Amazonian unity," according to Alvarez Lobo's (1984) formula, turned into reality, giving way to the establishment of international alliances that were up to the threat imposed by non-Amazonians, the number one enemies. In the words of an eighteenth-century Franciscan missionary, "There were infidels from all nations who prevented the passage and movement of Christians and missionaries. . . . This is a deeply rooted custom [of the Eastern Peru Indians]: they unite to challenge those who they call their common enemy, after which they . . . reassume their old quarrels" (Izaguirre 1922–29, 8:144, 159). The foundations of these latent military confederations are to be found in the particular characteristics of inter-Amazonian commerce. I will now summarize them on the basis of a previous work (Renard-Casevitz 1993).

First of all, this kind of commerce was exclusively Amazonian. It differed from commerce with the highland Andes, which, though undoubtedly important, mainly entailed forest products such as hardwoods to make weapons, medicinal plants, seeds such as *huairuro,* and birds. To describe this inter-Amazonian trade, we can adopt Godelier's (1969) definition: As soon as there is money there is trade, and money appears as soon as a product introduced into the trading network becomes a general equivalent (i.e., once this product goes through the whole chain of possible conversions). In the Peruvian Amazon, Campa salt is the general equivalent against which it is possible to barter anything else (e.g., cotton textiles, pottery, ornaments, or pearls). The Campa, initiators of Amazonian defensive solidarity, turned the Cerro de la Sal and its production of salt cakes into the center toward which vast commercial networks converged.

The salt extracted from the Cerro de la Sal was cooked, shaped into cakes, and accumulated in nearby depots. Salt makers followed the general scheme of a commercial system that demanded from every ethnic partner the introduction of a manufactured product of the highest quality and easily identifiable as their product. To elaborate salt cakes, the Campa used the red salt found in the vein of the largest hill (the divine Pareni) instead of the white salt found on a little neighboring hill (the daughter of Pareni).[18] These cakes were placed on high counters all along the Perené and Tambo rivers. Depending on how friendly were their relations, groups of traders could travel more or less closely to the heart of these commercial networks. According to an early Franciscan document, "All forest nations converge . . . towards the Cerro de la Sal. . . . They . . . come from so far away that it takes them six months to bring back the salt. . . . During the dry season, there were more than six hundred balsas and canoes" (D. Alvarez 1690, quoted by Alvarez Lobo 1984, 73; see also Vazavil 1921).

In truth, the lack of salt was not the main reason why these remote commercial partners came to the Cerro de la Sal. Though less important and easily accessible than the Cerro de la Sal, there are many salt mines in the Peruvian Amazon. Eighteen salt mines have been mapped in the Andean piedmont region between the Madre de Dios and the Lower Huallaga rivers (Hoempler 1953). These mines were locally exploited, and some were quite productive, such as the one in the Lower Huallaga–Chinchipe area. However, none was used for the production of salt cakes. As the only producers of this edible and perishable currency, the Campa developed a remarkable monopoly.[19] This monopoly explains the Campa's leading and structuring role in the constitution of ever-increasing commercial networks, which were the basis of important military federations.

Despite fluctuating margins, which are another result of the integrative processes, the spheres of integration are well delimited. Those who were related to the Masters of Salt, that is, the sphere of peaceful Campa who shared the same divine ascendancy and whose societies had been mythically founded through the establishment of internal peace (see references on the Yanesha later in this chapter), had the right to extract salt directly from the Cerro de la Sal or from the neighboring salt sources but not to make salt cakes. Cooked in earthenware pots, the unshaped salt blocks were (and still are) used for daily meals and for salting fish. The salt cakes obtained only through trade with salt cake makers, either by members or nonmembers of the Campa cluster, were used in a different way. Some were kept to serve as "money" and were disseminated beyond the borders demarcating the confines of the Campa trading network (a way of inducing new trading partnerships). Others were distributed during the celebrations organized by commercial partners, notably the great feast surrounding female puberty, which was common to both the Campa and the riverine Pano. On such occasions, every guest was given a piece of salt cake to dip into his or her soup or stew.[20]

Although all the Arawak and riverine Pano practiced horticulture, fishing, hunting, weaving, and pottery, the artistic and technical attention devoted to elaborating a specific product distinguished commercial partners. Thus, one could talk of an ethnic specialization, in which the Arawak were weavers, the Pano were potters, and the Piro were canoe builders. The main trait of Arawakan textiles was that the decorative motifs were entirely woven, in contrast to Panoan textiles, which were decorated with painted motifs. Arawakan weavers were also well known by the production of cotton textiles covered with feathers woven into the fabric. Pano pottery, generally adorned with black curvilinear designs over a rusty or creamy base, is famous for its high quality. In contrast, Arawakan pottery is dark brown, and its decoration is incised rather than painted. Other specializations included Campa and Piro feather goods and pearls, Pano "splendid *petates* or mats used to cover floors and walls" (Biedma 1685/1906, 319–28; San Antonio 1750/1906, 331–56), and finely decorated gourds, as well as Pano and Piro hammocks and oars.[21]

Among Amazonians, ordinary consumer goods were excluded from exchange. They were shared in the course of meetings, turning this parallel market into a hospitality market, which also provided the occasion to strike up pacts of brotherly friendship between hosts of different ethnic groups.[22] Additionally, the study of exchanged goods shows that only the marked and luxurious forms of everyday objects, which everybody produced in other forms, entered into the sphere of exchange.[23] Every set of partners was credited with a superior mastery in the production of certain artifacts, which engaged them in a specialized overproduction. This system can also be considered as a form of organizing artisan differences among groups that identified themselves as "forest people." By imprinting their label on specific products, each of them became an identifiable link in the panethnic luxury industry developed among Amazonians.

The Western notion of "Amazonians" or "forest people" is expressed in Arawakan language by the concept of "human being." To define this conception, or at least its range of application, I shall resort to the definition given by the Yanesha, who, although strongly influenced by Andean peoples, are definitely a lowland people. According to the Yanesha tradition, the Campa, Piro, Conibo, Shipibo, and other riverine Panoans "are included in the category *acheñ* because they think and act like human beings: they drink manioc beer, they share their food, and they wear the *cushma*" (Smith 1977, 71; also *acheñesha* or *acheñenesha*: 283, 290, 292; in Mojos language *achané* or *chané* [Eder 1985, 110]).[24]

Long commercial expeditions established a truce that allowed participants to associate in convoys and camp on the beaches opened during the dry season—which had the temporary status of no-man's land—to indulge in great collective fishing and to receive each other in riverine villages. This was an armed peace because along the route these coalitions released tensions by raiding the interfluvial Pano groups who were excluded from the commercial network because they were people without *cushma,* without beer, cannibals, and so on. These raids put to test the political alliances and the coordination of interethnic military exercises. Thus, the search for Campa salt cakes generated networks of trading partners and either seasonal spaces of peace along vast routes (the dry season beaches) or lasting peaceful relationships between pairs of "friends." Insofar as each traveler had at least one friend, the sum of their brotherly friendships allowed groups of travelers to overcome local conflicts and induce confederate processes, reinforcing the idea of political unity. The specialization of luxury products established the basis of a shared Amazonian identity made up of artisan interdependence, tracing the outline of a political community that materialized in large military confederations in case of threats or attacks launched by their common enemy, the non-Amazonians: Incas or Whites.

The analysis of the factors ensuring Campa cohesion shows how its members knitted among themselves a tight fabric of relationships, building a network of increasingly looser concentric circles and obtaining partners further and further away. Despite the distance, these partners could be engaged in military confederations extending over several hundred kilometers of rivers, which they had learned to navigate according to certain rules through their commercial expeditions. As in the Upper Xingu region but on a much larger political scale, the Campa built among the consumers of the salt money a multiethnic unity lacking supralocal political institutions that extended far beyond the frontiers of their nation. Following the definition of polity proposed by Menget (1993, 64, 73) for the Xingu, they constituted a "macropolity" whose shifting borders on the Amazonian side comprised a moral community.

This brief sketch, which contains only a few elements directly comparable to the data on the Mojos, cannot do justice to the rich sociopolitical complexity of this system. Keep in mind that a refined logic of the social, capable of promoting extended networks of political cooperation, is expanded by iteration of simple social models. These models or structures were tested at the level of the Campa cluster and purged of all the elements—linked to kinship, endogamy, or religious institutions—that promote increasingly closed or exclusive spheres of social relation. There are only short lineage segments that allow equal integration for all into an evolving network. Marriages, seen as exogamous, unite alternatively the close and the distant. There is neither a representative of the Campa cluster—except for the crystallized body of the goddess Pareni—nor a centralizing organ of its provinces, its regions, or even its kindreds. Leadership is multiple and unstable in essence and can do without representatives in cases of lack of vocation or ability. Other mechanisms restricted the power of shamans and war chiefs, always appointed case by case. Finally, internal peace and commerce establish spaces of cooperation and solidarity and show the open character that marks the institutions of the Campa cluster.

Campa Mojos Connections

From the beginning I have mentioned the regular interaction between the Matsiguenga of the Urubamba River and those of the Madre de Dios region. This contemporary evidence does not fill the gap of sources concerning the intermediate region between the Campa and the Mojos. Whereas the rivalry between the Jesuits of the Province of Maynas and the Franciscans of the Selva Central region during the seventeenth and eighteenth centuries has produced an abundance of documents for the Marañon and Ucayali valley, few are available when researching the Madre de Dios basin. The notorious difficulties of reaching the Madre de Dios region from Cuzco, together with the failure of the first Spanish military expeditions, chilled Spanish ardor for such a long time that it was not until the beginning of the twentieth century that the Dominicans attempted to establish themselves progressively in that region just after the upheavals of the rubber boom. Despite Spanish indifference, it is highly likely that during this period, the Campa continued upholding their system, which already under the Inca had allowed them to maintain their independence.

As for Spanish sixteenth-century texts, their precocity explains their great topographic and ethnic confusion.[25] By then, the legend of Paititi, a southern version of El Dorado, inspired the dreams and the cupidity of the Spanish. A mixture of information coming from the Inca, the Chunchos, and the Indians of the Audiencia de Buenos Aires originated the belief that Paititi was situated in the Sabana de los Mojos. Caught between Indian reports from Jujuy (Argentina) and Paraguay, mentioning the existence of a rich kingdom (the Inca) where gold came from, and those of the Inca and Quipucamayus, praising fertile lands of their allies, the Mojos, for a long time the Spanish believed that the rich lowland kingdom must be that of the Mojos.

What we do know for certain is that there were two groups of Mojos on the Tuiche and Mapiri rivers, which form the Beni River, in northern Bolivia.[26] The Quipucamayus mention them as gold diggers in a local mine, and we know that they were incorporated into Spanish *encomiendas* as gold washers or miners (Renard-Casevitz et al. 1986, chapters 6 and 9). In Inca times, these Mojo groups had submitted to the Inca, maintaining, however, an ambivalent position within a region that acted as a hinge between the highland Andes and the eastern, multiethnic lowlands. This position is similar to that of the Sati villages of Vilcabamba, very old pre-Andine Arawak colonies created at the time of the Huari empire (Renard-Casevitz et al. 1986, chapters 3 and 8). These highland Sati worked in local silver mines, and although they were subjected to the Inca they lodged Anti delegations traveling to Cuzco and served them as spies.

Both the Quipucamayus and the chroniclers (Renard-Casevitz et al. 1986, chapters 2–5) mention the presence of Anti and Mojos delegations in the ceremonies that the Inca celebrated in Cuzco in August (during the lowlands dry season). They also describe the exchange of very young people, who acted as hostages and guarantors of the political alliances between the Inca and the Antis or Mojos. Thus, there were occasions for regular contacts and information between the Campa and the Mojos in Cuzco. But above all, contact between these two peoples was maintained through the forest networks that extended from the Antis of the Urubamba River to those living in the Madre de Dios region, who in turn were neighbors of both the Mojos of the Tuiche and Mapiri rivers and the Machineri of the Lower Madre de Dios River.

In brief, we must take into consideration the Campa proclivity to develop systems of exchange and political alliance by means of interethnic trading networks, which increased in extension as a result of their own dynamics and in response to the expansion of the Inca empire—a proclivity shared by the Mojos. And if we recall that representatives of the lowlands—the Campa, the riverine Pano, the Mojos, and others—came regularly to Cuzco to trade and to participate in Inca celebrations, we have to give credit to the testimony of the Quipucamayus and of the Spanish chroniclers about the political collaboration between the Mojos and the Campa, insofar as contemporary testimonies perpetuate this long history. We must now examine the social system characteristic of the pre-Jesuit Mojos, given that, as we have seen, the Campa cluster is selective in its choice of interethnic trading partners, including the Cocama and riverine Pano but not the interfluvial Pano, who were conceived of as "savages," or the Andean peoples who were part of a hierarchical society united under the figure of the Inca "tyrant" (Renard-Casevitz 1991a).

The Pre-Jesuit Mojos

In a somewhat superficial way, because of the lack of thorough ethnographic data and despite a different ecosystem, there is a fascinating convergence between the social organization and way of life of the seventeenth-century Mojos and those of the Campa. When the Jesuits discovered the Sabana de los Mojos, they immediately described the ethnic and linguistic diversity of this vast region. Here I examine the reports concerning the Arawak-speaking portion of the Mojos and, in contrast, their oriental neighbor, the Arawak-speaking Bauré.

With regard to the 4,000–6,000 Arawak-speaking Mojos located in the central and southern part of the savanna, the Jesuits describe an extremely dispersed settlement pattern of people wearing long tunics. There were a "great number of villages and hamlets" (Marbán et al. 1676) that were "independent with respect to each other, insofar as they did not have a common leader to obey" (Orellana 1687/1906, 3).[27] They had "very narrow straw houses" each with a maximum five to eight hammocks and each with an adjacent small kitchen house (Orellana 1687/1906, 3).[28] Settlements were established in forest fragments on naturally high ground and in the *lomas,* or artificial hills, which allowed the residence of one to fifteen families.[28] When an artificial hill, or a clearing in a forest fragment, housed a village, houses (dormitories and kitchen) occupied the periphery and opened toward the interior, composed of a plaza, in the center of which were one or two houses. According to the Jesuits who slept in them, there was always a *bebedero,* or drinking house, and sometimes a temple. Dead people were buried in the drinking houses. It is clear, then, that these were "social houses" where celebrations were performed, temporary visitors were lodged, and dead people were buried. In other words, it was the place where communal activities were carried out regardless of gender and age differences.

The Bauré, located in the eastern portion of the savanna, lived in large fortified villages, each composed of several big *malocas.* Villages were headed by a hereditary chief controlled by an old man elected for this office every year. If the chief was not the eldest of a group of siblings, he was the son of a chief and the husband of a chief's daughter, and the couple was assigned servants, two young males for the man and two young females for the woman. There was an embryonic noble class derived from the marriage alliances established between some village chiefs. Whereas members of this group practiced local exogamy and rank endogamy, among the common people village endogamy was the dominant practice (Eder 1985, 85–86, 282).

The Jesuits represent the Bauré as people already civilized (Verdugo 1764, AGI Charcas 474, fol. 14v). In contrast, the Mojos seemed to them much more primitive because men and, even worse, women were rebellious and independent. Women were so "incapable of subjection and obedience" that it seemed that men did not have wives "for lack of dominion, insofar as women do not recognize subjugation to their husbands" (Orellana 1687/1906, 11).[29] Moreover, "a single ill word or disdain" of the husband toward the wife or of the wife toward the husband was enough for them to divorce. Instead of an overall paramount chief, they had, like the Bauré, a village chief, but elected for a year (a *cargo* chief): "There is no overall headman . . . and there were no village headmen. . . . Every year they elect a chief, but with so little subordination that nobody feels obliged to obey him" (Orellana 1687/1906, 11). This type of social order, without classes and a permanent visible hierarchy, baffled these attentive early observers. How was it possible to reduce the Mojos into missions if everybody refused submission, even in its very first manifestation: the physical punishment of children? What eluded Jesuit observers was both the individual internalization of law and morality and the forms of authority developed outside the field of coercion, which was relevant to the field of hunting and warfare rather than to the art of living in community.

The dispersed settlement pattern of the Mojos was based on that of the founding deities of their kindreds. Each matriuxorilocal settlement had its deity, or rather its deities, always presented to us as married divinities (*dioses casados*) placed at the head of a group by God. "They claimed that the origin of their ancestors was near their settlement, either in a lake . . . from whom the inhabitants of the village descended, or in a forest or grassland from where he raised the ancestors of other sites. Thus . . . God made their first ascendants different and independent from those of other villages" (Orellana 1687/1906, 8–9; Eguiluz 1884). As among the Campa, this type of mythical foundation substantiates the same symbolic model of social organization. If we disregard the kinship links between mythical founders, they all share common features: they are numerous, they appeared at the same time, already gendered and ready to have descendants, and they have a direct and identical relationship with the divinity who placed them in a given site. Their difference derives from the places in which they emerged and which they founded: a lake, a hill, or a grove. Thus, on a smaller scale, we find among the Mojos ideological and social schemes, and customs—from settlement patterns to social houses—similar to the Campa model. Although little is said about the Mojos system of kinship and marriage, we know that they married with people with whom they had no kinship link (exogamous ideology) and that their very well-documented uxorilocal residence rule differs starkly from the patrilocal system of the Bauré (Eder 1985, 83–84, 282ff.).[30]

Furthermore, in contrast with the Bauré, the Mojos also abided by the principle of internal peace, which extended, in accordance with the networks of political alliance, to multiple ethnic groups, either within the savanna or along the commercial routes connecting them to the Andean highlands. However, "they are in war" with other peoples, such as "the Cañacures villages" (Orellana 1687/1906, 2; Bolívar 1906, vol. 8). The ample ramification

of the communication networks connecting the Mojos with the Andean highlands is an expression of their antiquity and allowed the continuity of exchange even in the face of local conflicts. The internal peace within the Mojos cluster was a reflection of the everyday harmony respected within each
settlement. According to sources, "they never quarrel, even when anger flares"
(Orellana 1687/1906, 12; Eder 1985, 93), and just like the Campa, when facing
serious conflicts derived from sorcery, they put an end to them by discreetly
poisoning the accused sorcerer. Mojos drinking feasts had similar aspects to
the female puberty rituals celebrated by the Campa and riverine Pano: "They
wait for these occasions to settle their quarrels" in highly formalized public
duels (Orellana 1687/1906, 12; see also Eder 1985 and Eguiluz 1884).

There are other points of convergence between the Mojos and the Campa, such as the distinction between shaman healers and shaman thinkers, or
"wise men," as an Asháninka man called them. In the case of the Mojos, the
evidence seems to indicate not two types of shamans but rather two stages
in the development of a shaman's career, exactly like in the case of Asháninka and Matsiguenga shamans (independently of the category of sorcerers).
Thus, the Jesuits assert that there was only one term to designate shamans
but that some were healers (*encantadores y curanderos*) whereas others were
like wise men and priests (*como sabios y oficiantes* in Eder 1985, 109ff.; Orellana 1687/1906; see also Santos-Granero 1991, 1993b for another distribution
of the three categories among the Yanesha). It is worth noting that there were
both male and female shamans, although their ratio, ages, and roles are not
specified. It is clear that these data, taken out of their ideological and social
context, cannot be examined in greater depth. However, they allow us to assume that between the Mojos and the Campa there must have been a mutual perception of proximity based on sociopolitical homology, given that both
peoples had experienced cultural difference: the Mojos because of the multiethnic population of the Sabana de los Mojos and their periodic long voyages to the Andes—mainly in search of salt, stone, and metal—and the Campa because of their integrative multiethnic networks.

In synthesis, the Mojos were organized in networks of relations linking
small uxorilocal settlements in accordance with a structure of horizontal
connections or reticular system. There was no central ruling organ or unified representation of power, and every element of the system practiced self-
government within a large sphere of peace favorable to the multiplication of
Ego-centered relationships. This dense network of relationships constituted a latent force that could be mobilized in proportion to the seriousness of
external crises and threats. At a more global level, the Mojos economic and
sociopolitical schemes organized an egalitarian polity without hierarchical

structures operating at the ethnic or interethnic levels. It was an interethnic association open to a variety of partners—sometimes close neighbors, sometimes distant allies located along the routes of commerce—but offering the same structure of latent confederate strength.

Regressive History and Conjectures

If the Mojos social model is so similar to that of the Campa, the following question arises: Since when was this model prevalent in the Sabana de los Mojos among the Arawak-speaking core and its neighbors, lacking powerful headmen and practicing interethnic peace? Can we put forward the hypothesis that it is as ancient as that of the Campa, that is, that it goes back to at least the Middle Horizon (Huari, Tiahuanaco) or to the period immediately preceding the appearance of socially differentiated societies (Wankarani and the first phase of Tiahuanaco)? The key issue here is the type of social formation of the designers of the anthropogenic landscape of the Savanna. To build artificial hills, canals, wells, elevated roads, and earthen ridges, is it necessary to resort to a neo-evolutionist interpretation, like Steward's (1946–59), that links major infrastructure works to the existence of centralized power, in this case to the existence of powerful chieftainships? I would like to break away from this interpretation to suggest another hypothesis.

It is not known how many centuries it took to model the landscape of the Savanna, but it is known that the enterprise was already under way by A.D. 700 (Denevan 1980; Erickson 1980). According to local studies and more general aerial photographs, these works show an infinite variety in extension and concentration, suggesting in some places a family enterprise undertaken over several generations and in others "some evidence of integration at a higher scale" (Erickson 2000, 190). Globally, however, the image is one of a multiplicity of dispersed sites of uneven extension creating a complex landscape that can be read as the accumulated result of processes of fission and fusion, reproduction, and swarming. The pre-Jesuit Mojos seem to illustrate wonderfully well the way of life and organization of the ancient inhabitants of the savanna as they appear to us through the anthropogenic topography they modeled: the very dispersed settlement pattern, the variable size of the sites, and an anthropogenic network of connections.

There are many other regions in Latin America where people practiced an agriculture based on elevated fields and earthen ridges. This was the case of the sixteenth-century Taíno of Hispaniola, Arawak-speaking peoples who elevated their artificial hills with a digging stick (Sturtevant 1961, 73). It was also the case of the seventeenth-century Palikur, Arawak-speaking peoples of French Guyana (Rostain 1991; see also chapter 7). For the Beni archaeologists, "the earthworks did not necessarily involve the mobilization of large amounts of labor" (Erickson 2000, 192; see also Denevan 1980, 162). Let us not forget that the savanna landscape is but the eroded projection of the "collective multigenerational intervention" (Erickson 2000, 192). The descendants of each generation increased the height and size of the artificial hills on which they lived, prolonged the earthen ridges elevated by their forefathers, opened new canals, and created new hills.

Modern historical studies present the Mojos, the Bauré, and the Cayuvava as socially stratified agricultural peoples whose large population was distributed in large villages. We have seen that this is not true for the pre-Jesuit Mojos and that it was because of their high reputation among the Inca that Spaniards thought they constituted a kingdom. Likewise, generations of ethnologists tempted by evolutionism have attributed to them powerful chieftainships, whose existence is refuted by the rereading of early documentary sources. I argue that the greatness of the Mojos is associated with a type of social formation, which the West has been unable to read in the past and it seems to have forgotten today.[31]

It is not my intention to resolve whether the ancient inhabitants of the Sabana de los Mojos were Arawak. It is a question of opening an anthropological debate about sociopolitical forms of Amerindian polities. Therefore, I put forward the hypothesis that, like the pre-Jesuit Mojos, the ancient inhabitants of the Sabana de los Mojos had a social organization without a centralizing organ and that there is no necessary connection between the transformation of the landscape of the savanna and the existence of powerful chieftainships. Such a society would be composed of sets of farmers settled in dispersed sites varying in size and formed by a reticular system of exchange that develops internal peace (i.e., a type of society animated by a tribal dynamics with its phases of fusion and fission).[32]

Of course, such a scheme is opposed to interpretations strongly oriented by the process of Western globalization and homogenization of social diversity, with growing entropy. These interpretations are based on an unilinear model of social evolution that entails hierarchization in social classes, concentration of power in a ruling class, and a gradual move toward pre-state and, later on, state formations. Therefore, these interpretations neglect the possibility, indeed, the facticity of complexification and processes of sociocultural homogenization within relational networks forming polities or macropolities without governing bodies or class hierarchy, processes that are still at play. They impose a hegemonic scheme of sociopolitical organization, a scheme that is well represented but not universal. And thus they substitute a vertical hierarchical integrative structure for a possible, or real, horizontal heterarchical structure constituted by a network based on flexible connective processes of aggregation or of schism and colonization (in the sense of the swarming of human groups acquiring autonomy and decision-making power without losing memory of the place of origin and common ascendancy of the colonies).

The originality of this type of social formation had an irrevocable impact on Europeans at the time of the conquest of America. Thomas More's *Utopia*, which was inspired by these social forms, saw in their economies of sharing the solution for the deficiencies and worst evils of European societies. Thus, *Utopia* reminds us of the fundamental characteristics that separate this type of society from those of the Old World. These societies ensured the access of all their members to the means and instruments of production and to collectively possessed lands and rivers, each generation only making usufruct of the inherited or colonized territory. Each of them, in a structural way, brought about the competitive fragmentation of autonomous powers between prestige statuses within and between communities (groups or clans). And the large villages with strong chieftainships of the riverine Pano or the Bauré do not escape from this fragmentation and dilution of power. As a corollary, most of these societies were characterized by practices of redistribution of products either daily among co-residents or, on a larger scale, in periodic consumption celebrations. They also practiced the abandonment, destruction, or ritual burial of the material goods of deceased adults, often including their houses.

To put it in a negative way—that is, with respect to our ethnocentric perspective—there was no system of accumulation and conservation of movable and immovable property through dowry or inheritance, nor was there social differentiation through the individual appropriation of real estate property or through capitalization of production in benefit of a certain class. In other words, there was no feudal or mercantile economy. On the contrary, what we find are systems that organize the sharing or destruction of goods. From this point of view, Campa salt trade or Potlatch celebrations show the preponderance of social relations over capital. These traits, shared by numerous Amerindian societies, from the Canadian Algonquins to the Fuegians, are very well illustrated by the vast social formations of the Amazon, especially in this case: the pre-Andine Arawak and the Mojos, and even the Pano and the Bauré.

Despite the profound differences that separate these different clusters, most notably the presence or absence of the practice of endo-warfare, these social formations are based on the competitive or complementary presence of a multiplicity of similar units that connect with each other and produce local identities in accordance with systems of discrete differences: linguistic, ritual, or even productive. These societies seem to be organized by a reticular model based on simple iterative structures, which Carneiro da Cunha calls the "fractal model" (Hertz Conference, Paris). Thus, in many of these societies there is no evidence of a tendency toward a unified proto-state or state. This is so because they perpetuate the foundation of their society and their ideology: the egalitarian and sharing identity and the competition between multiple and locally restrained powers. This representative competition still goes on, as illustrated by the persistence of processes of fusion and fission that undermine the unified and centralized decision-making power of modern native Amazonian federations and confederations.

Notes

I wish to thank the organizers of the Comparative Arawakan Histories conference for inviting me to the first meeting of Arawak specialists and, especially, Fernando Santos-Granero for our debates and for his invaluable help in improving the translation into English of my essay. I am also grateful to the Smithsonian Tropical Research Institute for its warm welcome.

1. The pre-Andine Arawak cluster must be understood in a strictly sociopolitical sense. Despite their linguistic differences with respect to the Asháninka, Matsiguenga, and Nomatsiguenga core, who from this point of view are closer to each other, it comprises the Yanesha and some Yine (Piro).

2. Antisuyu, one of the four parts of the Inca Empire with a large unconquered tropical forest portion. On the evolution of the term *Anti* or *Andes,* see Renard-Casevitz et al. (1986, 37–38). With the passage of time, the Anti became the Campa for the Franciscan missionaries who entered into the Selva Central in the seventeenth century, and the Matsiguenga for the Dominican missionaries who entered the southern region in the twentieth century. The term *Chunchos* was used by the Inca to refer to several ethnic groups from the southern Montaña of Peru and northern Bolivia.

3. It is in the Vilcanota River, just below Ollantay Tambo, that the Matsiguenga used to perform an immersion rite that would make them masters of the relations with the Inca and nowadays with the highland Andean world.

4. Not to be mistaken with the creation myth, which also follows a quadripolar scheme but narrates the creation of the natural elements and living beings. The representatives of all the terrestrial species created through this act appeared already gendered.

5. The four primordial sibling-gods jointly appeared with attributes of eternity. Each of the following generations also appeared jointly, as immortal quadruplets. In contrast with the founding myths of the societies of the Vaupés River basin, there is neither ranking nor hierarchy according to a birth order or a gender inequality in the Campa versions.

6. Demigods are the entities begotten by celestial divinities but born on Earth, where they have lived and where, most of the time, they appear now under the guise of remarkable landmarks.

7. According to different levels and versions, marriages should take place between cross-siblings or first cousins. On the contrary, postmarital residence rule is always uxorilocal.

8. We should keep in mind that the Matsiguenga who have recently descended from Upper Timpia River after decades of isolation name themselves "Nantis," that is, "We, the Antis."

9. Thus, the mythical hero Shongabarini, literally "the revolutionary," gives his name to two or three real characters who enrich his saga with elements—most of the time hard to date—of their own post-conquest history.

10. The model of female fertility rate is built, as in the founding myth, on four or eight children with an equal distribution of sexes. Marriage follows rules of matriuxorilocal residence, local exogamy, and nonrepetition of alliances (see Renard-Casevitz, 1998–99). Thus, the resulting network is one of multiple connections established between distant localities.

11. Because it has Aymara or Quechua homonyms, the term *Campa* has been the subject of several interpretations. Under the form of *camba* it was used to designate all the native peoples of the Bolivian Lowlands. In Peru, the morpheme *kampa*, "to exchange" or "to trade," exists in the Asháninka-Matsiguenga language. Therefore, it is found in the term *Kampaříite,* or "the Master of commerce" (see Renard-Casevitz 1981, 124n.31, 128–30; 1993, 29, 40nn.3–4).

12. Six expeditions: two after the persecution of Tupac Amaru by García de Loyola (1572) by Fathers Montoya and Cartagena (Ocampo Conejeros 1923; Maúrtua 1906, vol. 7) and four smaller exploratory expeditions by Father Font and subsequent fellow Jesuits.

13. Thus, for instance, the Quipucamayus mention the fact that the Inca armies got lost in the forest when attempting, unsuccessfully, to subdue the Antis (Oliva 1895, 56–57; Cieza de León 1967; Renard-Casevitz et al. 1986, chap. 2).

14. Yine (Piro) villages and way of life from the sixteenth century to the beginning of the twentieth century are very similar to those of the nearby riverine Pano. Nevertheless, through this same period we have evidence of the existence of mixed villages, Yine-Asháninka or Matsiguenga-Yine, especially in the boundaries of their respective territories. These villages abided by the rule of internal peace, confining vendettas and raids to Yine and Pano villages and the "hinterland savages" and war to the Andean peoples.

15. According to the classic distinction between raids and war. The Campa used to raid the interfluvial Pano groups "in order to increase the number of members of their nation" (Izaguirre 1922–29, 10:190) and to wage war against their Andean neighbors.

16. This historiography describes in detail the battles that took place on the Iscaicinga, Manari, Manan Suyo, and Opatari borders—the Campa groups that extended from Huanuco to Madre de Dios—to resist Inca incursions (Renard-Casevitz et al. 1986).

17. The Iroquois League acted as a political unit beginning in 1690, adopting a very restrictive position with respect to old intra-Iroquois vendettas (Hunt 1960, 68ff.)

18. Drains dug out in the salt ore by means of water filtering from the pierced bottom of large gourds enabled them to detach hard slabs of salt. Once they were broken, the pieces were collected and mixed with water in ceramic pots. The salty liquid was then boiled and rid of impurities; once concentrated, it was poured into ceramic molds of two sizes. These molds were dried in sun or smoked; salt cakes were then carefully wrapped and tied up in big leaves. Salt cakes are called *tibipatsa* (Campa) or *kolpeto* (Piro).

19. Their subgroups controlled eight other important salt mines: The Matsiguenga controlled the salt mines located in the Upper Piñipiñi and Manu rivers, the Asháninka those in Quebrada Muchuy and the headwaters of the Pisqui River, the Yanesha the Agua de la Sal in Chumagua and the salt mines located in Uchiza and Tocache, the Yine those in Cachiacu (Hoempler 1953, map; personal fieldnotes). Used on a daily basis, these mines were not exploited for the production of salt cakes.

20. The inter-Amazonian trading network disappeared when the large Pano villages of the Ucayali River collapsed and when huge extensions of land were given to foreign firms during the rubber boom.

21. The Campa and Yine made beads of nacre, silver, and gold: "All these Indians are hardworking people and excellent traders. . . . What they desire most are pearls and, in order to obtain them they make long trips in which they sell canoes, textiles" (Izaguirre 1922–29, 9:47; see also Oricain 1790/1906, 373).

22. Friendship pacts are a key piece of the Campa model of sociopolitical organization. When uniting two men belonging to different ethnic groups, these pacts assumed the form of a sibling relationship. Openly political, they did not carry a ritual obligation. They were struck up by an uneven exchange of one product typical of the ethnic group of each partner. Above all, the pact implied permanent peace and mutual assistance between friends, even in case of conflict between their groups of origin.

23. The rareness of luxury products has been underlined by both Lévi-Strauss (1943) on commerce in the Xingu region and by Godelier (1969) on Baruya trade. Here there is a culturally oriented rareness.

24. A category that excludes both "Christians," that is, Andeans, mestizos, and whites, who are "demonized" for not having any of these practices; and the "bestialized" cannibals and the forest groups lacking the typical long tunic (*cushma*) or manioc beer.

25. Remember that the conquest of Peru started only in 1532 and that the first small expeditions into the Amazon lowlands were those of Mercadillo in 1538 to the Upper Marañón River, followed by that of Puelles to the Huallaga River in 1543.

26. I suggest that *Mapiri* is the Spanish transcription of *Mapïri*, a common Matsiguenga-Asháninka term for rivers whose beds are covered by stones and rocks (*mapï* = stone).

27. The large settlement in which the Jesuits chose to set up their mission was composed of "more than twelve houses in the midst of a dense forest" (Orellana 1687/1906, 21).

28. Note that the Sabana de los Mojos is flooded during half of the year and that the islands of forested land are rare and therefore much coveted.

29. Eguiluz (1884, 9) asserts, "No reconocían superior las mujeres a sus maridos" ("Women did not recognize their husbands as superiors"), and Eder (1985, 84) states, "Usaban la poligamia entre ellos: se halla un hombre con muchas mujeres y una mujer con muchos varones . . . (verdad que esto segundo es muy raro)" ("They practiced polygamy among them: a man with many women or a woman with many men [although in truth the latter is very rare]").

30. Jesuit missionaries were interested only in the native traits that could endanger their project or challenge their ideology: the great freedom that people, and especially women, enjoyed; infanticide; the dispersed settlement pattern; the absence of social classes and of chiefs worthy of that name; and the beliefs justifying their way of life. The missionaries also reported infanticide, polygyny, and polyandry with respect to the Campa.

31. On the basis of the Kachin cycle (*gumsa/gumlao* phases) of the highland Burma studied by Leach, Friedman (1975) proposed an analysis of tribal dynamics based on an alternation of fission and fusion processes. Many North American studies taking into consideration this type of sociopolitical mechanism are framed in neoevolutionist interpretations. For exceptions to this view, see Blitz (1999), Redmond (1998), and for the Mojos, Erickson (1980, 2000).

32. Village chiefs, war chiefs, and shamans are all statuses coupled with a random and temporary system of acknowledgment of the holder. They depend on the appearance of individuals with socially predefined personalities who are acknowledged in a consensual manner as appropriate to fill the position. In this system chiefs are only local, and "subjects" control their "king" by means of the institution of fragmentation, which allows a group to leave and create a new autonomous site with its own chief.

6 Piro, Apurinã, and Campa: Social Dissimilation and Assimilation as Historical Processes in Southwestern Amazonia

PETER GOW

> Further, it is beyond doubt that since the discovery of the Antilles, inhabited in the sixteenth century by Caribs, whose wives bore witness still, by their special language, to their Arawak origin, that processes of social assimilation and dissimilation are not incompatible with the functioning of Central and South American societies. . . . But, as in the case of the relations between war and trade, the concrete mechanisms of these articulations remained unnoticed for a long time."
> —Claude Lévi-Strauss, "Guerra e Comércio entre os Indios da América do Sul"

WHILE I WAS DOING fieldwork among the Piro (Yine) and Campa (Asháninka) people of the Lower Urubamba River in eastern Peru, my understandings of much of what I saw and was told ran along tracks laid down by my reading of the literature. As I have discussed elsewhere, the production of my own data and analyses forced me to radically rethink what I thought I knew about the history of relations between local people and nonindigenous newcomers (Gow 1991, 2001). But this has also been true of my understanding of the relations between Piro and Campa people, which was framed by my sense, derived from my reading, that these relations were very ancient and the product of an in situ differentiation between these two peoples. It has taken me a long time to rethink that issue and to be open to the possibility that the relations between these two peoples may actually be recent. This chapter outlines the process of that rethinking and what it implies.

Here I produce a conjectural history of the Urubamba Piro, which sees them splitting away from an ancestral population shared with the Apurinã people of western Brazil and then moving toward and eventually coming into direct and sustained contacts with the Campa and Matsiguenga in the Urubamba area (see map 5, p. 10). This historical reconstruction is unashamedly conjectural, although I hope to show that it is both interesting and plausible. I do not believe that, in itself, this historical reconstruction is particularly important. What really concerns me here are two different issues. First, I want to continue the dialogue between the sorts of data collected by ethnographers and the knowledge generated by linguists and archaeologists because this is an important route to historical understandings of contemporary indigenous Amazonian societies. Second, I want to develop analyses of indigenous Amazonian histories that accord with what we are learning about indigenous Amazonian people's own understandings of sociality.

Traces of an Unknown History

In the absence of other modes of accessing the pasts of indigenous Amazonian peoples, geographic location and linguistic classifications have played a key role in framing anthropological analyses of these societies. Peoples who speak related languages are assumed to constitute, inherently and unproblematically, natural units for analysis, in a way that has not been held to be true of speakers of unrelated languages. The most obvious example of such a natural unit is the Gê-Bororo peoples, which have produced their own subdiscipline, appropriately called Gêologia in Brazil. Other examples of such natural units are the eastern Tukanoans, Carib speakers, Panoan speakers, and speakers of Tupian languages. The obvious exception here is Arawakan and Maipuran speakers, a lacuna that this volume clearly seeks to redress.

I have no desire here to challenge the main heuristic device that underlies such analyses, for I believe that linguistic relationships offer important insights into the unknown pasts of the societies we study. Instead, I want to ask another question of such units: How do they conform to what we know of the sociologics of indigenous Amazonian peoples? One of the main problems with the natural units referred to earlier is that it is far from clear that any of them are genuinely meaningful for indigenous Amazonian peoples. For Europeans, genealogy and shared descent have powerful meanings, whether benign or alarming depending on context and one's point of view. They refer to socially operant entities, crucial to the building of nation states and supranational alliances and organizations. But if we have learned anything about indigenous Amazonian peoples, it is surely that genealogy and shared descent do not much interest them. Even in the few parts of indigenous Amazonia where we find descent groups, they have little to do with genealogy as such (Crocker 1979; S. Hugh-Jones 1979; Hill 1993). In the rest of indigenous Amazonia, we do not even find descent groups.

This in turn raises the question of the salience of such units as the Gê-Bororo and the Panoans for the peoples so described. It is not at all clear that Gê-Bororo peoples see themselves as a meaningful unit, nor that eastern Tukanoan peoples consider themselves to have more in common with each other than they do with their Cariban- and Maipuran-speaking neighbors and affines. Jackson's (1983) otherwise excellent account of eastern Tukanoan identity strangely offers no demonstration of the salience of "eastern Tukanoan speakers" as an exclusive unit to the people so described. Seeger (1987, 134) noted of studies of the Gê-speaking Suyá, "My impression of the Suyá and Lanna's characterisation of them could not have been more different. He saw a pale reflection of Upper Xingú societies; I saw a weakened picture of a Gê society. We were both probably correct. What it meant to be Suyá at the times of our visits was quite different."

Seeger's second major ethnography of these people therefore points toward an important problem: What meaning do such identities have for the indigenous Amazonian peoples who have them? What would an indigenous Amazonian account of such linguistic relationships, and hence of the histories they contain, look like?

This chapter explores certain problems raised by just such a linguistic unit, the pre-Andine Arawak, in southeastern Peru in the headwaters of the Ucayali and Madre de Dios rivers. This unit is formed by speakers of three closely related Maipuran languages: Piro, the various dialects of Campa-Matsiguenga, and Yanesha. A number of different terms have been used to name this unit, but I use *pre-Andine Arawak* in deference to its historical priority. The territories of the speakers of these three languages in this area form an unbroken bloc, bounded on all sides by speakers of very different language groups, such as the speakers of the various Panoan languages, Quechua, and Harakmbut. Therefore, the pre-Andine Arawak seem to represent a natural unit, and the differences between them seem to represent in situ modes of differentiation, related to different ecological orientations and differential historical contacts with neighboring peoples.

Such a unit, though real enough in the known historical record and in the present day, is unlikely to be an ancient phenomenon because one of its components, the Piro, seem to be newcomers to this bloc from far to the east. This in turn raises the questions of what this unit is, how it could have come into being historically, and how it is constituted. These questions involve direct engagement with indigenous Amazonian sociologics and raise further questions about how these sociologics unfold in historical time.

The Pre-Andine Arawak

To my knowledge, the first delineation of a pre-Andine Arawak grouping was proposed by Rivet and Tastevin (1919–24) on the basis of linguistic affiliations. They included within this unit the Piro-Chontaquiro, Kuniba, Kanamare, Anti-Campa, and Ipuriná languages.[1] Rivet and Tastevin's grouping was purely linguistic and had no cultural implications, and the name *pre-Andine Arawak* referred simply to the fact that these languages are spoken in southwestern Amazonia, closer to the Andes than most other Arawakan languages. A first point to note about this grouping is that three of the languages noted, Piro-Chontaquiro, Kanamare, and Kuniba, probably are better seen as dialects of a single language, Piro. I discuss this issue further later in this chapter.

By the time of the *Handbook of South American Indians* (HSAI, Steward 1946–59), Rivet and Tastevin's linguistic unit was replaced by a culture area approach. The pre-Andine Arawak who lived in the headwaters of the Ucayali and Madre de Dios rivers, closest to the Andes, were called Montaña peoples, and the rest, living further east in the valleys of the Yuruá and Purús rivers, were called Juruá-Purús peoples. The precise criteria for this distribution are not at all clear. The reason is part geographic propinquity and part gross cultural similarities. However, a major justification seems to be documentary: Our major knowledge of the Montaña peoples derives from Jesuit and Franciscan missionaries and travelers in what is now eastern Peru, whereas our major knowledge of the Juruá-Purús peoples derives from travelers in what is now western Brazil (as the spelling of the name implies). What this meant, for the case at hand, is that the speakers of a single language, Piro, were distributed between two separate culture areas. Of course, the culture areas of the HSAI were based on very scant information (see Myers 1974), and dividing lines had to be drawn somewhere. Unfortunately, such borders are highly replicative and have a habit of framing academic discourse for decades to come without ever being properly questioned. This is especially so when such borders reflect real international frontiers, a problem exacerbated in this case by different national languages and intellectual traditions.

Rivet and Tastevin's pre-Andine Arawak reemerged in Noble's (1965) study of Arawakan languages. This author did not add much to the specific case except to suggest that the ancestral homeland of speakers of the ancestral Proto-Arawak language lay in the headwaters of Ucayali and Madre de Dios rivers because migration downriver is easier than migration upriver. This suggests that the Yanesha, Campa, and Piro peoples represent the Arawak who stayed behind in their ancestral home. And Noble's work held out the hope that they may have preserved certain Ur-Arawakan cultural traits in the process, lost to their wandering cousins.

However, that same year, Summer Institute of Linguistics missionary Esther Matteson (1965, 1) produced the first structural linguistic study of a pre-Andine Arawak language, Piro, and concluded that it is "most closely related to Ipuriná: forty-eight per cent of the words of an Ipuriná vocabulary transcribed by Nimuendajú correspond to Piro words. Only about 19 per cent of the vocabulary of either Campa or Matsiguenga, spoken by the nearest neighbours of the Piro, correspond to Piro words."

Pre-Andine Arawak, as proposed by Rivet and Tastevin and defended by Noble, thus splits into two distinct sections: Piro-Apurinã and Campa-Matsiguenga. Matteson also noted the geographic spread of Piro speakers, living along the Cushabatay, Lower Urubamba, and Manú rivers (a north-south distance of almost 500 miles), and the presence of another dialect, Piro Manchineri, spoken 200 miles to the east of the Lower Urubamba on the Acre and Yaco or Iaco rivers. Manchineri (spelled *Manitineri* in Brazilian Portuguese) is almost certainly the dialect that Rivet and Tastevin called Kanamare. This indicated that the HSAI classification had distributed the speakers of a single language (in the sense of mutually intelligible dialects) between two culture areas.

In his study of Campa cosmology, Weiss (1975) proposed a unit he called Anti, comprising the Campa, Matsiguenga, and Yanesha, based on cultural similarities presumably with a minor linguistic element. Noting the high level of internal homogeneity of cosmological ideas within this Anti unit, he continued, "What is known of the Piros, who neighbor both the Campas and the Matsiguengas and, like them, speak an Arawakan language, shows their mythology to be quite different from that of the Anti tribes. In very few particulars can we recognize anything even remotely resembling what is encountered among the Antis" (1975, 482).

Therefore, the author of one of the earliest in-depth studies of a pre-Andine Arawak cosmology found that in this regard the Campa-Matsiguenga and Yanesha form a unit that excludes the Piro. It is a first indication that there might be something unusual about the Piro within the pre-Andine Arawakan grouping.

The major exponent of a pre-Andine Arawak unit has been Renard-Casevitz. In an early article, she identifies the Matsiguenga, Campa-Asháninka, Yanesha, Piro, and Mashco as the "Proto-Arawak" group, descendants of "an archaic branch of the [Arawak] family" (Renard-Casevitz 1972, 214).[2] In a later article she reidentifies this group as "sub-Andine Arawak," formed by "five self-designated sub-ensembles: Yanesha, Asháninka (four regional entities), Nomatsiguenga, Matsiguenga and Yineru or Piro, a name of Pano origin. The Yanesha to the west, influenced by long promiscuity and by linguistic cultural mixtures with neighbouring Pre-Incaic and Incaic neighbours, and the Piro to the northeast, under the often secular influence of the Pano, are distinguished, by language and certain cultural traits, from the very homogeneous complex formed by the other three sub-ensembles despite provincial variations" (1993, 26).

Renard-Casevitz's criteria clearly are more geographic than linguistic, although there is an implication that the linguistic divergences of both Yanesha and Piro are a result of extensive contact with Andean and Panoan neighbors, respectively. Although there is some linguistic evidence of this for the Yanesha (Wise, in Ribeiro and Wise 1978, 200), there is none for Piro. Piro shows remarkably little Panoan influence, either in lexicon or syntax.

The major focus of Renard-Casevitz's (1992b, 1993) work on this "sub-Andine Arawak" group has been to demonstrate its existence as a historically operant entity, which she does admirably. The Yanesha, Campa-Matsiguenga, and Piro people have a long and dense history of interrelations, marked by trading, intermarriage, political alliances, and warfare and most dramatically marked in the very impressive regional coalition formed by Juan Santos Atahuallpa. There is no question that this grouping can be identified in the historical record in a way that would have been meaningful to local indigenous peoples. But does this grouping form a natural unit in the thinking of local people?

I discuss contemporary Piro people's attitudes about this grouping later in this chapter, but two historical features raise questions about its analytical importance. First, the wider regional system identifiable in the historical record never seems to have coincided exactly with the sub-Andine Arawak: The Pano-speaking Conibo were also involved heavily in trading with Piro and Campa people and in the rebellion of Juan Santos Atahuallpa. And at no time in the past, as far as I can see, did Piro people coordinate their actions with those of their Maipuran-speaking neighbors in preference to their Pano-speaking neighbors.

Second, throughout their known history, Piro people from the Lower Urubamba showed just as much interest in contacts with other Piro communities far to the north, northeast, east, and southeast as they did in their neighbors to the west and south. There have always been Piro speakers in the Yuruá, Purús, and Madre de Dios areas, and Urubamba Piro have always traded with them.[3] Indeed, if one were to look for a regional system centered on the Piro rather than the Campa-Matsiguenga, it would not look like the sub-Andine Arawakan grouping.

Therefore, we are left with a problematic unit to analyze. Linguistically, the sub-Andine Arawak are spread out across a large area of southwestern Amazonia, stretching from the foothills of the Andes to the west and toward central Amazonia to the east. Culturally, by contrast, this linguistic grouping has been split by anthropologists into two: a Montaña component and a Juruá-Purús component. The first reflects a genuine historical entity, which Renard-Casevitz calls sub-Andine Arawak, between which the dense interactions of its subensembles is admirably well attested. Therefore, it looks like a tightly bounded unit, both geographically and linguistically. But one of these subensembles, the Lower Urubamba Piro, is in turn part of a larger set of Piro speakers spread out over a much wider area of southwestern Amazonia. Close contacts between these far-scattered Piro communities are historically well attested, and continue to this day (Gow 1991). The easternmost Piro communities are neighbors of the Apurinã, speakers of the language most closely related to Piro. Despite such close linguistic relatedness, however, the Apurinã have never been considered to have anything else in common with the Piro, and less still with the Campa or Yanesha, except with regard to language. How does all this connect to the ethnographies and ethnohistories of contemporary sub-Andine Arawakan peoples?

"People Like Us"

Obviously, we cannot expect indigenous Amazonian peoples to share our interests in their pasts. Anthropologists might want their knowledge to coordinate with that of the peoples they study, but these two forms of knowledge have such dramatically different origins that the anthropological task is likely to be very difficult in this regard. Equally, indigenous Amazonian people can hardly be expected to show much sympathy for our inquiries, given that they have been generated by interests totally alien to them. That said, however, a simple confirmation of our hypotheses would be if our indigenous Amazonian informants formulated them spontaneously for themselves or could at least recognize them when they were pointed out. Here I ask whether pre-Andine Arawak means anything to my Piro informants.

As far as I know, the close linguistic relationship between the Piro and the Apurinã is of no significance to Piro people living on the Lower Urubamba. To my knowledge, my informants had never heard of the Apurinã, who live very far to the east in a foreign country of which they know little. My very oldest informants had perhaps met Apurinã people when they lived on the

Purús River in the first decade of the twentieth century or had heard of such meetings with their parents and grandparents, but they had clearly not been sufficiently memorable to be recounted.

For what it is worth, when I first met Apurinã people in Acre in 1987, I do not remember any particular "click." Spoken Apurinã does not sound much like Piro, nor did anything in these Apurinã people's comportment signal them to be more like the Piro than the Kulina, Kaxinawa, and Yaminawa people I met there. By contrast, when I talked to Acre Manitineri people I had the sensation of being back among Lower Urubamba Piro.

The Campa-Matsiguenga loom far larger in Piro regard, for they are close neighbors and often their kinspeople. And Piro people do indeed recognize pre-Andine Arawak as a category, "people like us." In certain contexts, Piro people would point out to me that the Campa (Kampa, Gashanigka), Matsiguenga (Machikanko, Kiruneru), the Yanesha (Gamaysha) are "people like us" (Piro: yineru pixkalu, Ucayali Spanish: gente como nosotros). The basis for this identification is a shared way of being. For Piro people, the Campa-Matsiguenga and Yanesha are people who drink manioc beer, eat their food properly cooked and tempered, and wear clothing.[4] As such, they are potential spouses, and the Campa-Matsiguenga, and to a lesser extent the Yanesha, have a known history of intermarriage with the Piro. The Campa-Matsiguenga and Yanesha are thus "people like us," and Piro people often extend their own preferred term of self-reference, wumolene, "our kinspeople," to these neighbors.

But the basis of this "people like us" unit is not linguistic. They strenuously resisted my attempts to point out cognate words between Piro and Campa, the two pre-Andine Arawak languages most familiar to the people in the community I know best. I tried to point out (in casual conversation, I should stress) the basic similarities of the Piro and Campa words for "moon" (ksuru and cashiri), the similarity between the Piro kanru ("bitter manioc") and the Campa caniri ("sweet manioc"), and the differences between these and their equivalents in three languages familiar to my informants, Amahuaca, Quechua, and Ucayali Spanish (respectively, ushè, quilla, luna for "moon" and atsa, yuca, yuca for "manioc"). Linguistically, my Piro and Campa examples were very good cognates, reflecting consistent transformational phonetic patterns between the two languages, such as the loss of unstressed vowels in Piro and the loss of the mid-unrounded vowel in Campa. Even without phonetic transcription, I trust that these cognates are obvious to readers familiar with Spanish-based orthographies.

None of my informants was impressed by my analogies, and they pointed out that the Piro and Campa words were quite different, which I was forced to concede. After all, English and Dutch are very closely related languages, and I can make a decent stab at reading a Dutch newspaper, but Dutch radio absolutely defeats me. I remain convinced that multilingual speakers of Piro, Campa, and Matsiguenga, of whom there are many on the Lower Urubamba, must, at some level, be able to recognize the basic similarities of these languages as against Amahuaca, Quechua, and Ucayali Spanish, but I have never been able to get anyone to articulate this for me.

Indigenous people on the Lower Urubamba think of languages as being highly discrete entities, much as Sorensen (1967) reported for the northwest Amazon, and have no inclination to group them or to search for common words among them. Because knowledge of other languages is used for comprehension of speech and for talking itself, the identity or mere similarity of words between different languages is of no practical use; after all, identical or similar sounding words across different languages are as likely to be *faux amis* as to be aids to comprehension. This attitude toward other languages is even extended by Piro people to the other dialect of Piro with which they are familiar, *Yako gwachine tokanu*, "Yaco River people's language."[5] My Urubamba informants asserted that these people do not really speak Piro at all, but *tsrunni tokanu*, "ancient people's language." Similar attitudes were expressed toward Campa and Matsiguenga, which, despite their manifest similarities (which we would recognize as dialects), were consistently identified as two separate languages by my informants.

When Piro people asserted to me that the Campa-Matsiguenga and Yanesha were "people like us," it was almost invariably in one specific context: the contrast between "people like us" and "wild Indian" peoples, those who walk about naked, eat no salt, eat uncooked and disgusting food, and so on (see Gow 1991, 1993). The most common referent for "wild Indians" were the Amahuaca and Yaminahua, speakers of Panoan languages. However, again no comment was made on their Panoan languages, which at least to my ear sound remarkably different from Piro and Campa.

Indeed, language here seems to be quite irrelevant, for although Piro people very seldom admit to any similarities to the Amahuaca and Yaminahua (except perhaps in political discourses), they readily assert their similarity to the Shipibo-Conibo, close linguistic relatives of the Amahuaca and Yaminahua. And when Piro people say they are like the Shipibo and Conibo, they also emphasize their differences from both the Campa-Matsiguenga-Yanesha and the Amahuaca-Yaminahua. Like the Shipibo-Conibo, and unlike these others, Piro people are "people of the river," "people who know how to make canoes, pottery, designs," and so on. The Piro and their downstream neighbors, the Conibo, have a shared aesthetic of life, a shared vision of what constitutes *gig-*

lenchi, "beauty," which is not, they point out, shared by their Campa and Matsiguenga neighbors. The "people like us" unit that the Piro form with the Conibo and Shipibo does not involve much intermarriage, for these Panoan peoples are strongly endogamous. Many Piro men told me that they found Conibo women attractive but that the latter refused to sleep with them.

In the literature on the neighbors of Piro people, there is surprisingly little information of the former's views of the latter. Piro people seem to be far more interested in their neighbors than their neighbors are in them. From my own ethnography, I can say that Urubamba Campa people consistently criticize the Piro for their ignorance of the forest and for having too much contact with other peoples. One young Pajonal Campa man told me, as he gestured to the village of Santa Clara, "The people here are not my kinspeople, they are *shimirintsi* [Campa: "Piro"]. The *shimirintsi* are no good, they live too close to white people. My people are different, we live among ourselves." The moral worthlessness of the Piro in this regard is a byword on the Lower Urubamba, repeated as often by the local white elite as by Campa people in a convergence that I long ago learned to distrust.

My Pajonalino informant told me this during his prolonged stay in a Piro village, which had many Campa residents. At the time, I took it to be a piece of hypocrisy. However, it is a common statement by Campa people, but one that does not prevent many of them living with and intermarrying with Piro people. There are no ethnically homogeneous Piro communities, and all that I am familiar with have Campa residents. Furthermore, most Piro communities have spontaneously formed Campa "suburbs," affiliated communities located away from the banks of the main river, where Campa people can sustain this image of "living among themselves" while having access to the benefits of Piro people's easy relations with white people. This pattern intensified during the height of the civil war on the Ene and Tambo rivers (in the late 1980s and early 1990s), when many Campa fled to the Lower Urubamba, but it had existed before, probably long before.

My account here refers to these relations as they were enacted in the late twentieth century, and space does not permit tracking back through the historical records. However, nothing in the recent or more distant past suggests that the relations between the Piro and their neighbors were particularly different at any former time. In the present and throughout known history, we find Lower Urubamba Piro people as a remarkably cohesive unit engaged in dense relations with all their neighbors. Such relations undoubtedly are mediated by notions of similarity and difference, but all are equally marked by a more profound point: Piro people's sense of their own uniqueness and incomparability. In many contexts, Piro people assert themselves to be *yine potu,* "real humans," and in most contexts *yine,* "humans," has the primary referent, "Piro people."

This last point is important because the model of identities nested within more inclusive hierarchies implied by terms such as *pre-Andine Arawak* is quite alien to what we know about how indigenous Amazonian peoples think about identity. This raises the problem of what exactly we are to make of terms such as *pre-Andine Arawak* or *sub-Andine Arawak.* Are these simply analysts' terms, handy heuristics for our work, or are they to be imagined as native categories, sociological principles operant in the minds of indigenous people, and so revealed in our ethnographic data and played out in the historical archive?

My argument here is that terms such as *pre-Andine Arawak* are primarily analysts' heuristics, which reveal interesting things about the history of the project of ethnographic and ethnohistorical studies of indigenous Amazonian peoples, but that they should not further detain us. That said, several important points remain. First, the historical relationships between contemporary languages reveal historical processes that would be otherwise unknowable. Second, even if such historical processes are of no interest or relevance to the speakers of these languages, they must certainly have helped to shape features of contemporary people's lives. And much more importantly, such historical processes must have occurred in the *kinds* of relations we can observe in contemporary ethnographic accounts. By bringing the ethnographic data about identity and alterity I have been discussing here into alignment with what linguistic analysis can tell us about historical processes, we can formulate better accounts of the origins of the lived worlds we study and, more importantly, formulate ethnographically plausible accounts of what we know of those historical processes.

Maipuran Speakers in Southwestern Amazonia

In his overview of Maipuran languages, Payne (1991) makes some important points for the discussion here. Concentrating on the Maipuran languages that have been well described by linguists, he develops a reclassification of them. The most important point of his account for the present analysis is that he finds Piro and Apurinã to be more closely related to languages such as Bauré and Ignaciano, spoken in northern Bolivia, than they are to Campa-Matsiguenga while acknowledging that all of these languages fall within a single higher-order entity, southern Maipuran, which also includes the Terena of southern Brazil. This new unit, southern Maipuran, stretches along the eastern flanks of the Andes from the Gran Pajonal in the northwest to the

Pantanal in the southeast. The listed languages simply reflect those that have been well studied linguistically, and this unit unquestionably contains more and once contained many more. At the same time, Payne's reclassification solves the anomaly of Yanesha by placing it in a new family, western Maipuran, along with Chamicuro, spoken to the north in the Huallaga valley.

Payne's reclassification effectively decomposes the pre-Andine Arawak by subsuming the whole group into another one of a bigger scale. But it also suggests intriguing new historical possibilities for the Maipuran speakers of southeastern Peru. Far from representing the "Proto-Arawak," as Noble proposed, the Yanesha, Campa-Matsiguenga, and Piro may well represent recent geographic convergences within much older patterns of the geographic radiation of Maipuran speakers. If historical linguistics is to continue to aid anthropologists as it has done in the past, then anthropologists must continue to rethink the basic frames of their analyses in light of the changing views of linguists.

Genetic relationships between present-day languages, and the sequencing of protolanguages from which these languages are thought to descend, tell us nothing about the movements of peoples in the past except that such movements must have occurred. The fact that Yanesha and Chamicuro are related tells us nothing about where Proto-Yanesha or Chamicuro was spoken. It is as likely to have been spoken in present-day Yanesha territory or in present-day Chamicuro territory as in anywhere in between (or elsewhere, for that matter). In the absence of independent evidence, all we can say is that this ancestral language must have been spoken somewhere and that therefore the Yanesha, the Chamicuro, or both subsequently moved to their present territories.

That indigenous Amazonian peoples move around a lot is both obvious and well attested historically. I give three examples here. The movement of Piro people from the Lower Urubamba to the Cushabatay River 300 miles to the north occurred at the beginning of the nineteenth century (Izaguirre 1922–29, 9:33–35). Similarly, the Axaninka or Asháninka of the Amônia River in Acre moved there in this century. Another large group of Campa moved to the Chandless River in Brazil in the 1980s. The motivations for such movements clearly are complex and in the three cases cited are occurring, insofar as we know about them at all, in colonial contexts. However, as archaeologists make clear (Lathrap et al. 1985, 1987; DeBoer and Raymond 1987; Heckenberger 1996), such movements were also a feature of prehistoric Amazonia. We should keep their possibilities in mind when we consider historic and present-day Amazonia.

Payne's reconstruction of the linguistic history of southwestern Amazonia suggests three distinct components to the contemporary pre-Andine Arawak of southeastern Peru. First we have the Yanesha, speakers of a western Maipuran language. Second are the Campa-Matsiguenga, speakers of a southern Maipuran language that is notably divergent from its southern Maipuran relatives to the east. Third are the Piro, also speakers of a southern Maipuran language, divergent from Campa-Matsiguenga but very closely related to Apurinã spoken to the east and also to other southern Maipuran languages spoken very far to the southeast in northern Bolivia. Clearly, there has been a lot of movement, even if we have no idea in which direction such movements happened.

A Plausible Historical Hypothesis

If it is difficult to fit the known linguistic affiliations of the Piro to the pre-Andine Arawak scheme of in situ differentiation, is it possible to develop an alternative scenario? What follows is necessarily very speculative, but it has the virtue of both agreeing with the known linguistic relations and having a certain amount of independent support.

My hypothesis is that there was an ancient radiation of proto–southern Maipuran speakers within southwestern Amazonia, leading to the ancestral speakers of Proto-Campa-Matsiguenga being located in the northwest in southeastern Peru and the ancestral speakers of Proto-Piro-Apurinã-Bauré-Ignaciano being located in northern Bolivia. I make no inferences about actual directions of this ancient radiation.

I further hypothesize that, at a later date, the ancestral Piro-Apurinã moved out of northern Bolivia, north toward the Purús River, where they began the process of differentiation that led to the contemporary differences between Piro and Apurinã. Some of the ancestral Piro people moved west into the Purús headwaters and thence, following the many portage points, into the Yuruá, Manú, and Urubamba rivers. Those who moved onto the Urubamba thereby entered into contact with Campa people. It was on the Urubamba that these Piro people acquired many of the elements that they currently share with Campa people and, for that matter, with the Shipibo-Conibo.

This hypothesis accords with the linguistic relationships discussed by Payne, but it also accords with certain other features of the Piro and Apurinã. The first of these is that Piro and Apurinã cultures are remarkably different. The published ethnography on the Apurinã is slight, but even what little is known suggests some remarkable divergences (Ehrenreich 1948; Gonçalves 1991). I refer to the situation in the latter half of the nineteenth century, before the extensive changes caused by the rubber industry. Then,

Apurinã people lived away from the big rivers, Piro people lived on the riverbanks; Apurinã people depended more on hunting than fishing, Piro people depended more on fishing than hunting; Apurinã people stressed warfare as the key relation to the other, Piro people stressed trade. The Apurinã did not make or use woven clothing, the Piro did; the Apurinã slept in hammocks, the Piro did not; Apurinã pottery was crude with simple designs, Piro pottery was fine with complex designs.

I am not suggesting that the Apurinã maintained, into the late nineteenth century, a culture once shared with the Piro; the Apurinã must have changed a great deal, too. However, it is obvious that many of the differences between the Piro and Apurinã are most plausibly explained by the Piro's adoption of cultural forms originating in eastern Peru, such as a basic orientation to large rivers, woven clothing, fine painted pottery, and manioc beer, and consequently the abandonment of such cultural forms as hammocks.

Like all other such historical speculations, this could run in the opposite direction. Discussing the dispersion of southern Maipuran speakers from a putative heartland in eastern Peru, Urban (1992, 96) writes, "The Matsiguenga, Asháninka-Campa and Piro would have remained close to their geographical origin, and the Apurinã would have penetrated into the lowlands of the Purús." If this hypothesis is correct, then we could replay the scenario just proffered, but in the opposite sense: Here the Apurinã move to the east, losing various eastern Peruvian cultural traits and adopting those of Panoan and Arauan speakers in the Yuruá-Purús area, whereas the Piro remained closer to the place of origin and retained older traits.

Is there any evidence that would help us to determine which process occurred? To my knowledge, no archaeologists have worked on the Lower Urubamba or on these problems, but if Payne is correct and Piro-Apurinã are more closely related to languages in northern Bolivia than to Campa-Matsiguenga, then my hypothesis is slightly more probable than Urban's.

However, there are also a few scattered fragments in the known ethnography that support my conjectural history. In a major Piro mythic narrative, "The Kochmaloto Women" (Gow 2001), a woman is sleeping with her grandchild in a hammock next to a fire. Piro people do have hammocks, which are almost exclusively used by small babies; it is unusual to see adults sleeping in them, especially with a child in tow. But in twenty years, I have never seen anything that corresponds to this mythic image, for Piro hammocks are never strung next to a fire. This aspect of "The Kochmaloto Women," though logically necessary to the narrative, is sufficiently odd to have led one of my informants to comment on this scene, "Long ago, my fellow tribespeople slept in hammocks with their fires underneath, just like the Amahuaca people."

Piro people, like everyone else, say many things about their distant ancestors that are demonstrably untrue, but in this case I think the woman was correct, for there is corroborating linguistic evidence.

In most Maipuran languages, the word root "to sleep" forms terms for "hammock," which is readily understandable. This root is found in Piro: -mka/-maka, "to sleep." But this same root also forms words for clothing, hence *nomkalu*, "my *cushma* (cotton robe)," *nomkalnama*, "my skirt or my vagina clothing." The Piro term for "hammock," by contrast, is *shechi*. The most plausible explanation for this odd state of affairs is that as Piro people abandoned hammocks and adopted eastern Peruvian clothing, the word shifted in meaning from "hammock" to "clothing." This process has left two features to mark the unidirectional movement of history: an archaic practice appearing in a myth and the strange shared root of the words for "clothing" and "sleep."

The sense that the ancestral Piro came from the east, with a very different culture from the present one, is further confirmed by toponymy. The major tributaries of the Lower Urubamba, including those that have been most important to Piro people as residence sites, have Piro names that are clearly of non-Piro origin. *Ginoya, Mapoya, Supa, Pikiriya, Supawa, Miyariya,* and *Pakiriya*, which are standard and historically well-attested Piro toponyms, all seem to be of Panoan origin. This is most obviously seen in the -*ya* suffix, meaning "with or characterized by" in Panoan language: *Ginoya*, the Inuya River, clearly is Panoan *inoya*, "river with jaguars." There are river names of Piro origin on the Lower Urubamba, but with the exceptions of *Wawo* (Huau) and *Puyga* (Puija), these tend to be minor tributaries. This is in very marked contrast to the Campa and Matsiguenga toponymies of their respective territories, which are almost invariably analyzable in the local language (Weiss 1975; Renard-Casevitz 1972).

If we look to the east of the Urubamba, we find a very different situation. Here Piro river names abound. We find Manú (*Mano*, "Tarantula River"), Sotlija (*Sotluga*, "Stone River"), Curiuja (*Kolyoga*, "Small Catfish River"), Cujar (*Kokga*, "Coca River"), Curanja (a corruption of the older name *Curumahá*, from *Kolomaga*, "Green Scum River"), and Yavari (*Yawalu*, "Stone Axe River").[6] This suggests a greater time depth to Piro speakers' residence in the eastern area than on the Urubamba. It seems likely that as the ancestral Piro moved west onto the Lower Urubamba, they did so in relation to an earlier Panoan people from whom they then adopted the river names.[7] As with the earlier example of hammocks, such asymmetries are hard to explain if we posit a movement of Piro and Apurinã speakers from west to east.

The Search for Others

If this historical scenario is accepted as just as plausible as its alternatives, it becomes possible to ask what would have motivated the ancestral Piro to move onto the Lower Urubamba and, more specifically, to ask what in the known sociologics of indigenous Amazonian peoples would have led them to do this. My argument is that Piro people were attracted westward toward the Urubamba by an interest in the trade potentials of this area and that as they entered into trading relations with their new neighbors in the Upper Ucayali, they both intensified the role of trading in their social organization and adopted many new cultural forms from their new trade partners.

I return again to the Piro and Apurinã in the late nineteenth century. One of the most remarkable differences between these two peoples, so closely connected by language, lay in their primary orientation to other peoples. Gonçalves (1991, 134) reports, "Silva Coutinho tells us, in 1862, that this tribe is very inclined to warfare, and much of their time is taken up in the preparations and the adornments of war, and that they are well respected by other tribes." By contrast, Samanez y Ocampo (1980, 66–67) tells us, at about the same time, "The Piro, in general, are happy, communicative and real traders. . . . They show a great ability in everything, and energy in all work, *when they want to*, especially everything related to navigation, in which field they have no rivals along these rivers." For the Piro, such an outsider's judgment could be indefinitely multiplied across many centuries.

To be fair, the Apurinã also traded with their neighbors, and the Piro also made war on theirs and were feared by them, as noted by Santos-Granero (chapter 1). But more important than this symmetry, I think, is the radical difference between the Apurinã and the Piro in the latter half of the nineteenth century in their basic relations to their neighbors: warfare in the case of the former, trade in the case of the latter.

Long ago, Lévi-Strauss (1942/1976) pointed out that warfare and trade are two faces of the same relation in indigenous Amazonian societies. Lévi-Strauss's argument was expanded and generalized by Sahlins (1974) in his sociology of primitive exchange, such that warfare became one pole of a sliding scale of reciprocity constitutive of primitive society, going from generalized (in the domain of kinship) through balanced reciprocity (trade) to negative reciprocity (war). In this process, Lévi-Strauss's key insight, that trade and war are at some level the same thing in indigenous Amazonia, was unfortunately lost within this concern for reciprocity. Because the Piro preferred to trade with their neighbors, their "foreign policy" seems to us more social than that of the Apurinã, who preferred to raid theirs. Here, the profound analogies of Piro and Apurinã "foreign policies" are masked under an alien logic that equates positive reciprocity and the social.

This issue has been a major concern in the work of Viveiros de Castro, who developed an important new understanding of the global nature of indigenous Amazonian sociologics. Viveiros de Castro (1992, 1993) argues that indigenous Amazonian societies are not ordered by the local constitution of a social order that is subsequently turned outward to other social orders in trade and war but by the key relation to distant and often hostile others that exists before and above the constitution of the local social order and gives the latter its form. The global form of such a social order is a symbolic economy of predation wherein predator-prey relations are the cosmological model of all social relations.

Whereas interethnic trading in southeastern Peru is well attested and the subject of numerous studies, little has been written about its social form. The fine-grained studies concern intraethnic trade relations (see Bodley 1970 and Schäfer 1991). How exactly interethnic trade relations were thought about and socially constituted by indigenous peoples is little known. However, one point does stand out from a consideration of such interethnic trading: The trade relation did not seem to affect the identity of its terms. That is, when Piro people traded with the Campa or Matsiguenga or Conibo, there was no sense in which this relation led to a merging of identities. Indeed, I suspect that the trade relation was what constituted such terms. Following Viveiros de Castro, it is the global relation to the other that constitutes the self: It is the fact that the Campa and Conibo exist as trade partners that constitutes the Piro, and reciprocally.

This perspective elucidates two apparently contradictory features of Piro people's visions of their neighbors and their motivations for trading. On one hand, Piro people seem to believe that any form of knowledge is held in a better form by a neighboring people; thus the Campa and Matsiguenga weave and make bows and arrows better than they do, and the Conibo paint and make pottery better than they do. This establishes the motivations for trading. On the other hand, Piro people show a surprising lack of interest in how their own actions might benefit their neighbors. Though fascinated by the details of their neighbors' lives, Piro people do not seem to think of themselves as part of an organic totality that includes those neighbors and themselves. They do not seem to think of themselves as in any way serving their neighbors. Instead, they seem to treat their neighbors primarily as resources for the production of their own social lives.

From this point of view, therefore, interethnic trading in southeastern Peru does not take the form of an organic regional division of labor, but rather a series of predatory relations on the specialist knowledges of neighboring peoples. The productive knowledge of neighboring peoples becomes the point from which selves ("real people") are made. In this scheme, the differentiation of selves from others must be both maintained and preferably constantly exaggerated so that selves might continue to come into being.

This argument has two correlates important for the present analysis. First, it corresponds to the known contours of the region under consideration. Despite the time depth of very close relations between, for example, Piro and Conibo or Campa peoples, there is no sense that these peoples, as identity positions, are merging. This is especially notable on the Lower Urubamba, where Piro and Campa coreside and intermarry extensively. Although the identities of specific persons vary depending on context, there is no ambiguity about what such identities might be: Piro, Campa, or both. Intermarriage mixes identities, but it cannot create or transform them. Such identities have a very potent referent in language, for there is no "Piro-Campa" creole that would correspond to such mixed identities: Piro and Campa languages remain highly distinct, as noted earlier.

Second, this approach helps to explain the historical processes that underlie my conjectural history. Viewed in this way, as Lévi-Strauss noted, trade and warfare are the two faces of the same relation with the other. It therefore becomes clearer how the ancestral Piro-Apurinã people gave rise to two such different descendants, the Piro and the Apurinã. All we have to assume is that the proto-Piro began to emphasize a trade relation to the other, whereas the Apurinã emphasized a war relation. Over time, this slight difference of emphasis and its manifold ramifications would have led to the major difference between these two peoples despite the great similarities of their languages.

My account here even allows us to posit why this occurred. As they differentiated, the proto-Piro seem to have been located more to the west, and the proto-Apurinã were located more to the east. Therefore, the ancestors of the Piro were much closer to the complex portage system in the headwaters of the Purús and hence to the dynamic trade network of southeastern Peru. I suggest that it was access to this trade network, and its linkages both to the Andes and to the Central Amazon north along the Ucayali, that motivated them to move onto the Lower Urubamba via the portages between the Purús and Urubamba rivers.

Once they reached Lower Urubamba, the range and complexity of the trade network accessed by Piro people as they came into direct contact with the Campa-Matsiguenga and the Ucayali Panoans would have increased the volume and variety of wealth items available to them. A consequence of such an intensification of a trade-oriented relation to others, and a consequent increase in trading activities, would have been the genesis of new practices and manners of production and consumption. Thus the ancestral Piro people would have acquired and later started to produce clothing, pottery, and other items of the form common in their new area and to develop new ritual forms. This process seems to have been most intense in relation to the riverine peoples of the Ucayali, insofar as Piro material and ritual culture most closely resembles that of the Conibo and is so perceived by both peoples. But it would also have been true of relations with the Campa-Matsiguenga and, beyond them, the Yanesha.

The process of cultural homogenization that I am suggesting for the Piro in relation to the Campa-Matsiguenga would correspond in many of its features to other known multiethnic systems in indigenous Amazonia such as the Alto Xingú system (Galvão 1979; Basso 1973, 1995; Heckenberger 1996) or the northwest Amazon (Goldman 1963; Galvão 1979; Jackson 1983; Hill 1996b). The linguistic heterogeneity of these multiethnic systems reveals them to be the products of complex historical processes, and their cultural homogeneity reveals them to be a recent historical phenomenon. But such multiethnic systems would also benefit from social analysis of how linguistic heterogeneity and cultural homogeneity are mapped onto indigenous Amazonian sociologics.

In the case of the pre-Andine Arawak, I have suggested that the linguistic heterogeneity of this unit reflects a past more complex than has been envisioned heretofore and that the manifest cultural homogeneity of this unit, where it exists, can best be understood as the result of recent interactions rather than ancient in situ differentiation. I have also argued that this cultural homogeneity perhaps has precise sociological coordinates in indigenous Amazonian notions of the relation to the other as foundational of social existence. Whatever their historical origins, an indigenous Amazonian people who choose to emphasize trade as their privileged relation to the other will end up looking like those others, by sheer dint of the accumulation of those other peoples' things.

Assimilations

In the concluding sections of this chapter, I want to briefly consider some of the implications of my analysis, particularly the implications for historical understandings of indigenous Amazonian peoples of Lévi-Strauss's and Viveiros de Castro's approach to relations of self and other as processes of assimilation and dissimilation of a very distinctively Amazonian kind. I begin with assimilations.

Elsewhere, I have analyzed the power of using indigenous Amazonian notions of self-other relations in elucidating the history of the Piro and their relations with white people (rubber traders, hacienda bosses, missionaries, and state officials) from the 1880s to the 1980s (Gow 2001). That century saw many important transformations in Piro life, such as the rise in debt slavery, the escalating use of imported technology and clothing, mass conversion to Seventh-Day Adventism and Evangelical Protestantism, and the importance of literacy and schooling, which come to make sense in Piro terms when "white people" are seen from a Piro perspective as the privileged other that guarantees the ongoing potentials of Piro social life.

My argument there is that many of these changes, which anthropologists tend to view as acculturation and culture loss, are in fact fairly simple consequences of Piro people's decision, in the period immediately before the rubber industry's expansion into the area, to increase their relations with traders from central Amazonia, such that these traders became the key other operating in the genesis of local Piro social life. Although we necessarily know very little about it from a Piro perspective, that decision was undoubtedly motivated by the trade potentials these new traders offered. The consequences of this decision do indeed look like acculturation and culture loss, for Piro people were precisely interested in the wealth items, knowledge, and cultural forms of these "white people," but they wanted these things in order to be Piro. It was the relation to white people that mattered, for it is in that relation to the term *white people* that *Piro people* becomes a term. Concepts such as acculturation and culture loss are unhelpful here precisely because they posit the merging of these terms, a process that was assuredly not happening in the Lower Urubamba over the century discussed.

The recent history of relations between Piro and white people is an example of assimilation in the sense used here. Piro people have no desire to become white people; *kajitutachri,* "one who behaves like a white man," is a very serious insult between Piro people. Instead, Piro people want to become *themselves* through their relations with white people. The sociologic here is identical to the one I posited earlier in this chapter for the earlier period of developing relations with the Campa and Conibo, and indeed has the same basic form of importing the things and knowledge of the other for the genesis of selves. The positing of such historical continuities in self-other relations has the advantage that we can use contemporary ethnography as a guide to historical processes that we can know only through the traces they have left in the contemporary world.

The position defended here is the one that was called uniformitarian in nineteenth-century geology in that historical processes are held to be uniform:

The kinds of processes that built the current world are currently operating in the world. This was opposed to catastrophism, which insisted that historical processes were nonuniform: The kinds of processes that built the current world were of a radically different order from those that currently operate. Catastrophism has had a long period of dominance in the historical understanding of indigenous Amazonian peoples, for such accounts have long been centered on the singular catastrophe, for local indigenous peoples, of European colonial insertion into the region. Indeed, so dominant has this catastrophism been that it has generated a sort of Edenic vision of precolonial Amazonia. After all, if almost all changes in Amazonian history are referable to European colonial insertion, then prehistoric Amazonia must indeed have been a land without history, as Euclides da Cunha famously put it.

This is the import of historical linguistics for ethnographers of contemporary indigenous Amazonian peoples, for it shows us powerfully in the traces of relationship between contemporary languages that the region had a long and complex prehistory, and it seems reasonable to posit that the social processes governing that complex prehistory continued into the colonial history of Amazonia and into the present. For this reason, I assert that the relationship of assimilation between Piro and white people can help us to understand the earlier assimilation between Piro and Campa people, an event posited on linguistic grounds and supported by other data. Assimilation and dissimilation are uniform processes in Amazonian history, I suggest, and we should begin to look beyond the undoubted catastrophe that indigenous Amazonian peoples have suffered to try to see the uniform sociologic that must equally have informed their responses to that catastrophe.

Dissimilations

Finally, I return to an aspect of my conjectural history. If, as I have argued, the pre-Andine Arawak, at least in the Piro-Campa case, are an example not of in situ differentiation of a common stock but rather of a more recent assimilation in the sense used here, then this does not mean that such differentiations do not occur. Indeed, my model depends precisely on such a differentiation, that between Piro and Apuriñã. In the vocabulary used here, such differentiations are dissimilations. What do such dissimilations look like in practice?

I noted earlier that the Urubamba Piro know little or nothing about the Apuriñã, so nothing from my ethnography of the former would help to elucidate the problem. However, following the uniformitarian principle, we do have a contemporary issue that can serve as a model: relations between

Urubamba and Yaco Piro. When Urubamba Piro discuss the Yaco Piro dialect, they note certain word differences and consistently attribute those differences to the fact that the latter speak *tsrunni tokanu,* "ancient Piro people's language." For example, the Yaco Piro word for "plantain" is *sapna,* a
word limited in Urubamba Piro to wild *Heliconia* spp. Speakers of the latter
dialect also asserted that *sapna* was the old word for "plantain" and therefore that Yaco Piro preserves an ancient usage, replaced in Urubamba Piro
by a new word, *paranta.*[8] This pattern is quite consistent. However, although
Urubamba people assert the primordiality of Yaco usage, they in no sense
assert its authenticity; for them, the "real Piro word" (*yineru tokanu potu*)
for plantain is *paranta,* not *sapna.*

From a Western point of view, this attitude seems strange, which undoubtedly has much to do with our attitudes toward legitimacy, primordiality, and
genealogy. In the Piro case, I think we are looking at the sociologic of dissimilation: From the point of view of Urubamba Piro, the Yaco people are
dissimilating by remaining like the ancestors rather than changing their
speech, as Urubamba people have done. For these latter, the neologism *paranta* has replaced *sapna* as the true Piro word, and if Yaco people want to speak
yineru tokanu, "human language," they should keep up. This feature of local perception of language use was brought forcibly to my attention in 1995,
when I returned to the Lower Urubamba after an absence of seven years
because of the civil war. I would say something and local people would respond, "We no longer say that, now we say this," or, "When you lived among
us, we used to talk about X, but now we talk about Y." They are highly conscious of linguistic innovation and seek to "keep up"; indeed, young people
openly criticize or ridicule old people for failing to do so.

In these two examples, what counts as the proper way of doing things is
the manner in which a coresident group of interacting people currently do
these things, and deviations from this current mode are rejected as archa-
isms. This is not particularly surprising. Piro people place a very high value
on peaceful coresidence with kin and the consequent transformation over
time of coresident nonkin into kin and parallel transformation of non-cores-
ident kin into nonkin (see Gow 1991). Minute attention to transforming language use therefore marks out an ongoing history of such relations, which
dissimilates this group of coresidents from others, who are consequently seen
to be archaic and therefore different. Such dissimilations could be overcome
only by renewed assimilations in everyday life through renewed coresidence.
If this does not happen, they tend to expand.

If linguistic differentiation through social dissimilation expands long
enough, dialect formation takes place, and if continued longer, mutually

incomprehensible languages develop. This, presumably, is what happened to Piro-Apuriña. From this perspective, it is not necessary to assume that the ancestral Piro-Apuriña people split into two isolated populations that then differentiated as language communities. All that is necessary to assume is that ongoing dissimilations stopped being reassimilated and were exacerbated to the point at which speakers of the two new languages came to see them as distinct entities.

Dissimilation reiterates the point made earlier about the value of uniformitarian historical analysis in the study of indigenous Amazonian history. Just as assimilations reflect decisions indigenous Amazonian peoples make about which others to be interested in and therefore to target for the production of themselves, dissimilations reflect decisions about whom to cease being interested in and therefore to ignore. Dissimilations are relations in their trajectory of being unmade though indifference to their content. Dissimilations, lack of interest, ignoring, being bored by—all these are things unlikely to stimulate interesting ethnography or ethnographic questions. But they are the processes that we need to investigate if we want to link our understanding of how contemporary indigenous Amazonian peoples have historically come to live the lives that they do to our understanding of the meanings that these lives have for them. The unnoticed can be profitably brought to mind.

Notes

I would like to thank Fernando Santos-Granero and Jonathan Hill for their invitation to the conference at which the original paper was presented and Eduardo Viveiros de Castro and Christina Toren for their help in formulating the ideas. Fieldwork on the Lower Urubamba and in Acre between 1980 and 1999 was funded by the Social Science Research Council, the British Museum, the Nuffield Foundation, and the British Academy.

1. The Kuniba in this list should not be confused with Pano-speaking Conibo, and the Kanamare should not be confused with Katukina-speaking Kanamarí.

2. The "Mashco" usually are identified today with the various Harakmbut-speaking peoples of the Madre de Dios region and were once thought to speak an Arawakan language; current linguistic thinking (Payne 1991) questions their inclusion in this family and certainly excludes them from the Maipuran grouping. However, *Mashco* or *Mashco-Piro* is also used locally to refer to two other groups: the Piro speakers of the Manú River and the uncontacted speakers of a language identical with or very closely related to Piro, also living on the Manú, Yaco, and Purús rivers.

3. There were also the Iñapari people, speakers of a language very similar to Piro, in the area between the Purús and Madre de Dios (Rivet and Tastevin 1919–24; Payne 1991). These people are thought to be extinct, but it is possible that the uncontacted "Mashco-Piro" (see note 2) are survivors of these people.

4. The Campa and Matsiguenga do eat certain foods that Piro people will not (such as frogs and shrimps), and the Piro eat certain things (deer and large catfish species) that the Campa and Matsiguenga will not.

5. The "Yaco River people" call themselves Manxineru, Manchineri, or Manitineri. This name is considered illegitimate by Urubamba people, who assert that the Manxineru were an ancestral group of their own.

6. *Cujar* was the name by which the entire Purús mainstream was once known in Peru.

7. The most likely candidates for these original inhabitants would be the ancestors of the contemporary Amahuaca, who continue to have a special place within Piro people's regard: The Amahuaca (along with the Matsiguenga) are the only neighbors of the Piro who have a real Piro name, *Gipetuneru,* or "Capybara People."

8. *Paranta* clearly is a borrowing of Amazonian Quechua, *palanda,* but this fact was never commented on by any of my informants, for whom it was self-evidently different from the Quechua term.

7 Both Omphalos and Margin: On How the Pa'ikwené (Palikur) See Themselves to Be at the Center and on the Edge at the Same Time

ALAN PASSES

> Then Ohokri [God] said to the Pa'ikwené king, "You're the strongest king but I can't have you staying here for you would take command of all the other [i.e., white] nations." So Ohokri sent him away, far from all the other kings, to Aúkwa.
>
> —From a story told by Kamavi, a Pa'ikwené informant

IT IS NOW ACKNOWLEDGED that the Conquest meant not only the immediate decline or extinction of some Native South American societies, but the growth, albeit short-term, of others in respect of territory, trade, and political and military power (Dreyfus 1992; Whitehead 1993a, 1994; Arvelo-Jiménez and Biord 1994). There also occurred the ethnogenetic formation of new indigenous entities through the aggregation of diverse preexisting and often ethnically and culturally different groups and elements of groups as a result of or, it has been argued, as a strategy of resistance to European expansion (Hill 1996a, 1996c; see also Garcés Dávila 1992, 72–73). This chapter is concerned with one such case, that of the Pa'ikwené or Palikur,[1] and the process whereby they turned a remote area of northern Brazil first into a zone of safety for themselves and other Amerindians fleeing the European presence and then into the hub of an important panregional polity.[2]

The People of the Middle

Conventionally labeled a coastal society (Gillin 1963; Lévi-Strauss 1986a),[3] the Pa'ikwené or Palikur occupy a wide and environmentally varied territory,[4] comprising a far-flung relational network that, they tell you, was even more extensive in the past. It reached north, as now, into French Guiana, where they claim to have had communities since before the Conquest, but also south, into mid- and southern Amapá state (Brazil), and on the Amazon (see map 7.1). As we shall see, there might be reason for believing the Pa'ikwené originated further south than that. Although their present-day habitats range from marshland to periurban, perhaps the Pa'ikwené could best be described as a riverine people in the sense that their existence can be plotted, from a Western historical perspective, in terms of a trajectory between two rivers—the Amazon and Oyapock—and a relationship with a third, the Urucauá, a tributary of the Uaçá, which flows into the southernmost reaches of the Bay of Oyapock, at the base of Cape Orange in the northeast corner of Brazil.[5]

Situated roughly midway between the Oyapock, which forms the frontier between Brazil and French Guiana, and the Cassipore rivers, the Urucauá (*Rocawa* in French) and the ecologically rich region around it are known in the Pa'ikwené language, Pa'ikwaki, as Aúkwa.[6] Whether actually living there or not, today's Pa'ikwené, no less than those studied by Nimuendajú (1926/1971) in 1925, regard the territory as their homeland (settlements are located

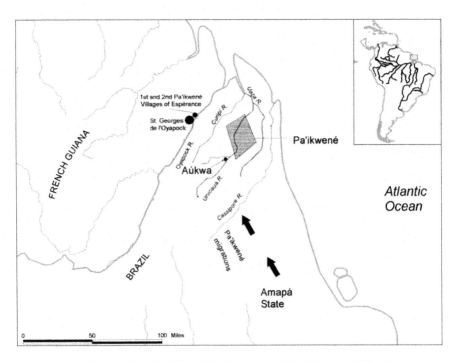

Map 7.1. Present Location of Pa'ikwené Settlements and Past Routes of Migrations

mostly on the middle stretch of the Urucauá). It is here that their clans have their two traditional cemeteries (Nimuendajú 1926/1971, 15, 60; Arnaud 1984, 32), where the dead customarily were buried even if they died far from home (Barrère 1743; Fauque 1839). Spatially, materially, and affectively, Aúkwa seems for the Pa'ikwené to embody Augé's (1997, 42–74) notion of "anthropological place," as one experienced and valued by its inhabitants as the meaningful locus of relations, identity, and history.

However, not only is it possible that the Pa'ikwené have not always inhabited Aúkwa, but, with nearly half the present population dwelling in French Guiana (Passes 1998, 7–8), not all of them do so now. Moreover, because of the intricate wider interethnic framework in which their society is set, they simultaneously live within four cultures and languages: their own, the Brazilian, the Créole, and the French. The centrality, culturally, emotionally, and in relation to identity and history, of Aúkwa, comprises one pole, or omphalos (i.e., navel) of the contemporary Pa'ikwené's stance toward the modern world (see chapters 8 and 9 on the importance of the center in Arawakan thinking). The other pole, or antiomphalos, is evinced by a feeling of marginalization within two nation-states (Brazil and France), though not in the political-economic sense intended by Frank (1967) or Wallerstein (1974). It is primarily this double-sided situation and its relation to the historical context wherein it evolved that this chapter explores.

The name *Pa'ikwené* is composed of two terms. The first, *Pa'ik*, comes from *pakwa*, which, according to informants, "is the same as *aúkwa*, which means the middle." Indeed the Pa'ikwené sometimes also call themselves the Aúkwayené. However, F. Grenand and P. Grenand (1987, 22) suggest that the Aúkwayené are possibly not the Pa'ikwené globally but a subgroup constituting one (northern) section of a bipartite entity, an issue I will return to. The second term, *wené* or *yené*, means "people." The use of this or a phonetically related term to indicate "people" or "humans" exists elsewhere among Arawakan speakers (see Gow 2000, 48–49; chapter 6). Etymologically, then, the Pa'ikwené constitute "The People of the Middle" (Dreyfus 1981; Ricardo 1983, 19; Arnaud 1984; F. Grenand and P. Grenand 1987, 22; Montout 1994, 26; Passes 1998, 2–3).

This they are by virtue of geography and cosmology. Aúkwa—the "Middle River"—is so named because it lies between two others: the Wassa (Uaçá) and the Kwip (Curipi in Brazilian), which is described as "to the east," in line not with terrestrial bearings but with their mirror reflection in the night sky, where Aúkwa is said to sit in the middle of the "great river" of the Milky Way, with Kwip on its right-hand side and Wassa its left (Dreyfus 1981, 301–2).

According to Dreyfus (1981, 302), it was their neighbors on the Kwip and

Wassa—the Karipuna, Galibi, and so-called False Galibi, a mixture of Arúa
and Itútan (both now extinct) and others—who conferred the name *Palikur.*[7]
The distinction the Pa'ikwené themselves make between ethnonym and auto-
ethnonym illustrates how they can also be regarded as the "central" people
in an ethnocentric sense. Whereas *Palikur* is widely used as a synonym for
generic *Indian,* Pa'ikwené is reserved for a specific and special type: themselves.[8] In other words, in Pa'ikwené thinking, a Pa'ikwené person is Palikur
similarly to members of the other indigenous peoples insofar as they are all
inclusively "Indians," but he or she alone is Pa'ikwené.[9] This interpretation
of the two appellations is bound up with the Pa'ikwené's self-image as a
unique and exclusive nation, *naoné*—an example of the widespread Amerindian theme whereby only one's own people constitutes "real humanity"
(Lévi-Strauss 1967; see Viveiros de Castro 1998, 474–77; Gow 2000)—although
there might be a common level of identity with others.

Indeed, *naoné,* which the Pa'ikwené translate in Créole as "nation" (they
also use the word *naowatunyé*), does contain an in-built acknowledgment
of others: The term polysemically means all foreign (i.e., indigenous non-
Pa'ikwené) ethnic entities barring enemy ones (*givétúnya*); all the native
groups of Amapá, including themselves; each of the clans of the Pa'ikwené
people; and, finally, that people collectively (see also F. Grenand and P. Grenand 1987, 16–17; see Lagrou 1998, 10ff., on the Pano-speaking Cashinahua).
This multiple concept introduces us to a key issue: the fact and composition of the Pa'ikwené's clan society and its evolution into a greater geopolitical entity through amalgamation with and absorption, enculturation, and
(occasionally) Arawakization of various non-Pa'ikwené groups or elements
of groups.

Native history reports that there were once eighteen clans in all, of which
today seven or eight (depending on the researcher) remain.[10] Whether they
are originally Pa'ikwené or foreign and Palikurized, no linguistic distinction is made between them, all being equally designated Pa'ikwené, nor are
they graded in terms of political status. As an example of dual organization
(Lévi-Strauss 1986b, 108, 132ff.), the clans are divided into two subsets: inner clans (an "original Pa'ikwené" nucleus) and outer or peripheral ones
(later incomers). Each clan used to have its own territory, but this is no longer the case. After the migration of the southern ones to Aúkwa, the clans
structurally split into two segments, the Walavidi and Kwapi, residing respectively on the left bank of the Lower and Upper Urucauá, and each possessing its own cemetery (Nimuendajú 1926/1971, 15, 60). Today, however,
the members of the surviving clans are "all mixed together," to quote
Nimuendajú (1926/1971, 17), who, on his visit to Aúkwa in 1925, also found

them to be living "without any laws," his take on the egalitarianism of Palikur community life (Passes 2000a).

Politically the clans were autonomous, with no clan leaders as such, but they recognized the overall authority of a sort of supraclan superchief. Clan affiliation is patrilineal and marriage interclan exogamic, with mythic evidence suggesting a changeover from endogamy probably in the seventeenth or eighteenth century (F. Grenand and P. Grenand 1987, 17). Today, although marriage choices are still regulated by clan affiliation, its prominence as a factor of social organization seems somewhat undermined by the establishment, since the mid-1960s, of multiclan communities based on and to a significant extent divided by an increasingly superseding (Christian) sectarian affiliation.

In the past the clans were partitioned along geographic lines, and they are still so classified. The Pa'ikwené identify thirteen of the eighteen clans as northern, or originating above the Araguari River and mainly in the Curipi-Urucauá-Uaça region (asterisk denotes "inner clan"): Akamaiyené (extinct), Auniyené (also known as Nasisyené), Kwimyúné* (extinct), Maiúyené (extinct), Paimioné, Pa'úyené, Uwanyúné* (extinct), Wadayené, Waïvayené*, Washiyené, Wakapúyené*, Wakaoyúné (extinct), and Yatúwéyené (extinct). Four are listed as southern, from the Amazon region—Kawakúkyené*, Kamúyené (extinct), Masamainé (extinct), Túkúwené (extinct)—and a fifth as coming from between the Araguari and Amazon, Maikyúné (extinct).

The Pa'ikwené's tendency to situate themselves center stage—an attitude Dreyfus tautologically labels "aukwa-centrism" (1981, 302)—reflects their pivotal historical and political role in the region and is compounded by a deep and almost mystical attachment to Aúkwa. This feeling obtains not only among its inhabitants but also among Pa'ikwené who have moved to or were born in French Guiana. I even heard it expressed by certain extremely creolized Pa'ikwené who had never set foot in Aúkwa and are mostly the descendants of people who crossed into French Guiana in 1900, when the long dispute between France and Brazil (and, before that, Portugal) over possession of Amapá was resolved by Swiss arbitration in favor of Brazil. These people, many of whom no longer speak Pa'ikwaki and appear, at least on the surface, thoroughly acculturated, tend to live along the Oyapock, by the Créole town of St. Georges and in several small communities between there and the delta, as well as in various scattered settlements further north.

Native to Aúkwa or not, many Pa'ikwené say this is where their nation originated (Dreyfus 1981, 304; Montout 1994, 26) and that they have "always" been there. Others will tell you that their nation's provenance is located much further south (see Nimuendajú 1926/1971, 16–17). There are two significant factors that seem to bear out the latter claim. The first is linguistic.

The Linguistic Evidence

As will become clear, it is appropriate before starting to restate the uncertainty inherent in relying on language distribution as the prime criterion (along with ceramic distribution) for establishing either migrations and diffusion or sociological, cultural, and ethnic distinctions when seeking to describe ancient or historically obscure Amerindian societies (Whitehead 1994, 33–34; see Dreyfus 1992; Roosevelt 1994, 17–18).

Pa'ikwaki seems to be only distantly related to other Arawakan (or Maipuran) languages spoken in the Guianas apart from that of the Pa'ikwené's extinct neighbors in Amapá, the Arúa.[11] Rivet (1924) postulated an intimate connection between Pa'ikwaki and the language of another extinct local group, the Maráon, on the erroneous grounds that they and the Palikur were the same people (Deyrolle 1916; Rivet and Reinburg 1921), an assumption cogently rebutted by Rivet's contemporary, Nimuendajú (1926/1971, 11–12), and the Pa'ikwené themselves, who label Maráon a Carib language (F. Grenand and P. Grenand 1987, 38, 44; Lombard 1723/1857). However, it is classed as Arawakan in the literature.[12]

Noble (1965), glottochronologically bracketing Palikur with Maráon on the same linguistic branch as Arawakan languages spoken today in Upper Xingu (e.g., Mehinaku), posits a bifurcation between the two subgroups some 2,000 years ago. Yet as F. Grenand and P. Grenand (1987, 30) point out, because there is almost as statistically high a correspondence of Palikur with Mojo (a Maipuran language of Bolivia) as with Mehinaku, the presumed relatedness of Palikur and Xingu languages probably is unsafe, the more so when one also considers the fact that no two studies before Noble's categorize Palikur identically. Thus, Rivet (1924) qualifies it as pre-Andine Arawak and Loukotka (1968) as northern Arawakan, as does Aikhenvald (1999a). Matteson (1972b, 234–38) sets it in the proto–eastern Newiki subgroup with various Arawakan languages of the Upper Rio Negro such as Baniwa, Curripaco, and Tariana. Derbyshire and Pullum (1986), Payne (1991, 489), and the Summer Institute of Linguistics (2001) all classify Palikur as eastern Maipuran. Other research includes Goeje (1928), Greenberg (1956), H. Green (1960), Wise and Green (1971), H. Green and D. Green (1972), Dooley and Green (1977), Derbyshire and Payne (1990), Wise (1990), Green et al. (1997), and Aikhenvald and Green (1998).

None of these studies can be said to situate irrefutably the Pa'ikwené people's precise point of departure, be it in the south, the southwest, or elsewhere—assuming that there was one. This is not a foregone conclusion because even if Pa'ikwaki can be traced back to its source with any certainty, it does not follow that all of its present-day speakers originated in the same place.

Pa'ikwaki, alternatively called Kamúyúné, was not always their language, according to today's Pa'ikwené. It was initially the language of the Kamúyené, "People of the Sun," or peripheral Sun Clan, which all the other Pa'ikwené clans took up, probably between 1630 and 1760 (F. Grenand and P. Grenand 1987, 54). The Kamúyené (recently extinct) brought this language with them on migrating to northern Amapá from the south (Arnaud 1968, 7; F. Grenand and P. Grenand 1987, 23, 25, 30–31). In the past, say the Pa'ikwené, each of the eighteen clans had its own language (possibly different dialects of the same language for F. Grenand and P. Grenand 1987, 30). Except for Kamúyúné, all these languages, and most of the clans that used them, have vanished.

Before the collective adoption of Kamúyúné, interclan communication occurred by means of Kíaptúnka, "the language of respect" (*kíapta* = respect; *únka* = word), originally an elite ceremonial and diplomatic language spoken by chiefs (F. Grenand and P. Grenand 1987, 31–33; Passes 1998, 93–95; see Rivière 1971; Sherzer 1983, 91–99). Today moribund, it lingers in certain songs performed at dance and cashiri-drinking events, themselves increasingly on the wane because of the radical influence of Protestant fundamentalism, which many or most of today's Pa'ikwené have adopted in both Brazil and French Guiana. Sometimes shamans also use Kíaptúnka for communication with supernatural entities (Passes 1998, 94, 213). Two other reasons for its entropy are demographic: the loss of speakers resulting from epidemics that decimated the Pa'ikwené population between 1900 and 1920, and the subsequent abandonment of the different clan territories previously ensuring the language's use; and the rising death rate of people of the present older and middle generations who still know it, however patchily (F. Grenand and P. Grenand 1987, 31–32). In direct proportion to its progressive decline, what was originally a political tool has acquired an almost sacred status and high affective value. Today's Pa'ikwené, including youths who know not one word of it, categorize Kíaptúnka in Créole as *langue grammaticale* (grammatical language), the purest and most correct form of language (Passes 1998, 93–95).

Kíaptúnka was not limited to intra-Pa'ikwené communication but also was used in relations between the Pa'ikwené and other Amerindian peoples. Some of these became incorporated over time as clans in the Pa'ikwené federation (e.g., the Kamúyené, mythically the product of a non-Pa'ikwené woman and a Pa'ikwené man) and the Paragoto. In other instances, it was subgroups of foreign entities that were absorbed; thus the Washiyené and Auniyené clans developed from Maráon and Arúan elements, respectively, and (inner) clan

Kawakúkyené are said to derive from the marriage of Pa'ikwené women with Karipuna migrants on the Amazon.

This brings us to the second factor pointing to the Pa'ikwené's genesis somewhere south of the present northern Amapá homeland and the settlements in French Guiana. This factor is historical and documentary. It consists of both written European records and indigenous oral ones and commentaries on these. I shall begin with the former sort.

The Etic Historical View

As with many Amazonian societies, a definitive history of the Pa'ikwené is doubtful, given the many gaps in our knowledge of their past (P. Grenand 1987, 76; Dreyfus 1988, 21; see Nimuendajú 1926/1971, 16). It appears that in the immediate pre-Conquest period the Pa'ikwené, held to be linked to the so-called Mazagão-Aristé civilization,[13] were a dominant entity in Amapá, consisting of two primary, interrelating groups, one based in the circum-Amazonian area and the other in northern Amapá. Amapá was then characterized by a profusion of diverse ethnic groups, clans, and languages (Arawak, Carib, Tupi), out of which there seems to have developed a unified (though not homogeneous) culture, entailing peaceful and interdependent relations and interethnic trade, festivities, and marriage (see Butt Colson 1985; Dreyfus 1992; Whitehead 1993a; Arvelo-Jiménez and Biord 1994, on the Guianas). It was both conducive to and underwritten by a panregional macropolity regulated by a "unificatory chiefdom," with linguistic differences being resolved through a common diplomatic-cum-ceremonial language (F. Grenand and P. Grenand 1987, 51–52; Whitehead 1994, 40). Until about 1550 European invasiveness was minimal and scarcely felt, save for the arrival of groups gravitating toward northern Amapá under the growing Spanish pressure in the Antilles and northwest Guianas (e.g., the Yao).

It was noted earlier that, according to Dreyfus, their indigenous neighbors in northern Amapá bestowed the Pa'ikwené's ethnonym *Palikur*. However, the term was used by whites right from the start of actual contact with or at least reported sightings of the Pa'ikwené/Palikur in the *south*. The first, by Vicente Yañez Pinzón in 1500 C.E., the very year of Cabral's landing in Brazil, relates to their territory on the north bank of the Amazon delta, which Pinzón (1513, in Nimuendajú) records as the province of the Paricura, under which name (with orthographic variations) it subsequently figured in European cartography.[14] Hard data proved elusive, and a description by Jesse de Forêt (1624/1914) of a Paricores River, a small confluent of the Amazon, represents it as the home not of the Pa'ikwené but of the Maráon. By contrast,

European reports of the latter people, whose territory in both southern and northern Amapá is now known to have been coevally inhabited (or traveled through) by Pa'ikwené, are comparatively abundant during the period in question (late sixteenth to mid-seventeenth century).[15] A not quite so rare example of a contemporary reference to the northern Pa'ikwené is provided by de Gomberville (1644 in Dreyfus 1992, 82, 93).[16]

The low documentary profile at that time of some groups, as opposed to others, arguably is ascribable to two causes, as suggested by Whitehead (1996a, 21). First is the poor intelligence in the early colonial period about the regions into which such groups were retreating from contact (as European expansion grew, so did their knowledge of the indigenous populations). Second, and maybe more important, is the fact that these groups were engaged throughout the epoch in a process of evolution that resulted not only in the disappearance of some preexisting formations but also in the ethnogenesis of others into new formations along with a continual forging of identities, sometimes involving the creation or adoption of new names. As we will see, the Pa'ikwené themselves were then undergoing unceasing transformation and renewal, and they also migrated (away from the Portuguese in the south). Moreover, Europeans knew a number of groups who were or became Pa'ikwené by other names. For example, the Carib-speaking Paragoto, or Paracostes or Pararweas, became the Pa'ikwené and the Arawak-speaking clan Pa'úyené probably at some stage in the sixteenth century, during their migration to Amapá away from Spanish intrusion in the northwestern Guianas. Conversely, the Ourouraroura, Ouranarioux, or Ouraroyou, the Tocoyennes, Tokoyen, or Tocujos and the Maika, Maycas, or Amaycas were all actually Pa'ikwené clans: Uwanyúné, Túkúwené, and Maikyúné (F. Grenand and P. Grenand 1987, 12–14, 20, 24, 26–27).

More significant perhaps was the persistent erroneous conflation by outsiders of the Pa'ikwené and Maráon, noted earlier. However, Biet (1664), a French missionary based in Cayenne who in 1653 expressly went searching for the Palikur, specifically distinguished between them and the Maráon. However, Biet himself took the Yao and, like Moquet (1617), the "Caripous" for the Palikur (Nimuendajú 1926/1971, 4, 11–12).[17]

Equally incorrect, according to F. Grenand and P. Grenand (1987, 21–22), was Keymis's (1596) and Harcourt's (1613/1906) mistaking of the Pa'ikwené or Palikur for the Arikare. But the Grenands propose that the Pa'ikwené or Palikur *were* the Arricouri, Arricours, or Arracoory, reported respectively by Keymis (1596) and Forêt (1624/1914) on the Cassipore and by Harcourt (1613/1906) between the Cassipore and "Arracow" (i.e., Urucauá [Aúkwa]). Therefore, not only did the name Palikur rarely appear in the colonial records, but when it did, it tended to be attributed to several other peoples rather than to the Pa'ikwené themselves.

The increasing two-pronged European penetration in southern Amapá and the Guianas, involving the Portuguese, Spanish, French, English, and Dutch, and their rivalry over possession of territory or resources initiated the deportation and atomization of the indigenous groups and their flight toward northern Amapá. This coincided with and probably contributed to (P. Grenand and F. Grenand 1988a) a period of inter-Amerindian conflict. A protracted war, remembered still today, occurred between the Galibi and (though not exclusively) the Arawakan groups, notably the Pa'ikwené, who in about 1590 joined forces with the Yao and some Maráon subgroups under the famous Yao chief Anakayúri (Keymis 1596; Harcourt 1613/1906; Mocquet 1617; Forêt 1623–24/1914). Some sixty years later, the Pa'ikwené, who also produced great leaders of their own such as Ipero (F. Grenand and P. Grenand 1987, 18), had come to dominate the area between the Cassipore and Uaçá. Like other native groups, they were embroiled in the struggle between France and Portugal for control of northern Amapá, a prize that from at least 1580 also attracted diverse English, Dutch, and Irish colonists and traders (Barre 1666; De Oliveira 1994, 100). In exchange for aiding the French, the Pa'ikwené secured weapons and munitions for their long-standing war with the Galibi and protection against Portuguese slave raids (Nimuendajú 1926/1971, 4–6).[18] In the early 1720s, when depopulating southern Amapá of its remaining native communities, the Portuguese were warned off from pursuing the Pa'ikwené beyond the Cassipore by the French authorities in Cayenne (Hurault 1989; Nimuendajú 1926/1971, 6). Three quarters of a century later, still seeking to deprive the latter of indigenous allies, the Portuguese again "ethnically cleansed" the area right up to the Oyapock (Nimuendajú 1926/1971, 8; De Oliveira 1994, 105).

By 1735, the Pa'ikwené were installed on the Urucaúa and Upper Uaçá (Coudreau 1893). Relations with their neighbors, both Arawak and non-Arawak (e.g., the Arúa, Maráon, and Mauyuné), were good. The larger Uaçá region and the Lower Oyapock constituted a safety zone for the different indigenous groups seeking refuge from intensifying European geopolitical pressure. Among them, according to Pa'ikwené records, were their southern clans—Masamainé, Túkúwené, Kawakúkyené, and Kamúyené—and, from Central Amapá, the Maikyúné.

During this period (mid-eighteenth century) began the process of interethnic fusion from which eventually evolved three distinct entities: the Karipún (a mixture of "acculturated" Amerindians and caboclo-ized whites and blacks), the "False Galibi," and the Pa'ikwené. Native history relates that the latter people grew out of a corpus of nine original clans (inner and pe-ripheral), which coalesced with nine non-Pa'ikwené groups, Palikurized as peripheral clans, under a "super-chief" (F. Grenand and P. Grenand 1987, 17–29) such as Youcara, an important ally of the French (Fauque 1736/1839). This process of accretion continued into the nineteenth century, with elements of the depleted groups (e.g., Itútan, Arúa, Maráon, and Kúkúyúne) being progressively absorbed into the Pa'ikwené clans (Leprieur 1843; Nimuenda-jú 1926/1971, 17).

Starting in the 1680s, northern Amapá and southern French Guiana also underwent several Christian, and especially Jesuit, missionary campaigns. From the late 1720s the Pa'ikwené were effectively caught between the French Catholics, out to convert and missionize them, and Portuguese slavers, of-ten aided by other Amerindians such as the Wayapi from the Upper Oyapock (P. Grenand 1979, 4). By the 1790s, under the cumulative effects (fighting, deportation, slave raids, flight, and diseases) of the European presence, they were demographically much depleted.

Little is known about the Pa'ikwené during the next hundred years, but it seems they were firmly established not only in Aúkwa but wider afield, on the Uaçá, Curipi, and Lower Oyapock. Left in peace by the French authori-ties wielding de facto power in northern Amapá, they led an untroubled existence in an ecologically bountiful territory. Catholic missionary activity subsided, although a push in the 1890s netted some converts. At that time the Pa'ikwené, under Chief Rousseau, again were concentrated mainly around the Urucauá. Contacts with other indigenous societies on the Oyapock were maintained, in part through interethnic marriages, as were trade relations with outsiders, especially the French Guianese Créoles, whose cultural and linguistic influence was to grow ever stronger.

In due course, the Pa'ikwené, their population having risen to 200 to 300 (Coudreau 1893), emerged as a powerful entity. When Brazil was finally grant-ed possession of Amapá (1900), most chose, at the invitation of the authori-ties in Cayenne, to settle on the French side of the Oyapock, arguably less of an immigration than a return to a territory in which some of them had been born (Dreyfus 1981, 306), one that had harbored Pa'ikwené communi-ties as far back as the early 1500s (P. Grenand and F. Grenand 1988a), if not earlier. By 1915, however, with the new community decimated by a series of epidemics, the bulk of the survivors had returned to Aúkwa. A decade later about 50 Pa'ikwené remained in French Guiana out of about 240 (Nimuenda-jú 1926/1971, 15). A rough census I did in 1994 made it 790 for the "Brazilian" community and 720 for the "French Guianese" one.

Later waves of migration from Aúkwa began in the early 1960s, one important one triggered by a shamanic war (Arnaud 1970, 14–15, 1984, 46; Dreyfus 1981, 306–8). Another significant factor was the impact of Protestant fundamentalism. When, due largely to Summer Institute of Linguistics (SIL) proselytizing in the mid-1960s, a wide section of the population adopted Evangelical Pentecostalism, an opposing group of Seventh-Day Adventists settled in Premier Village Espérance (or La Savane), by St. Georges. This community was largely inhabited by creolized Pa'ikwené who had remained, or were descended from people who had remained, after the large-scale return to Aúkwa between 1910 and 1920.

The departure to French Guiana of an Assembleia de Deus leader around 1980 prompted further migrations and the founding of new settlements (notably at St. Georges and Macouria) whose populations continue to this day to be replenished by a steady stream of Aúkwan incomers. Movement across the Oyapock is not solely one way, however; not only does it enable a flow of modern concepts and artifacts into the "Brazilian" communities and a reinfusion of old concepts and ways into the "French" ones, but it is cohesive. Any split among today's Pa'ikwené has less to do with country of residence than with two other causes. The first is religion, in the form of antagonisms between Christians and non-Christians and, especially, between converts to the different Protestant sects. The second is language, with a sizable proportion of French Guianese Pa'ikwené opting for Créole (and a Créole-type lifestyle) at the expense of Pa'ikwaki and another group self-consciously and determinedly sticking to Pa'ikwaki. Thus, for example, although a language shift has occurred (especially in the younger generation) in the Adventist community of Premier Village Espérance, it has not done so in the neighboring one, the more recently established Evangelical-Pentecostalist Deuxième Village Espérance (or Persévérance). As a member of that community explained, although they value Créole, the regional lingua franca, as a practical tool for certain contexts, they also hold that not having your own "Indian" language signifies no longer being "Indian" (see Passes 2001; D. Thomas 1982, 19; Santos-Granero 1991, 87–88). This is precisely how they regard the Karipún, whose present language is Créole and before that *lingua geral.*

The two contemporary bodies, the "Brazilian Pa'ikwené" and "French Guianese Pa'ikwené," not to mention the Protestant and non-Protestant Pa'ikwené, may be said to be continuing a historical process whereby their nation has consistently comprised two subgroups of various and intersecting kinds: inner clans and outer clans, northern clans and southern clans, "original Pa'ikwené" clans (inner and outer) and clans (outer) produced from foreign groups or elements or remnants of such groups, and Aúkwa moieties

Walavidi and Kwapi. I shall now look at some of these issues from an emic historical perspective.

Minikwak ("Long Ago"): Pa'ikwené Representations of the Past

It has been argued (Vansina 1980, 1985; R. Thomas 1990) that memory operates on history in such a way as to transform it over time and, as a function of given circumstances and the ever-changing tactical needs of actors, into the stuff of myth, with the latter type of representation growing more subjective, emotive, and fantastical (i.e., "untruthful") the further from the original (and "factual") source it travels and the more etiolated that historical root becomes. In other words, this view manages both to assume a "true" (if occluded) historical foundation to myth and to endorse the rationalist conception whereby, in contrast to history, myth is "unfactual" and thus "untrue" (see Vernant 1974; Detienne 1980; Hill 1988; Tonkin 1990; Overing 1995; Rapport and Overing 2000, 269–82). However, to the extent that history may underpin myth, it does not determine or dictate it (Chernela 1988, 48). Rather, it provides the base metal of experience and often the psychic aftermath from which, through the means of myth, culture forges an assimilable and understandable narrative.

Although for Amerindians myth often is an affective and psychologically cathartic medium (Basso 1985, 351; Ireland 1988), it cannot be extrapolated that it is also therefore an untrue one, although it may well be "fictional," which is quite another matter (see R. Thomas 1990). But rather than debating the issue of what is real and true or unreal and untrue in relation to myth and history, it is perhaps more appropriate here to consider indigenous myth to be, like history, a cultural mode of social consciousness (Hill 1988; Turner 1988), which is used not just for remembering the past and orienting oneself in the present but for creating an ever-renewed understanding of the former from the perspective of the latter. This it achieves through a permanent reproduction, reshaping, reinterpretation, and recycling of memory and tradition and of the narratives (re)formulating them (Samuel and Thompson 1990), in a manner whereby the narratives reflect the present just as much as they do, actually or supposedly (R. Thomas 1990), the past.

Unlike some Amazonian peoples, such as the Wayãpi (F. Grenand 1982) and Waurá (Ireland 1988), the Pa'ikwené do not seem to distinguish linguistically and formally between history and myth. This does not mean that they do not recognize history and try, "cold society"–like, to deny or annul it through the device of myth (Lévi-Strauss 1974, 231–44, 256ff.; see also Fabian 1983; Hill 1988, 3–5; Turner 1988, 235–39, 243–53; Gow 1991, 252–74, 2001; Overing 1995). Rather, the Pa'ikwené conjoin what we classify as history (and historical consciousness) and myth (and mythic consciousness) in a unitary process and see "mythic consciousness" itself as a dynamic one in which temporality is acknowledged.

All Pa'ikwené narratives of the past, be they in our sense myth or history, are called *inétchit,* which is the generic term for "story" and related to the verb "to converse," *kinét(ch)iwa.* Thus, as in the Romance languages, there is an identical word for story and history, and *inétchit* translates in Créole as *histoire* (story or history). A frequently used alternative word is *estúwa,* by way of *histoire* or the Portuguese *estoria.*

As Walter Benjamin (1973) argues, the spoken story is itself a temporal process, a historical product that, in its realization, is repeatedly recreated in the present. But it is more than stories that relive. It is also the past, or "tradition," in the sense not of a detached reification but of the existential experience of prior others that the stories tell. And for Benjamin, the key aspect and purpose of the storytelling act has less to do with the representation of the past in the here and now than with the transmutation of the experience of those who lived in the past *into* that of those who live in the present and who in their very listening are agents in its reproduction. (On the constitutivity of listening and interpreting to the process of verbal intercommunication, see Hymes 1986; Duranti and Brenneis 1986; Ochs et al. 1988; Basso 1995, 29–32; Passes 2000b.)

Discussing their people's past with me, a group of Pa'ikwené, all Protestant fundamentalist converts, stated that before their people acquired knowledge of God (*Ohokri*) it was the Time of Ignorance and Sin (Passes 1998, 187ff.). I will now consider three examples of *inétchit* relating to this period, which these informants seemed to regard as some sort of primal dark ages but also, as examples B and, particularly, C will reveal, as a time of lost greatness. Regrettably, A and B are decontextualized, having been prompted by my solicitation for "Pa'ikwené stories"; thus, though by no means private tellings, they were somewhat artificial.

Example A: A Faraway Time, a Faraway Place

The following extract concerns three pairs of male siblings: two sons of Avakni, the harpy eagle spirit; two Pa'ikwené brothers; and two birds—Súyen (a type of small parrot) and Kaú (a blue macaw?)—who are half-spirit, half-human brothers possessing the same Pa'ikwené father. Learning of Avakni's intention to destroy and eat the Pa'ikwené because of his anger at the younger human brother taking his younger son from the forest to raise him as an "Indian," Súyen and Kaú warn their father, and the evil plan is thwarted. But Avakni seems to have got his own back, for, in the words of Kamavi, the narrator,[19]

> In their land were many *kohivra* [birds] for the Pa'ikwené to hunt, a lot of birds to eat. And they held feasts and sang songs to them. But the Maráon people came and killed and ate Kaú and Súyen. The Pa'ikwené were angry and left that land, and went to another one where there was a lot of *puigné* [animals] to catch, and they stayed there. This place was called Mapérepkit. It is not here . . . it is far from here [Aúkwa] . . . in the South. The Pa'ikwené built a village there and called it Waïnli. But Kaú and Súyen's father did not stay in this new country because there weren't many *kohivra* there, though there was much fish. And he went back to live in the old country, the name of which was Uméyoni. It is even farther away from here than Mapérepkit . . . a long way away . . . far, far in the South.

"Yes, very far!," some listeners interjected, "Farther even than Macapá. . . . It's as far as Belém [actually south of the Amazon]." "And the time that had gone by [Kamavi continued], from when Kaú and Súyen's father came to the second country until he went back to the first, was three months."

In this narrative, were one to adopt a Western rationalist perspective, myth and history are intertwined. To the information about spirit and half-spirit entities, the narrator has added data on actual (negative) relations between the Pa'ikwené and their erstwhile neighbors and on known place names, both of which are not merely descriptive but also meaningful to a Pa'ikwené audience. In particular, the "far, far away" Uméyoni, where the killing of the birds happened, and which translates as the "river of canoes," is their name for the Amazon River.[20] This reference alone shows that, contra Dreyfus (1981, 304, 1988; see Nimuendajú 1926/1971, 16), contemporary Pa'ikwené have not forgotten their origin in the "old country" in the south (see also the story of the genesis of the Kamúyené clan in their "land of the southeast," i.e., the Amazon delta, in Nimuendajú 1926/1971, 17–18; see F. Grenand and P. Grenand 1987, 59–62). Furthermore, the recounting of the different journeys—from Uméyoni to Mapérepkit, located between the former place and Aúkwa (where the story was told), and the subsequent one back to Uméyoni—demonstrates that the migrations were not consistently unidirectional (south-north) or the relocations permanent. Thus, time is not ignored or denied in this account, for though plainly not a chronology of specific calendar dates, it cannot be said to be a frozen past-present, evincing a belief in a temporal sameness (Lévi-Strauss 1974, 217–44).

The linkage of the two narrative elements pertaining to time and place appears to substantiate Benjamin's (1973, 84–85) theory that although stories and storytelling fall into two archaic archetypes, one pertaining to experiences and tales of the past and of home, the other to those about faraway places (which the original storyteller brings home), the "most intimate interpenetration" of the two kinds has developed.[21] As this *inétchit* seems to indicate, the Pa'ikwené's collective experience reproduces and combines memories of the temporally and spatially remote and of home, in such a way as to represent and understand their "home," or social life, and the meaningful places connected with it, as something that has continuously relocated over space and time while remaining itself (i.e., Pa'ikwené), which, it has been proposed, is a very "Arawakan" trait (Santos-Granero 1998; chapter 8).

This story might do more than confirm that there is a southern basis to Pa'ikwené society and that they remember it still to this day. It could shed light on some other questions, such as the consistent mistaking by sixteenth- and seventeenth-century European travelers of the Pa'ikwené for the Maráon.[22] It is tempting to speculate whether de Forêt's aforesaid recording of the Amazon tributary Paricores as the territory of the Maráon might not have been the Pa'ikwené land referred to in the *inétchit,* which the Pa'ikwené had temporarily abandoned, for de Forêt makes no mention of any Pa'ikwené or Palikur being there.

Also, although involving an unspecified clan, the story shows that the Pa'ikwené's migration north, whether because of European or (as is the case here) Amerindian pressure, did not happen in such a way that all the clans decamped simultaneously and at the same rate. On the contrary, and the historical evidence is clear, whereas some clans moved north, others stayed in the south to head north later (e.g., the Kamúyené). Nor did they all in the first instance make for northern Amapá, let alone Urucauá (Aúkwa). Some settled in Central Amapá (the Maikyúné) or on the Cassipore (the Maiúyené) before eventually moving on. Finally, some seem to have been in northern Amapá and French Guiana from before the Conquest.

Example B: The Mightiest King of Them All

Kamavi also related the following:

A long time ago, Ohokri [God] made a man who was very strong and the king of all the Pa'ikwené. Next, Ohokri made a white chief, the king of the French. He was a strong king but not as strong as the king of the Pa'ikwené. Then Ohokri made another king, the king of the English. Lastly he made the king of the Portuguese and Brazilians. These kings were strong too but not as strong as the

French one and even less strong than the Pa'ikwené's. All these kings told king's stories. Then Ohokri wanted to test the French king's strength, and asked him to cut a rock with his knife. He did the same with the kings of the English and the Portuguese and the Brazilians. They all cut the rock, but only a little bit. Then he got the king of the Pa'ikwené to test his strength too. The Pa'ikwené king exerted his strength . . . not all of it, just a little bit of it . . . and cut the rock in two. Then Ohokri said to the Pa'ikwené king, "You're the strongest king but I can't have you staying here for you would take command of all the other nations." So Ohokri sent him away, far from all the others, to Aúkwa.

A tale of simultaneous creation and exile, this parable-like *inétchit* touches on three historical issues central to the present discussion: chieftaincy, Pa'ikwené-white contact, and the link between the Pa'ikwené polity and the Urucauá area.

Before the dissolution of the clan territories through demographic decline, the Pa'ikwené had a pan-clan chiefdom, *úkiwara,* being "governed," as noted earlier, not by clan or (as tends to be the case today) village leaders, *híaptihi,* but by a confederation superchief. At various times in their history, such as the war with the Galibi, panregional alliances linking the Pa'ikwené to other groups were similarly under the authority of a single leader (e.g., the aforementioned Yao chief Anakayúri). Today, Pa'ikwené chieftaincy is non-hereditary, although it might have been in the past, as was the case among other Arawakan groups as well as non-Arawakan ones in the region, such as the Galibi, Guayano (Ralegh 1592–96/1928), and Yao (Whitehead 1994, 40). Fernandes (1948, 219) indeed has claimed that the office of chief was hereditary among the Palikur until the end of the eighteenth century, when the joint influence of the French authorities and Catholic missionaries put an end to the practice.

Then as now, chiefs maintained power on the basis of leadership skills. A crucial one was diplomacy, given that people like the eighteenth-century chief Youcara were what Françoise and Pierre Grenand (1987, 19) call "peace chiefs," whose function was primarily to establish and maintain harmonious relations both at the interclan, intra-Pa'ikwené level and at the interethnic one. As in other groups, provisional war chiefs were appointed if and when necessary (Boyer du Petit Puy 1654; F. Grenand and P. Grenand 1987, 18). Although it may appear so at first sight, the chief as "peace maker" need not contradict the depiction given in Kamavi's story. The representation of the Pa'ikwené king's (superior) strength in physical terms may be said to symbolize not martial power but a political and moral one, a power necessary not only for the protection of the Pa'ikwené *naoné* (nation) from European invasiveness but for the reproduction and upkeep of concord intrasocially and with other indigenous entities, the members of the wider regional *naoné* (see Basso 1995, 91–189).

The Pa'ikwené's understanding of the asociality of seeking and appropriating power for personal ends is well expressed in the story, a variation of Kamavi's, in which a superchief announces, "I cannot make war; I am so strong I would win, and then there would soon be no other nations but mine" (in F. Grenand and P. Grenand 1987, 18, my translation).[23] Interestingly, here it is not divine dictate but human agency, expressed through peacefulness and forbearance, that underwrites the absence of war.

Kamavi's story's conclusion, the sending away of the Pa'ikwené king (and implicitly his people) to Aúkwa, may be seen not only as a banishment. In that it is a cosmologically endorsed declaration of Pa'ikwené supremacy, it is also a triumph, one compounded by historical success. For under the old chiefdom system, the Urucauá region, and northern Amapá generally, became not just a safe haven but also a viable home for the Pa'ikwené clans and other groups fleeing European expansion and oppression, some of whom the Pa'ikwené made alliances with and some they federated with and absorbed. Viewed in this light, the metaphorical wilderness into which their mythic leader is cast paradoxically turns out (also) to be Eden if one goes by the present-day Pa'ikwené's positive evaluation of Aúkwa, described earlier.

Example C: We Were Giants Once

The preceding *inétchit* establishes the Pa'ikwené's two-edged accession to power; the next registers their fall. I present it first as recounted by Moisés Yapara and collected by Harold Green, an SIL worker, then give a brief and slightly different version that I myself heard, along with some comments from a Pa'ikwené listener. Moisés Yapara's version begins by stating that "long ago" there were many Pa'ikwené and that they once decided to have a dance on an island where they became very drunk and thus unable to protect themselves from a surprise attack by slave raiders:

> After midnight, suddenly they heard frightening screams. All of the ancestors were drunk. The Ceará people came suddenly during the people's drunkenness. They captured all the men and women. Also, all the children. The Ceará people disemboweled them. They peeled off their skin. Then they left in canoes with our ancestors and went to their own land. Whoever died was thrown in the water. That is how, long ago, our people began to be finished off. (Moisés Yapara, in H. Green 1988)

The second version, narrated by Karinai, my host in the village where I lived, arose spontaneously out of a discussion he, his wife, Susana, and I were having with some others about Pa'ikwené population figures. It is interesting because, although it tells the same basic story, the Portuguese are implicated: They not only accompany the Ceará raiding party but are directly responsible for it. Given that the Portuguese policy of enslavement, introduced in the eighteenth century, continued well into the nineteenth, the "long ago" that situates the recounted events could just as easily refer to a given moment in either century. Another crucial difference in the second account is that one Pa'ikwené, being less drunk than his fellows, manages to avoid capture. He then wages war single-handedly against the Portuguese and slays many of them before finally being killed. Karinai used the story to illustrate a demographic point, namely that the slavery and killings by or at the instigation of the Portuguese are responsible for the small number of Pa'ikwené alive today.

According to Susana, it is also the reason for their present small stature. Before that time, she said, the Pa'ikwené were all giants, which is why, although the word for ancestor is *amekené*, the "first ancestors" such as those referred to in the story are also called *imúwad*—in Créole, *les grands*, the "great ones" or "tall ones." Since the death of that particular ancestor, the unnamed freedom fighter, all the Pa'ikwené have been little—just like her husband, she stressed, and like all other Indians.

As in the previous *inétchit* (example B), bodily states (bigness or tallness and smallness) serve as metaphors to express real demographic and political states in the form of greatness and decline. Also, in myth and folklore a giant stature is not just the distinguishing feature of monsters and ogres. It sometimes indicates freedom and autonomy, with an impressive physique and bodily strength constituting stereotypical folk hero qualities used in the defense of integrity and egalitarianism against an imposed hierarchy (Johansson 1990).

In Ancient Greek thinking, *mythos* constituted the first speech, *logos*, which was impelled to break the preexisting speechlessness of the world, a seminal act whose memory lives on in the related Latin word *mutus*, "mute" (Vico 1970, 85). For the Greeks, then, myth names the world through fabulous discourse, and as we can see in respect of the slave raid, it does indeed give the unspeakable a voice. Moreover, it makes it comprehensible through the very action of hearing, a process not epistemologically alien to the Pa'ikwené, for whom the word "to hear," *tchimap*, also means "to understand," a common Amerindian trait (Passes 1998, chap. 4; also Seeger 1981, 83ff.; Kidd 2000, 116).

Like the Waurá myths described by Ireland (1988), the account of the slave raid works as a way to make sense in a comprehensible cultural idiom of incomprehensible events and their psychological and emotional legacy. Myth thus seems to be an intrinsic human tool for processing historical experience and its traumatic aspects, which in the Amerindian context since the Conquest mostly implies the actions of whites. It can also constitute an act of opposition. For instance, in regard to concentration camp inmates, it has been argued that myth making is itself a means of active resistance against unendurable circumstances (Bravo et al. 1990).

Conclusions

This chapter has explored the ethnogenetic formation, from 1500 C.E. onward, of the Pa'ikwené nation through a continuous process of accretion, absorption, and unification, in which a prior multiclan base agglomerated with other indigenous groups that became Palikurized as outer clans and, if originally non-Arawak-speaking, Arawakized. Out of this emerged a polity comprising at its height (probably the end of the eighteenth century) eighteen clans, under the unifying authority of a pan-clan chief and joined in shorter or longer-term alliances with other ethnic entities in a panregional macropolity, again under a single leader.

Although European expansion undeniably affected the evolution of Pa'ikwené confederation, it would be incorrect to consider it a determining cause. Rather, because a strategy of interethnic political amalgamation seems to have been already under way before contact, it probably accelerated or intensified a preexisting process. As F. Grenand and P. Grenand (1987, 54–56) note, despite the shrinkage of their territory under European expansion, many of the diverse ethnic groups in Amapá did not disappear but survived (and continue so to do today) in and as the Pa'ikwené clans or as members of similar composites, such as the Karipún and "False Galibi."

However, the Pa'ikwené, like other northern Amapá peoples, are not to be seen as the fragmented escapees of a cataclysm wrought by the Conquest. Rather, their nation, *naoné*, comprises the reconstructed units, both "originally Pa'ikwené" and initially foreign, that evolved through resistance to European colonialism and bonded around a strong central Pa'ikwené core grounded in and remaining consistently true to basic endogenous values (see F. Grenand and P. Grenand 1987, 55–56). Thus the Pa'ikwené's transformation, whatever their society may have been like before Columbus, embodies not a passive response to colonialism but a proactive one.

That the Pa'ikwené's Arawakan language constitutes proof of their ethnic identity as Arawaks is problematic, history having shown in regard to Native South America that language does not necessarily determine ethnicity. Language barriers are fluid and permeable, and there exists a high degree of linguistic exogamy and, consequently, multilingualism. As noted, each Pa'ikwené clan once had a different (Arawakan) language, and they communicated among themselves, and also with non-Pa'ikwené groups, through the elite lingua franca, Kíaptúnka, before eventually adopting their present, collective everyday language, Pa'ikwaki or Kamúyúné. It is presumably on this language, initially belonging to a "southern," "outer" clan of partly non-Pa'ikwené ancestry, that the linguistic research has been carried out. However, the aforementioned disagreement over what type of Maipuran Pa'ikwaki really is must obviously extend to its point of origin (Xingu? Upper Rio Negro? the Pre-Andine?).

But even if its birthplace were incontrovertibly proven, one could not conclude that that is where the contemporary Pa'ikwené nation began its journey as a purportedly homogeneous Arawak-speaking whole, if only because the historic evidence reveals that at least one of its constituents (Pa'úyené clan) was originally a non-Arawak-speaking foreign group (the Paragoto), which became Arawakized during the Pa'ikwené nation's progress from south of the Amazon toward the Oyapock, a process that started before contact and continued after it. In short, as others have indicated, language is not an entirely reliable indicator of a people's geographic matrix or ethnic identity (Dreyfus 1983–84, 1992; Roosevelt 1994; Whitehead 1994; see Klein 1994).

Notwithstanding claims to the contrary (Dreyfus 1981, 304, 1988), the Pa'ikwené have not forgotten their migrations from the south. They say they carry them, and other matters relating to their past, "at the bottom of the head"—the literal translation of the Pa'ikwaki word for memory, *ú[k]tchiwik*. These historical events are spoken of both conversationally and in formal accounts. In either case, through such talk, there occurs a re-creation of Pa'ikwené society not just as it was but as it is now. As Turner (1988, 276–81) argues, native representations of the past are aspects of a process by which society defines itself in relation to others and thereby reproduces itself. Or, to put it somewhat differently—and assuming the social and psychological cofunctionality of myth (Cohen 1969)—each telling of a Pa'ikwené story does more than recreate that particular narrative. In its transmission it also, in the Benjaminian sense, reanimates the life experiences of dead significant others for the "community of listeners" (the social group, Benjamin 1973, 91) and in so doing recreates and perpetuates—socially, morally, and existentially—that community.

Such a reproduction is radically unlike the structuralist one, where myth comprises the endless reconstruction and "projection of sameness or likeness across space and time" (Urban 1991, 82). Thus, an *inétchit* (story) such as that about the Pa'ikwené man who left Uméyoni, his land on the Amazon, when his half-bird sons were hunted and killed by the Maráon but then

missed it so much that he went back (Example A) is not to be seen as a return to an ahistoric Eden and therefore as an expression of some unconscious
impulse to negate or freeze history by mythically replicating an immutable
time (Lévi-Strauss 1974, 217–44; Urban 1991, 81–83). Rather, Pa'ikwené *inét-
chits* acknowledge and express the dual capacity of things (society, nation)
to historically transform and yet integrally stay themselves.

At another level, though, Uméyoni does represent a lost paradise. And one
wonders how many such returns and how many flights there were before the
final "expulsion" and when Aúkwa replaced Uméyoni as Eden. Although we
cannot (in European terms) know for sure, except that it had to be post-
Conquest, the move from the one (Amazon) to the other (Urucauá) constitutes a process of the shifting center.

As other contributors writing about northwestern Amazonia have shown
(see chapters 5 and 8–11), centrality of place appears to constitute for Arawak-
speaking peoples a major ideological theme.[24] For the Pa'ikwené, *Aúkwa*—
"middle," "center"—is both a keyword and key metaphor. It is the former,
in the sense used by Williams (1976) and Baumann (1987, 143–44), inasmuch
as it refers to an experience or state of being common to the collective and
fundamental to its social life and expresses shared ideas, lifeways, and values
(see Woolard 1998). Thus the term *aúkwa* does more than identify the
Pa'ikwené topographically; it also embodies them. As I have tried to show,
they are the "people of the middle" not only in respect to three rivers (Curipi, Urucauá, Uaçá) but also in a broader historical, multiethnic, and multi-
cultural (and multilinguistic) environment. From that perspective, *aúkwa* has
efficacy and value (epistemological, axiological, and affective) as a trope, with
the word not just illustrating and evoking the Pa'ikwené's central place in the
scheme of things but also acting to (re)produce it. For it is instrumental in
the ongoing creation of the native experience of tradition, distinctiveness in
relation to others, and continuity within a process of constant transformation, reinvention, and appropriation of and adaptation to foreign influences
from different sources (Amerindians, Europeans, and Créoles) and of different types (political, linguistic, religious, technological, and economic).

For the Pa'ikwené, in respect of fellow Amerindians such as the Paragoto
or the remnants of the Arúa, this process typically has taken the form of incorporation and acculturation. But the traffic has not been one way, as evidenced, for example, by the introduction and adoption by the collective of
the language of one incoming group, the Kamúyené, who according to myth
also brought with them a material innovation, metal graters.

There is a Western tendency to confer on peoples such as the Pa'ikwené a
peripheral (and inferior) status in terms of their place on the social, cultur-

al, and economic map of the state and globalization. The Pa'ikwené are not blind to that scheme of things or to their marginality within it. However, as I have tried to show, the "People of the Middle [River]" also know themselves, in connection with a different order, to be *central*—not just etymologically and geographically and notwithstanding the ambiguity inherent in their worldview whereby Aúkwa is both heartland and, as stated so concisely in the story of the Pa'ikwené king, exile (omphalos and *ultima thule*). In some ways, their perspective calls to mind the Buddhist concept according to which there is no margin, for wherever a person is, there is where the center is also.

Notes

I wish to thank Fernando Santos-Granero and Jonathan D. Hill for their helpful comments and for their invitation to participate in the conference on Comparative Arawakan Histories, to which an earlier draft of the present work was submitted. My gratitude also goes to Karinai and Susana Labonté, their children, and many other members of Deuxième Village Espérance (French Guiana) too numerous to list, and to "Capitaine" Louis Norino of Premier Village Espérance and Chief Tchikoi of Kúmené village, Aúkwa (Brazil).

1. Given the almost universal use by modern observers of the given name *Palikur* rather than the autodenomination *Pa'ikwené*, and in an attempt to avoid confusion, I shall here use the former whenever the circumstances appear to demand it. At all other appropriate times I prefer to use the native term.

2. I wish to record here my indebtedness to Françoise and Pierre Grenand's article, "La Côte d'Amapa, de la bouche de l'Amazone à la baie d'Oyapock à travers la tradition orale palikur" (1987), which proved of invaluable help in writing this chapter.

3. See also tribal distribution maps such as Roosevelt's (1994, 21), which places them nearly on the Atlantic, east of their true contemporary location in Brazil, and omits their presence in French Guiana altogether.

4. For a critique of the ethnological tendency to classify indigenous Amazonian peoples in terms of one specific milieu, their supposed natural habitat, when many of them concurrently or sequentially occupy various different kinds, see Butt Colson 1985; F. Grenand and P. Grenand 1987, 22; Dreyfus 1992, 88; Whitehead 1993a, 291–93, 1994.

5. In connection with settlements on the outskirts of French Guianese towns such as Régina, St. Georges, and Macouria, a fact that, among other things, consolidates the Pa'ikwené's close links with the Créole community, which date back at least to the nineteenth century.

6. The Urucauá-Uaça ecosystem, like that of Amapá generally, is based on flooded savanna and marshland. Horticulture is practiced on the rocky and forested islands where the different Pa'ikwené subgroups have their settlements and gardens (see Nimuendajú 1926/1971, 12–14, 48–51; F. Grenand and P. Grenand 1987, 14–15). In French Guiana their limited access to land and remoteness from good hunting sites mean that the Pa'ikwené's situation is ecologically poorer, and there is a growing involvement in the market economy (P. Grenand 1981; P. Grenand and F. Grenand 1988b; Rostain 1991).

7. The Pa'ikwené's "traditional enemy" and a branch of the Kariña/Kaliña of the northern and western Guianas, who around the end of the seventeenth century had a significant presence in French Guiana. A small number apparently have resettled recently in the Uaçá River region, according to my Pa'ikwené informants (1995).

8. As a Pa'ikwené friend put it, "All Indians are Palikur. The Yanomami, Araweté, Wayapi, Emerillon, Wayana, Galibi are Palikur—but we Pa'ikwené are the most Palikur."

9. From a Pa'ikwené perspective, all these different Palikur, including the Pa'ikwené, are Indians in relation to whites (pa'asi), Brazilians (parahna), and blacks (atiwi). The Pa'ikwené also distinguish themselves from Asian Indians, of whom there is a sizable community in French Guiana and whom they call by the Créole term Coolie.

10. In 1925 Nimuendajú (1926/1971, 15–16) listed seven extant clans and four extinct ones; Arnaud (1984, 31–32), six extant, five extinct; and F. Grenand and P. Grenand (1987), seven extant, twelve extinct. Passes (1998, 8–9) reports eight surviving ones, seven rated "real" by informants, and one "false" yet legitimate: the Auniyené (the indigenous name for the Arúa, whose remnants comprise the clan).

11. See F. Grenand and P. Grenand (1987, 37–39, table 3, 42) for other defunct Maipuran groups in Amapá.

12. Schmidt (1926/1977), Loukotka (1935/1968, 145–47), Mason (1950), Meggers and Evans (1957), Noble (1965), Dreyfus (1981), Aikhenvald (1999a).

13. Through funerary tradition to the Mazagão and southern Aristé of the Lower Amazon, and through ceramic tradition to the northern Aristé of northern Amapá (F. Grenand and P. Grenand 1987, 46–54).

14. Maps of Vesconto de Maiollo, 1515, 1527; Diego Ribeiro, 1598; and Robert Dudley, 1646.

15. By, for example, Keymis (1596), Harcourt (1613/1906), de Forêt (1623–24/1914), Laët (1633).

16. Concerning a break in Kariña-Palikur hostilities.

17. As did Lombard (1723–33/1857), Fauque (1729–36/1839), Barrère (1743), De Préfontaine (1749), Buache (1787, in Nimuendajú 1926/1971, 8).

18. On the political advantages to and agency of Amerindian groups involved in such alliances, see Dreyfus (1992), Whitehead (1992, 1993a).

19. Or Léon Orlando, to use his Western name. For the full narrative, see Passes (1998, 239–40).

20. F. Grenand and P. Grenand (1987, 23, 26) render it "Uumeuni" and caution against confusing it with a creek of the same name on the Cassipore.

21. Although Benjamin's essay is specifically concerned with the historical evolution of European storytelling, I see no reason why his premise cannot in principle be extended to the non-European.

22. The Pa'ikwené report of the Maráon in the land of Uméyoni confirms early Western references to their presence both in southern Amapá (e.g., de Forêt 1623–24/1914) and the north (Keymis 1596, Harcourt 1613/1906, Forêt 1623–24/1914, and others). According to the Pa'ikwené, the Maráon had also started off in the south then evolved into a northern group based in Urucauá and Lower Oyapock and a southern one on the Amazon, which was eventually deported by the Portuguese and went to join the others in the north, where both groups later died out (F. Grenand and P. Grenand 1987, 36).

23. The Pa'ikwené also have a mythic leader, Tchalbé, probably deriving from the Créole folkhero 'Ti Albè (Petit Albert), who becomes so powerful and self-seeking that he abandons them to become "the chief of foreigners" (including all the whites).

24. Although it is not limited to them, as evidenced by Echeverri's recent work (1997) on Huitoto, Bora, and Andoque speakers.

PART 3

Power, Cultism, and Sacred Landscapes

8 A New Model of the Northern Arawakan Expansion

ALBERTA ZUCCHI

WHEN WE OBSERVE the number of languages that belong to the northern Maipuran groups and their wide distribution in South America, several questions arise regarding the location of ancestral areas, the characteristics and causes of this population dispersal, the processes of linguistic and ethnic differentiation, and the archaeological evidence of these processes and their antiquity. During the last three decades archaeologists have proposed models that tried to answer some of these questions (Lathrap 1970b; Meggers 1987, 151–74; Rouse 1985, 9–21; Oliver 1989; Zucchi 1991a, 113–38, 1991b, 1–33, 1991c, 202–20, 1991d, 368–79, 1992, 223–52), using archaeological materials from the Amazon and Orinoco areas. As a result, the process of dispersal of this population has been associated with six different ceramic traditions: zoned incised and Barrancoid (Lathrap 1970b; Meggers 1987, 151–74; Rouse 1985, 9–21), ancient Amazonian polychrome, macro Tocuyanoid, and macro Ronquinoid (Oliver 1989), and the incised parallel line (Zucchi 1991a, 113–38, 1991c, 202–20).

In 1970, Lathrap provided the groundwork for the first model of Arawakan expansion, explaining the conditions in which demographic increments arose in the Middle Amazon and how they related to domestication and improvements of the most important crop: manioc. In a later work (Lathrap 1977, 713–50) he proposed that the revolution of floodplain and estuarine agriculture provided the conditions for expansion and colonization of similar eco-niches. Although the later models were strongly influenced by Lathrap's ideas, most of them failed to provide new details of this impressive process of population dispersal. In this chapter I present recent data related to the following aspects of the Arawakan expansion: ancestral homelands; exploratory travels, permanent migrations, and the occupation of new territories; and the archaeology of the Upper Orinoco–Lower Ventuari–Atabapo and Upper Negro–Guainía–Casiquiare subareas.

The Ancestral Homelands

Historical linguistics is a powerful tool for reconstructing ancient population movements and past demographic processes and for explaining questions of origins and cultural change. Noble (1965) carried out the only comprehensive application of lexicostatistical methods for historical purposes in the Arawak language family. Another important breakthrough in Arawakan studies came a few years after the publication of Noble's monograph in studies of the major branches of the Arawakan family. These works followed the lexicostatistical method and produced chronological estimates. Although these estimates cannot be taken as absolute values, they provide a useful indication on the time span involved (Lathrap 1970b, 72). According to Noble (1965), Proto-Arawak diverged from Proto-Equatorial around 4,000 to 3,500 years B.P. A second surge of divergence, which Noble reconstructed as Proto-Maipuran, took place between 3,000 and 2,500 years B.P. Out of this second surge further separations developed, and Proto–Northern Maipuran evolved into a group of languages and dialects.

When the focus is narrowed to include only northwestern Amazonia, it reveals a different variant of this overall chronology. Nimuendajú (1927/1950, 125–83) hypothesized a three-stage occupation of the northwest Amazon. According to this author, the most ancient inhabitants of the region were several groups of seminomadic hunters and gatherers generically known as Makú. Various Arawak and Tukano groups, who migrated into the area from regional centers, represented the second occupational stratum: Arawak from the Upper Orinoco–Guainía area in Venezuela and the Tukano from the eastern part of the continent. The third stratum was represented by a hybrid culture that was formed as a consequence of the encounter between Arawaks, Tukanos, and Europeans. The Arawakan invasion was supposed to have taken place in successive waves; the major Arawakan groups settled in the Negro Basin as follows: the Baré along the Middle and Upper Rio Negro and its tributaries; the Warekena on the Xié and Lower Isana; and the Baniwa on the Isana and Vaupés, particularly in the upriver region around the Querari River. The Tariana arrived at the Isana after the Baniwa had settled there but later migrated through the Upper Aiary to the Vaupés, finally settling along its banks around the Juareté and Papurí rivers.

Oral traditions of several northern Arawakan groups support some of

Nimuendajú's ideas but also provide additional information. Several groups of the Isana, Vaupés, and Upper Negro (i.e., Curripaco, Baré, Warekena) and from the Guaviare-Inírida (i.e., Baniwa, Piapoco) consider the Hípana rapids a sacred place ("the world's navel") from whence their first ancestors were extracted in a mythical order. The Baré provide additional information on this process, indicating that the first three brothers extracted from Hípana were the ancestors of the Hohódene, the Baré, and the Waríperi-dakéenai, and other brothers followed later; and that when these ancestors settled in the Upper Negro, the climate was different. "There was a terrible summer," the river was dry, and the people were very hungry because "there was no food" (Vidal 1993, 74; Wright 1981, 11).[1]

This ancestral order of emergence is also supported by other groups (i.e., Warekena, Baniwa, and Curripaco) (Vidal 1993, 73–74). Meanwhile, oral histories of the Hohódene and Kadapolitana add that their first ancestors inhabited the region of the Upper Uaraná, a tributary of the Aiarí, whereas the Kadapolitana occupied the area around Tunuí and above on the Isana River. In addition, these oral histories indicate that in those times of ancestral emergence they all were the same people and that the early ancestors relied on fish as the principal food resource. The early ancestors are said to have had pottery, although some of them lacked agriculture.

Combining linguistic, archaeological, ethnological, and local historical evidence, it is possible to hypothesize that between 4,000 and 3,500 years B.P. several groups of Proto–Northern Maipuran groups settled in the Isana subarea. From the Isana subarea, several of these groups gradually moved to the adjacent areas (e.g., the Upper Negro, Lower Guainía), and a few others migrated to distant areas (e.g., the Middle Orinoco) of northern South America. Some of these early groups had no agriculture or depended only minimally, if at all, on major crop plants, and fish was their most important food resource.[2] The early settlements in the Isana and Upper Negro subareas occurred during a period when the food was scarce, probably because of a drier climatic phase.

Exploratory Travels, Migrations, and the Occupation of New Territories

Wright (1981), Hill (1983), and Wright and Hill (1986, 31–54) have indicated that Arawakan mythical cycles are fundamental for the study of their societies because they contain the basic principles that render possible sociocultural reproduction and continuity. These myths explain how conditions, institutions, and orders were begun in a mythical past and given for all people but also create a bond of continuity between each Arawakan group and the ancient people of the mythical times who performed the actions.

The mythical history of Arawakan groups can be divided into two main cycles. The first of these cycles refers to Iñapirrikuli, Káali, and their kinsmen in a mythical past and establishes a distant and closed symbolic space-time in which cosmogonic processes of creation unfold within the framework of rules and axioms that give order to everyday social experience (Hill 1983, 92). According to these myths, Iñapirrikuli, the Creator, extracted five ancestral brothers in hierarchical order from a specific place, and he gave to each one of them a totemic name, a symbol, a territory, an occupation, the spirit of tobacco, and other ritual instruments. In a second myth cycle about Kúwai, the primordial human being, the violent and incomplete space-time of the mythical past was transformed into the social, natural, and supernatural worlds in which the Arawakan groups live today.

Both mythical cycles also refer to voyages that these two mythical figures and their companions made to different places in South America, and the sacred chants specifically mention several fluvial and terrestrial routes that were opened during the voyages of Kúwai (Hill 1993; chapter 9), which are called the roads of Kúwai. These roads are an indication of the geographic knowledge of South America that northern Maipuran groups have acquired through time, and they have been constantly used in trade and migrations (Vidal 1987, 127).

Migrations are selective historical processes, variable in time and space, which represent one of the mechanisms or alternatives through which a population can cope with social, economic, ecological, political, and cultural changes in their homeland or in a new area. The research that Vidal (1987, 22) has carried out among the Piapoco provides the best information on the general characteristics of northern Maipuran migrations, the routes that were used by some of the groups, and the specific places where important processes of re-creation of their societies occurred. Although the author identified four types of migration, in this chapter I will refer exclusively to permanent migrations.

Northern Maipuran permanent migrations apparently involved three distinct and successive phases: the exploration of new lands, the migration proper, and the adjustment of the migrants to new environmental and social conditions. During the first of these phases, the head of the migrants and a group of males carry out one or more exploratory voyages to the probable receiving areas to evaluate the local conditions, establish contacts and negotiate permits with local groups, select possible settlement sites, open the first agricultural plots, and build the first houses. When these tasks are accomplished the explorers return to their homeland. Once there, the head or captain of a migrant group ritually returns to the time of "the beginning of the world" and becomes Kúwai. As a symbolic Kúwai he assumes the organization and control of all aspects of the migration proper and also selects the route that will be used. It is precisely at that moment when the "roads of Kúwai" become of great importance (Vidal 1987, 127–33).

Once the migrants have arrived in the new area, other important ritual and secular processes take place: first, the re-creation (reorganization) of the group and the distribution of the social units in the new land, and, second, the transformation of the new land into the migrants' territory. To perform the first of these processes, the head of the group ritually assumes the shamanic powers of Iñapirrikuli and re-creates the people, or the descent units with their hierarchical position, and distributes them in the new land. After the first settlements are established, other social, economic, and political adjustments are made, and formal procedures are established with the neighbors, which will shape their insertion and interaction with the new physical and social environment.

Oral histories of several northern Arawakan groups provide an abundance of information on ancient migrations. These accounts usually include the relation of their first ancestors with a specific Arawakan social unit or society from which they separated and descriptions of the route that was followed by their ancestors when they migrated from their mother group or society to the area that their descendants consider their traditional territory. In addition, the oral histories recount the specific geographic places where re-creation processes of their societies occurred and, sometimes, the names of the phratries or sibs that were involved in these processes (Bourgue 1976, 117–43; Vidal 1987, 144; Wright 1981, 11–12; Zucchi 1991a, 113–38; 1991c, 368–79).

Some groups have also mentioned that once the mythical emergence (arrival) in the Isana area had occurred, the first ancestors dispersed. The Hohódene (keepers of the Isana rapids) expanded from the Uaraná (Yukuali) to the Ayarí and its adjacent areas; the Waríperi-dakéenai went to the Pamari River, and the Baré moved to the Papuri (tributary of the Vaupés) and the Apaporis. Many Baré returned to the Caurés (Cauari), through the Negro penetrated the Branco River, and finally occupied the Cauaburi, the Casiquiare, the Upper Orinoco, and some of its tributaries (Vidal 1993, 7–77).

Although several groups provided information on the early migrations of their ancestors, at present the migration of the Piapoco still is the best-documented case. According to Piapoco informants, their ancestors migrated in ancient times from the Ayarí to the Guaviare. Although they do not remember the name of the social unit from which they separated, they recall that they were related to one of the Wakuénai groups (Vidal 1987, 140–41). Among the Hohódene, a Wakuénai phratry living at Hípana on the Ayarí River, oral traditions state that in ancient times one of the Wakuénai subgroups called Dayzo-dakénai living in the Ayarí migrated to the Guaviare (Wright 1981, 11–12). Vidal (1987, 141) believes that the name *Dayzo-dakénai* could be related to the Piapoco self-denomination (Dzáze, Tsáse, or Cháse) or with the name of their highest-ranked phratry (Tsáse-itáakenai).

The oral history of this group also mentions that after the separation of the ancestral sib in the Ayarí (map 8.1), the migrants moved to the Upper Guaviare (Waá-veri) where they remained for a period. During that time in "the house of the Kúwai-seri," located in the Zamuro rapids, the first process of re-creation took place. Through it the ancestral group was transformed into a phratry with four sibs: Tsáse-itakeenai, Káwiriali-itakéenai, Malai-itáakenai, and Neri-itákeenai. After this process, the people moved along the Guaviare and reached the mouth of the Uva River, where the population separated. The Neri-itákeenai entered and settled along this river, while the rest of the population remained along the Guaviare. With time the

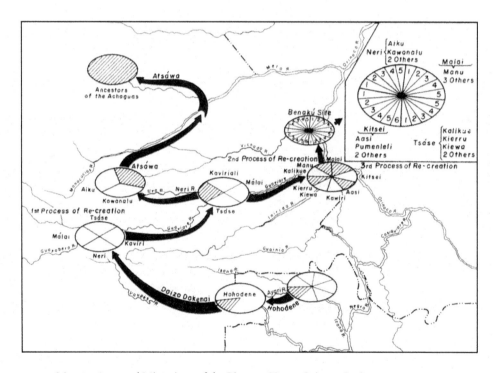

Map 8.1. Ancestral Migrations of the Piapoco, Upper Orinoco Basin

population of the Uva River had increased, and a new phratry with three sibs (Néri-itákeenai, Aiku-itákeenai, and Atsáwa-nai) was created. Soon after, the Atsáwa-nai sib separated from the phratry and through a savanna trail moved to the headwaters of the Uva and Manacacías, and later to the headwaters of the Meta River. The Piapoco indicate that although these people never returned to live in the Uva, they continued to visit their "Neri grandparents," despite the fact that they were no longer their "captains" and that the Atsáwa-nai had become a different people *"que ya no escuchaba (hablaba) Piapoco"* ("who did not heed (talk) Piapoco"; Vidal 1987, 143; Zucchi 1991a, 126).

Later, the rest of the population extended toward the confluence of the Guaviare-Atabapo-Orinoco, where another important process of re-creation, which marked the ethnic differentiation of the Piapoco, took place (Vidal 1987, 143–44). This process occurred at La Punta, an area within the present-day town of San Fernando de Atabapo, and through it, each of the present day sibs of the Tsáse, Kawirri, and Malai phratries were created. After a time people of the Kierru and Aási sibs and of the Malai phratry moved from the confluence of the Guaviare, Orinoco, and Atabapo rivers and also along the Orinoco up to the mouth of the Vichada. Because other people occupied this river, they obtained permission to establish a settlement in Benakú (Santa Rita), from where they gradually extended along the Vichada River. After a time they invited the Neri, Kalikué, Kiéva, and Kítései to an important ceremony where another process of re-creation of the society occurred. Through this process the territory was divided, and each part was formally assigned to one of the various descent units.

The second process that takes place after a permanent migration is the ritual transformation of the new land into "the group's territory" through the construction of a cosmographic model. Schama (1995, 10) has recently indicated that landscapes are the result of the application of human agency to specific natural settings over time; it is precisely through human agency and perception that a landscape becomes the carrier of the "freight of history" and its scenery, which is constructed "as much from strata of memory as from layers of rock." Other authors (Bender 1993; Feld and Basso 1997; Friedland and Boden 1994; Hill 1989, 1993; Rappaport 1989; Renard-Casevitz and Dollfus 1988; Santos-Granero 1998) have also emphasized the importance of landscape as another means of encapsulating and transmitting historical memory among literate and nonliterate societies.

Although at present we do not know exactly when the first process of topographic writing took place or who were its main actors, it is possible to assume that religious specialists must have played a central role. Two recent studies (Ruette 1998; Vall 1998) on the cosmography of the Warekena of the

San Miguel River and of the Baniwa and Curripaco settled along the Aki River indicate that the cosmological models of these three northern Arawakan groups are the result of mythical and historical events that were molded into the landscape, the memory of the people, the narratives, and the sacred chants. No dependent relationship exists between the physical characteristics of places and the narratives associated with them. This indicates that their cosmological models operate within culturally established limits and that a specific topological trait or meaning can be selected from a whole gamut of possibilities. The place is the basic spatial unit through which temporal and symbolic meanings are expressed. Because the mythical and historical narratives are spread within the landscape, they allow the coexistence of different times and symbolic events in each space. As a consequence, a place can express discontinuities, which encapsulate different mythical and historical processes and also different types of social behavior (figure 8.1).

Because the experience of places evokes different pasts, time and space become two indivisible dimensions. The semanticity of space and the con-

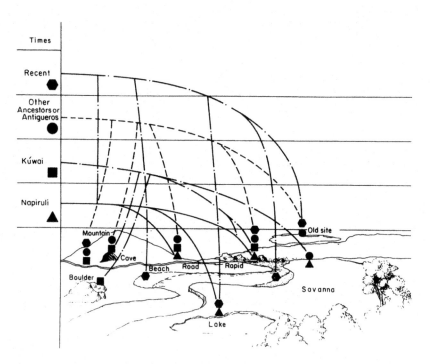

Figure 8.1. Process of Landscape Construction among the Curripaco, Baniwa, and Warekena of the Guainía River

struction of places involve a process of interpretation of the past through which new places are named or new meanings are assigned to places previously constructed. The spatial distribution of narratives confirms these ideas and indicates that these groups have used narrative discourse and ritual performances of sung and chanted speech to write mythical and historical events into the landscape (see Santos-Granero 1998). The spatial distribution of narratives about the beginning of the world and their temporal and symbolic frontiers are related to the exercise of power by the dominant segments of the society. Spatial frontiers are constructed with narratives that legitimize the existence of male-controlled secret societies. As a result, some of the spatial limits of the San Miguel and Aki rivers are structured in terms of age and gender and impose prescriptions and restrictions on behavior. In this way, the spatial representation becomes a perfect medium to transmit and impose on the everyday life of these groups the contents of the mythical and historical narratives that legitimize the present-day order (Ruette 1998; Vall 1998; Zucchi et al. 2001).

Another aspect that should be mentioned is the occupation of one territory by two different northern Maipuran groups. The research carried out among the Baniwa and Curripaco who are occupying the Aki River has revealed the existence of two superimposed cosmographies (Ruette 1998). For the Baniwa the Aki River is the heart (core) of the territory that was given to their ancestors by the Creator (Iñapirrikuli) at the beginning of the world. On the other hand, for the Curripaco whose ancestral territory is in the Isana, the Aki River is a peripheral area, which is perceived exclusively through the mythical map that was constructed by the travels of Kúwai (Ruette 1998, 202).

Although the places that are recognized by the Baniwa and Curripaco coincide spatially, the Curripaco cosmography synthesizes only some of the Baniwa contents (e.g., names and location of places). This has allowed the Curripaco to establish new discontinuities in a previously continuous space and add new meanings to it. The differences in the meanings and the names of certain places were the result of their assignment of different temporal and symbolic contents during the semantic processes. Although the Curripaco have adopted the Baniwa spatial distribution of places, they have constructed new representations for them. Consequently, although there are similarities in the names, meanings, and spatial location of certain places that are recognized by the two groups, it is possible to identify two distinct cosmographies in the Aki River, which are differentiated by the narratives on the Kúwai and of his travels.

Based on this information, it is possible to conclude, first, that the similarities and differences between these two cosmographies are expressions of past and present relations between two groups who have synthesized, integrated, and interpreted mythical and secular information. Second, the existence of two cosmographies is an indication of two processes of appropriation of a territory that are based on the continuous assignment of mythical and secular meanings to a space and to its places. Finally, the superimposition of the two cosmographies suggests that the two groups share the same mythical history and the same model of landscape construction. The adoption by the Curripaco of the Baniwa location of places and of certain names and meanings is an indication of their later arrival into the Baniwa territory. Furthermore, the differences in the meanings of certain places that can be observed in the Curripaco cosmography indicate that even though another Maipuran group occupied the land, the Curripaco constructed their own cosmographic model, and in doing so they converted this land into their new territory.

Santos-Granero (1998, 140–41) has designated the process of writing based on landmarks resulting from the agency of human or mythical beings as topographic writing. He calls the elements of the landscape that have acquired their configuration through past human or mythical actions topograms. Human-made topograms include not only components of the landscape modified by human activities (old gardens, house sites, mines) but also petroglyphs, paintings, and other intentionally made signs. When topograms are combined in sequential manner to form longer narratives, they become topographs. Through this process of writing specific events of a common mythical history into new landscapes, the different northern Maipuran groups that migrated from the Isana at different times apparently extended the early geographically reduced mythical map of the world centered in the Isana region to other adjacent and distant territories. The successive instances of topographic writing that occurred at different times and in different places have contributed to the maintenance of a sense of cultural and ethnic identity among the different northern Maipuran groups, even among those who inhabit distant areas.

According to ritual specialists of several northern Maipuran groups, early ancestors made the petroglyphs that are found in specific areas of the northwest Amazon "when the rocks were still soft." Some of them can be classified as topographs because they recall a sequence of mythical events. One such case is the petroglyphs of the Hípana and Enúkoa rapids, which according to ritual specialists narrate in a sequential manner the principal events of the two mythical cycles (González Ñáñez, personal communication, 1997).

Based on this information it is possible to hypothesize that the first process of topographic writing could have taken place along the Isana River after the arrival of the first Arawakan groups. Through this process specific elements of the Isana landscape (e.g., the rapids of Isana and Enúkoa) were transformed into the "navel of the world," where the basic events of the mythical creation and transformation of the world occurred and from where the mythic ancestors and their human descendants emerged. According to the informants, early ancestors made the petroglyphs that are found in the rocks of these rapids as permanent reminders of the mythical events that occurred there. For this reason, ritual specialists regularly visit these sacred places. The petroglyphs that are found in other areas are reminders of specific mythical events (e.g., Hiwa, Aki), figures (e.g., the Kúwai), or of past processes of re-creation (e.g., La Punta site at the confluence of the Atabapo, Guaviare, and Orinoco rivers) (Vidal 1987, 143–44; Zucchi 1991a, 113–38).

Finally, it is possible that it might have been precisely through this kind of ritual process of topographic writing, which converted specific elements of the landscape (e.g., rocks, caves, beaches, lakes, savannas, rapids, and mountains) of a newly occupied area into topographs and topograms, that a new land was transformed into a group's own territory. The initial appropriation of a new land was gradually reinforced through a continuous process of topographic writing through which new events of the particular history of each group are encapsulated into new or already named places or elements of the landscape. Based on this information it is possible to hypothesize that ritual power was a fundamental component of the northern Maipuran expansive process, as is indicated by the ritual adoption of Iñapirrikuli's and Kúwai's magical powers to plan and organize migrations, re-create the society in different spatial and temporal contexts, construct new landscapes, and distribute the population within a new territory.

New Archaeological Evidence

In 1984, a new ceramic series called Cedeñoid was identified along the Middle Orinoco and in the adjacent Venezuelan Llanos or savannas. The carriers of these ceramics occupied these areas between 1000 B.C. and A.D. 1500 (Zucchi and Tarble 1984, 293–309; Zucchi et al. 1984, 155–80). At the time of the research, the available archaeological evidence indicated that early Cedeñoids were small groups of fishers, hunters, and gatherers with no or an incipient type of agriculture who had settled in the area at approximately the same time as the Saladoids, or even earlier.

Cedeñoid pottery has a soapy texture and is tempered with small clay pellets and vegetable fibers. The decoration usually is incised, and motifs consist of groups of fine, straight parallel lines, notches, or short incisions placed on vessel rims; however, a few sherds with polychrome painting were also found. Open bowls are the most common vessel shape, but small jars and ollas were also identified. All specialists working in the Middle Orinoco have described this pottery (Howard 1943; Roosevelt 1980; Rouse 1978, 203–29; Vargas 1981). However, because of its low frequency, it was usually considered part of the Saladoid tradition.

The large collection obtained at the Aguerito site, as well as in other sites of the area (Zucchi and Tarble 1984, 293–309), allowed the isolation of this component as pertaining to a distinct social group that apparently entered the area during the first millennium B.C. or even earlier. The Cedeñoids shared the Middle Orinoco area with La Gruta (the earliest Saladoid site of the area, 1000 B.C.–200 B.C.) and the later Ronquin people (200 B.C.–A.D. 400) (Zucchi and Tarble 1984, 293–309; Zucchi et al. 1984, 179).

In 1986, Zucchi began a research project on human settlements along blackwater (Upper Orinoco, Atabapo, Negro, Casiquiare, Lower Guainía, and San Miguel) and whitewater (Orinoco) rivers of the Amazon state of Venezuela. This large area was divided into seven subareas where thirty-seven pre-Columbian settlement sites were located and tested (five along the Atabapo, sixteen along the Orinoco, four in the Lower Guainía, four in the Upper Negro, two along the Casiquiare, and six on the San Miguel, an important tributary of the Lower Guainía) (Zucchi 1991a, 113–38; 1991b, 1–33; 1991c, 202–20, 1991d, 368–79; 1992, 223–52). The pottery from these sites belongs to five ceramic complexes that have the following chronological positions: Iboa (400 B.C.–A.D. 200), Nericagua (A.D. 600–800), Carutico (100 B.C.–A.D. 500), Pueblo Viejo (A.D. 600–800), and Garza (A.D. 1450–1600).

When these ceramics were compared with the pottery described for other areas of South America (e.g., Middle Orinoco, Central Amazon, Brazilian Guiana, and Guyana) it became clear that despite their geographic distance and chronological differences, some of these materials shared the same basic pattern of formal, technological, and decorative traits. To visualize these similarities and interpret their meanings, these ceramics were grouped into five subareas. Table 8.1 shows the types of temper that were used in each of them. It can be observed that with the exception of the Jauarí and other pottery of the Central Amazon (Hilbert 1968), all others are characterized by the use of more than one type of organic and inorganic tempering material.

Although eight vessel shapes were identified in the Middle Orinoco material, only six of these shapes are found in the pottery of the other areas (figure 8.2). The remaining two shapes (7 and 8) exhibit a more limited spatial and temporal distribution. As was the case with the Cedeñoid material of the Middle Orinoco, the qualitative and quantitative changes that can be observed in each of the local sequences seems to be the result of internal

Table 8.1. Types of Organic and Inorganic Temper

Phase or Complex	Ceramic Type	Organic					Inorganic						
		Cauixi	Caraipé	Fibers	Charcoal	Ash	Conch	Sand	Mica	Quartz	Feldspar	Clay	Crushed Sherds
Jauarí	Wide-line incision	X											
Manacapurú	Fine-line incision[a]	X											
Caiambé	Fine-line incision	X											
Paredão	Fine-line incision	X											
Santa Luzia	Fine-line incision	X											
	Red paint	X											
	Incision in red	X											
Iboa		X	X		X			X					
Nericagua		X	X					X					
Monouteri			X					X					
Carutico			X	X	X			X					
Nofurei	Gamitana incised		X		X			X					
Vichada	Ocuné fine		X		X			X				X	
Mabaruma	Aruka incised												
	Mabaruma plain							X		X			
	Hosororo plain							X			X		
	Koberimo plain							X	X				
Taruma	Kanashen incised												
	Yachó plain				X			X					
	Mawiká plain		X					X					
	Kalumyé plain				X				X				

Table 8.1. Con't

Phase or Complex	Ceramic Type	Temper Types											
		Organic							Inorganic				
		Cauixí	Caraipé	Fibers	Charcoal	Ash	Conch	Sand	Mica	Quartz	Feldspar	Clay	Crushed Sherds
Mazagão	Anauerapucú incised												
	Mazagão plain								X		X		
	Picacá incised												
	Vilanova plain		X										
	Jarí scratched								X				
	Camaipí plain		X							X			
	Daví incised							X					
Aristé	Flexal scratched							X		X			
	Aristé plain							X		X			
El Caimito					X	X	X	X	X	X			X
Musiepedro													
Hond. del Oeste													
Río Verde	Río Verde diagonal incision												
	Río Verde incised				X	X	X	X	X	X			X
Río Joba	Joba incised						X						
	Joba zoned-incised												
	Joba diagonal-incised												

a. Fine rectilinear incision and curvilinear incision without cross-hatching.

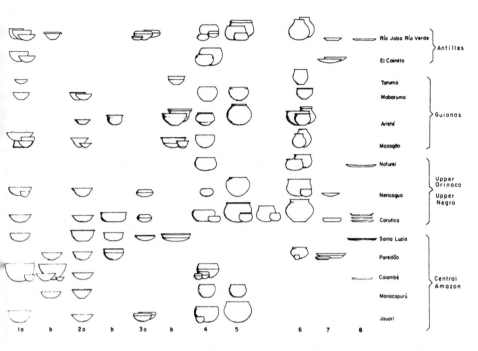

Figure 8.2. Vessel Shapes Characteristic of the Parallel Line Incised Tradition

processes of change and also of different types of interaction between the carriers of this pottery and other local groups. Although some of the later materials exhibit certain trait differences (e.g., new rims, variants of vessel shape 8), the basic pattern of diagnostic elements persists.

The decoration of these ceramics also exhibits amazing similarities with the Cedeñoid material (figure 8.3); in all of them the fine line incision is the most popular decorative technique, and the incised motives are characterized by the use of multiple vertical, horizontal, and diagonal straight lines and of vertical and horizontal curved lines. In addition, all styles display the use of incised composed elements such as angles, circles, squares, triangles, diamonds, and spirals (square, round, and triangular) (Zucchi 1991c, 202–20). The formal, stylistic, and technological traits of this pottery; the wide geographic distribution of the sites where it was found, which are located in six different subareas of South America (Central Amazon, Negro Basin, Middle Orinoco–Llanos, Guyana, Brazilian Guiana, and the Western Antilles); and a chronological position that extends between 1000 B.C. and A.D.

Phases/Sites	Incised Motives
Río Joba Río Verde	
El Caimito	
Taruma	
Mabaruma	
Aristé	
Mazagão	
Nofurei	
Nericagua	
Carutico	
Santa Luzia	
Paredão	
Caiambé	
Manacapurú	
Jauarí	
Apostadero	

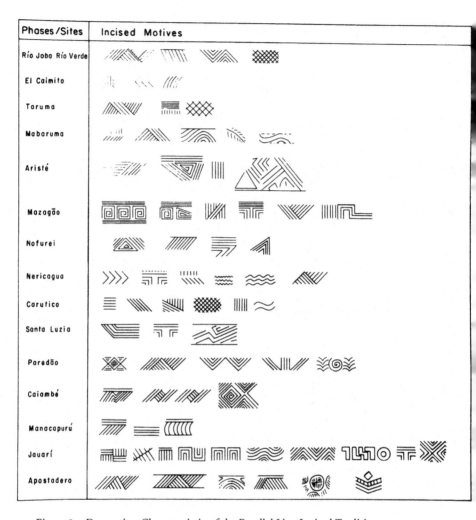

Figure 8.3. Decoration Characteristic of the Parallel Line Incised Tradition

1800 permitted the establishment of a new tradition that has been called the parallel line incised tradition (Zucchi 1991c, 202–20).

Most social anthropologists agree that in a certain sense unique cultures are the result of the existence and viability of ethnic groups (Barth 1969, 9–38; Honingmann 1959, 873; Mason 1976, 349–67). This idea provides a means to test the significance of ethnicity in archaeological terms through indirect evidence. However, the relative scarcity of unambiguously located archaeological sites with ethnic affinities unequivocally supported by primary historical documents is the main weakness of this approach. To this we must add that the remains of a single community at a particular point in time cannot be taken to represent the totality of the society of which it was part. Similarly, the establishment of a particular assemblage does not preclude the possibility of a similar assemblage being something else at another site. The complexity and scale of social and cultural transformation that have occurred within the Maipuran population through time militate against a simplistic one-to-one correlation of particular artifacts or assemblages and specific ethnic identification wherever they occur.

Mason (1976, 360) argues that the relative rarity of historically fixed sites, migrations and fissioning of populations, the origin of sociological reference of group names, and emergent ethnicities following the commingling and disappearance of earlier groups are not just traps for the unwary but also multifaceted research opportunities. Ethnic affiliation of archaeological materials can be analyzed through two major complementary approaches, called site-unit and territorial ethnicity. The strength of the first lies in its highly specific localization in space and time of the remains of named groups. However, as mentioned earlier, the site-unit approach is problematic when unsupported by primary historical documents or when the remains of a single community in a particular historical moment cannot be taken to represent the totality of the society of which it was part.

On the other hand, territorial ethnicity does not require tight historical documentation on specific localities but only on a subarea or area. This permits a way of approaching the identification of archaeologically represented ethnicities, even when discrete localities that are mentioned in the historical literature have not been found. The weakness of this approach is its vagueness regarding time and place, which may result in ethnic identifications that by the inclusiveness "part more from the constitution of original, real societies than is the case with site-unit approach" (Mason 1976, 360–62). The establishment of these ethnicities must be as multidimensional as possible "not only for the indispensable purposes of opportunities for convergent verification but to approach the study of the whole societies represented by the cultural fragments called "sites"" (Mason 1976, 361).

Archaeologists have long been interested in methods for assessing the ethnicity of sites and assemblages, especially because of the growing emphasis on the archaeological contributions to the study of the processes by which societies adapt to their circumstances and how cultures evolve along new lines. To establish the archaeologically represented ethnicities of the parallel line incised ceramic tradition, I analyzed, compared, and combined the available archaeological, chronological, ethnological, historical, and environmental data with the information provided by the oral histories of several northern Arawakan groups.

This process has allowed me to hypothesize that the pottery that belongs to the parallel line incised tradition is related to the expansion of northern Maipuran and with non-Maipuran groups that were closely related to them (e.g., the Tarumas). The geographic distribution of these materials indicates their occupation of the Negro Basin and their gradual expansion to adjacent areas (e.g., Lower Guainía, Upper Orinoco, Casiquiare, and Atabapo) as well as the outward migrations of some of these groups (e.g., Proto-Igneri, Proto-Lokono) from their ancestral homeland to other areas of northern South America and the Caribbean (e.g., Middle Orinoco, Guyana). The types of interaction that each Maipuran group maintained through time with other groups varied in nature, time, and space, and this variability should be reflected in the corresponding archaeological contexts. As a consequence, the interpretation of archaeological contexts not only reflects the interaction (adaptation, compatibility, and necessity) between two or more ceramic traditions but also different types of factors that are variable in time and space. When one observes the different modes of initial inception and the later developments of this kind of pottery in each of the local, subregional, and regional contexts, it is possible to suggest that these differences were the result of migrations or of different types of interaction that the migrants maintained with the new physical and sociocultural environments (Zucchi 1991d, 368–79, 1993, 131–48). The different modes of inception of this kind of pottery in the local and subregional contexts also suggest that the penetration and settlement of these northern Maipuran groups in other areas were attained through peaceful mechanisms.

Conclusions

The combination of linguistic, archaeological, ethnographic, mythical, and historical data has permitted the construction of a new yet still somewhat tentative model of the northern Maipuran diaspora. Although several propositions have been made regarding the probable place of origin of Proto-Arawak, concrete evidence is still lacking. For this reason, we begin our model in the Isana subarea, a region that the oral traditions of several northern Maipuran groups consider as the place of emergence of their first ancestors. Regarding the chronological position of the earliest divergences of and differentiation within the family, Noble (1965) suggested that between 4,000 and 3,500 years B.P. Proto-Arawak began to diverge into its six or seven main branches. He also calculated that by at least 3,000 to 2,500 years B.P. a second surge of divergence, which he reconstructed as Proto-Maipuran, had already taken place. Out of this second surge further separations occurred, and Proto–Northern Maipuran evolved into several languages and dialects.

Another aspect that should be considered in relation to these early periods (4,000–2,500 B.P.) is the climatic fluctuations that apparently occurred in the tropical lowlands of South America during the Quaternary (Haffer 1987, 6–22; Meggers 1979, 252–66). Although the Quaternary history of the Amazonian rain forest is still poorly understood, the recent data indicate that although climatic anomalies occurred during the Holocene, reduced precipitation was never enough to fragment the forest in the Amazon lowlands (Colinvaux et al. 2000, 141; Haberle and Maslin 1999, 27–38).

According to certain specialists (Markgraf et al. 2000, 132), one of the most dramatic and important ways in which climatic change can affect ecosystems is by altering the frequency, intensity, and extent of forest fires. They also stressed the importance of the role of El Niño–Southern Oscillations (ENSOs) in modulating fire regimes on global scales, as suggested by the occurrence of extensive wildfires in Indonesia, Australia, Central America, and Amazonia during the recent El Niño events of 1982–83 and 1997–98. The occurrence of drier phases has been recorded in the Amazon Basin between 6,000 and 4,000 B.P., 2,700 and 2,100 B.P. and about 1,500, 1,200, 700, and 400 B.P. (Absy 1985; Van der Hammen 1972, 641–43, 1974, 3–26, 1982, 61–67; Wijmstra and Van der Hammen 1966, 88). The combination of climatic change and human impact on ecosystems is of critical concern in both the tropical and temperate zones.

Research carried out in the San Carlos area (Upper Negro, Venezuela) suggested that under drier climatic regimes, wildfires might have destroyed large areas of forest, resulting in a large-scale mosaic of successional forests. Charcoal has been found in the soils of mature terra firme and caatinga forests of this area (Sanford et al. 1985, 53–55). Charcoal samples taken from an oxisol and ultisol in two terra firme areas of the San Carlos region provided dates that ranged from 250 ±50 B.P. to 6,260 ±110 B.P., whereas the soil charcoal from the caatinga forest was dated at 1,400 ±140 B.P. Charcoal is also abundant in the anthrosols of the area, and the oldest evidence of human presence was provided by a thermoluminescence date of 3,750 ±20 B.P. taken from an ultisol close to a side stream near the town of San Carlos.

It is possible that the occurrence of drier climatic periods affected the subsistence resources exploited by the human groups of the tropical lowlands, especially those that were occupying areas of lower productivity such as the Negro Basin, and that "the demographic consequences of these events (lowered density, increased mobility, migration and extinction) should be reflected in patterns of linguistic distribution" (Meggers 1979, 252–66). Based on these premises and on the information presented in the previous sections of this chapter, I will present a new model for the northern Arawak expansion, which will be confirmed, rejected, or modified through future research.

Because we lack concrete evidence on the ancestral area of Proto-Arawak, the model begins somewhere in the Amazon basin between 4,000 and 3,500 years B.P., when Proto-Arawak began to diverge into several main branches.

1. Between 4,000 and 3,500 years B.P., the beginning of a dry phase and a gradual reduction of the aquatic resources probably influenced the redistribution of the Proto-Arawak population and the separation of the different Proto-Maipuran linguistic groups (northern, pre-Andine, southern, and eastern).

2. One of these early groups apparently moved along the Rio Negro and settled in specific areas of the basin, causing the separation of the Proto–Northern Maipuran or Proto-Newiki linguistic group.

3. According to the oral traditions of several northern Maipuran groups (e.g., Warekena, Baniwa, Piapoco, Baré, Wakuénai (Curripaco), Kabiyarí, Yukuna, and Tariana), one of these ancestral settlement places was the Isana subarea. This information also indicates that the first three Proto–Northern Maipuran groups that settled in this subarea were the ancestors of the Hohódene, Baré, and Waríperi-dakéenai, and that other groups followed later (Vidal 1987, 1993).

4. The ethnographic evidence recently obtained from northern Maipuran groups that inhabit the Lower Guainía subarea (Ruette 1998; Vall 1998), indicates two important facts: first, that northern Maipuran groups construct their cosmographies through continuous processes of topographic writing, through which mythical and historical events are associated with specific places in the landscape; and, second, that it is precisely this process that allows the transformation of a new land into a group's territory.

Because several northern Maipuran groups consider the Isana subarea to be the navel of the world and the place of emergence of the first ancestors, it is possible to hypothesize that the first ritual process of topographic writing could have taken place precisely once the settlement of the first ancestral groups had occurred and that it was precisely through this kind of process that certain natural elements and places of the Isana landscape (e.g., the Hípana and Enúkoa rapids) were ritually transformed into the scenario where the basic episodes of the mythical creation and transformation of the world (Iñapirrikuli and Kúwai mythical cycles) occurred and, consequently, also in the place of emergence of the first ancestors and their descendants.[3]

5. Between 3,000 and 2,500 years B.P., the probable arrival of other northern Maipuran groups into the Isana subarea, together with more efficient agricultural techniques, interethnic marriages, and processes of ethnic aggregation, were factors that contributed to increase the local population.

6. An increase in the local population probably made necessary its redistribution within the land. As a result of this geographic redistribution of the population, certain subgroups expanded into adjacent areas or distant areas. The second surge of linguistic separations that occurred between 3,000 and 2,500 years B.P. within the northern Maipuran group of languages probably was influenced by the migrations of certain social units (sibs or phratries) of the ancestral groups that were settled in the Isana subarea to other subareas of the Rio Negro basin or to adjacent and distant territories (e.g., the Colombian Llanos, the Orinoco basin, the Guainía River). The oral traditions of several groups provide information about the routes that were used during these migrations as well as the specific places where ritual processes of re-creation of their societies took place.

7. Archaeological evidence (e.g., the number and size of archaeological sites) from the area suggests that between A.D. 800–1300, the local population of the Upper Orinoco–Lower Ventuari–Atabapo subarea increased greatly.

8. Historical documents of the seventeenth and early eighteenth centuries indicate that during this period the northern Arawakan groups occupied vast territories (Vidal 1987). The Piapoco had a large territory that began in the right bank of the Meta River (between the Duya and Guanapalo) and included the Guaviare, Vichada, Inírida, Orinoco, and Atabapo rivers. The Achagua were located in northwestern Venezuela (states of Falcon, Lara, and Barinas), along the Apure, Casanare, Ariporo, Ele, Pauto, Manacacías, and Meta rivers, as well as in certain areas of the Airico River. The Caquetío were found in the islands of Aruba and Curaçao, along the coasts of the Falcon, Lara, and Yaracuy states along the Upper Sarare, Apure, and Orinoco rivers and also in the Airico between the Vichada and Uva rivers (Aguado 1906, 165; Carvajal 1892, 172; Cassani 1967, 143–45, 201–37; Gilij 1965, 2:280; Rivero 1883, 19, 21).

The Maipure occupied the right bank of the Orinoco from the Maipures rapids to the mouth of the Yao River and also several tributaries (e.g., Sipa-po, Guayapo, Autana, Tuapo, and Lower Ventuari) (Gumilla 1963, 202; Gilij 1965, 1:58–59; Caulín 1841, 67, 71). The Guaipunavi, who arrived in the Upper Orinoco during the eighteenth century, occupied the Atabapo River and its tributaries, the Caname and the Chamoquini. They finally settled in Maracoa (the town of San Fernando de Atabapo), and later they moved to the Upper Orinoco, Lower Guaviare, Inírida, Sipapo, Parú, and Patavita (Cuervo 1893, 3:327; Vega 1974, 117–35).

The Warekena were found along the Guainía, Tiriquin, Itiniwini, Atacavi, Upper Atabapo, and Muruapo, a tributary of the Casiquiare River (Caulín 1841, 70, 75; Cuervo 1893, 3:244, 322–27). The Baniwa were settled along the Upper Guainía, Patavita, Aki, and Upper Xié, a tributary of the Upper Negro (Caulín 1841, 75; Cuervo 1893, 3:322–23; Sweet 1975). The Yavitero were initially settled along the Xié and Tomo (Cuervo 1893, 3:322–25; Sweet 1975). Later they are mentioned along the Temi and Tuamini (Cuervo 1893, 3:245; Ramos Pérez 1946, 319–20). The Baré occupied a large territory that extended from the Middle Rio Negro, the Casiquiare, and its tributaries (e.g., Ajuana, Marié, Iá, Siapa, Pamoni, Pasimoni, Pasiba, Baría) (Caulín 1841, 73; Cuervo 1893, 3:324). Toward the end of the century two Baré subgroups were mentioned among the population of the Japurá-Caquetá (Llanos and Pineda 1982, 59). In the Upper Orinoco there were other Maipuran groups (e.g., the Guinau and Anauyá) about which there is very little information.

The Manao were occupying the Middle Negro and its tributaries the Urubaxi, Daráa, Padauiri, Anjurim, Xiuará, Cauaburis, and Uneuxi, and also the Timoni Island (Sweet 1975; Hemming 1978; Wright 1981). The Curripaco were around the Isana and its tributaries and also along the Vaupés and some of its tributaries (e.g., Papuri and Querari).

The Tariana were occupying an area located between the Isana, Vaupés, Papuri, Yuareté, Tiquié, and Japurá (Cuervo 1893, 3:325; Llanos and Pineda 1982, 57–67; Wright 1981, 9). The Yucuna and Kabiyarí were part of the population of the Japurá-Caquetá and occupied the Comarca de Araracuara, the rapids of Cupatí or La Pedrera, and the Apaporis River. The Yumana-Passé were settled between the Putumayo, Caquetá, and Tiquié (Llanos and Pineda 1982, 25, 57–59, 66–67), and the Resígaro occupied the Lower Caquetá–Putumayo and the headwaters of several tributaries of the Upper Cahunari and of the Upper Igará–Paraná (Llanos and Pineda 1982, 54–56). The Wainuma occupied the Cahuinari River and the area located between this river and the Ipi (Llanos and Pineda 1982, 92). Other Arawakan groups on which there is little information, such as the Caboquena, Carapiten, and Anuvicena, inhabited the Lower Rio Negro during the sixteenth and seventeenth centuries (Sweet 1975; Hemming 1978).

9. Because the traditional territories and specific settlement sites of several northern Arawakan groups (e.g., Baré, Baniwa, Warekena, Piapoco, Maipure, and Guaipunavi), which have been reconstructed through oral traditions and the colonial documents of the seventeenth and eighteenth centuries, coincide with the archaeological subareas that have been established in the Upper Negro–Casiquiare–Upper Orinoco–Lower Guainía and Atabapo region, it is possible to hypothesize that the archaeological materials that were found in these subareas are related to the occupations of these groups. Consequently, because the ceramic complexes that have been established belong to the parallel line incised tradition, this ceramic tradition can be tentatively related with the northern Maipuran occupations.

10. The available information on the mechanisms of northern Maipuran migrations seems to suggest that the northern Maipuran diaspora was attained through peaceful mechanisms based on an open and inclusive type of sociolinguistic organization linked to a transformational notion of the world and a marked flexibility toward change that facilitated processes of negotiation and aggregation and also the establishment of cross-linguistic ties, transethnic identities, and extended regional alliances and trade networks (see chapter 1).

The information presented in this chapter reveals the complexities of the northern Arawak expansion. Although the reconstruction I have presented is hypothetical and must be tested against new data, it certainly demonstrates that a multidisciplinary approach can provide the best results. Using this kind of approach, it is possible to obtain a more significant and integrated interpretation of the groups that inhabited the tropical lowlands of South America during precontact and early colonial times. To attain these results it is necessary to visualize the archaeological remains as evidence of the prehistory of the indigenous populations that are mentioned in the historical documents and to study the oral histories of the different autochthonous groups whose descendants still inhabit the areas where the remains are found.

Notes

Research on human settlements in the Amazon State of Venezuela was sponsored by the Consejo Nacional de Ciencia y Tecnología (SI-1729), the Instituto Venezolano de Investigaciones Científicas, and UNESCO Man and the Biosphere Program (MAB 11). I am very grateful to Berta Perez for reading the first version of this chapter and to Jonathan Hill, Fernando Santos-Granero, and Michael Heckenberger for their important comments and suggestions. Carlos Quintero made all the drawings.

1. The first people to emerge (to arrive in a place) are recognized as "grandparents" (Van der Hammen 1992, 128; Vidal 1993, 75).

2. At present, the oldest evidence of human presence in the Upper Negro subarea is a thermoluminescence date of 3,750 B.P. ±20 percent (standard deviation), which was obtained from a ceramic sherd found in a side stream located near the town of San Carlos (Sanford et al. 1985, 54). The oldest carbon-14 date obtained during the archaeological survey of the area was 1,800 ±80 B.P. (Beta 253954) and corresponds to the Carutico site along the Upper Rio Negro (Zucchi 1992, 237).

3. According to northern Arawak ritual specialists, a patch of black soil that is found in one of the banks of the Hípana rapids is believed to be the place where the Kúwai was consumed by fire (González Ñáñez, personal communication, 1996).

9 Shamanism, Colonialism, and the Wild Woman: Fertility Cultism and Historical Dynamics in the Upper Rio Negro Region

JONATHAN D. HILL

THIS CHAPTER has two interrelated goals. First, I will explore the concept of culture area as it developed in the ethnology of Lowland South America in the twentieth century and suggest ways in which the concept can be retheorized to restore its utility in current anthropology. Particular attention will be given to rethinking culture areas in Lowland South America in relation to the concern for culture, power, and history. A second goal of the chapter is to demonstrate how such a retheorized concept of culture area can be used in developing a dynamic regional interpretation of long-term historical processes that have generated contemporary ethnolinguistic geographies in the northwest Amazon/Upper Rio Negro region. Drawing on ethnographic research with the Arawak-speaking Wakuénai of Venezuela and previous analyses of their complex mythic and ritual practices, I will argue that northwestern Amazonia, as known through twentieth century ethnographic studies, emerged through a complex intertwining of two distinct historical processes: indigenous fertility cultism and Western colonial and national state expansions.

The northwest Amazon region provides a highly suitable context for retheorizing the culture area concept in South America. Beginning with Goldman's (1963) monograph on the Cubeo, ethnographers have documented the cosmopolitanism of the region's indigenous peoples and the complex historical relationships between communities with diverse cultural and linguistic practices. Jackson's (1983) regional analysis of social and linguistic organization among the eastern Tukanoan groups of the Vaupés basin in Colombia demonstrated the complexity and fluidity of regional ties. There are no comparable regional studies of northern Arawakan peoples living in the Isana-

Guainía drainage area east and north of the Vaupés basin, in part because of the tripartition of their ancestral territories among three separate national states (Colombia, Brazil, and Venezuela). However, recent ethnographic works on the Baniwa of Brazil (Wright 1998), the Curripaco of Colombia (Journet 1995), and the Wakuénai of Venezuela (Hill 1993) support the emergence of a more balanced perspective of the northwest Amazon region as a whole. In addition, studies of eastern Tukanoan peoples who live in the transitional zone between the Central Vaupés basin and the Isana-Guainía drainage area have provided important clues to the region's historical and cultural dynamics (see Chernela 1993 on the Wanano; Reichel-Dolmatoff 1985 on the Desana; and Goldman 1963 on the Cubeo). In the 1980s and 1990s, researchers working in all three subregions (eastern Tukanoan, northern Arawakan, and transitional) began to focus greater attention on long-term processes of colonialism, missionization, rubber gathering, and the role of indigenous cosmologies and ritual practices in interpreting and acting on these processes (see Hill 1996b for an overview of these sources).

What sets the northwest Amazon region apart from other areas of Lowland South America is the existence of strongly hierarchical forms of sociopolitical organization. Among both eastern Tukanoan and northern Arawakan groups of the region, local communities are linked together into phratries, or confederations based on ideologies of shared mythic descent from a group of brothers. Descendants are ranked according to the birth order of mythic brothers, with highest rank attributed to the oldest brother's descendants and lowest rank to the youngest brother's descendants. Among eastern Tukanoan peoples living in the central Vaupés basin, phratric ranking occurs in the absence of geographic localization of communities within a shared territory, and there is no linkage between principles of rank and marriage practices (Jackson 1983). Among the Arawakan Wakuénai and Baniwa of the Isana-Guainía drainage area, marriage is linked directly to rank, especially for highly ranked men and women. Highest-ranked men intermarry with women of highest rank in different phratries. Among lower-ranked individuals, there is little or no concern for relating rank to marriage. This linkage between marriage and rank, or "rank endogamy," among Arawak-speaking peoples was combined until the fairly recent past with localization of phratries in shared riverine territories. Taken together, the features of rank endogamy and localized phratries institutionalized the reproduction of hierarchy and its political implementation among Arawak-speaking peoples of northwestern Amazonia. The absence of these same features among eastern Tukano-speaking peoples has led to the conclusion that phratries there are epiphenomenal (Jackson 1983). The distribution of ranking principles in northwestern

Amazonia strongly implies that hierarchical ranking of local communities into larger groupings, or phratries, originated among the Arawak-speaking peoples and was adopted at some later time by eastern Tukanoan peoples. Localized phratries and the linkage between ranking and marriage are found among eastern Tukanoan peoples only among the Cubeo (Goldman 1963) and Wanano (Chernela 1993), and both of these peoples inhabit the transitional zone located along the border between eastern Tukanoan and northern Arawakan peoples.

By turning to the study of long-term historical processes in northwestern Amazonia, researchers have opened up new possibilities for comparing the region's unique configuration of ethnolinguistic practices to similarly complex ethnoscapes found in other areas of Lowland South America. Comparison between northwestern Amazonia and the Montaña region of the eastern Peruvian lowlands is particularly feasible in this historical perspective. Both areas are strongholds for Arawak-speaking peoples who have survived through centuries of colonial and more recent changes. Both areas are located in geopolitically marginal zones at the borders between colonial and national states, and this marginality resulted in similar policies of missionization and colonization.[1] Indigenous peoples in both northwestern Amazonia and the eastern Peruvian lowlands recovered from their losses of lands and population during the early nineteenth century while the Wars of Independence decimated missionized indigenous groups in the Andes and the northern lowlands of Colombia and Venezuela.[2] And in both regions, the neocolonial demand for rubber in the late nineteenth to early twentieth centuries led to genocidal campaigns of forced labor, interethnic warfare, and internecine struggles. These macrolevel historical similarities allow the development of a cross-regional comparative perspective that embraces and controls for major issues of history and power.

Another very important dimension of comparison between northwestern Amazonia and the eastern Peruvian lowlands is what makes the project a specifically Arawakan historical comparison. I refer here to the multitude of ways, both similar and divergent, in which Arawak-speaking peoples in the two regions have registered the effects of long-term historical processes in their cosmologies, ritual practices, trade relations, and everyday social worlds. In both regions, Arawak-speaking peoples have engaged the flow of historical changes in ways that reveal how local and regional histories are constructed and interpreted. Integration of these indigenous Arawakan histories with macrolevel historical studies of Upper Amazonia and the growing ethnographic knowledge of Lowland South America can lead to a critical historical approach to regional and cross-regional comparison.

Clearly such a critical historical approach to culture areas and comparative studies poses challenges and problems even as it promises to yield opportunities and insights. Like other world regions, the ethnology of Lowland South America has grown exponentially in recent decades. Writing about the Montaña region of eastern Peru, Murdock (1951, 429) observed that the region's "cultures are described with a degree of inadequacy unusual even for South America." The same dearth of ethnographic knowledge characterized most other areas of Lowland South America at mid-century. In the 1970s, Lyon (1974) bestowed her famous label of "the least known continent" on South America. By the late 1970s, however, the number of publications in Lowland South American ethnology began to grow at a rapid pace, reflecting both the increasing significance of Amazonia as a testing ground for anthropological theories and the emergence of new communities of anthropological scholarship in Brazil, Peru, Colombia, and Venezuela.

The growth of anthropology has created similar problems for researchers working in Melanesia and other places. "Gaining mastery of regional ethnography or history is not just a lost art; it is almost impossible. The range of relevant sources skyrockets. Geographical as well as disciplinary markers blur as they get scrutinized" (Knauft 1999, 7). The proliferation of anthropological knowledge in formerly unstudied or understudied regions may lead some researchers to withdraw into the apparent safety of ethnographic and historical specificity at the expense of comparative theory. However, as Knauft (1999, 7) points out, the glut of ethnographic information calls for renewed attention to regions because "they provide an analytic context that can be rigorous, responsive to cultural differentiation, important in geographic scope, and conducive to broader comparisons." Moreover, comparative theory in anthropology can develop only to the extent that specialists in different areas write for one another in ways that are informed by readings of each other's published works (Strathern 1996).

Retheorizing the Culture Area Concept in Lowland South America

The increasing difficulty of mastering ever-expanding amounts of ethnographic, historical, and other kinds of knowledge is only one of the obstacles to retheorizing the culture area concept. If the goal is to restore the concept's utility as an analytic context capable of supporting broader comparative generalizations, then it is not sufficient to start from the old descriptive and taxonomic definition of culture areas as "trait lists." Murdock's (1951, 416) elaboration of twenty-four South American culture areas was intended as a taxonomic device for organizing indigenous cultural diversity according to such traits as linguistic affiliation, subsistence economy, sexual division of labor, crafts and other material technology, political organization, and patterns of kinship and marriage. It is interesting to note that all of Murdock's culture areas are linguistically heterogeneous, hinting at a richer picture of historical and ethnopolitical dynamics behind the classificatory façade. Arawak-speaking groups are present in nine of the twenty-four culture areas, often listed as intrusions, or minorities surrounded by speakers of other language stocks. The two areas forming the main foci of the present Comparative Arawakan Histories conference are the only ones labeled as mainly Arawakan, and then only in tandem with Panoan, Cariban, or Tukanoan groups (Murdock 1951, 429–32). The use of culture areas as descriptive, taxonomic devices made sense in mid-twentieth-century anthropology, when the ethnology of Lowland South America was still quite underdeveloped. However, it is not possible to bring the culture area concept up to date simply by expanding the list of traits to include issues of history and power.

Instead, what is needed to restore the culture area concept's usefulness as an analytic tool for broader comparisons is a politico-historical approach to macrolevel, long-term processes of change that also allows room for the diversity of culturally specific ways of constructing histories that have developed in Lowland South America. We need to acknowledge that contemporary indigenous societies are products of historical processes that have resulted in geographically dispersed clusters of peoples without resorting to the view that today's societies are merely remnants or fragments of an earlier time. The areas of greatest cultural diversity in the twentieth century are located in contested spaces that were at the margins of competing, expanding colonial states or in remote interior regions of modern national states. In many of these areas, new patterns of interethnic trade and alliance have emerged through amalgamations of various smaller groups. Such processes of ethnogenesis unfolded not only in zones of direct interethnic relations with Western states but also in remote areas having little or no direct contact (Basso 1995). These macrolevel historical processes must be integrated into the culture area concept from the outset rather than added on as an afterthought. However, it is equally important that indigenous ways of interpreting and acting on historical changes be integrated into a retheorized culture area concept. Without a concern for these local principles of history and power, current ethnolinguistic geographies in Lowland South America would be reduced to mere reflections of macrolevel political history. As Knauft (1999, 218) points out, "The underside of this timely concern with the global, the hybrid or diasporic, and the late modern or postcolonial is that it underemphasizes and sometimes totally misses the tenacity and richness of received cultural orientations. These persist even as they twist and redefine amid forces of change."

From a macrolevel perspective, northwestern Amazonia clearly illustrates how geopolitical marginalization in remote frontier areas between competing colonial or national states allowed and even promoted the flourishing of indigenous cultural diversity. Being located at the headwaters of the Rio Negro gave Arawak-speaking peoples of the region a degree of strategic flexibility for coping with colonial pressures of disease, missionization, and enslavement. Because most of these forces before the 1750s emanated from downstream areas of Portuguese Brazil, local peoples were able to take temporary refuge in the Vaupés, Guainía, Casiquiare, and other river basins beyond the range of direct contact. Similarly, when the murderous campaigns of the rubber boom descended on the Curripaco, Warekena, Baré, and other Arawakan peoples of Venezuela in the early twentieth century, they survived by moving across the frontier into Brazilian territory until it became safe to move back into Venezuela after World War II. The history of northwestern Amazonia is filled with these kinds of population movements, or "survival migrations" without which there would be little if any of the rich cultural diversity found in the region today.

Contrary to this scenario of survival through strategic migrations across colonial frontiers and national borders, indigenous Arawakan groups living in more accessible areas along the Middle Orinoco and Lower Negro rivers and across the Llanos of northern South America were decimated by diseases, warfare, and other changes during the colonial and early nationalist periods. More so than any of the other main language families of Lowland South America, the northern branch of Arawakan languages before the colonial period displayed a continuous, flowing distribution along the Orinoco, Negro, and Amazon rivers (see map 1, p. 2). The decimation of downstream coastal and Llanos groups has left northwestern Amazonia and a few other disjointed areas from what was formerly an enormous, interconnected set of riverine and coastal territories spreading across the northern lowlands of South America. From this macrolevel perspective, it would be easy to label northwestern Amazonia as a mere fragment of the precontact diaspora of riverine, Arawak-speaking peoples.

However, the Wakuénai (or Baniwa or Curripaco) do not see themselves as inhabitants of an isolated region, nor do they understand their history as a simple process of losses and fragmentation. Instead, they see themselves as the inhabitants of a mythic center of the world that continuously opens up, or expands, into the riverine and coastal areas that were formerly inhabited by other Arawak-speaking peoples. This indigenous historical vision of a dynamic social universe that expands through political and economic relations of trade along riverine and interfluvial pathways is discernible in two major genres of cultural performance. First, a cycle of mythic narratives about the second creation of the world outlines the basic principles of social development and interaction that generated the pattern of trade relations between peoples living in different river basins. Second, a genre of ritually powerful chanted and sung speeches, called *málikai*, connects these developmental and interactive principles to specific peoples and places throughout northwestern Amazonia and northern regions of Lowland South America.

These performances form the central core of male and female initiation rituals, and they result in very different but overlapping historical and geographic maps depending on the gender of people undergoing the transition to adulthood. In both male and female initiations, the musical naming of peoples and places constructs a flowing, continuous expansion of historical space that follows major rivers. The chants for female initiation result in a mapping of the home territories, or ancestral lands, of Wakuénai phratries in the Isana-Guainía drainage area of Venezuela, Colombia, and Brazil. In male initiation rituals, however, the chanting of place names encompasses a far larger set of riverine and coastal areas that stretch across the entire northern half of Lowland South America. This contrast between male and female initiation rituals gives substance to the importance of gender as a basic principle of indigenous history, or the idea that gender differentiation and competition are forces that generated a series of historical expansions away from and back to the mythic center. Both mythic narratives and ritual performances point to the importance of controlling the potentially disruptive forces of gender differences by transforming them into complementarity and connection between the sexes.

In contrast to the geopolitical marginality of northwestern Amazonia in macrolevel political and historical terms, Wakuénai mythic narratives and ritual performances continue to assert the ethnopolitical centrality of this headwater area for Arawak-speaking peoples who live north of the Amazon River. This view of northwestern Amazonia as a cultural center makes sense when combined with the ritual mapping out of riverine territories across the Orinoco and Negro basins. In this perspective, northwestern Amazonia is centrally located along the riverine connections between the Orinoco basin and Llanos to the north and the Negro and Amazon basins to the south. Before the decimation of Arawak-speaking peoples living in these downstream areas during the colonial period, Wakuénai lands along the Isana, Guainía, and other headwater rivers were strategically positioned to control trading networks between the two largest river basins of South America, the Orinoco and the Amazon.

Fertility Cultism in Northwestern Amazonia

The specific aim of this chapter is to demonstrate how the culture area concept, when retheorized along the lines just discussed, can be used to develop a critical historical understanding of northwestern Amazonia. The core of this ethnohistorical demonstration will consist of an overview of Wakuénai cosmology and ritual practices as a dynamic process of fertility cultism. From this starting point I explore some of the ways in which indigenous experiences of Western societies have become integrated into a gendered historical consciousness through the interpretive figure of Amáru, the primordial human mother or woman. The analysis focuses mainly on indigenous ways of classifying Western peoples, diseases, and technologies from the colonial period before 1750. In a later section I consider macrolevel political changes of the late colonial period, including the way Arawak-speaking peoples of northwestern Amazonia are portrayed in the Watunna, or the creation myths of the Yekuana.

The concept of fertility cults, or male-controlled ritual hierarchies concerned with symbolic fertilization of nature and regeneration of community, has proven to be useful for analyzing diverse religious practices in New Guinea (Whitehead 1986). By focusing on the processes of symbolic linkage between natural fertility and social reproduction, the concept of fertility cult encompasses a broader range of variable gender relations than the more narrowly focused concept of men's cult. Whitehead draws an analytical distinction for New Guinea between two kinds of fertility cult: cults of manhood and cults of clanhood. In the former, substances and symbols of fertility are entirely male-controlled and are used in developing adult men whose identities are defined primarily through this manhood, regardless of their kin-group identities (Whitehead 1986, 84). Cults of clanhood (found mostly in highland areas of New Guinea) use a similar theme of making men, "but the ceremonies devoted to it become adjunct to the celebration of agnatic group unity and ancestral fertility" (Whitehead 1986, 84). In these cults, women play important roles in the ritual fertilization of nature and regeneration of community, but they achieve ritual positions not as women per se but "through their status as *clanswomen*" (1986, 85). The distinction between cults of manhood and cults of clanhood is one of "relative salience" of sex- versus kin-defined identities, and "both components occur in virtually all fertility cults" (1986, 85).

As I argue elsewhere (Hill 2001), Whitehead's distinction between cults of manhood and cults of clanhood, with some adjustment and refinement, can be useful for interpreting the varieties of male-controlled ritual hierarchy in Amazonia. From a theoretical perspective, the main limitation of Whitehead's model is its functionalist sociological orientation (Weiner 1988). In addition, Whitehead's model does not hold up well against the full range of ethnographic variation in New Guinea (Knauft 1993, 143; Biersack 2001). These problems notwithstanding, Knauft (1993, 115–16) credits Whitehead with having taken "a very important first step in initiating this kind of integrated analysis," or a combined concern for cosmological dimensions of gender and "the historical patterns of power and practice through which they were actualized." Because the terms *manhood* and *clanhood* are sociologically complex and problematic in both New Guinea and Amazonia, I suggested that Whitehead's terms "cult of manhood" and "cult of clanhood" be replaced with more neutral ones of "marked" and "unmarked" fertility cults, respectively.

The distinction between marked and unmarked fertility cultism is not a static, taxonomic division between types of social or religious organization but a reflection of different processes of constructing male ritual hierarchies in contradistinction to everyday social relations characterized by egalitarian relations between men and women. In marked fertility cultism, the strong emphasis on gender oppositions and exclusion of women from ritual activities often is backed up by threats of physical or sexual violence against women and accompanied by male guilt about acts of violence against outside enemies or inside women and children. In unmarked fertility cultism, women are ambiguously included and excluded from male-controlled ritual activities, which provide ways of coordinating male and female processes of socialization and of asserting the interdependence of men and women as agents of social reproduction.

Perhaps the clearest indicators of marked fertility cultism are male ritual practices that dramatize a vehement severing of social ties between male children and their mothers and that symbolically deny the role of maternal nurturance. In marked fertility cultism, male-controlled rituals assert male potency and reproductive leverage over and above female fertility. Although some of the same elements of gender opposition and antagonism are to be found in unmarked fertility cultism, these elements have distinctly different social meanings when they are being used as a point of departure for constructing relations of complementarity between men and women and for affirming the significance of female fertility in male-controlled ritual performances. In unmarked fertility cultism, the symbolic weighting shifts from processes of severing maternal bonds and denying the role of maternal nurturance to the building of enduring connections between parents and children, men and women, mythic ancestors and human descendants.

The religious beliefs and practices of the Wakuénai of northwestern Amazonia offer a very clear illustration of unmarked fertility cultism. One of the most important sacred rituals in Wakuénai religion consists of the two sets of *málikai* chants performed for the parents of newborn infants. A first set of chants is designed to link the newborn's spirit with its father's ancestral tobacco spirits through naming all the tools, weapons, and objects of the father's everyday subsistence activities. After this first set of chants, the father hunts for game animals in the forest, the mother cooks the game meat in hot peppers, and both parents offer the cooked meat to a ritual specialist, called *málikai liminali* ("chant-owner" or "master chanter"). A second set of chants focuses on the pot of cooked game meat and the spirit-naming of all edible animal species so that the parents can resume their normal diet without causing harm to their child (see Hill 1993, Chap. 4).

Wakuénai childbirth rituals are an orchestration of contrasting sets of male and female imagery into an integrated whole of male and female bodily and cosmic places. The social context of ritual chanting also aims at an integration of male and female qualities and activities. Both mothers and fathers of newborn infants observe the same restrictions (seclusion, fasting, and sexual abstinence) during the week after birth, and both the male activity of hunting and the female activity of cooking are required to produce the pot of sacred food for the second set of málikai chants. The general significance of childbirth rituals is that of transposing the "overly close" biological relationships of newborn infants with their mothers (Lévi-Strauss 1969, 335) into overly close spiritual and emotional connections between newborn infants and their fathers. The ritual process thus supports the infant's arrival into human society as a member of the father's patrilineal descent group. However, the newborn's social identity is not complete until the overly close relationship with its parents has been socialized, or "stabilized," through the parents' act of eating the sacred food (*karidzamai*). Much like the mythic transformation of primal (incestuous) sexual relations into imagery of fasting and eating, the second set of chants in childbirth rituals embodies the transformation of sex- and gender-based activities into those of cooking and eating. Sharing of supernaturalized food replaces the sharing of sexual substances as the social means for signifying the biological family's participation in a local community defined through ritual as a hierarchical ordering of empowering mythic ancestors, powerful chant-owners, and empowered human descendants.

The umbilical cord serves as a unifying symbol for the first set of chants performed in Wakuénai childbirth rituals. In his chanted journey in search of an infant's mythic ancestors, the Wakuénai chant-owner travels along an internal, spiritual umbilical cord, connecting the newborn infant with its father and marking the transition from unborn fetus who receives nourishment inside its mother's womb to newly born child who consumes foods produced by its father. The mother's nurturing role is not denied so much as complemented and expanded to the social and economic connectedness between fathers and their children. It is significant that many spirit names in these first chants refer to long, thin objects of the father's work activities: vines, palm fibers, leaves, and grasses, which men must cut from the forest to use them to tie things up, bind together house poles, weave baskets, and make fish traps. Like these long, thin materials for binding and weaving things together, the chants themselves are long, thin strands of sound and meaning stretching across an invisible cord inside the infant's body and creating multiple connections between parents and children, husbands and wives, and mythic ancestors and human descendants.

The overriding importance of connectedness between fathers, mothers, and newly born infants is given additional expression in Wakuénai childbirth rituals through the second set of *málikai* chants. The naming of edible animal species over the pot of sacred food acknowledges the complementarity of the father's hunting and the mother's cooking of game meat. The protective powers of these chants is believed to pass from the mother to her newborn child via her breast milk after she and her husband have consumed the pot of sacred food. Thus, whereas the first set of chants extends the mother's biological nurturing of the infant to the father's social role as provider of food, the second set of chants connects this social relationship back to the mother's postuterine role as nourisher of the child during its first stage in the life cycle.

In both male and female initiation rituals, the primary focus of *málikai* singing and chanting is a pot of hot-peppered, boiled meat (*karidzamai*). Unlike childbirth rituals in which eating the sacred food signifies the stabilizing of parents' dynamic relationship with newborn infants, initiation rituals are contexts in which eating the sacred food embodies the more dynamic processes of "chasing after the names" and the mythic creation of an expanding world of peoples, animal and plant species, and geographic places. In a similar manner, initiation rituals are a dynamic transformation of the biological and culinary imagery used in childbirth rituals. The significance of sacred food as a source of continuity and shared substance across generations within the local descent group transforms in initiation rituals into the embodiment of dynamic exchanges and movements between local descent groups.

The transformation from internal to external relations is concretely expressed in the verbal and musical dimensions of *málikai* singing and chanting for the sacred food of initiates. These performances begin with a sing-ing-into-being of the celestial umbilical cord (*hliépule-kwa dzákare*) that connects the sky world of mythic ancestors to the navel of the terrestrial world of human descendants. The use of several different pitches is a musical con-struction of the celestial umbilical cord, the vertical power relationships gov-erning the transitions between developmental stages in the human life cycle and the turning over of generational time. Chant-owners use a sacred whip to tap out a percussive rhythm on an overturned basket covering the pot of sacred food, adding yet another dimension to the movement from internal to external worlds. After naming the mythic center at Hípana, the opening song modulates into a chanted naming of plants and animals in different places. In a long series of chants, the verbal naming of places away from the mythic center is musically expressed through use of different starting pitch-es, microtonal rising, accelerations of tempo, and loud-soft contrasts. The final chants return to the naming of places near the mythic center, and a clos-ing song using the exact same set of pitches as the opening song returns to the more stabilizing, vertical dimensions of power (i.e., the celestial umbil-ical cord). Overall, *málikai* singing and chanting in initiation rituals outlines a verbally and musically dynamic set of movements away from and back to the mythic center, or the musically stabilizing movements between distinct, sung pitches.

After the *málikai* singing and chanting are completed, the initiates come out from their place of seclusion to face the ritual advice of chant-owners and other elders. The initiates' mothers bring the pots of sacred food out-side and place them on woven mats, where the initiates must stand to receive the elders' advice. The initiates' senior kin, both male and female, participate in these ritually aggressive speeches. At the end of the advice, chant-owners lift a morsel of the hot-peppered food to the initiates' mouths on the ends of sacred whips before lashing the initiates' backs. In effect, the use of loud percussive sounds to signify the transformation from inner to outer worlds has reached a conclusion. The initiates' bodies, in full view of an assembled group of senior kin, have become percussive instruments that, through eat-ing the sacred food, carry within themselves the dynamic, expanding world of the second mythic creation.

Málikai singing and chanting over the sacred food and the elders' speeches of advice form a core of activities that is common to both male and female initiation rituals. However, the social organization and symbolic meanings of the two rituals are distinctly different, or even opposing. Female initiation rit-uals are small, localized gatherings held when an individual girl experiences her first menses. The young woman's loss of menstrual blood is associated with

alienation from her ancestral dream soul, and the long set of *málikai* chants
for the girl's sacred food is understood as a process of chasing after her dream
soul so that she will be a healthy and fertile adult woman. Female initiation
rituals are called *wakáitaka iénpiti* ("we speak to our child"), a label that highlights the significance of the elders' ritual advice as an arena for attaching sacred moral significance to the individual girl's physical maturation as a fully
sexual being. *Málikai* singing and chanting for female initiates begin at noon
and end at sunset. The naming of places in *málikai* chants starts at Hípana,
the mythic center, moves across the major river basins in the Upper Rio Negro region, and ends at Mutsipani, the mythic home of Amáru (see map 9.1).
The chants outline a process of movement away, or displacement, from the
mythic center at Hípana, a theme consistent with the situation of women who
have reached marriageable age in a patrilineal, patrilocal social world.

   In male initiation rituals, the pattern of place naming and movements in
málikai chants reverses and greatly expands upon the movements outlined

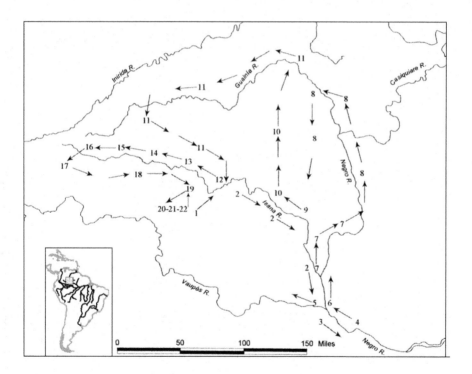

Map 9.1. Place Naming in Chants for Wakuénai Female Initiation Rituals
The numbers 1–22 represent sacred chants in the order of their performance during female initiation rituals.

in chants for female initiation rituals. Chants for male initiates begin at
Amáru's mythic home (Mutsipani) and end at the mythic center (Hípana)
after traversing a vast range of riverine territories throughout the Amazon
and Orinoco basins (map 9.2). The overall effect of place naming in the
chants is to highlight movements back to the mythic center at Hípana. Male
initiation rituals are large social gatherings in which chant-owners and elders from two or more local descent groups initiate a group of adolescent
males. The name for male initiation rituals is *wakapétaka iénpitipé* ("we show
our children"), referring to the period of instruction during which adult men
show the group of male initiates how to make and play the sacred flutes and
trumpets. *Málikai* singing and chanting for the initiates' food takes place on
the final night of ritual activities, and the elders give their speeches of advice
just before dawn.

Like childbirth rituals, male and female initiation rituals use social and
symbolic contrasts between the sexes to build an integral whole that not only
includes but also depends on female as well as male participation. Ritual

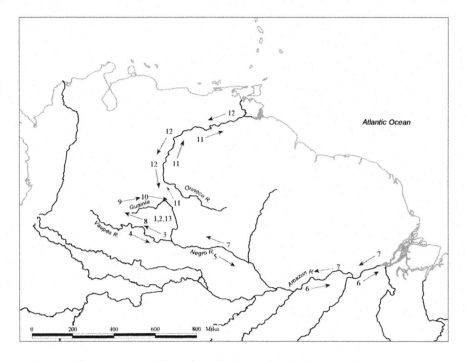

Map 9.2. Place Naming in Chants for Wakuénai Male Initiation Rituals
The numbers 1–13 represent sacred chants in the order of their performance during male initiation
rituals

activities sometimes require strict separation of the sexes, particularly when adult men teach male initiates how to make and play the sacred flutes and trumpets. However, women are not excluded during performances of *máli-kai* singing and chanting, and they are active participants in the giving of ritual advice to male and female initiates. Female reproductive anatomy— wombs, umbilical cords, and menstrual blood—supplies much of the symbolic content for male controlled activities of *málikai* singing and chanting. Ritual appropriations of women's reproductive anatomy do not portray women's fertility as a source of pollution that threatens an all-male realm of purity but as an ambiguously charged, life-giving and life-taking power that must be harnessed to collective processes of producing socialized people and reproducing the interlocking social realms of adult women and men.

The Gendering of History in Northwestern Amazonia

Wakuénai fertility cultism is rooted in a complex set of mythic narratives about the life cycle of the primordial human being, Kúwai, and his mother, Amáru. These creation narratives are preceded and surrounded by other cycles of narratives about the mythic trickster, Iñapirríkuli, and his brothers, Dzuli and Kaali. These narratives describe the continuing efforts of various animal-humans to destroy Iñapirríkuli, but the trickster always manages to outsmart his enemies, who end up becoming victims of their own murderous schemes. Out of this background of unceasing violence, there emerges a cycle of myths about Kúwai, the son of incestuous sexual relations between Iñapirríkuli and Amáru, his paternal aunt. Iñapirríkuli and his brothers take Kúwai from his mother to live in a corner of the sky. Kúwai breaks out of this place of confinement and creates all the species of plants and animals by humming and singing their names. In the remaining myths of the cycle, this world-creating musical and verbal force is brought down to the ground at Hípana, the center of the world, and implanted into human society as the *málikai* songs and chants of sacred rituals. The cycle ends when Iñapirríkuli and his brothers push Kúwai into a great fire, and the world shrinks back to its original miniature size. This first creation cycle outlines the coming into being of a hierarchical ritual structure in which chant-owners and elders mediate between the creative powers of mythic ancestors and the life cycle transitions of younger generations of human descendants.

In the second cycle of creation narratives, the ashes of Kúwai transform into trees and vines used for making sacred flutes and trumpets. Amáru and her female followers take these musical instruments away from Iñapirríkuli and the men. The world opens up for a second time as Amáru and the women

flee from the mythic center and play the sacred flutes and trumpets in various river basins. When Iñapirríkuli finally catches up with Amáru at a lake
near São Gabriel along the Rio Negro, Amáru escapes with the flutes and
trumpets back to her home at Mutsipani through a secret underground passageway. In the end, Iñapirríkuli and the men regain control of the sacred
musical instruments of Kúwai and trick Amáru into believing that the instruments have transformed into various wild animal and bird species. This
second cycle of creation myths poetically describes the coming into being of
a dynamic, expanding universe of peoples living in different river basins
through a series of movements away from and back to the mythic center of
the world. History, or the reproduction of social relations, is driven by the
struggle between men and women for control over the life-giving powers
embodied in the sacred flutes and trumpets of Kúwai.

The second cycle of creation narratives provides a basic template for understanding history and power in ways that are culturally specific to the
Wakuénai of northwestern Amazonia. Like the latticework of streams and
rivers that traverses the equatorial rainforests of the region, history flows in
a continuous movement away from the mythic center of the world at Hípana. The mythic figure of Amáru embodies a feminine agentive power for
constructing history by playing the sacred instruments of Kúwai, thus opening up a cultural landscape of distinct peoples and places. The cycle of myths
also makes room for the sudden, discontinuous twists and turns of history
through the metaphor of Amáru's return to the mythic center via a subter-
ranean passageway.

Although this cycle of creation myths does not make explicit reference to
the specific events of colonial history, one important episode does implicitly comment on the colonial past through an explanation of how *lingua geral*
(or *yeral*, in Spanish) originated. When the trickster arrives at Amáru's hide-
out on a lake near São Gabriel de Cachoeira, he disguises himself as a *geral*
person and speaks to Amáru in *geral*, or *nheengatú*.

> Kamena rúnuka uñaísre.
> "Eh, nudaké," pidaruaku, "kjeti pinu?"
> "Aaa, nunu pukjuete, abo, Kurukwikjite," pidaliaku.
> Kákukani Ñéngatuliko. Kamena likeeñuéetaka Ñéngatú até pandza jekuapi.
> "Kapjá pikaapa Iñapirríkuli, nudaké?" pidaruaku.
> "Karrú pakaapa, abo, karrutsa nuajnédaka Iñapirríkuli," pidaliaku rujliú.
> "Iñapirríkulipami iájniri jieekuítajni jnua," pidaruaku. "Kadzu karru nuájni-
> ka nudáwaka," jniwa pidaruaku.
> "Jnua matsiádaru iéemaka nudzákaleliko," pidruaku.

"Liúkakja waíkajle pandza abó nuíinuákaru mitjani," pidaliaku, "jnua mit-ja íinuani,"pidaliaku.

"Oojontja, nudaké, píinua mitja nudza Iñapirríkuli nukawiña mitja pjiá jor-ré," pidaruaku lisriú.

Already she was coming down to the port.

"Ee, my grandson," she said, "Where are you coming from?"

"Aaa, I am coming from downstream, grandmother, from São Gabriel," he said.

They spoke in *lengua geral*. That is how the *geral* language that is spoken today began.

"You haven't seen Iñapirríkuli around here, my grandson?," she asked.

"I have not seen anything, grandmother, I do not even know this Iñapirríku-li," he replied.

"That shameless Iñapirríkuli goes around persecuting me," she said. "That's why I go about in hiding."

"I live well here in my village," she said.

"If only he were to arrive here today I would kill him," he said, "I'd be sure to kill him."

"If only it were so, my grandson, if you were to kill Iñapirríkuli, I would pay you plenty," she said. (my translation)

At this point, Iñapirríkuli asks Amáru whether he can stay overnight, and she shows him where he can hang his hammock in a house full of men. The men are obligated to stay in seclusion in a separate house so that they will not be able to see Amáru and the women playing the sacred flutes and trumpets for the first female initiation ritual.

Amáru ia líkajle. Rudée lirawa apada kuya padzáwaru.

"Óojon, nudaké, pira padzáwaru," pidaruaku lisriú.

"Joo, abó," pidaliaku. Lira pida tsutsa. Lidieeta rujliú.

Rukaapa pikárrumitsa.

"Pishenina?" pidaruaku.

"Óojon, abó, nuísrenina."

"Paaa," pidaruaku, "mairakatsa nuada pjiá, nudaké. Jliá dekjá Iñapirríkuli-pami, nudaké, jliá dekjá ira jorré," pidaruaku.

"Karrú dekje jnua," pidaliaku. "Karrú nuíraka kadzu Iñapirríkuli íraka pid-za," pidaliaku.

Amáru approached him. She brought a gourd full of manioc beer for him to drink.

"Here, my grandson, drink some beer," she said to him.

"Okay, grandmother," he said. He drank very little, then returned it to her. She saw that the gourd was still full.

"You already drank?" she asked.
"Yes, grandmother, I already drank."
"Paaa," she said, "you drank nothing, my grandson. That shameless Iñapir-ríkuli, my grandson, he really drinks a lot," she said.
"I do not do that," he replied. "I do not drink like Iñapirríkuli," he said. (my translation)

In this dialogue, the trickster uses his verbal skills to create a new language, or *lingua geral,* to conceal his true identity from Amáru. He also refers to her as "Grandmother" and refuses to take more than a mouthful of manioc beer, convincing Amáru that he is really not the trickster but a polite youngster whose presence (except for his masculine gender) is harmless. Irony gives the trickster a limited ability to control the shape of historical change.

The figure of Amáru is connected through this myth with the origins of *lingua geral,* a Tupí-Portuguese trade language introduced in northwestern Amazonia in the late seventeenth or early eighteenth century. It is significant also that the myth points to São Gabriel as the place where *lingua geral* originated, thereby giving mythic significance to the colonial expansion of Portuguese forces up the Rio Negro from a southeasterly direction. In other myths, Amáru is strongly associated with the eastern horizon, the sun's heat as it rises to light up the day, and the biological power of fertility and giving birth. When these associated meanings are coupled with the world-opening powers of Amáru's movements away from and back to the mythic center with Kúwai's instruments, the figure of Amáru makes perfect sense as a metaphor for registering the profound historical changes set in motion during the colonial period.

In ritual performances of *málikai* songs and chants, the name *Amáru* serves as a category of spirits encompassing the new technologies and diseases introduced by European colonizers. Tsimukani Amáru, or "the hot things of Amáru," is the mythic ancestral name given to steel tools, firearms, motors, and other manufactured items in *málikai* chants performed at the birth of children. In curing rituals, *rupapera sru Amáru,* or "the paper of Amáru," is used to categorize measles, smallpox, and other Old World diseases brought by Europeans. All these uses of Amáru's name place the indigenous experience of conquest and colonization into the framework of the mythic expansion of the world during the second creation of the world.

The use of Amáru's name is also important in *málikai* chants for male initiation rituals. In these performances, the naming of peoples, places, and natural species is a highly dynamic, musical process of "going in search of the names" (*wadzújiakaw nakuna*). Just as Iñapirríkuli had to search through every corner of this world to find Amáru and the sacred flutes, so must chant-owners explore every nook and cranny of the collective historical experience of their people in searching for the initiate's souls. However, with the exception of their own patrilineal groups, chant-owners do not use everyday social names for different peoples but the mythic, ancestral names of places and animal species.

The arrival of European peoples into northwestern Amazonia is given active expression through naming of places and animal species. Mythic, ancestral names for the places of European colonization are most prevalent in the chants describing the Rio Negro and other downstream locations to the south and east of Wakuénai lands at the headwaters of the Rio Negro. These European sites are given names in *lingua geral* and include several settlements (Barcelos, Camanão, and Fortaleza) along the Rio Negro that no longer exist but are identifiable in colonial accounts. In addition, these towns are brought into the sacred language of *málikai* chants by combining each of them with the term *dzakare-kwa* ("village-place"). These towns were mission settlements, military outposts, and trading posts near the river port of São Gabriel, and they formed the points of entry for European peoples, material culture, and diseases into the Upper Rio Negro region during the colonial period.

Following the indigenous logic of using animal names to designate peoples in *málikai* chants, the European colonizers who inhabited early colonial settlements are not named according to nationality or other social criteria but through the names of animal species that they introduced into the Upper Rio Negro region. The general name for European colonists in the chants is *rucampo ruyeni Amáru*, or "the children of Amáru's pasture." This categorization of Europeans in the mythic domain of Amáru is consistent with other uses of Amáru's name as a class of "things" brought into the region by Europeans during the colonial period. Within the general category of *rucampo ruyeni Amáru*, the Europeans receive two other mythic ancestral names in *málikai* chants for initiation. *Jnarekada éenunai*, or "the whitish forest animal-spirit," designates the pig, and *natsuwana éenunai*, or "the horned forest animal-spirit," is the mythic ancestral name for cattle. By using animal names as metaphors for the Europeans who colonized the Upper Rio Negro region, the Wakuénai have created collective representations of Western colonial power as part of the dynamic musical opening up of the mythic primordium into an expanding world of peoples and places. By giving ancestors to the pigs, the Wakuénai have socialized colonial history by placing Western colonial power into the framework of hierarchical relations between mythic ancestors and human descendants.

In *málikai* songs performed to counteract the effects of life-threatening witchcraft, the southeasterly direction is given further recognition as the place from which deadly diseases entered Wakuénai territory. This sacred song outlines a mythic journey going from southeast to northwest, beginning at São Gabriel and ending at Maapakwa Makakwi ("The Great Honey Place") near the headwaters of the Rio Guainía. The victim of witchcraft is laid out in a canoe made of beeswax at São Gabriel and begins to recover as he ascends the Isana River. By the time he reaches Maapakwa Makakwi, the man is well enough to walk again, and he travels to a remote village on the Vaupés River. There he is cared for by an elderly woman, who hides him from enemy witches living downstream. The story of the first victim of witchcraft often is performed in shamanic curing rituals. Through this song, the Wakuénai have musically commemorated the historical importance of movements to remote headwater areas to escape the lethal effects of diseases, which entered their lands from the southeast during the colonial period.

It is important to note that this shamanic discourse ends by placing the witchcraft victim under the care and protection of an elderly woman. Wakuénai sacred narratives and ritual discourses often are rooted in metaphors derived from female procreativity: the internal umbilical cord that binds fathers to newborn infants, the cosmic umbilical cord that connects mythic ancestors to human descendants, and the old woman who nurtures and protects witchcraft victims from the lethal gaze of powerful enemy witches. The dangerous creativity of Amáru, the mythic Wild Woman, is socialized in ritual performances by fusion with such images of feminine nurturance, protection, and regeneration. Likewise, it is through the mythic figure of Amáru that the Wakuénai couple the tremendously disruptive forces of colonial history to the socializing powers of shamanic ritual and mythic ancestors. Through ritual performances, images of historical disruption and gender antagonism are transformed into flowing continuity and the interdependence between men and women.

Late Colonial Expansions into Northwestern Amazonia

Through sacred narratives and associated ritual performances, the Wakuénai have preserved a historical memory of how Arawak-speaking peoples engaged the arrival of European peoples into northwestern Amazonia during colonial times. This indigenous vision of colonial history is oriented in a southeasterly direction toward the Lower and Middle Rio Negro in Brazil, thereby converging with written historical sources that demonstrate the overwhelming influence of Portuguese Brazilian colonialism in the region. By the late colonial period, the extensive network of trade relations linking indigenous peoples of northwestern Amazonia to the Manao and other Arawak-speaking peoples of the Lower Rio Negro basin had been largely severed and replaced by new regional patterns of interethnic trade with eastern Tukanoan peoples in the Vaupés basin (see Hill 1996b).

One noteworthy feature of this regional historical scenario is the absence of any reference to Spanish colonialism in Wakuénai narratives and rituals. All evidence points to the pronounced influence of Portuguese Brazilian colonial power: *lingua geral,* Brazilian settlements along the Lower Rio Negro, and the arrival of European diseases from the Lower Rio Negro. One explanation for the invisibility of Spanish colonialism in local histories is that the Spanish did not make formal claims in the area until the late boundary expeditions led by Francisco Solano in the 1750s. Only fifty years later, the Wars of Independence began in the Llanos and coastal areas far to the north, and the thin line of Spanish mission settlements and forts fell into neglect as political energies were expended elsewhere. There is no doubt that Spanish colonial presence was weaker, later, and less systematic in northwestern Amazonia than that of Brazil. However, there is another important reason why Spanish colonialism has remained so absent from regional history: the Yekuana-led uprising in the Middle and Upper Orinoco basin in 1776.

The Spanish recognized the importance of the Upper Orinoco as a buffer against Portuguese incursions from the south and established settlements at La Esmeralda, Solano, Maroa, San Carlos de Rio Negro, and other strategic locations. After a brief initial period of cooperation in which the Spanish lavished goods on the Yekuana, a Carib-speaking people of the Ventuari and Cunucunuma rivers, relations between the Spanish and their indigenous hosts turned sour during the 1760s and 1770s. According to Guss (1986, 420), "By 1767 the Spanish had embarked on a more aggressive policy of colonization of the Upper Orinoco. In an attempt to secure the entire region, an expeditionary force was sent out to build a road and 19 small forts connecting Angostura with La Esmeralda. This ambitious plan, which to this day has never been accomplished, was to cut directly through the homeland of the Yekuana. Refusing to cooperate, the Yekuana were forcibly relocated and set to work on chain gangs. This also marked their first exposure to Christianity, as Capuchin missionaries were dispatched to actively convert them. Amazed by this sudden change in behavior, the Yekuana decided that this was not Iaranavi, but rather a different species altogether. Fañuru, as they called him, was a creation of Odosha. Along with their allies, the Fadre (Padres, priests), they had come from Caracas to overrun their friend Iaranavi in Angostura." Conflicts between the Yekuana and the Spanish reached a climax in 1776, when a Yekuana-led coalition of indigenous groups rebelled and destroyed all nineteen forts, driving the Spanish out of their territory for the next century and a half.

What is remarkable about the story of Yekuana resistance to Spanish colonialism is that they were unusually successful at repulsing Spanish military forces from their territory. Whereas other sedentary, horticultural peoples of the Llanos and tropical forests were simply overpowered and engulfed by missionization and frontier expansion, the Yekuana constructed a social barrier that halted Spanish expansion just as effectively as the natural obstacle of the Atures and Maipures rapids along the Middle Orinoco. Had it not been for the successful Yekuana uprising, many other indigenous peoples of the Venezuelan Amazon would almost certainly have suffered the same fate as the Maipure, Achagua, and other missionized peoples living in accessible areas.

Today the Yekuana remember these historical events in a highly poeticized set of mythic and historical stories that form a continuation of their cycle of creation myths, the Watunna. Like many other indigenous histories in South America, the Watunna situates the indigenous society in a very ambivalent relationship to expanding colonial and national states. The mythic creator (Wanadi) furnishes a limited number of "Good White People," firearms, and generous supplies of trade goods, whereas the creator's destructive brother (Odosha) provides an infinite number of "Evil White People," rivers filled with corpses, enslaving missionaries, and rapists who were "looking for people to kill and eat." The Watunna not only commemorates the violent events of the late colonial period but also creatively reworks major facts and events of the past into a social discourse. For example, the Yekuana compress the complex act of rebellion against the Spanish into the supernaturally powerful figure of Mahaiwadi, a great shaman capable of transforming into mythic predators who kill and eat the Spanish soldiers and missionaries.

Before leaving this world, Wanadi created healing medicines and a source of material wealth so that his people, the Yekuana, would not remain defenseless in the violent world controlled by Odosha and the Spaniards. According to Civrieux (1980, 160), "Wanadi went to the edge of the Earth, to the shore of the sea, to find Hurunko [the Dutch] and his village, Amenadiña. Hurunko was wise and powerful. He was a good man. . . . Wanadi went to his house in the Sky, in the North, on the other side of the sea. He got shotguns, hooks, machetes, knives, shirts. He brought it all back and gave it to Hurunko. Then he started walking again. He made more houses. He made the other tribes. He made the Piaroa, the Makú, the Yabarana, the Warekena, the Baniwa, the Makushi. He made them all. He made lots of people to fight Odosha and his Fañuru [Spaniards]."

Wanadi's final act of mythic creation was to make the Saliban, Arawakan, and other indigenous peoples of the Upper Orinoco and Negro rivers to help fight against Odosha and the Spaniards. The Watunna thus provides insight into a profound historical truth: The Yekuana-led uprising of 1776 created a social barrier that gave indigenous peoples of the Upper Orinoco and Negro rivers a chance to survive Spanish colonialism in the late eighteenth century.

This Yekuana interpretation of late colonial history is important because it connects the activity of resistance against Spanish colonial authority to two related historical processes. First, the Watunna relates the 1776 uprising to the repositioning of the Yekuana within the scheme of competing colonial powers in northern South America such that they could continue to have access to firearms, steel tools, and other trade goods via the Dutch trading posts along the Essequibo River. And second, the Watunna associates the uprising with the creator-god's making of "the other tribes"—including Arawak-speaking peoples of the Upper Rio Negro region—as allies forming a coalition against the Spanish. These two processes interact synergistically because the routes taken by the Yekuana to reach their new source of trade goods went south to the Rio Negro, over to the Rio Branco in Brazil, and then north to Guyana and Suriname by traveling east of the Roraima highlands. After the 1776 uprising, the Yekuana could no longer travel directly north and east to reach the Dutch trading posts along the Essequibo because of the strong Spanish presence along the Lower Orinoco and its southern tributaries, such as the Caroní River (Guss 1986). Thus, to carry out their new alliance with the Dutch, the Yekuana had no choice but to travel through Baniwa, Warekena, and other Arawak-speaking peoples' territories in the Upper Orinoco and Negro river basins.

Conclusions

In this chapter I have outlined some of the ways in which the culture area concept may be retheorized from a descriptive, taxonomic device into an analytical context for making broader comparative generalizations. In particular, I have suggested that the culture area concept can be retheorized by integrating it within a macro-level political approach to history and articulating it with the analysis of indigenous histories that register, engage, and creatively rework this political history. The result of this integrated approach is an understanding of culture areas as products of the intertwining of two or more formerly distinct histories into a single colonial history open to multiple interpretations. Thus conceived, the culture area concept can serve as a middle ground between local and global levels of analysis by encompassing sociocultural phenomena that persist over long periods of historical time and that are spread across vast geographic and political spaces (Knauft 1999, 7).

This chapter also suggests that another way of retheorizing the culture area concept is by exploring culturally specific interpretations of history and power. These indigenous perspectives of history and power are not focused solely on local communities but also include a concern for complex and dynamic intercommunal, even interregional relations. The Wakuénai story of the second mythic creation and its expression in ritually performed chants, for example, shows an indigenous awareness of movements to and from regions that are geographically distant from the mythic center of the world. Likewise, the Yekuana story of making "the other tribes" covers a vast region spreading from the Middle Orinoco basin in the north to the Rio Branco basin in the south and from the Rio Negro in the west to the Essequibo River in the east. Moreover, these indigenous histories are constructed in ways that presuppose culturally specific relations of power and that seek to resolve contradictions between these local forms of authority and the alien forms of power introduced into Lowland South America by colonial governments. In both the Wakuénai and Yekuana historical narratives, the process of socializing these alien forms of power is directly tied to the commemoration of past events, places, and processes. Infusing the culture area concept with a concern for history and power, both at the macropolitical level and in terms of indigenous ways of defining history and power at local and regional levels, is another way to restore the concept's utility as an analytic context capable of supporting broader comparative theory.

In addition, this chapter supports the conclusion that the valorizing of culturally specific idioms of history and power offers a valuable corrective against the tendency to give too much weight to global dimensions of social change. For the most part, histories of South America have been written from masculinist or ostensibly gender-neutral perspectives.[3] The Wakuénai use of the mythic figure of Amáru as a primary historical trope provides insight into a gender-inflected mode of historical consciousness. The indigenous view of history as a process of transforming gender antagonism into complementarity, and the corresponding view of regional space as an actively expanding, continuous network of political-material relations, enriches the existing anthropological and other scholarly ways of conceptualizing culture, power, and history.

Notes

1. Geopolitical marginalization in relation to Euro-American states does not imply that the two regions were marginal in terms of indigenous ethnopolitical relations. The Montaña area of Peru was at the center of extensive trade relations between the Incan and earlier states of the Andean highlands and the tropical forest societies of the Amazon basin.

Northwestern Amazonia is located along the main fluvial passageway connecting the Orinoco and Amazon river basins of Lowland South America.

    2. The comparison must be qualified because the Peruvian Montaña region underwent an earlier period of missionization, population losses, and recovery in the mid-eighteenth century. In northwestern Amazonia, intensive European colonization did not commence until the mid-eighteenth century.

    3. See Silverblatt (1987) for an exception.

10 Secret Religious Cults and Political Leadership: Multiethnic Confederacies from Northwestern Amazonia

SILVIA M. VIDAL

The contemporary Baré and Warekena are two Arawak-speaking groups that inhabit several townships of the Upper Guainía–Rio Negro region in the Venezuelan Amazon (map 10.1). There are about 600 Warekena and 2,000 Baré in Venezuela, who are part of a macroregional sociopolitical system with some other 40,000 Tukanos, Makús, and Arawaks living in Venezuela, Colombia, and Brazil (map 10.2). This system is characterized by extensive multilingualism, exogamy, and varied modalities of interethnic relationships (Chernela 1993; Hill 1983, 1993; Jackson 1983; Vidal 1993, 1999; Wright 1981).

Although European colonization of the Upper Orinoco and Rio Negro basins began in the middle of the seventeenth century, the occupation and the definitive control of the Amazon region did not occur until well into the eighteenth century. Indeed, it is only by the middle of the eighteenth century that one can speak of the implantation of the colonial system and of the intensification of social, ethnic, and cultural relationships between European and indigenous peoples. From the sixteenth to the mid-seventeenth centuries, the ancient forefathers of the contemporary Arawak-, Tukano-, and Makú-speaking groups were part of the Manoa and Oniguayal (also known as Omagua) macropolities (or "macro-regional political and economic systems"; see Vidal 1993) of the Northwest and Central Amazon. These macropolities were multiethnic, multilingual, sociopolitical, and economic systems, which had an internal interethnic hierarchy led by a paramount chief ("lord" or "king") and a powerful elite of secondary chiefs; leadership was hereditary (Whitehead 1994; Vidal 1993). Early European documents of the great river basins of the Orinoco and the Amazon refer to the existence of extensive connections between groups (riverine and hinterland peoples) within and between macropolities (Acuña 1864; Almesto 1986; Cuervo 1893–4; De la Cruz 1986; Federmann 1916; Llanos and Pineda 1982; Simón 1882; Whitehead 1988, 1993a). According to Whitehead (1993a), these connections were based on regional trade systems. But I consider these regional trade systems to be only one of the more visible dimensions of Amerindian sociocultural connections and political relations.

European colonization of the Rio Negro basin began in the mid-seventeenth century. However, Portuguese, Spanish, Dutch, French, and British colonial empires were competing with each other and with some of the more powerful Amerindian groups of local macropolities to establish control over indigenous populations and regional trade systems of the Orinoco and

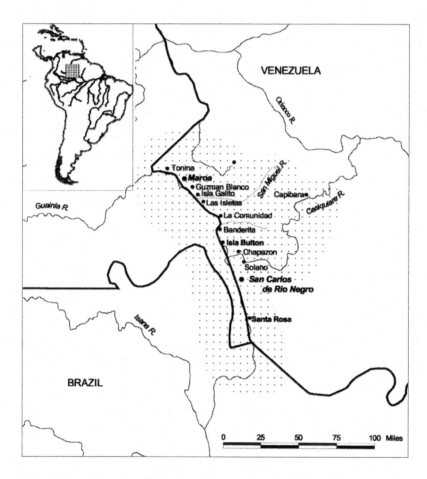

Map 10.1. Present Location of Arawakan Townships in the Rio Negro Basin

Map 10.2. Present Location of Amerindian Peoples in Northwestern Amazonia

Amazon rivers. Although Oniguayal leadership disappeared by the early seventeenth century, the powerful leadership of the Manoa macropolity appears to have been able to survive until the late 1650s, when it began to lose its political and economic hold on the region. By the end of the seventeenth century, the Manoa and other macropolities of the Negro, Orinoco, and Amazon rivers were experiencing dynamic processes of transformation and disintegration. Internal sociopolitical contradictions and conflicts, the demographic decimation of Amerindian populations (diseases, enslavement, and the like), and the European colonization of the Negro and Orinoco rivers led to radical disruptions. Such processes caused the mobilization and regrouping of indigenous peoples, and by the early eighteenth century they gave rise to new sociopolitical formations, which I call "multiethnic confederacies" (Vidal 1993).

By the eighteenth century the forefathers of contemporary Warekena and Baré were groups belonging to different multiethnic confederacies. European written documents describe these powerful Arawak-speaking groups as being associated with each other through trading networks, indigenous rebellions, the religions of Kúwai, and sacred places. In this chapter I examine how the integration and relationship between male ritual societies and the religion of Kúwai constitute the sociopolitical and religious basis for the regional leadership of powerful Arawak-speaking chiefs and groups. I also analyze the key role played by the relations between their sociopolitical structure and secret religious cults in the emergence of multiethnic confederacies.

The Warekena and Baré Sociopolitical and Religious Structure

Contemporary Warekena and Baré groups share not only important aspects of their cultural and political histories but also an internally hierarchical sociopolitical structure that is organized in several patrilineal, localized, and exogamic phratries. Each phratry consists of two or more sibs ranked according to the birth order of the ancestral mythic brothers.

Hierarchy is a criterion by which people and place are classified into a given status, and it influences both intragroup and intergroup alliances. It also plays an important role in processes and mechanisms of ethnogenesis and social reproduction. Each phratry and sib is identified with a specific area within its group's territory in the San Miguel, Guainía, Casiquiare, Upper Orinoco, and Upper Rio Negro. Localized phratries and sibs exercise political and economic control over rivers, sacred places, and natural resources of their territories. However, this territorial control can be negotiated through economic bargaining and political alliances between phratries and groups. For example, in the written sources of the seventeenth and eighteenth centuries (Acuña 1864; Betendorf 1910; Ribeiro de Sampaio 1825; Vidal 1993, 142–43) it is pointed out that there were territorial boundaries well defined among the Baré, Manao, Cariaya, Wirina, Mepuri, and Mavez. However, these boundaries were flexible enough to allow partialities of each group (the Manao-Urumanao) to inhabit or exploit the territory of partialities of the other (the Baré-Mariarana).

Exogamy makes it possible for these groups and their subgroups to associate with each other and with other societies. Warekena, Baré, and other Arawak-speaking groups practice a nonlinguistic exogamy and place all their in-laws ("the other") in a single category, allocating to them ambivalent and contradictory meanings ("people," "nonpeople," "relative" or "brother-in-law," potential "ally" or "enemy," and so on) (Hill 1987, 190–91; Vidal 1987,

1993, 1999). These social relationships are deeply embedded in systems of religious belief as well as the potential for constructing both vertical and horizontal hierarchical structures. These symbolic and organizational factors have influenced their forms of leadership, control over and expansion of their alliances, and the emergence of interregional political alliances and multi-ethnic confederacies.

Cross-cousin marriage is practiced among the Baré and Warekena, but their marriage system is focused mainly on expanding alliances to incorporate other groups with whom they are not related by traditional affinal links (Vidal 1987, 1993, 1999).[1] This is the result of a complex relationship between these practices and the service paid by sons-in-law to fathers-in-law, the localization of the descent units, the rule of patrilocal residence, the establishment and increment of political networks, and the cycle of ceremonial exchange of goods of different class or value (i.e., smoked fish and other aquatic and terrestrial animals for vegetable products) between affines.

The enormous potential that the Baré and Warekena system of marriage networks has for politicoregional alliances is also evident in the prohibition of marriage between individuals that belong to descent units sharing the same totemic symbol and possibly the same mythical ancestors (Vidal 1993). This rule supports the inclusion as kin of a larger number of segments and populations both at a regional level in the category of "siblings" ("we" or "us") and in the amplification of alliance networks between affinal kin of diverse groups ("they" or "the others").[2] This system of regional exogamy, in turn, is related to and based on their religious system as well as their traditional beliefs regarding the origin of the world and the ancestors.

This social structure and associated political networks of peoples is grounded in the shared Kúwai (also Kuwé, or Yuruparí) religious system. This religious system is divided into two or more mythical cycles; each cycle, consisting of a corpus of narratives (e.g., stories, myths, chants, songs, prayers, advice), ritual knowledge, puberty rites, male secret societies, and festivals, comprises a wide variety of ideological symbolic and practical codes. These codes teach important knowledge that has been associated with Kúwai and the Trickster Creator (Napirríkuli or Nápiruli). Moreover, these codes have influenced and oriented indigenous peoples' strategies to face events and situations of their ritual and secular lives.

For the Warekena, Baré, and other Arawak-speaking groups, the origin of people is linked with a unique and special place that is shared by all groups. In this place, the first ancestors emerged in a hierarchical order from older to younger siblings, and from there they dispersed throughout the Orinoco-Amazon region. This hierarchical emergence not only refers to each Arawakan phratry and sib but also to each non-Arawak-speaking group of the northwest Amazon.

Both their historical interpretation and their mythic representation of the world, natural beings, society, and humankind are closely related to the Warekena and Baré's system of ancient beliefs. Mythic narratives and oral history constitute two complementary genres influencing one another through which these people can narrate, tell, and interpret their present and past processes of change.

The Religion of Kúwai and Male Ritual Societies

According to Filintro Rojas (1994), a Wakuénai historian, in the "beginnings" (*miyaka*) or genesis of the universe (and of the Milky Way and of the planet Earth), the Unique Spiritual Being (only thought) was the epicenter of a big emptiness (there was neither place, space, nor time), and everything was in silence. Here that being is known as Makuku, or silence.[3] Then Makuku with his thought begins the creation of all life, separating time and space, and speaks to the universe. At that moment, after speaking, he becomes Dukuku, and his speech, song, and voice (as a thunder) divide both the universe between darkness and light and the creation in six steps. In each one of the stages one of their child-spirit creations speaks. In the fifth step, Kúwai, the magnifier or enlarger of the firmament and voice of the world, is heard.

For contemporary Warekena and Baré groups, Kúwai, Kuwé, Kúai, Katsimánali,[4] or Yuruparí[5] is the voice of the creation that opened up the world. He is described as a monstrous, primordial human being (Hill 1993, xvii) whose body is made of all elements of this world (except fire, which could have destroyed him). He is the master of all visible and invisible beings (Wright 1993), and capable of controlling the sky and the universe through his powerful knowledge. Thus, he came to this world to teach people all his sacred ritual powers.

Kasimájada (in Baré) or *Kasíjmakasi* (in Warekena) is the name of rituals dedicated to the cult of Kúwai and the forefathers or first ancestors and of puberty rites of young boys and girls. In these rituals, Kúwai, his troops, and the elders reproduce the time-space and the actions of the beginnings: the creation of the first people and their sociopolitical organization. And the elders also transmit their history and important knowledge to the new generations.

Kasimájada ceremonies are held by a group of men who include ritual authorities, prominent elders, and initiated adult men. This group of men is associated with a hierarchical political and religious structure, or male ritual society, which represents Kúwai and his troop. This politico-religious structure organizes all initiated men into a hierarchical order that includes from higher to lower status the positions of chiefs, masters, warriors, shamans, and servants.

In theory, chiefs are charismatic political leaders who have training in the arts of war, speak several indigenous languages, and possess valuable knowledge on history, myths, and rituals. They also have extraordinary shamanic powers. However, in the present day, chiefs are the leaders or "captains" of their communities. Masters are ritual specialists with profound knowledge of myths, dances, songs, prayers, and oral history of the group. Also, masters lead dances and songs during rituals, and they teach this knowledge to newly initiated men. They also act as advisors about Kúwai rituals to chiefs and shamans. Warriors are men who possess important knowledge in the arts of war. They can manage all type of weapons, guard their communities during the celebration of Kuwé rituals, and defend all members of the secret male society and the teachings of the Kuwé against intruders and outsiders. Shamans are mediators between the world of human beings, the natural environment, and that of supernatural beings and ancestral spirits.[6] They perform important rites during Kúwai celebrations such as blessing and blowing tobacco over the initiate's food. Servants collect plentiful amounts of tobacco cigarettes and other ritual paraphernalia, including food and drinks sufficient for all the people. During Kuwé festivals, they help shamans and masters with their ritual tasks.

The close relationship between mythical Kúwai and his troop and male ritual society, or politico-religious hierarchy, is based on the association that Arawak-speaking groups establish between mythic or first ancestors (*Inépe mikí náwi*) and the living elders (*pjénawi*). *Inépe mikí náwi* can be real or mythic ancestors from a very distant past such as Nápiruli, Kuwé, and others. *Pjénawi* or *péinjli-náwi* are living adults with great wisdom and important historical, mythical, ritual, and practical knowledge.

At present, Kasimájada rituals are carried out once or twice a year (in the summer or in the rainy season) and can last three or more days. On the first day, with the arrival of Kúwai and his troop, women, children, and all non-initiated people hide in a place (in the village or in the forest) where they cannot see the sacred animal instruments. Later, that same day, young boys are confined in the Táli, or sacred place outside their town, where Kuwé and his troop are also located and where all of them will remain until the final day of the ritual. The girl-initiates remain in their community under the custody of one or more old women. During the whole ceremony, all the people fast, and they consume only water, *yucuta*, or *seje* juice. This collective fast concludes with the ritual of "tasting" the food by young boys and girls who are undergoing initiation into adulthood. The shaman blows tobacco over this ritual food, which consists of several types of fish, different meats of game animals, wild fruits, and manioc breads and flour. After this ritual, the rest of the food is distributed among those attending the ceremony.

After the young boys are told and shown the secrets of Kúwai, all the participants of the ritual, including the boy- and girl-initiates, are lashed on their backs and chests with whips (*adábi*), made with strong lianas or branches of trees knitted with *curagua* (a fiber), in whose tips animal teeth and bones are placed to lacerate or mark the skin.

During the ceremony of Kasimájada, Kuwé's sacred instruments are played, collective dances are performed, and beautiful songs relating the history of the first ancestors are sung. For the last dance, when the men already initiated return to their community, all the people dress properly, paint their bodies with *chica* (a red coloring), adorn their heads with beautiful attire made of feathers, and draw on their backs the sacred totems of their sibs and phratries.

In Kasimájada rituals Kuwé's knowledge is learned not only by young boys and girls but also by men in their secret meetings to perform Kúwai rituals and dances. Although women are initiated in the religion of Kúwai during their puberty rites, they do not belong to secret societies. But they also learn important aspects of oral history, myths, and ritual knowledge related to the teachings of Kúwai, and for that reason women often advise men during the celebration of Kúwai rituals.

The religion of Kúwai is also associated with Kuwé Duwákalumi, a complex set of geographic, geopolitical, ecological, botanical, and zoological teachings and knowledge (Vidal 2000).[7] Kuwé Duwákalumi also includes mythical journeys and a complex network of land and water routes that connects different regions of South America. These routes also represent the location and connection with sacred places related to the creation of the world, people, and social order and to the performance of ceremonies of Kuwé's religion and shamanic rituals; sacred and secular strategic resources (i.e., gold, silver, and stones); and peoples and places for sociopolitical, migratory, and commercial purposes. In sum, Kuwé Duwákalumi illustrates not only the different routes opened up by the Kuwé of each Arawak-speaking group but also the extension of the explored geographic areas, the location and limits of each ethnic territory, and certain places or landmarks in South America that have been used for secular or sacred purposes by each of the Arawak-speaking groups and their allies.

The Religion of Kúwai in Oral History and Myths

The mythico-historical and ritual narratives of the Warekena and Baré can be separated into three cycles or sets of narratives that comprise and outline complex processes of ethnogenesis and cosmogenesis. The first cycle of narratives begins at Jípana or Hípana, an ancient community located on the Ayarí River, which is considered the mythical place of the Beginning of the World. Nápiruli (the trickster creator) created the first world and was entrusted to eliminate all the dangerous animals and imperfections. At that time, Nápiruli, Amáruyawa (primordial woman), the first Kuwé and a group of human-animal beings inhabited the world. However, this first world was destroyed by a great flood from which only Nápiruli, Amáruyawa, and some human-animal beings survived.

The second cycle narrates the expansion of the miniature first world until it reaches its natural size, with mountains, rivers, and forests. Nápiruli inhabited this second world, the three sons of Nápiruli, Amáruyawa, the second Kuwé, Káli, some human-animal beings, and the first ancestors. This cycle explains the life and death of Kuwé. He taught agriculture (*kalítani*) and the sacred rituals of initiation to the first ancestors. Nápiruli killed Kuwé in a great fire at the end of the first ritual Kuwé performed for the first ancestors. Then he left this world and went to heaven. From his ashes sprouted the materials for making the sacred flutes and trumpets ("his voice"), which are played in initiation and other sacred rituals today. Later, Amáruyawa and other women stole the sacred instruments from the initiated men, and this act of Amáruyawa and her troop of women set off a long chase, opening the world for a second time, starting on the Ayarí and Isana rivers and spreading to different places in the Orinoco, Negro, and Amazon basins. This long chase ends when Nápiruli and his men regain control over Kuwé's instruments.

According to the Warekena and Baré, the death of Kuwé and Nápiruli's chase after Amáruyawa and the women were two of the most important moments in their history because they changed forever the culture and society of their forefathers. Since then, the forefathers of contemporary Arawak-speaking groups gathered together to celebrate initiation rituals.

The third cycle of narratives relates social and political relationships between peoples, between people and their ancestors, and between human beings and powerful spirits from other parts of the cosmos. This cycle also tells the connections between different regions of the cosmos. It narrates the human past of mythic ancestors such as Nápiruli, Amáruyawa, Purúnamínali ("giver of names"), Puméyawa, Kuámasi, and some other real and mythic forefathers. This set of narratives takes place mostly in Warekena and Baré ancestral lands and is also connected with some of their economic, migratory, commercial, political, and shamanic activities.

The oral history of the Warekena and Baré (the history of their ancestors) can be divided into three important phases or periods that implied processes of unification of different peoples and of sociopolitical and religious transformation. The first phase occurs in the Isana River, when the world was created, and it is related to the first cycle of mythical narratives. The second one deals with the transformation of rituals of initiation and Kuwé cult into a religion that includes a warrior organization and male ritual societies. It began during the time of the grandfathers Deréderé (-náwi) and Benábena, when they introduced initiation rites for young girls. First, by Kuwé routes they traveled to different places inviting relatives, in-laws, and friends to the ritual, and all the people gathered at Maracoa (now known as San Fernando de Atabapo, in the Upper Orinoco). Later, in Capihuara and other places of the Casiquiare basin, the forefathers performed an important initiation rite for the daughters of grandfather Siwali (an ancient powerful leader of the Warekena). There was a great concentration of different peoples (ancestors of the Baré, Warekena, Baniva, and so on), which was led by Dépenabe, the master of the rite and Dzúli as the great shaman. Since then, the forefathers of the Warekena, Baré, and many other groups related to them and their in-laws and allies started to celebrate puberty rites for both men and women. In this way the religion of Kuwé began.

The third period begins when the Kakáhau people murder Puméyawa and her husband in the Aguachapita River, an affluent of the Casiquiare River. They killed her because Puméyawa saw their Kuwé, and in this way she broke the sacred laws of the religion of Kúwai. Before dying she gave birth to Kuámasi (or Kuámati, in Baré), who was protected and raised by the Inámalu and Inilíwiyu peoples. When he grew older, Kuámasi drove a war against the Kakáhau people, their allies, and in-laws. Kuámasi and his men killed captain Ipíchipiméjli and most of the Kakáhau people. The victory of Kuámasi generated a new process of sociopolitical reorganization, which started another generation of groups or peoples.

In these oral histories the names of some of the mythical and historical ancestors of the Warekena and Baré are intermingled, especially those of Nápiruli, Purunamínali, and Kuwé with names of famous warrior-chiefs of the eighteenth century such as Cocui, Davipe, Cabi, Cayama, and Basimúnare. It is also interesting to highlight that in these narratives the ancestors are portrayed as a group of men building and opening roads, writing messages and teachings on riverine stones (petroglyphs), and traveling by Kuwé routes. Warekena and Baré oral traditions recount that along Kuwé routes there were many places and limits that demarcated the borders between two or more ethnic groups, which were watched over by Kúwai and his troop. It is also said that in those places, and elsewhere when they met, each Kúwai and his troop (i.e., men from different male ritual societies) greeted each other, challenged each other, and engaged in symbolic or real combat.

In the beginnings, during his lifetime, Kuwé and his troop traveled through different regions and places in Amazonia; after his death, other mythical ancestors and living elders continued traveling north, west, and east of the Amazon basin. During the eighteenth century, some powerful Warekena and Baré leaders were impersonating Kuwé and his troop and were traveling, migrating, trading, and battling, following the teachings and knowledge of their mythical first ancestors. For the Arawak-speaking groups, the integration and relationship between male ritual societies and the teachings and knowledge of the Kúwai constitute a model of and for their societies and sociopolitical relationships. In present and past historical situations, the integration and relationship between male ritual societies and the cult of Kúwai formed the sociopolitical and religious basis that sustained the regional leadership of powerful Arawakan chief-warriors.

Secret Religious Cults, Regional Leadership, and Multiethnic Confederacies

By the eighteenth century, the forefathers of contemporary Warekena and Baré were affiliated with different multiethnic confederacies. The multiethnic confederacies were flexible and varied in their ethnic membership and were led by charismatic shaman-warrior chiefs. Most of these confederacies can be described as having a "theocratic-genealogical" mode of leadership (Whitehead 1994, 39), in which powerful chiefs based their political authority on their ability to build a personal following (kinfolk, in-laws, and allies), their skills as regional traders (especially of European goods), and their shamanic knowledge and power. However, by the second half of the eighteenth century there were some Arawakan partialities and groups who privileged a "trading-military" mode of leadership (Whitehead 1994, 39) because they were influenced by both their continuous insertion within colonial regimes and their close relationships with Caribs and eastern Tukanoan groups. This mode of leadership was based on control over people through military subjugation and the conversion of trading partners into political supporters and military allies.

From 1700 to 1770 there were as many as fifteen multiethnic confederacies led by Arawak-speaking groups (tables 10.1, 10.2, and 10.3). For the period between 1700 and 1725, the forefathers of Warekena and Baré groups and their

Table 10.1. Arawak-led Multiethnic Confederacies in the Orinoco–Rio Negro Basin, 1700–1725

1. The Manao Confederacy
   Groups: Manao, Baré, Makú, Tiburí, Mabazarí, Javarí, Bumajana, and Mayapena
   Principal warrior-chief: Ayuricawa o Ajuricaba
   Other chiefs: Debajarí, Bejarí, Basuriana, Caricuá, Camandary, Aduana

2. The Cauaburicena Confederacy
   Groups: Baré and other peoples of the Middle and Lower Rio Negro
   Principal warrior-chief: Curunamá
   Other chiefs: (?)

3. The Aranacoacena Confederacy
   Groups: Baré and other groups of the Middle and Upper Rio Negro (?)
   Principal warrior-chief: (?)
   Other chiefs: (?)

Source: Silvia M. Vidal, "Reconstrucción de los Procesos de Etnogénesis y de Reproducción Social entre los Baré de Río Negro, Siglos XVI–XVIII" (Ph.D. diss., Centro de Estudios Avanzados, Instituto Venezolano de Investigaciones Científicas, 1993).

Table 10.2. Arawak-led Multiethnic Confederacies in the Orinoco–Rio Negro Basin, 1725–55

1. The Demanao Confederacy
   Groups: Baré, Manao, Warekena, Cubeo, Makú
   Principal warrior-chief: Camanao
   Other chiefs: Maça, Manacaçari, Ignacio, Ioa, Mababire, Jauinuman, Immo, Cocui, Dauema, Auajari, Juviary, Cayamu, Murú, Cauínarao, Mabé, Inao, Yune

2. The Madáwaka Confederacy
   Groups: Baré, Mabana, Warekena, Yahure, Guinau, Anauyá, Baniva, Desana, Makú, Guariba, Yekuana
   Principal warrior-chief: Guaicana (1725-45), Amuni (1745-54), Mavideo (1755-60)
   Other chiefs: Mabiú, Mará, Amuni, Arucuní, Cavi or Caavi, Tape, Guarena, Guaipure, Guarape, Yurico, Mapure

3. The Boapé-Pariana-Maniva Confederacy
   Groups: Baniwa or Curripaco, Mabana, Meoana or Arapaço, Mäbei, Cubeo, Yapoa, Makú, Baré, Warekena, Puinave, Desana, Tariana, Chapuena, Guaipunavi
   Principal warrior-chief: Cunaguari or Cunaguasi
   Other chiefs: Yavita, Boapé, Macapu, Cuceru or Cruceru

Source: Silvia M. Vidal, "Reconstrucción de los Procesos de Etnogénesis y de Reproducción Social entre los Baré de Río Negro, Siglos XVI–XVIII" (Ph.D. diss., Centro de Estudios Avanzados, Instituto Venezolano de Investigaciones Científicas, 1993).

Table 10.3. Arawak-led Multiethnic Confederacies in the Orinoco–Rio Negro Basin, 1755–70

---

1. The Darivazauna Confederacy
   Groups: Baré, Warekena, Piapoco, Puinave, Cubeo
   Principal warrior-chief: Mara
   Other chiefs: Davipe or Dauipe, Dojo, Mabiú

2. The Amuisana Confederacy
   Groups: Baniva, Baré, Yavitero, Desana
   Principal warrior-chief: Amuni
   Other chiefs: Dauiba, Teyo, Arucuná, Yavita

3. The Tariana-Maniba Confederacy
   Groups: Tariana, Curripaco, Uanano, Cubeo, others (?)
   Principal warrior-chief: Boapé
   Other chiefs: (?)

4. The Guaipunavi Confederacy
   Groups: Guaipunavi, Parcune, Docionavi, Puinave, Megepure, Warekena, Macirinavi, Parrene, Maipure, Caverre
   Principal warrior-chief: Cuceru
   Other chiefs: Capi, Guayucava, Mabari

5. The Marabitana Confederacy
   Groups: Baré, Manao, Guinao, Catarapene, Yahure, Makú, Guariba
   Principal warrior-chief: Immo (1755-64), Cocui
   Other chiefs: Cocui, Cayamu, Inao

6. The Madáwaka Confederacy
   Groups: Baré-Madáwaka, Baniva, Haruca, Mawakwa, Anauyá, Yekuana
   Principal warrior-chief: Davillape or Davicape
   Other chiefs: Caavi

Source: Silvia M. Vidal, "Reconstrucción de los Procesos de Etnogénesis y de Reproducción Social entre los Baré de Río Negro, Siglos XVI–XVIII" (Ph.D. diss., Centro de Estudios Avanzados, Instituto Venezolano de Investigaciones Científicas, 1993).

allies were regrouped in three multiethnic confederacies: the Manao confederacy, the Cauaburicena confederacy, and the Aranacoacena confederacy. Between 1700 and 1730, most of these confederated groups and their leaders were devoted to intensive trading of their own commercial products and slaves with each other and with Portuguese, French, Spanish, and Dutch colonies in exchange for guns and other European goods. During this period there were many different European camps, also known as *arraiales,* or corrals, which were used to keep captive indigenous slaves and for the control of indigenous and European trade between colonies.

On one hand, the instability of these new ethnic formations, their possession of a great number of European weapons, and their definitive integration into the colonial commercial networks of European goods led to competition and internecine conflicts between leading groups of these indigenous confederacies. On the other hand, European economic ambitions and fears of these powerful indigenous peoples pushed colonial authorities not only to intensify their explorations and patrols of some of the more important commercial routes but also to compete with the Amerindian polities and other rival colonial powers to gain control over strategic areas of the Negro and Orinoco river basins. Thus, the European colonial system itself and interactions between European and indigenous peoples were decisive for the creation and transformation of these new ethnic sociopolitical formations.

For the period between 1730 and 1755, important reorganization and fusion processes took place that gave rise to four new multiethnic confederacies: the Demanao confederacy, the Madáwaka confederacy, the Boapé-Maniva confederacy, and the Guaipunavi confederacy. The violent wars between several indigenous groups and the defeat of the Manao by Portuguese colonial forces were the causes that generated both important Amerindian migrations toward the Upper Rio Negro and Upper Orinoco and the emergence of the Guaipunavi confederacy. Crossing the borders between Portuguese, Spanish, and other European colonies was a common strategy used by the Guaipunavi and other Arawakan groups (see chapter 9).

The process of European economic dominion over the Amerindian political economy began in the 1750s and continued into the late 1770s. During this period the Crowns of Spain and Portugal signed a delimitation treaty to demarcate their respective overseas possessions. The border demarcation implied the expansion of colonial frontiers, whose goal was to obtain definitive territorial control by expelling intruders and competitors. Achieving a forced political, legal, economic, and cultural amalgamation implied the integration of indigenous populations to Imperial Crowns.

As a consequence, new sociopolitical changes and violence took place in the Orinoco–Rio Negro region. Between 1755 and 1767, there were many indigenous rebellions in the Middle and Upper Rio Negro and in the Upper Orinoco River (Caulín 1841; Fernández de Bovadilla 1964; Ferreira 1885, 1886, 1887, 1888; Mendoça Furtado 1906; Ramos Pérez 1946). While some rebel groups were defending their lands and sacred places against European encroachment, others were fighting to regain control over strategic trade networks. Yet these events meant a deeper involvement of these indigenous groups with the colonial system. This involvement produced a continuous desertion of some indigenous groups from European towns and villages, and for other groups it entailed a decline of their economic and political autonomy.

Between 1756 and 1760, Spanish and Portuguese expeditions were made to define their limits in the Upper Rio Negro–Upper Orinoco region. Military and civilian authorities tried to impose some changes in the organization of their respective colonies; the foundation of new towns and fortress-es began, and mission towns were transformed into secular villages under the control of imposed European and indigenous authorities. Europeans even prohibited indigenous peoples from freely moving within and between co-lonial territories.

A great contingent of Portuguese soldiers, officials, and experts traveled along the Rio Negro and began using indigenous chiefs and groups as me-diators and ethnic militia against other independent indigenous groups. This Portuguese campaign generated a great indigenous rebellion in 1757. Indeed, several allied indigenous confederacies along with indigenous in-dividuals and groups from mission towns confronted the Portuguese army at São Gabriel Falls.

This war broke indigenous-Portuguese relationships and caused a num-ber of indigenous migrations from Middle Rio Negro basin to the Spanish colony in Upper Rio Negro–Upper Orinoco region. However, Spanish au-thorities induced more changes with their intervention in the nature of in-digenous-European interactions. Spaniards tried to negotiate their political protection against the Portuguese and ethnic soldiers in exchange for indig-enous subjection to the Spanish Crown. By 1759, many powerful indigenous leaders of major confederacies were performing public ceremonies of vas-salage to Spanish authorities. This vassalage weakened the leadership exer-cised by Arawak-speaking groups and directly affected the viability of their confederacies, causing their progressive disintegration.

These events meant a deeper involvement of Amerindian groups in the colonial system. But these processes also produced a continual desertion of some indigenous groups and individuals from European towns and villages, and the regrouping of other Amerindian groups in new multiethnic confed-eracies. In fact, while the Guaipunavi and Madáwaka confederacies were fighting to survive, the Marabitana, Darivazauna, Umasevitauna, Urumanavi, and Amuisana confederacies were emerging as the powerful leaders of the Upper Rio Negro, Casiquiare, Guainía, and Upper Orinoco rivers.

After the 1770s, most of the village sites along the major river routes (Up-per Orinoco and Upper Rio Negro) were largely uninhabited (Ferreira 1885, 1886, 1887, 1888; Humboldt 1956, vol. 4; Jerez 1960a, 1960b; Ribeiro de Sam-paio 1825), and several groups of the Rio Negro had been changed from *gen-tiles,* or independent peoples, into *abalizados,* or assimilated individuals and families (Neto 1988) or groups undergoing drastic reductions in their polit-ical autonomy (Vidal 1993). During this same period, a new kind of indige-nous category was established, that of *canicurú* or "traitor" (Neto 1988, 52–53; Stradelli 1929, 395). The Manao, Baré, and other groups of the Upper Rio

Negro region used this term to refer to both individuals and groups who were at the service of the colonial powers.

By the end of the eighteenth century, the European colonial system came to dominate the Orinoco–Rio Negro region. However, some indigenous groups managed to survive and resist this colonial domination by transforming their sociopolitical structure, redefining their identities, and reinstating their religious beliefs and mythico-historical teachings and knowledge.

Regional Leadership and Male Ritual Societies in the Eighteenth Century

Both European written records and the oral history of Arawak-speaking groups lead to the conclusion that multiethnic confederacies' powerful indigenous chiefs, captains, or caciques and their followings celebrated big multiethnic ritual festivals that were related to the Kuwé religion and included sacred places, special men's houses, whipping and fasting ceremonies, and musical performances such as dancing, singing, and the playing of trumpets, flutes, and drums.

Besides their important esoteric and religious value, sacred places were also strategic places for the defense and trade of indigenous leaders and groups (Vidal 2000). The eighteenth-century written records refer to different sacred ritual places and indigenous market centers that were highly valuable to both European authorities and indigenous leaders (Morey 1975; Sweet 1975; Hemming 1978; Whitehead 1988). These places include Cumarú, Atures and Maipure Falls (in the Upper Orinoco River), Yauita or Yavita (a site and town located at the Temi Creek in the Upper Atabapo basin), Cocorubi Falls (in São Gabriel das Cachoeiras), Marié River (in the Middle Rio Negro basin), Maracoa[8] (southern part of the present city of San Fernando de Atabapo, at the confluence of the Atabapo and Upper Orinoco rivers), Autana River (in the Upper Orinoco basin), Inírida River (in the Lower Guaviare basin), Pasiva River and lagoon, and other places in the Casiquiare basin, Tomo River (in the Guainía basin), Vaupés Falls (in the Vaupés basin), and Isana Falls (in the Isana basin) (Altolaguirre y Duvale 1954; Gilij 1965; Humboldt 1956; Llanos and Pineda 1982; Mendoça Furtado 1906; Ramos Pérez 1946; Ribeiro de Sampaio 1825; Sweet 1975; Vega 1974; Vidal 1993, 1999; Wright 1981). However, the best example of these sites is Cumarú (later known as the city of Poiares). This site was located between the Arirá (or Arirajá) and Unini rivers in front of the mouth of the Rio Branco (Ribeiro de Sampaio 1825, 102–3) and received the name *Juruparíporaceitáua,* or "place where Juruparí or Kuwé dances." The Caburicena (ancient forefathers of contemporary Baré and other Arawak-speaking groups) and many other groups held their ritual festivals in this site (Ribeiro de Sampaio 1825), but Cumarú was also a place where Amerindian and European goods and peoples circulated through an important trading route connecting the Japurá and Upper Amazon rivers with the Branco and Orinoco rivers and the Guayanas.

The European explorers also made reference to special ritual houses that were used as men's houses for religious festivals (Arriaga 1954; Daniel 1916; Ferreira 1886; Ramos Pérez 1946; Ribeiro de Sampaio 1825). In every Amerindian town besides their particular homes, each paramount chief or *capitán* had another house much bigger and roomier that was used in common by all men, where they smoked their tobacco and carried out their war meetings, parties, drinking, dances, and other business (Daniel 1916, 359; Ribeiro de Sampaio 1825, 21). In these houses men gathered together for their secret meetings (Arriaga 1954, 272), and the initiated men performed their sacred ritual festivals and whippings.

These ritual festivals could last for more than eight days and were described as ceremonies in which men, or men and women, danced and slashed each other with a whip, made of dolphin, tapir, deer leather, or well-knitted and bent branches of trees. These whips had in their tips solid, sharp objects (Ferreira 1888, 14–16; Ribeiro de Sampaio 1825, 21–22). They slashed with whips in pairs, standing with their arms raised up. After the lashes, the men gathered together, smoking tobacco, snuffing *yopo*, and drinking fermented beer. Rituals were accompanied by martial and festival musical instruments that included drums, trumpets, and flutes. Women were not admitted to dances with these instruments; if they participated, shamans could sentence them to death. Also, the purpose of these rites was to recruit new soldiers or to initiate young boys into the "virile state" (Ferreira 1888, 16).

However, ritual whippings, dances, and festivals were held not only at men's houses but in other places such as open plazas in bigger towns, as in Crucero village, home of the famous leader of the Guaipunavi confederacy (Arriaga 1954; Ramos Pérez 1946), or in Cumarú village (actually Poiares) in the Middle Rio Negro (Ferreira 1887, 19; Ribeiro de Sampaio 1825, 102–3); caves in mountains, such as those held by Boapé, chief of the Tariana in the Vaupés River (Amorim 1928); and sacred rivers and creeks, such as the Tomo River in the Guainía basin (Humboldt 1956).

By the second half of the eighteenth century, multiethnic confederacies associated with the forefathers of contemporary Warekena and Baré were the Guaipunavi, Marabitana, Urumanavi, Darivazauna, Umazebitauna, and Amuisana. Crucero, Imu, Cocui, Inao, Mará, Davipe, and Amuni were the powerful chiefs who led these confederacies. The Guaipunavi were described as a warring nation devoted to intensive trade with Portuguese, Dutch, and many Amerindian groups and dominating various indigenous groups of the Upper Orinoco, Atabapo, Guaviare, and Ventuari rivers (Arriaga 1954; Humboldt 1956; Ramos Pérez 1946). Crucero was the cacique or leader of a number of secondary chiefs of the Guaipunavi, Caverre, Puinave, Parrene (Yavitero), Maipure, and other indigenous groups. In their village of Maracoa, the Guaipunavi had fourteen houses, one for the cacique Crucero, and another (a barrack or quarter) where men gathered together for their parties and where women were not allowed to enter (Arriaga 1954, 272; Ramos Pérez 1946, 299). According to Arriaga (1954, 266), the Guaipunavi had the idea of a god who created everything and preserved the world, but they also believed in another being to whom they rendered worship to protect the newly born children of the caciques and to guarantee the production of their agricultural, hunting, and fishing activities. They also worshipped this divinity when young people tasted the sacred food for the first time and when men went to war. This cult was accompanied by sacrifices that consisted of lashings with whips.

Gilij (1965, 3:184–85) also mentions that before attacking the mission town of Atures, Imo and his men performed a sacred ritual, which included playing flutes, trumpets, and drums. However, the best descriptions of Kuwé ceremonies are those provided in the oral history of the Tariana people of the Vaupés River (Amorim 1928, 11–77). In those narratives, it is told that the Tariana men held Kúwai rituals every night at Iauipáne, a cave near their village, especially before they went to war (Amorim 1928, 11). Some Tukanoan and Arawakan groups of the Vaupés and Isana basins also shared Tariana's Kúwai rituals.

By the end of the eighteenth century, when most of the multiethnic confederacies were losing their political autonomy or breaking apart, some of their leaders such as the Marabitana Cocui and the Umasevitauna Davipe were able to continue the religion of Kuwé at the Cocui Mountain site and by the Tomo, San Miguel, and Tiriquín rivers. By the end of the 1770s, Fray Xerez (1954, 313) stated that the Capitán Cocui was well respected by his men and many other groups of the Rio Negro, but he also mentions that it was very hard for him to abolish the whipping festivals and rituals Cocui and his followers were still celebrating at that time. Between 1799 and 1800, when Humboldt was exploring the Negro and Orinoco rivers, he was able to listen to the sacred flutes and trumpets of Kuwé (or *botutos*) at the Tomo River; Humboldt also learned about the great achievements and powerful ritual knowledge of Cocui, the last great chief of the Marabitana.

Conclusions

Ethnological literature of the northwest Amazon region has highlighted the importance of the rites and secret societies associated with the Kúwai or Yurupari. Many scholars have even formulated interpretations about the relevance of this ritual system for the cultural history of that region.

At the end of the nineteenth century, several scientists and explorers mentioned the existence of these rituals, which they considered to be a group of beautiful native legends, myths, and poetry (Amorim 1928; Stradelli 1929; Wallace 1969). However, as researchers began to come out from that region with new data, a series of important contributions arose that enabled the development of new understandings of the cult of the Kúwai (González Ñáñez 1980; Hill 1983, 1993; S. Hugh-Jones 1979; Mich 1994; Reichel-Dolmatoff 1989; Van der Hammen 1992; Vidal 1987, 1993, 2000; Wright 1981, 1993). Although some of these works have highlighted the association between Kúwai rituals and myths with biological and social aspects of the indigenous groups of the northwest Amazon (i.e., exogamy) (Reichel-Dolmatoff 1989), other authors point out that this cult could represent the highest expression of the religious life of Arawakan and Tukanoan peoples. The relationships between this religious system and the sociopolitical organization and the cultural history of these groups are much more complex phenomena that warrant more than a single or simple interpretation (Hill 1993; S. Hugh-Jones 1979; Vidal 2000; Wright 1981).

The religion of Kuwé implies complex relationships because it involves the association between living and mythic elders, male ritual societies, and political and religious authorities. This articulation of knowledge and activities of wise elders, powerful shaman-warrior chiefs, and secret forms of political organization also is related to the social, political, and economic reproduction of society and identities. Santos-Granero (1986b, 1993a) argues that in Amazonian indigenous societies where shamans are also political leaders, their power is of an economic nature insofar as their ritual knowledge is considered indispensable to ensure the success of productive and reproductive activities. This is also true for the Arawakan peoples of the northwest Amazon, where the religion of Kuwé is linked to collective death and rebirth, world destruction and renewal.

The evidence presented in this chapter shows that the religion of Kúwai has been part of the ritual and sociopolitical traditions of northern Arawakan groups from at least the eighteenth century; Tukanoan and Makuan groups of the northwest Amazon have also shared these traditions. The evidence also demonstrates that there was a close relationship between the cult of Kuwé and the male ritual societies of powerful Arawakan chiefs who led different multiethnic confederacies. This relationship represented a political and religious strategy, which allowed the Warekena and Baré ancient leaders to build political communities and new cultural identities within the colonial regime of the eighteenth century. The Baré and Warekena forefathers used this strategy not only to participate in the trading network of indigenous slaves and European goods (especially firearms, knives, and machetes) but also to evade or challenge colonial domination.

Wright (1993) mentions that among the Arawakan Hohódene, the religion of Kúwai represents their notions of territoriality and collective identity as well as their sense of cumulative historical knowledge, including their experiences of contact, trading networks, and wars with other ethnic groups. Hill (1993, 156) states that "the cult of Kuwái and of the ancestor spirits has continued to serve the Wakuénai as a power resource for negotiating interethnic relations along Lower Guainía River in Venezuela." Thus, the integration and relationship between the male ritual societies and Kuwé teachings and knowledge constitutes a model of and for their societies and their geopolitical relations. This religious system, as an ideological support of military trading polities, also came to favor the emergence and continuity of a pan-indigenous politico-religious hierarchy in the northwest Amazon during the nineteenth century. This pan-Indian organization came into action during the Rubber Boom era as powerful indigenous shaman-prophets led millenarian movements (Hill and Wright 1988; Wright and Hill 1986).

Notes

I would like to thank Jonathan Hill and Fernando Santos-Granero for organizing the "Comparative Arawakan Histories: Rethinking Culture Area and Language Family in Amazonia" conference, an amazing and important contribution to the understanding of Amazonian cultural history. I also thank my Warekena, Baré, Baniwa, Wakuénai, and Piapoco friends and colleagues for sharing with me their forefathers' knowledge and history.

1. The forefathers of the Warekena and Baré used to practice marriage alliances between phratries and sibs of the same rank in their regional and local hierarchies. For example, Crucero, the great warrior-shaman chief of the Guaipunavi confederacy and member of the sib of highest rank in his phratry, was married to Bolmo-Caro, also a member of a phratry of the highest rank among the Parrene (later known as the Yavitero) Indians of the Guaviare, Negro, and Atabapo rivers (Altolaguirre y Duvale 1954, 267–68, 279).

2. See Jackson (1983) for a comparison of this amplification of kin networks of the Arawakan peoples with that of the Tukanoan societies of northwest Amazon.

3. In the Arawakan languages, the prefix *ku-* and the suffix *-ku* are related to an archaic word that means "sacred or shamanic language." This is the reason why this prefix or suffix is present in sacred names such as *Kúwai, Makuku,* and *Dukuku.*

4. *Katsimánali* or *Kachimánali* means "shrimp eater" in Baniwa and Baré. Other names for Kúwai among the Arawak-speaking groups are *Kúwaiséiri* (Piapoco), *Cuaygerri* (Achagua), *Kué* (Tariana), and *Kuéti* (Maipure).

5. *Yuruparí* is the name of Kúwai in the *neêhengatú* or *lengua geral* language. He is also known as He among the Tukanoan peoples, as Boom among the Puinave, and as Idn Kamni among the Makuan peoples.

6. Among the Warekena and Baré, five levels of shamanic knowledge exist, which can be interpreted as a hierarchy of the ritual, botanical, zoological, ecological, and anatomical knowledge, mediating between natural and supernatural worlds. This hierarchy is integrated by Biníji, or the one who knows and cures with herbs; Makakána, or the one who knows and cures by means of blowing tobacco; Uyákali, or the one who knows about harmful and poisonous beings, substances, and spells, and cures by means of suction; Sibunítei, or the one who is a seer or foreteller and cures by means of the divination and through dreams; and Maríri, or the one with wisdom that dominates the other four specializations, can turn into different species of animal-spirits, and can travel to the different levels of the cosmos.

7. *Kuwé Duwákalumi* literally means "where Kuwé passed by." In some maps of the eighteenth, nineteenth, and twentieth centuries, Kuwé routes appear under the names *Pasos del Diablo* ("Passages of the Devil") and *Yuruparí.*

8. *Maracoa* (*malákua*) means "place where they (Kuwé and his troop) came down." This was the Arawakan name for the village of Crucero, the Guaipunavi chief. Later this place was renamed as the city of San Fernando de Atabapo.

11 Prophetic Traditions among the Baniwa and Other Arawakan Peoples of the Northwest Amazon

ROBIN M. WRIGHT

THIS CHAPTER EXPLORES prophetic traditions among Arawak-speaking peoples of the northwest Amazon seeking, through a comparative and historical view, to determine what seem to have been critical elements of the Baniwa religious imagination that came to be expressed in historical prophetic movements. It begins with a regional perspective on the Arawakan peoples of the northwest Amazon, focusing on the Rio Negro and, in particular, the Upper Rio Negro valley. Both the written sources and oral histories attest to the existence of vast regional networks of commerce, exchange, and ceremonial interaction among Arawak-speaking peoples as well as intense cultural interaction with non-Arawak-speaking peoples, particularly the Tukanoan and Makuan peoples (see chapter 10). Recently, ethnographers have also drawn attention to religious traditions among diverse Arawak-speaking peoples, suggesting the perception of a wider linguistic and cultural identity among the Arawak-speaking peoples of the northern Amazon, in contrast with non-Arawak-speaking peoples with whom they have been in contact throughout history.

With this broad perspective, I then focus on the Baniwa in Brazil and the nature of prophetism in their culture. In previous publications, Jonathan Hill and I have analyzed the history of various messianic and millenarian movements, including conversion to evangelical Christianity (Wright and Hill 1986; Hill and Wright 1988; Wright 1992b, 1998). Here I present an in-depth interpretation of diverse aspects of the Baniwa religious imagination to illustrate how notions that seem to be similar to Western ideas of "purity" and "contamination" are central to prophetism and the dynamics of historical religious movements. I illustrate this through shamanic discourse, myths, sickness and curing rituals, and eschatology.

In these, the notion of a protected place, or sanctuary, appears to be of fundamental importance where, for example, the sick may recover and where sickness and death-dealing elements are prevented from entering. Powerful shamans and prophets have concretely translated this notion into historical millenarian ideology and practice. In a similar way, such notions have been fundamental to conversion to evangelical Christianity by defining Baniwa expectations of the coming of a savior, their representations of this figure, and the concrete utopia, which they have sought to realize in practice.

This chapter concludes by returning to the comparative, historical view examining similarities and differences with other Arawakan and Tukanoan prophetic movements in the northwest Amazon. I first compare indigenous representations of two prophetesses, both extraordinary cases in the long history of religious movements in the region, and then suggest ways in which, based on this discussion, the anthropological notion of culture area may be rethought based on the ethnographic material from the northwest Amazon.

Arawak-Speaking Peoples of the Northwest Amazon

The Arawak-speaking peoples of the Upper Rio Negro valley today include the Baniwa and Wakuénai (including the Curripaco) of the Isana and Guainía river basins, the Warekena of the Xié River in Brazil and Caño San Miguel in Venezuela, the Baré of the Upper Rio Negro between Santa Isabel in Brazil and San Carlos in Venezuela, and the Tariana between the Middle and Lower Vaupés in Brazil. Further north are the Piapoco of the Guaviare and Inirida and the Baniwa of the Upper Guainía and Atabapo; to the southwest are the Kabiyarí and Yukuna of the Mirití-paraná and Apaporis River regions in Colombia.

The earliest historical sources from the eighteenth century indicate a large number of other Arawak-speaking peoples in the Rio Negro region about whom we know very little, such as the Maríarana, Amaríavana, Mepuri (probably related to a group of the same name on the Orinoco), Carnao, Kavaipitena, Tibakena, Iaminari, and many others. All of these are simply mentioned in the sources with at most a few details about their location and language. By the end of the period of Portuguese slavery in the eighteenth century, they no longer existed as distinct peoples. It is nevertheless important to remember that all of the Rio Negro valley, from the mouth to the headwaters and including many of its major tributaries such as the Vaupés, and a large part of the Upper Orinoco were the territory of northern Arawak-speaking peoples and had been for centuries before European expansion began in the late seventeenth or early eighteenth century. The Upper Rio

Negro valley thus was located practically in the heart of this vast territory and at the center of a network of peoples connected through alliances, intermarriage, commerce, and exchange.[1]

A quick look at the ethnographic map of the Upper Rio Negro valley today shows that the population of Arawak-speaking peoples has been drastically reduced and restricted to the northern part of the region and that Tukanoan-speaking peoples now predominate over a greater part of the Vaupés and its tributaries (see map 10.2, p. 250). Colonial penetration (slavery), epidemics, and migrations would account for why Arawakan peoples who once dominated the region were, by the nineteenth century, reduced to a few small enclaves on the Vaupés: Jauareté and Ipanoré rapids, traditional places of the Tariana; the Querary River, where various Baniwa phratries were located; and the Yaviary River off the Lower Vaupés, also territory of the Baniwa. Over time, each of these groups diminished in number and, increasingly surrounded by Tukanoan-speakers, either withdrew deeper into Arawakan territory (e.g., the Baniwa groups of the Querary who migrated to the Isana beginning in the second half of the nineteenth century) or gradually adopted the Tukanoan language (e.g., the Tariana and several phratries of Cubeo). However, this did not mean that they abandoned Arawakan culture; on the contrary, both Cubeo phratries and the Tariana today, though Tukanoan-speaking, retain much of the mythology, shamanic traditions, and other cultural elements of their Arawakan ancestry.[2]

In 1959, Brazilian ethnologist Eduardo Galvão proposed a reformulation of Steward and Murdock's earlier definition of "culture areas" of South America to better reflect the realities of indigenous cultures in Brazil known at that time (the late 1950s). He divided the country into eleven large culture areas, several of which are further subdivided into smaller areas. The "decisive criterion" for the delimitation of areas was the "contiguous spatial distribution of culture traits, both material and socio-cultural" (1967, 185). Galvão's proposal further took into account other important factors: geography, the contact situation and relations to pioneering national frontiers, and, above all, the "occurrence of intertribal acculturation." To the extent that this proposal emphasized dynamic processes of culture contact, it represented an advance over Steward and Murdock's typology.

Nevertheless, the determining criterion of Galvão's proposal focuses predominantly on external factors defined by historical contact with the national society or with neighboring indigenous cultures, not to any extent on criterion that may have been important to native societies. Thus Galvão represents the region of the northwest Amazon as a subdivision of a vast northern Amazon culture area, which extends from the Rio Negro in the west to the Atlantic Coast in the east. The principal characteristics of the northwest Amazon were a predominantly extractive national pioneering frontier, which had produced a situation of "permanent contact" and "accentuated acculturation" and a consequent "cultural uniformity" among the indigenous peoples, principally Baniwa and Tukano.

If, following the proposal of the Comparative Arawakan Histories Conference, we shift our understanding about the decisive criterion from external factors based on colonial history to perspectives that indigenous peoples have of their histories as well as of their insertion within broader cultural contexts, then the configurations of a culture area change in scope and nature. One of the central objectives of this chapter is to explore this possibility.

Recently, various ethnographers of northern Arawak-speaking peoples have focused attention on certain lengthy sacred traditions that are chanted during initiation rituals. These traditions, I suggest, may provide us with a clue as to how the notion of culture area may be related to native conceptions of cultural unity. Jonathan Hill (chapter 9) likewise analyzes these traditions in terms of a native notion of a historically produced culture area. Remarkably similar in content, they concern the mythical voyages of the first woman, Amáru, who played the sacred flutes and trumpets representing the body of her son the culture hero Kúwai, throughout a vast region of the northern Amazon.[3]

The voyages generally begin at the rapids of Hípana on the Aiary River—considered the sacred center of the world by the Piapoco, Hohódene, Dzauinai, Adzanene, Warekena, Kabiyarí, Yukuna, Baré, and other Arawakan peoples of the northwest Amazon—and from there Amáru and the women, pursued by the men who seek to regain possession of the sacred instruments, travel to all parts of the known world. The chanters of these traditions name in a specific order all the places where the women stopped and played the instruments, thus leaving the music for all future generations. The Hohódene tradition describes a series of five voyages corresponding to ever-widening loops that cover the major arteries of the Rio Negro, Orinoco, and Amazon to the ends of the world known to the Hohódene and, finally, back to the center and origin-place at Hípana.

Much can be said about these traditions; here I only wish to mention the principal conclusions of my study of the Hohódene traditions (1993) and comparisons with others. First, these traditions appear to represent notions of territoriality of the phratry to which the specific tradition belongs, of collective identity vis-à-vis other peoples on the peripheries of these territories, and of the cumulative historical knowledge that each phratry has of distant peoples and places. Second, there are numerous coincidences between the traditions of different peoples, such as the origin point (Hípana), routes of the voyages, place naming, and knowledge of the extreme points of the voyages. As Hill (1983, 1984, 1989, 1993, 1996b, 1999; chapter 9) notes, if we compare the ethno-maps of these voyages with maps of the linguistic distribution of the peoples of the northern Arawak language group, there are correspondences indicating that these traditions may collectively represent a conception of the greater cultural and linguistic unity of the Arawakan-speaking peoples north of the Amazon. Third, the traditions display extraordinarily extensive geographic knowledge of the entire Amazon Basin. For example, the Hohódene tradition covers an area from the foothills of the Andes in the west to the mouth of the Orinoco in the north, to the Upper Solimões in the south, to the mouth of the Amazon in the east. In the Warekena version, once the chanters reach the mouth of the Orinoco, they proceed along the northern coast of the continent descending to the mouth of the Amazon and then back up to the Rio Negro. Vidal (1987) suggests that such extensive knowledge embodied in these traditions may refer to ancient patterns of migration and networks of intertribal commerce among the northern Arawak (Wright 1981).

Other oral traditions of the Hohódene (ACIRA/FOIRN 1999) of the Aiary River, also offer interesting evidence of ancient cultural exchanges, connections, and migrations. Hohódene myths of the emergence of their first ancestors from the rapids at Hípana on the Aiary River state that the first people to emerge were the "Daizo dakenai," who, in remote times, migrated north to the Guaviare River. According to Vidal's (1987) investigations, these may have been a phratry of the Piapoco whose migration tradition coincides with the Hohódene myth. Hohódene oral histories also refer to another elder-brother phratry called the Mulé dakenai, whose name is similar to that of the Piapoco phratry Mali itakenai, strengthening the historical connections between these two peoples. The Hohódene and their affines, the Walipere dakenai and the Dzauinai of the Aiary and the Isana rivers, add other interesting information to these emergence stories. They include both the Tariana and the Desana as kin groups agnatically related to Baniwa phratries who emerged after the Baniwa phratries.[4] The link with the Tukanoan-speaking Desana (in Baniwa, Deethana) is at first unexpected, yet it suggests again the hypothesis that at least some Desana sibs originally were Arawak speakers (Dominique Buchillet, personal communication, 2000). Early eighteenth-century maps of the northwest Amazon locate the Desana on the Isana River further north from where they are located today (Wright 1981).

I believe that further research along the lines of comparing religious traditions may deepen our understanding of northern Arawakan culture patterns and history. To that end, this chapter seeks first to explore in depth the predominant patterns of symbolism in Baniwa prophetism in order to compare with other prophetic traditions in the northwest and finally return to the question of culture areas in the northern Amazon.

Ethnography of the Baniwa in Brazil

The Baniwa live on the frontier borders of Brazil, Venezuela, and Colombia. The majority live on the Brazilian side, a total of approximately 4,100 people distributed in ninety-three communities along the Isana River and its tributaries, the Cuiary, Aiary, and Cubate; in several communities of the Upper Rio Negro; and on the Lower Xié and Vaupés rivers. In Venezuela and Colombia, where they are known as Wakuénai and Curripaco, their population is perhaps as many as 8,000 people living in communities along the Guainía and its tributaries, and the Upper Isana.

Horticulture and fishing are their principal subsistence activities, although a long history of contact has involved them in various forms of production for markets and extractive labor. Their society is organized into approximately a half-dozen phratries, the Hohódene, Walipere-dakenai, and Dzauinai being the principal ones located on the Aiary and Isana rivers. Traditional religious life was based largely on the mythology and rituals of the first ancestors, represented in the sacred flutes and trumpets called Kúwai; the importance of shamans and chanters; and a variety of complex dance festivals, *pudali,* coordinated with seasonal calendars. In the latter half of the nineteenth century, prophets emerged to create a tradition called the "song of the cross" or the "religion of the cross," the memory of which is still active in several communities of the region. In the 1950s the Baniwa converted en masse to Protestant evangelicalism and since then have consolidated a specific form of Christianity adapted to their spiritual needs.

Beginning in the 1980s, invasions of their lands by gold panners and mining companies and military proposals to reduce their lands posed grave threats to Baniwa communities in Brazil; nevertheless, indigenous political mobilization and participation in the pan-Indian Federation of Indigenous Organizations of the Rio Negro (FOIRN), founded in 1987, has guaranteed the defense of their land rights and culture. In 1996, after years of negotiation, the federal government of Brazil decreed the creation of a large and continuous land reserve for the Indians of the Upper Rio Negro.

The Baniwa have had a long history of contact with nonindigenous society dating from the first half of the eighteenth century (see Wright 1981, 1983, 1987–89, 1991, 1992c, 1998). Yet little was known of their society and culture until the beginning of the twentieth century, when German ethnologist Theodor Koch-Grünberg traveled for several months on the Isana and Aiary rivers, leaving the first reliable ethnography on record (1967). From then, at intervals of nearly every twenty-five years, ethnographers have worked on the Isana and its tributaries in Brazil.

Baniwa Prophetism

Research I have been conducting since the beginning of 1999 in the northwest Amazon region has led me to rethink the dimensions of what I called in my book (1998) "Baniwa millenarian consciousness." There are other features of this consciousness, and one of these consists of a contrast between notions that have to do with what could be thought of as "purity" or "purification" and "contamination." I will illustrate how this contrast appears in numerous areas of religious discourse and practice beginning with cosmogony and cosmology, followed by the discourses of shamans regarding the qualities of the world, notions of sickness and curing, and eschatology.[5]

I am fully aware that the terms *purity* and *contamination* have markedly Western connotations, as a number of participants in the Comparative Arawakan Histories conference pointed out. Nevertheless, I will try to show how both have specific connotations in Baniwa shamanic, mythic, and ritual discourse. The idea of "contamination" is most nearly translated by the Baniwa notion of *-nupa,* which has to do with sickness or the danger of life-threatening conditions that could bring on death. Such conditions result on the most general level from the mixing of substances that should be kept apart and on specific levels to breaking prohibitions on such things as eating cooked food or having sexual relations during periods of ritual seclusion.

The notion of *-nupa* is highly ambivalent, however, for it condenses both danger and creativity. The sacred flutes and trumpets of Kúwai, for example, are exceedingly dangerous and may kill those who are prohibited from seeing them (women and the uninitiated); at the same time, they produce music unequaled in its polyphonous beauty, which creates new generations of adults. The term *kanupa* also refers to menstruation: Women's menstrual blood is considered highly creative as the sign of new life, but it is exceedingly dangerous to shamans, for it "causes a sickness in their blood," and during his apprenticeship a would-be shaman cannot even look at a woman, for the ideal is to remain celibate for the period of training. In the myth of Kúwai, during the first ritual of initiation, Kúwai declares to boys about to be initiated, "so dangerous (*kanupa*) am I, you must remain restricted (secluded, *itákawa*) for three dry seasons." Seclusion, or separation, from that which is considered life-threatening, together with the consumption of life-giving substances that "revive" (*iafétawa*) or strengthen the individual's "heart-soul" (*ikaale*), define the process of purification or purity. It is thus specifically this dialectical opposition between *nupa* and *itákawa* that, I argue, corresponds to Baniwa notions of contamination and purity.[6]

The images of the primordial world presented in Baniwa myths confirm its violent and catastrophic nature, moribund and chaotic, in which the creation of order constantly suffers the threat of being dismantled. The very beginning of the cosmos is marked by terrifying and disastrous events. Such a possible condition was never totally eliminated, and humanity today remembers its presence. On the other hand, the primordial world is the source of renewal and change. Spiritual creativity eternally transcends the destruction of the material world; this is the essence of the Creator/Transformer Nhiã-perikuli. Spiritual creativity is the source of abundance and happiness that sustains life and creates meaningful existence for the future, for the "others who will be born," as the Baniwa say.

This mythical discourse develops through a series of themes related to the end of the primordial world and the beginning of the new order created from the vestiges of the old. The new order contains traces of the old, for Nhiã-perikuli never totally eliminated the chaotic forces of the beginning: Sorcery and witchcraft still are seen as the most persistent causes of human death, despite the norms to control them. The catastrophic destruction of the world also remains a possibility, according to some, for when it seems that the world is overrun by insupportable evil—as this is represented in the myths—the conditions are sufficient for its destruction and renewal. The history of the cosmos attests to this pattern: Before Nhiãperikuli brought forth the first ancestors of humanity, he caused a great flood to wash the world and force the spirits of the forest and of death to flee. Later, he burnt the world. Only afterward, he looked for the first ancestors.

Both cosmogonic myths and the shamanic discourses emphasize that this world is intrinsically flawed by evil, misfortune, and death. Like a sick person, this world constantly needs to be healed, restored to a state of integrated spatial-temporal order (which would be the equivalent, for the Baniwa, of the notion of salvation). For that reason, the shamans have the vital task of sustaining ordered life and preventing the "death of the world," which means, concretely, when the world collapses in total darkness, when humans are consumed by fatal sicknesses and epidemic diseases.

The shamanic quest is characterized in terms of the protective, beneficial, and aesthetically correct: "To make the world beautiful," "to make this world and people in it better and content," "to not let this world fall or end," and "to retrieve lost souls and make sick persons well" are all phrases that appear in shamanic discourses. In fact, it is as though the specific objective of the shaman's frequent journeys to the Other World—that is, to retrieve lost souls—were so interconnected with the larger concern of making the world better that it is impossible to separate them. In all phases of this journey, the beauty, goodness, unity, order, and truth of the Other World stand in contrast with This World of multiple pain and evil. In one sense, then, the shaman's quest seems to be one of "beautifying" This World by sustaining order and preventing chaos.

Shamans classify the principal kinds of sicknesses, according to their sources, in the following groups: "Sicknesses of people," referring to sicknesses provoked by the actions of sorcerers who, through the blowing of spells, put sickness on their victims that may be so serious as to lead to death; "poison" (*manhene*), or plant substances (berries, leaves) mixed in food or drink by witches; "sicknesses of the forest,"[7] provoked by spirits of the forest, rivers, and air, called *iupinai;* "sicknesses of the universe," which include ailments and epidemics that occur during dangerous periods of the annual cycle such as seasonal transitions or during meteorological phenomena such as eclipses of the sun; sicknesses sent by other shamans; and sicknesses of the whites.

This classification may be seen to correspond to a concentric model of social space, coherent with similar models in other areas of Baniwa culture. The types of sickness correspond to a series of concentric circles. The innermost refers to a sphere of the greatest social proximity, for sorcery most often occurs among members of the same descent group and sib; the second, poisoning by witches, most often occurs among affines, members of different and spatially distant phratries. The third type, sicknesses of the forest, occurs in the relations between humans and animals, the spirits of the forest, rivers, and air. These sicknesses often result from failure to observe rules of fasting or bodily hygiene during periods of ritual seclusion, which is consistent with the rigorous norm to maintain purity during rites of passage. Finally, the last three types correspond to the circle of widest inclusion, the sicknesses of the universe or the sicknesses that occur in the relation between man and the cosmos or between native peoples and outsiders (especially whites) and those that are caused by shamanic warfare. This is where the risk of contamination is the greatest, including epidemics, which come from outside, from afar, or from unknown sources such as the shamans of other peoples. One may presume that it is in these cases that shamans are called on to "heal the universe" (*pamatchiatsa hekwapi*) through their cures (see figure 11.1).

Particularly instructive for our analysis is the category of sicknesses introduced by whites. The Baniwa explain the origin of the sicknesses of whites

Representing this model:

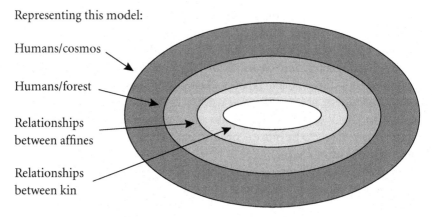

Humans/cosmos

Humans/forest

Relationships
between affines

Relationships
between kin

Figure 11.1. Model of the Social, Natural, and Spiritual Worlds in Baniwa Shamanism

through a myth about Amáru, the first woman and mother of Kúwai, the "owner of sicknesses." After the war between Nhiãperikuli and Amáru over the possession of the sacred flutes—the transformed body of Kúwai—the men sent the women to the four ends of the earth. There, Amáru became the "mother of the whites," and in each place the women made factories. Informants affirmed that Amáru's knowledge was as great as that of Nhiãperikuli, so she could produce factories, the source of all the whites' merchandise. In these factories there are pots of various kinds of metal: gold, silver, iron, and aluminum. Constantly heated by fire, poisonous smoke from the pots spreads over the world, and it is the smell of this poisonous smoke that causes diseases associated with whites—flu, whooping cough, dysentery, measles, malaria—all of which produce high fever. The shamans say that Amáru has her hair tied up with a cloth, and this cloth is the cause of flu among the Baniwa. Amáru weaves cotton of various colors, and it is this cotton that in Baniwa curing orations symbolizes the flu.

The poisonous smoke spreads from the periphery of the world back to the center, where the Baniwa live. How? By the planes that bring merchandise, for the motors of the planes are produced in the factories of the women, and it is the smell of oil and gasoline that also causes sickness. The Baniwa also say that when a person dreams of a plane, it is a warning of the imminence of the whites' sickness. Boats are also a source of the whites' sicknesses, for they are painted in various colors, and it is the smell of the paint that provokes diarrhea and dysentery among the Baniwa. Orations to cure the sicknesses of the whites must name all the things of Amáru that may produce sicknesses: her factories, her cloth, planes, boats, cars, and *cachaça* (rum).

The image of a factory that produces motors and poisonous smoke that arises from the pots may be understood as a symbolic elaboration on an image found in traditional shamanism that refers to "sicknesses of the universe" that occur during seasonal transitions: At these times sickness spreads, as though through the air, originating from great pots of fruits located in various parts of the cosmos. A novel semantic category, "sicknesses of the whites" has thus been grafted onto preexisting categories and symbolic processes of sickness to elaborate an explanation for the historical reality of contact and the epidemics it has produced.

In a parallel and complementary fashion, sicknesses of the whites or those that accompany their merchandise is a theme repeated in other myths and curing orations that explain the origin of the whites. A myth tells how an aquatic serpent devoured the younger brother of Nhiãperikuli and carried him, alive, inside his belly far downriver to the end of the earth. There, the victim managed to kill the serpent, escape from death, and begin to return to his home upriver. From the rotting body of the serpent, Nhiãperikuli extracted two larvae, one white and one black, and from these, he made a white man and an Indian. He ordered each to take a shotgun and shoot; the white man's gun fired, the Indian's didn't. Therefore, Nhiãperikuli left the shotgun and the "knowledge to make all merchandise" with the white man, and the Indian was left with the blowgun and the knowledge to produce indigenous objects.

But, informants stated, "Nhiãperikuli didn't want the White Man to stay on the lands of the Indians." For that reason, he put the white man in a boat and sent him away, to the east, where (presumably) he joined up with Amáru and the women. Here we have another instance of how mythic consciousness provides the imagery for reflecting on history, but not merely as the concrete problem of who gained what but on the more abstract difference in knowledge between Indians and whites and their consequences.[8]

Whereas the orations to cure the sicknesses resulting from the women's factories are spoken to prevent or neutralize their effects, the orations that accompany the myth of the aquatic serpent can be understood in terms of reversing the disastrous effects of epidemics caused by historical contact through a return from the periphery to the sacred center of Baniwa territory, which is a sanctuary, a place of refuge and protection. The orations recreate the slow process of recovery by tracing a canoe voyage that he makes with his brother, starting from the east, downriver, and proceeding upriver, to the west, to the central region of Baniwa territory. During the voyage, Nhiãperikuli extracts the nectar of various species of flowers and gives it to his brother for him to drink and so "sweeten his heart or soul" (*iputidtha ikaale*). The refreshing effects of the nectar and the purest honey of bees calm the victim's fear of death and cool the fever from his body. In each place where the brothers stop, the heart or soul of the sick gets a bit better until they finally reach the center of Baniwa territory, the place of mythical origin of the Baniwa people, the rapids called Hípana. There, the sick person, now fully recovered, is able to paddle the canoe by himself and to get up and walk on his own. In short, the spatial movements described in the formula reflect a gradual process of return from the periphery to the sacred center, to a place of collective origin, which represents a sanctuary allowing the full revival of the person.

As Hill (1993) argues in his book on Wakuénai chant-owners, these formulas and the narrative establish a wider contrast between the areas to the east, where sicknesses afflict the body, and more isolated areas to the west, where these sicknesses are reverted. This contrast reflects historical consciousness in the sense that it represents the regeneration of the Baniwa in their flight from the calamitous effects of epidemics that began to penetrate their territory, coming from regions to the east, during the colonial period. These regions were the points of greatest contact between colonial society and the indigenous peoples beginning in the eighteenth century. The written sources describe various epidemics of measles, smallpox, and other diseases that devastated the indigenous peoples of the region at that time. During the epidemics of 1780, for example, the main rivers of the region were practically abandoned, and the survivors of the epidemics sought refuge in remote areas.

The image of a sanctuary and space of regeneration strongly marks cosmogony, curing practices, and the ideologies of historical prophetic movements. A sanctuary represents protection and recovery from a catastrophic loss, or historical reempowerment. It offers a haven from the disastrous effects of contact and the possibility of regeneration through purification. In other protective orations, for example, we find the notion of a vertical sanctuary to protect a house against the attacks of witches. In this case, the orator creates with his words a protective fence around the house and sends the collective soul of its inhabitants to a place in the Other World "where there are no sicknesses," under the protection of the primordial shaman.

Sanctuaries are likewise fundamental to curing rituals, for victims of serious ailments (poisoning, for example) must remain isolated from the rest of the community by living for the period of the cure in a shelter especially constructed for them in the forest near a stream. Only the shaman and a member of the family designated by him to visit the sick, prepare his food, and so on are allowed to visit him. If another, "unauthorized" person visits the sick, breaking these restrictions, he or she puts the life of the sick in danger. Simply by looking at the patient, he or she brings about his death. (For example, a son of the shaman Mandu, bitten by a snake, was put in seclusion; without thinking, one of his brother's wives visited him to bring him food. The man didn't resist and soon died from a worsening of the snake poison.) The notion here, again, is that of a sanctuary, a protected place, that allows a process of purification to occur from the sickness that contaminates the person. The process of internal purification revolves again around the idea of *inupa:* If a person undergoing restrictions because of sickness, poisoning, or periods of ritual passage consumes or does what he or she should not, that person violates the rule, and the sickness and pain will worsen. In cases of sicknesses that could be transmitted to the rest of the community, such as flu and other whites' diseases, isolating the sick from the rest of the community prevents the transmission of the sickness.

Myth and History

How have these notions been translated into historical action? Here, we will mention three ways: in interethnic relations, in historical prophetic movements, and in Baniwa conversion to Protestant evangelicalism. The written sources and oral histories are replete with instances of flight and refuge, of the abandonment of villages out of fear of sicknesses, and of the dread the Indians have demonstrated at the terrorizing presence of the whites. It is no exaggeration to say that the Baniwa have been traumatized by contact at various moments in history (the rubber boom and its aftermath, for example). And there are various cases on record of entire villages decimated by diseases or outbreaks of witchcraft as a result of the intervention of whites in their lives.

Certainly these were important factors in the various prophetic movements since the mid-nineteenth century. The Baniwa Venâncio Kamiko, who prophesied a world conflagration that recalled mythic images of world destruction and renewal, led the first recorded prophetic movement. Oral histories recount the miraculous powers of Kamiko to produce things, to escape from the death planned for him by white soldiers, and to revive rejuvenated. Kamiko instructed his disciples to avoid contact with the whites, to observe periods of fasting, and to give him their total fidelity. The utopia that he promised was a place free of "sins" and "debts" to the whites. At the end of the nineteenth century or beginning of the twentieth, another messiah, probably Venâncio's son Anizetto, was attributed the creative power to produce things and to make gardens grow miraculously simply by making the sign of the cross. Like Kamiko, he was known as a miraculous curer and was identified with Jesus Cristu. He established a sort of sanctuary on the Cubate

River, where he and his disciples sought refuge from the rubber bosses and the military.

Half a century later, the prophet Kudui, a shaman of great prestige among the Hohódene, prophesied the realization of a utopia where "there would be no more sicknesses," which could be understood as an earthly sanctuary equivalent to the Other World, where there is no sickness. He spoke of the "place of happiness," *kathimákwe*, equivalent to the "city of God." Like the other messiahs before him, he was identified with Nhiãperikuli, with whom he communicated constantly in his dreams, and with Jesus Cristu; thus, the Hohódene considered him "our salvation." His village, located on an island of the Uaraná stream, was the mythical dwelling place of Nhiãperikuli. He preached not so much autonomy of the Baniwa from the whites as the coming of the whites to the area, for which the Hohódene had to prepare themselves, above all by respecting the laws of living. Although he never preached an "end of the world," he did prophesy imminent changes.

As Kudui's son declared to me in early 2000, to suggest—as the Protestant evangelicals did—that the world will come to an end is unthinkable. Individuals die, and their worlds come to an end, but the world as a whole has never come to an end and never will. Following this line of thinking, when prophets of the past announced the "end of the world" this may have been understood to mean that certain political, economic, social, or historical conditions, or states of culture (e.g., the practice of warfare) would come to an end, but not *hekwapi*, "this world."

The evangelical movement began among the Baniwa in the 1950s as a millenarian movement. The first Protestant missionary was a North American woman, Sophie Muller, who single-handedly evangelized the Baniwa, Wakuénai, and Curripaco. There are various indications—from the records of her travels and from Baniwa memories of her—that she came to be seen as a new messiah, as the one who announced imminent transformations in the world and its regeneration, and as one who had extraordinary powers to produce things, to make gardens grow. In short, she was seen according to the patterns of Baniwa prophets who had preceded her.

The majority of the Baniwa (approximately 80 percent) converted to the new religion she brought. In the beginning, the movement to convert had all the trappings of a millenarian movement; today, evangelicalism has established itself as the predominant religion among the Baniwa. It is a church, in the same way as other traditions of native churches are, such as the Hallelujah religion among the Carib-speaking peoples of the Guyanas. But why did the Baniwa see Sophie as a new messiah? Why did they follow her demand to abandon their culture, their traditions, and the ways of their ancestors? When I put this question to one of the current political leaders of the Baniwa associations, who is an evangelical, he answered me in the following way: At the time Sophie first came, some Baniwa shamans had foreseen the imminence of a series of great transformations that would occur in the world. One of these was the return of the world to the primordial times, the world of the beginning, the ideal and paradisiacal world.

In the history of the cosmos, this man recounted, there have been various moments when the world was destroyed and later regenerated. In the very first world, only one being existed; about this being and the world in which he existed, very little is known. It was a world in which everything was possible: Gardens grew by themselves, and so on. But that world came to an end when the great world tree called Kaalikathadapa—which connected the Other World with This World—was cut down. When this happened, Nhiãperikuli obtained *pariká*, the shaman's snuff, which is today the only means by which one can move between the two worlds.

The felling of the tree initiated the second period of the universe, which is the epoch in which Nhiãperikuli walked and obtained things in this world: the earth, the gardens, day and night, cooking fire, fish—in short, all things with which humanity could live in this world and prosper. As narrators state, Nhiãperikuli foresaw how things should be in this world for all future generations (*walimanai*, "for all those who will be born"). This period ended with the felling of another great world tree, or *axis mundi*, which likewise connected this world with the other world and was produced from the body of Nhiãperikuli's son Kúwai, who was burned to death at the end of the first rite of initiation. When this great tree was felled, Nhiãperikuli produced the first sacred flutes and trumpets, the body of Kúwai, with which the men initiate their children today. That is, the sacred flutes represent the principle of social and cultural reproduction—the means by which culture is transmitted over time—and in fact everything that Nhiãperikuli had obtained, which was left for all future generations to reproduce. After this, Nhiãperikuli washed and burned the world, ridding it of all predatory beings and malignant spirits, and then with the sacred flutes brought forth the ancestors of humanity.

According to this man, humanity today lives in the third period. But this third period, evangelicals believe, will likewise come to an end. Shamans are the only ones considered capable of knowing when the end of the world will occur. At the time of Sophie's coming, he said, some of them foresaw that great transformations would occur and that the world would return to its initial paradisiacal and miraculous state. Indeed, Sophie announced that the end of time was at hand.

But why would they believe in a white woman who simply ordered them to throw away their traditions? It happens that she was not seen as a normal white person, perhaps because she, unlike most whites before her, communicated to them in their language, and perhaps because of her eccentricities, such as praying in the forest alone at night, which many people associated with the nocturnal spirits. According to the Curripaco whom Nicolas Journet (personal communication, 1996) interviewed, her legend was that she was not like other women. She was considered to be "pure, chaste, she had no menses, and she only ate powdered milk," an image of a nonhuman, plausibly a messenger from the other world.

In their accounts of her message to them, the Baniwa remember that she sought to implant a morally puritan style of life—consistent with her real background—which forbade the use of tobacco and alcohol, sexual relations, and contact with the whites because this would lead to the damnation of their souls. People were supposed to only "think holy."

How did believers translate this message into practice? The historical project of the evangelicals—their "concrete utopia," to use Alicia Barabas's term (1989), that is, a utopia that is realized in practice over time—was to create an exclusivist community with its own distinctive style of life. This style of life included everything from the construction of their houses, which are notably different from the house styles of the Catholics; everything was to reflect the ideal of moral purity. In short, this was to be a utopia on this earth, here and now. Because the evangelicals prohibited everything related to the ancestors' ways of life, this meant that the vertical connection between the Other World of Baniwa divinities and This World had been severed. In the believers' new world, there were no more shamans, there were no more rituals of initiation, nor sacred flutes—in short, everything that connected humanity to its past and to the primordial world. It is as though all of the history of the universe had been wiped clean to begin a new world and utopia of the believers. If, before, the vertical Other World had represented the ideal, orderly, and beautiful, with the new generation of believers, the vertical had become superimposed on the horizontal plane of the earth. Utopia became here and now on this earth, not of the primordial past in the sky.

To what extent have the believers succeeded in creating and maintaining this utopia? They have never succeeded, and indeed it would be impossible to eliminate all of the evils, as the Baniwa conceive them, that plague the world. Believers die because of sorcery and witchcraft; they are still contaminated by the envy, jealousy, and anger that lead people to practice witchcraft. And with the participation of youths in the political movement, the risk of these young men getting lost from the way of moral rectitude is even greater.

Comparative Prophetic Traditions of the Northwest Amazon

In table 11.1 I have summarized all information available on prophetic movements among indigenous peoples of the northwest Amazon from the mid-nineteenth century, when we have the first records of such movements, to the present. The connections between prophets and their disciples are not readily apparent by a simple list in a table. From the sources, it is possible to determine that the most important of the Baniwa prophets, Venâncio Kamiko, taught all other Arawak-speaking prophets until his death at the beginning of this century. Among the Tukanoans, the first prophets were disciples of Baniwa prophets; however, the most important of the Tukanoan prophets was unquestionably the miraculous Desana girl María, whose disciples elaborated her teachings and preached among numerous Tukanoan-speaking peoples of the region.

Thus, there are actually two distinct prophetic traditions in the region, not one that was simply passed from one group to the other. The earliest cults, in the mid-nineteenth century, were Arawakan, and these were introduced among the Tukanoans of the Vaupés. But according to oral sources, the first Tukanoan movements didn't last very long; by contrast, the Arawakan tradition maintained its continuity on the Isana and Acque rivers until the early twentieth century. Among the Tukanoans, it was in the last quarter of the nineteenth century that two important foci of cult activities emerged: one on the Lower Vaupés, led by Arapaço shaman Vicente Christu, and the other, on the Papury River, beginning with the Desana girl María.

The first appears to have been very similar to its Baniwa counterpart led by Anizetto, which took place during the same period. In both movements, the shaman-prophets were seen as great healers who protected their people from the rubber bosses and merchants, who promoted the growth of plantations, relieving people from hunger and debt. Among Vicente's prophecies was that the rubber bosses would soon be expelled from the Vaupés region. Both were strongly influenced by the popular Catholicism of the region because Saint Anthony was considered a great protector of the Indians on a par with indigenous divinities: Nhiãperikuli for the Baniwa, and Tupana for the Tukanoans of the Vaupés.[9] Both movements had strong tones of rebellion, but neither sought to gain the whites' wealth, nor was there a suggestion of cargo. Vicente further prophesied that missionaries would soon come to the Vaupés because he had requested them from Tupana.

With the Desana girl María, the Tukanoan tradition appears to elaborate

Table 11.1. Millenarian Traditions of the Northwest Amazon

Years	Prophet's Prophets	Prophet's Group	Oral Following	Locations	Traditions	Written Sources
1857–1902	Venâncio Anizetto Kamiko	Dzauinai (Baniwa)	Baniwa, Baré, Tukano	Isana (Brazil), Acque (Venezuela)	Dzauinai, Hohódene, Tariana	Wright 1981; Wright and Hill 1986
1858	Alexandre	Baniwa	Tukanoan and Tariana	Lower/Middle Vaupés (Brazil)		Wright 1981; Wright and Hill 1986
1858	Basílio Melgueira, Claudio José, Cypriano Lopes	Baré Warekena (?) Warekena (?)	Baré, Baniwa, and Warekena	Xié River (Brazil and Venezuela)		Wright 1981; Wright and Hill 1986
1858	Caetano	Baniwa (?)		Vaupés		Wright 1981
1875–1903 (approx.)	Anizetto	Baniwa	Baniwa, Tukano	Cubate River		Wright 1981, 1998
Late 1870s/ early 1880s	Vicente	Arapaço (Tukanoan)	Indians of Vaupés	Japú Igarapé (Lower Vaupés)		Wright 1981, 1998; Hugh-Jones 1989
a	Joaquim Parakata	Tukano	Tuyuka, Karapaná, Tariana, Desana, Pira-tapuya	Papuri, Tiquié rivers		Hugh-Jones 1989
Late 19th century	Maria	Desana	Tukano, Desana, Pira-tapuya, Makú, and others	Papuri, Tiquié, Vaupés rivers	Desana	Panlon Kumu and Kenhíri 1980; Freitas 1983; Brüzzi da Silva 1977

Late 19th century	"Bishop" Paulino	Tukano	Tukano, Desana, Pira-tapuya, Makú, and others	Turí igarapé	Tukano	Freitas 1983
Early 20th century	Yewa, or Lino Sêwa ("Santo Lino")	Tukano	Tukanoan	Montfort (Papuri River), Vaupés, Tiquié	Desana	Hugh-Jones 1989; Fanlon Kumu and Kenhíri 1980; Brüzzi da Silva 1977
Early 20th century	Raimundo	Tukano	(?)	Turí igarapé	Desana	Hugh-Jones 1989
1948–50	Sophie Muller, Vítor Correa	North American, Curripaco	Curripaco, Baniwa, Cubeo	Isana, Aiary, Cuiary, Querary, Guaviare, Guainía	Baniwa	Wright 1998
[a]	Tukanoan and Bará emissaries	Tukanoan	Barasana, Bará, Arapaço, Tatuyo	Pira-paraná (Colombia), Tiquié	Barasana	Hugh-Jones 1989
1960s–70s	Kudui	Hohódene (Baniwa)	Baniwa, Wanano	Aiary River	Hohódene	Wright 1998

a. No specific information is available on these years because the information is obtained from oral traditions.

in directions that were distinct from that of the Arawakans. It is nevertheless instructive to continue the comparison, for it leads us back to representations of Sophie Muller, all the more interesting because these are the only
two female prophets in the region about whom there are oral traditions.
According to the version presented by Desana narrators Panlon Kumu and
Kenhíri (1980, 86–87; my translation), María was an important figure because
she provoked a great change in the eschatology of the Desana. Before her, "By
order of Boléka, the ancestor of the Desana, the souls of common people
[deceased] were sent to a house called *wahpíru wi* [a lake near where María
was born on the Papury]. The souls of all Desana of lesser or no power [i.e.,
who were not shamans or chanters] returned there, as is the case of women
and children. In this house, the soul of the deceased would remain as if it were
inside the body. The living at times heard the music of the sacred flutes being played by these souls, as well as their laughter and conversations. For many
centuries the souls of the ancients returned to this place, until there occurred
something which changed this custom."

The tradition goes on to recount María's life:

> At the headwaters of the Macu River, the wife of a Desana, without living
> much with her husband, conceived and gave birth to María. At two years of age,
> she played differently from other children. At three she sang songs differently
> from other children—stuttering, but melodious songs. At five, she and her
> friends made a cross with sticks. At 13, she asked her father to make her a drum
> and a cross of brazilwood, which he finally did. She also urged her friends to
> persuade their fathers to make them crosses. Every afternoon, they sang songs,
> but no one knew where the songs had come from.
>
> At 15, she told her parents that it was Kirítu [Jesus Cristu] who had taught her
> these songs, that he came from heaven advising her to sing these songs to par-
> don sinners. Her parents didn't know who Kirítu was, but she convinced them
> that they should believe in him. She began singing the song of the *kurúsa* [cross],
> the song of Bália [María], of Yusé [José], of Mentre [Master], Olha Santo [the
> saints], and Pardon of Sins. When there appeared men who had committed grave
> sins, she would fall on the ground because she felt the weight of their sins on
> her body. She said that in heaven there was a strong God who one day would
> come amongst them. Her fame spread among the people of the Papuri, Tiquié,
> Vaupés, and Pirá rivers who came to hear her message and sing her songs. Thus,
> the elders began to believe in Kirítu and all that María was saying.

The tradition then says, "It was at that time that the souls who were in
wahpíru wi disappeared. It seems that the song of *kurúsa* [the cross] took
them to the sky." According to this tradition, "evil men" who wanted to test
her poisoned María: "If she had power, she would not die. But she died." After

her death, another prophet emerged from the Papury. He was a Tukano sha-man called Yêwa or Lino Sêwa. It was he who foresaw the coming of the missionaries to the region: "The men of God who would be called *paiá*" (priests) and "virgins dressed in black with white habits" (nuns).

Another tradition cited in Hugh-Jones (1989, 27) asserts that "The White people sent her [María] a box containing a flag and other ornaments used by the *caboclos* for their saint-day festivals and in it they put a curse which caused a measles epidemic amongst her followers. After the epidemic, María announced the end of the world, a time when all sinners would be turned into animals with horns and eaten by jaguars and spirits. She added that deer and cows had once been people who were punished for their sins."

In the version summarized by Brüzzi Alves da Silva (1977, 284), an elder Tukano named Paulino, also from the Papury—and who may have been the same as Lino Sêwa—later elaborated on the rituals begun by María. He erect-ed a great cross on the plaza in front of his house where people often prayed, sang, and danced. They brought him presents, including red ribbons, which he wore around his neck. He came to be known as Bishop Paulino. His ritu-al consisted of people dancing three times around the cross, and with the nectar of flowers he baptized the people. With water that dripped from the wood, which he collected in a bottle, he worked cures on the sick.

To compare the two figures, María and Sophie, it is essential to remember that it is the *representations* the indigenous people made of them that are of interest and that reveal the imagery of prophetic consciousness. Both are represented as extraordinary people different from normal humans. María was conceived without a father and began to have visions as a child; like Sophie, she had no menses, was pure and chaste. Both are represented as urging their followers to dedicate their lives entirely to a new religion, which they transmitted through their direct connections to Christian divinities. Sophie urged her followers to "think holy," to sing and read the New Testa-ment; María taught hers to devote themselves to the cross and to sing. Both were considered saints. Both are represented as having provoked great changes in cosmologies related to the ancestors. For Sophie's followers, this meant a rupture in the vertical connection to their ancestral past; for María, there occurred a vertical dislocation of the houses of the souls of the dead. Both warned of the imminent end of the world. Sophie's followers translat-ed this warning into mythic images of catastrophic world destruction; María spoke of punishment through a catastrophic transformation of humans into animals of prey.

Characteristic of messianic myths, both figures are represented as having been persecuted, as struggling against an opposing force. In the case of Sophie, her followers say that the Baniwa who refused to follow her attempted to kill her and by exactly the same means that the whites used to kill the messiahs of the past (by drowning). In the case of María, the white men sought to destroy her through a measles epidemic, which, although she escaped, decimated her following. In both cases, shamans were important to the creation of messianic representations. Baniwa shamans announced Sophie's coming; María's principal disciple, a Tukano shaman, announced the coming of the Catholic missionaries.

To be sure, there are important differences in the representations of these two figures, particularly in relation to the new order they sought to introduce. Sophie's followers recalled her orders to "leave everything of your ancestors behind"—which was the great transformation that everyone expected—and obey a set of rules of living founded in a puritan morality. Traditions of María simply speak of the songs, dances, curing rituals, and devotion to the cross—in other words, new ritual forms but not a new morality or a rejection of ancestral ways.

Conclusion

This chapter has sought to contribute to the question of rethinking the concept of "culture area" in relation to Arawak-speaking peoples in the following three ways. First of all is through a comparative and ethnohistorical approach to the Arawak-speaking peoples of the northwest Amazon. Both written and oral sources demonstrate that the region of the Rio Negro Basin was inhabited since pre-contact times by Arawak-speaking peoples whose societies were interlinked through dense networks of political, social, economic, and ceremonial ties. Eduardo Galvão's proposal (1967) for the definition of a northern Amazon culture area based on external criteria, regardless of language differences, is inadequate, for if we take seriously the content of the oral traditions of the northern Arawak-speaking peoples, the contours of such culture areas turn out to be very different. That is, ethnic definitions of collective identity and alterity provide us with an altogether different view of the Arawakans' relations to their territory or culture area. Religious traditions of various Arawak-speaking peoples of the northwest Amazon define an ethno-map of places where peoples of the Arawak language family have left their mark in the form of sacred, world-creating music. Interestingly, this native point of view of their culture area coincides in large part with linguists' mapping of Arawak-speaking peoples north of the Amazon. Furthermore, these religious traditions are particularly sensitive to historical change, including places native peoples have come to know and even to occupy in historical (i.e., colonial) times.

Second, an in-depth interpretation of Baniwa shamanism, myth, and ritual discourse brings to light some of the central concepts related to sickness, ritual seclusion, and restrictions. These concepts, roughly equivalent to Western notions of contamination and purity, refer specifically to forms of behavior that produce or avoid life-threatening situations. On the more general level, these concepts refer to exceedingly dangerous yet highly creative powers to produce society. Myths, cosmology, and shamanism elaborate these concepts, among other ways, by contrasting the primordial and present-day worlds. Ritual specialists especially have the power to assume the attributes of key divinities involved in the creation and expansion of the primordial world from its original miniature size to its present-day size. In effect, they are responsible for the process of migration and the creation of new village and ritual spaces. Baniwa prophets are powerful shamans who announce and initiate the process of seeking a "good earth" free from sickness and life-threatening elements or conditions.

It is worth noting here that this explanation adds a new dimension to the central question of Max Schmidt's classic monograph on the Arawak-speaking peoples (1917)—that of the so-called Arawakan expansion—by focusing on native cosmology and ritual discourse as well as sociopolitical and economic processes. This question also received major consideration in the "Final Statement" of the Comparative Arawakan Histories conference.

In relation to the concept of culture area, I suggest that, for the Baniwa at least, this comprises a "sacred center" (the rapids called Hípana) from which the ancestors emerged and that represents an eternal source of refuge and creative power, surrounded by a large area defining the territories of the diverse Baniwa phratries of the past and present, interconnected through social, political, and ceremonial alliances; and a "peripheral zone" of extreme danger (some associate this with the city of São Gabriel da Cachoeira, others with further downriver), which opens up to a world inhabited by the whites and other "mixed" non-Arawak-speaking peoples.

Third, this chapter explored the similarities and differences between historical Arawakan and Tukanoan prophetic traditions, further illustrating the complexity of historical exchanges between the two cultures. I briefly compared the indigenous representations of two movements, both notable in having women as prophets (one a nonindigenous outsider), showing how the cosmologies of both peoples were transformed through the changes they introduced. Here my method centered on a controlled comparison of two cultures within a specific region who had experienced many of the same external forces of contact throughout history. Although there were certainly influences between the prophetic movements of the Arawakans on the Tukanoans, each developed its own culture-specific forms and practices related to their cosmologies and eschatologies. In this century, the mass movement of conversion to evangelical Christianity affected primarily—though not exclusively—the Arawak-speaking peoples. This raises the interesting question of whether this might not be related to a specifically Arawakan way of transforming ritual power to control the situation of contact. Indeed, the Comparative Arawakan Histories conference in Panama pointed to such processes "linked to transformational notions of the world and a marked flexibility in the face of change" as important dimensions of Arawakan cultural identity.

Notes

I am grateful to Dominique Buchillet, Jonathan Hill, Fernando Santos-Granero, Marcello Massenzio, Cristina Pompa, and Hanne Veber for their critical comments on earlier versions of this chapter.

1. The Manao people of the Middle Rio Negro were an extremely important connection in this network, as traders in a chain that linked sub-Andean chiefdoms (Tunebo, Chibcha) with the peoples of the Amazon and Solimões (Yurimagua, Aisuare) and with the kingdoms of the Guyanas. It is also evident that the peoples of the Isana, Vaupés, and Upper Negro river basins were connected by a series of overland trails and waterways to the peoples of the Solimões, Japurá-Caquetá, Putumayo, Branco, Orinoco, and Guaviare rivers.

2. In May 2000, the Tariana of the Vaupés River published a volume of their sacred stories, *Upíperi Kalísi. Histórias dos antigos Taliaseri-Phukurana*, edited by the União das Nações Indígenas do Rio Uaupés Acima, and the Federação das Organizações Indigenas do Rio Negro.

3. Hill (1993) has analyzed these traditions among the Dzauinai phratry of the Wakuénai; Vidal (1987), for the Piapoco of the Llanos in Colombia; González-Ñáñez, among the Warekena of the Caño San Miguel; and I, for the Hohódene of the Baniwa in Brazil (1993).

4. A Dzauinai elder of the Lower Aiary affirmed that there were four "moments" of emergence corresponding to four different phratries: in the first, the Daizo dakenai, Hohódene, Hipátanene, and Maulieni emerged; in the second, the Walipere dakenai, the Kamarheruene, and the Mauikulieni; in the third, the white people; and in the fourth, four Cubeo groups and the Desana.

5. For more detailed information on Baniwa shamanism, see Saake (1959–60) and Wright (1992a), and on chanters, see Hill (1993).

6. Even in daily practice, this opposition includes personal cleanliness and hygiene.

Daily bathing, for instance, is considered essential to avoid the attacks of sickness giving forest spirits, *iupinai,* which "become angry" with the "smell" of unclean persons.

7. The distinction between sorcerers and witches is based on the Baniwa distinction between the use of spoken formulas to inflict sicknesses (sorcerers) and the use of plant poisons (witches, or *manhene iminali* = "poison owner").

8. Indeed, Baniwa shamans appear to have elaborated a "cosmology of the whites" parallel and partially assimilated to the "cosmology of the Baniwa." Also, as a result of their contact with Afro Brazilian religions, they appear to have elaborated a series of parallelisms between rituals of *macumba* and shamanic practice.

9. In 1976–77, the cult of St. Anthony still claimed a large following on the Lower Vaupés River, where an old woman claimed to be able to communicate with the spirits of the dead and the saints and counseled those who requested her advice.

References Cited

Absy, Maria Lucía. 1985. "Palynology of Amazonia: The History of the Forests as Revealed by the Palynological Record." In *Amazonia.* Ed. Ghillean T. Prance and T. J. Lovejoy. 72–82. Oxford: Pergamon Press.

ACIRA/FOIRN. 1999. *Waferinaipe Ianheke: A Sabedoria dos Nossos Antepassados—Histórias dos Hohódene e dos Walipere-dakenai do Rio Aiary.* Trans. and revisions by Robin M. Wright. *Coleção Narradores Indígenas do Rio Negro 3.* São Gabriel da Cachoeira, Brazil: FOIRN.

Acuña, Cristoval de. 1864. "A New Discovery of the Great River of the Amazons." In *Expeditions into the Valley of the Amazons, 1539, 1540, 1639.* Ed. Clements R. Markham. 90–120. New York: Hakluyt Society.

Adam, Lucien. 1878. *Du parler des hommes et du parler des femmes dans la langue caraïbe.* Paris: Mémoires de l'Academie de Stanislas.

Aguado, Pedro de. 1906. *Recopilación historial.* 5 vols. Bogotá: Imprenta Nacional.

Aikhenvald, Alexandra Y. 1995. *Languages of the World: Materials 100.* Munich: Lincom Europa.

———. 1998. "Warekena." In *Handbook of Amazonian Languages.* 4 vols. Ed. Desmond C. Derbyshire and Geoffrey K. Pullum. 4:225–439. Berlin: Mouton de Gruyter.

———. 1999a. "The Arawak Language Family." In *The Amazonian Languages.* Ed. Robert M. W. Dixon and A. Y. Aikhenvald. 65–106. Cambridge: Cambridge University Press.

———. 1999b. "Areal Diffusion and Language Contact in the Içana-Vaupés Basin, Northwest Amazonia." In *The Amazonian Languages.* Ed. Robert M. W. Dixon and A. Y. Aikhenvald. 384–416. Cambridge: Cambridge University Press.

———. 2001. "Areal Diffusion, Genetic Inheritance and Problems of Subgrouping: A North Arawak Case Study." In *Areal Diffusion and Genetic Inheritance: Problems in Comparative Linguistics.* Ed. Alexandra Y. Aikhenvald and R. M. W. Dixon. Oxford: Oxford University Press.

Aikhenvald, Alexandra Y., and Diana Green. 1998. "Palikur and the Typology of Classifiers." *Anthropological Linguistics* 40(3):1–53.

Alès, Catherine. 1981. "Les tribus indiennes de l'Ucayali au XVIe siècle." *Bulletin de l'Institut Français d'Etudes Andines* 10(3–4):87–97.

Almesto, Pedrarias de. 1986. "Jornada de Omagua y Dorado." In *La Aventura del Amazonas*. Ed. Rafael Díaz. 99–223. Madrid: Historia 16.

Altolaguirre y Duvale, Angel. 1954. *Relaciones Geográficas de la Gobernación de Venezuela, 1767–68*. Caracas: Ediciones de la Presidencia de la República.

Alvarez Lobo, Ricardo. 1984. *Tsla: Estudio Etno-Histórico del Urubamba y Alto Ucayali*. Salamanca, Spain: Editorial San Esteban.

Amich, José. 1975. *Historia de las Misiones del Convento de Santa Rosa de Ocopa*. Lima: Milla Batres.

Amorim, Antonio Brandão de. 1928. "Lendas em Nheêngatú e em Portuguez." *Revista do Instituto Historico e Geographico Brasileiro* 100(154):1–445.

Anghiera, Pietro Martire d'. 1530. *De Orbo Novo*. Compluti: Apud Michaele d'Eguia.

Anthony, David W. 1990. "Migration in Archaeology: The Baby and the Bathwater." *American Anthropologist* 92:895–914.

Arnaud, Expedito. 1968. "Referências Sôbre o Sistema de Parentesco dos Indios Palikúr." *Boletim do Museu Paraense Emílio Goeldi* (Nova Série Antropologia) 36:1–21.

———. 1970. "O Xamanismo entre os Indios da Região Uaçá." *Boletim do Museu Paraense Emílio Goeldi* (Nova Série Antropologia) 44:1–22.

———. 1984. "Os Indios Palikúr do Rio Urucauá: Tradição Tribal e Protestantismo." *Publicações Avuls: Museu Emílio Goeldi* 39:23–47.

Arriaga, Julián de. 1954. "Viaje del Excmo. Señor D. Josef Solano Marques del Socorro en la Provincia de Guayana, Siendo Capitán de Fragata de la Real Armada, y Comisionado por el Estado con D. Josef de Iturriaga, Jefe de Escuadra, D. Eugenio de Alvarado Marques de Toveloso, Coronel de Infantería, y D. Antonio de Urrutia, Capitán de Navío, para efectuar los Acordados Límites de los Dominios del Rey y del Rey Fidelísimo, en la Parte Septemtrional de la América Meridional." In *Relaciones Geográficas de la Gobernación de Venezuela, 1767–68*. Ed. Angel de Altolaguirre y Duvale. 243–88. Caracas: Ediciones de la Presidencia de la República.

Arrom, José Juan. 1999. Introduction to *An Account of the Antiquities of the Indians* by Ramón Pané. xi–xxix. Durham, N.C.: Duke University Press.

Arvelo-Jiménez, Nelly, and Horacio Biord. 1994. "The Impact of Conquest on Contemporary Indigenous Peoples of the Guiana Shield: The System of Orinoco Regional Interdependence." In *Amazonian Indians from Prehistory to the Present: Anthropological Perspectives*. Ed. Anna C. Roosevelt. 55–78. Tucson: University of Arizona Press.

Augé, Marc. 1997. *Non-places: Introduction to an Anthropology of Supermodernity*. London: Verso.

Baldi, Philip, ed. 1990. *Linguistic Change and Reconstruction Methodology*. Berlin: Mouton de Gruyter.

Barabas, Alicia. 1989. *Utopías Indias: Movimientos Socioreligiosos en México*. Mexico City: Grijalbo.

Barnard, F. M., trans. and ed. 1969. *Herder on Social and Political Culture*. Cambridge: Cambridge University Press.

Barre, Lefebvre de la. 1666. *Description de la France équinoctiale*. Paris: I. Ribov.

Barrère, Pierre. 1743. *Nouvelle relation de la France équinoxiale*. Paris: Piget.

Barth, Frederik, ed. 1969. *Ethnic Groups and Boundaries*. Boston: Little, Brown.

Bartra, Roger. 1994. *Wild Men in the Looking Glass: The Mythic Origins of European Otherness*. Ann Arbor: University of Michigan Press.

Basso, Ellen B. 1973. *The Kalapalo Indians of Central Brazil*. New York: Holt, Rinehart and Winston.

———, ed. 1977. *The Carib-Speaking Indians: Culture, Society, and Language*. Tucson: University of Arizona Press.

———. 1985. *A Musical View of the Universe: Kalapalo Myth and Ritual Performances*. Philadelphia: University of Pennsylvania Press.

———. 1995. *The Last Cannibals: A South American Oral History*. Austin: University of Texas Press.

Bateson, Gregory. 1980. *Naven: The Culture of the Iatmul People of New Guinea as Revealed through the Study of the "Naven" Ceremonial*. (1936). London: Wildwood House.

Baumann, Gerd. 1987. *National Integration and Local Integrity: The Miri of the Nuba Mountains of the Sudan*. Oxford: Clarendon Press.

Bender, Barbara. 1993. "Introduction: Landscape-Meaning and Action." In *Landscape, Politics, and Perspective*. Ed. Barbara Bender. 1–17. Oxford: Berg.

Benjamin, Walter. 1973. "The Storyteller: Reflections on the Works of Nikolai Leskov" (1955). In *Illuminations*. Ed. Hannah Arendt. 83–109. London: Fontana.

Bennett, John. 1989. "An Arawak-English Dictionary." *Archaeology and Anthropology* 6(1–2).

Bennett, Wendell C. 1936. "Excavations in Bolivia." *Anthropological Papers of the American Museum of Natural History* 35:329–507.

Beraún, Bartolomé. 1981. "Carta del Capitán . . . al Gobernador D. Francisco de Elso y Arbizu" (1686). *Amazonía Peruana* 4(7):177–78.

Betendorf, João Felippe S. J. 1910. "Chronica da Missão dos Padres da Companhia de Jesus no Estado do Maranhão." In *Revista do Instituto Historico e Geographico Brasileiro*. Vol. 72 (1). Rio de Janeiro: Imprensa Nacional.

Biedma, Manuel. 1906. "Relación e Informe . . ." (1685). In *Colección de Documentos que Apoyan el Alegato de Bolivia en el Juicio Arbitral con la República del Perú*. Vol. 2: 319–28. Buenos Aires: Cía. Sud-Americana de Billetes de Banco.

———. 1981. *La Conquista Franciscana del Ucayali*. Lima: Milla Batres.

Biersack, Aletta. 2001. "Reproducing Inequality: The Gender Politics of Male Cults in the Papua New Guinea Highlands and Amazonia." In *Gender in Amazonia and Melanesia: An Exploration of the Comparative Method*. Ed. Thomas Gregor and Donald Tuzin. 69–90. Berkeley: University of California Press.

Biet, Antoine. 1664. *Voyage dans la France equinoxiale en l'Isle de Cayenne*. Paris: F. Clouzier.

Biord-Castillo, Horacio. 1985. "Contexto Multilingüe del Sistema de Interdependencia Regional del Orinoco." *Antropológica* 63–64:83–101.

Blitz, John M. 1999. "Mississippian Chiefdoms and the Fission-Fusion Process." *American Antiquity* 64(4):577–92.

Boas, Franz. 1928. *Anthropology and Modern Life*. New York: W. W. Norton.

Bodley, John H. 1970. "Campa Socio-Economic Adaptation." Ph.D. diss., University of Oregon.

———. 1984. "Deferred Exchange among the Campa: A Reconsideration." In *Networks of the Past: Regional Interaction in Archaeology.* Ed. Peter D. Francis, F. J. Dense, and P. G. Duke. 19–28. Calgary, Alberta: Archaeological Association of the University of Calgary.

Bolívar, Gregorio de. 1906. "Relación de la Entrada del P. Fray Gregorio de Bolívar a las Provincias de Indios Chunchos en 1621." In *Exposición de la República del Perú . . . en el Juicio de Límites entre el Perú y Bolivia conforme al Tratado de Arbitraje de 30 de Diciembre de 1902.* 15 vols. Ed. Víctor M. Maúrtua. 8:205–37. Barcelona: Imprenta de Henrich y Comp.

Bono, James J. 1995. *The Word of God and the Languages of Man: Interpreting Nature in Early Modern Science and Medicine.* Vol. 1: *Ficino to Descartes.* Madison: University of Wisconsin Press.

Boomert, Arie. 1995. "Island Carib Archaeology." In *Wolves from the Sea: Readings in the Archaeology and Anthropology of the Island Carib.* Ed. Neil L. Whitehead. 23–36. Leiden, The Netherlands: KITLV Press.

Bourdieu, Pierre. 1993. *Outline of a Theory of Practice.* (1972). Cambridge: Cambridge University Press.

Bourgue, François. 1976. "Los Caminos de los Hijos del Cielo. Estudio Socio-Territorial de los Kawillary del Cananarí y del Apaporis." *Revista Colombiana de Antropología* 20:101–46.

Boyer du Petit Puy, Paul. 1654. *Véritable relation de tout ce qui s'est fait et passé au voyage que M. de Brétigny fit à l'Amérique Occidentale.* Paris: P. Rocolet.

Bravo, Anna, Lilia Davite, and Daniele Jalla. 1990. "Myth, Impotence, and Survival in the Concentration Camps." In *The Myths We Live By.* Ed. Raphael Samuel and Paul Thompson. 95–110. London: Routledge.

Breton, Raymond. 1665. *Dictionnaire caraïbe-français.* Auxerre, France: Giles Bouquet.

———. 1666. *Dictionnaire français-caraïbe.* Auxerre: Giles Bouquet.

Brett, William Henry. 1868. *The Indian Tribes of Guiana: Their Condition and Habits— With Researches into Their Past History, Superstitions, Legends, Antiquities, Languages.* London: Bell and Daldy.

Brinton, Daniel G. 1871. "The Arawack Language of Guiana in Its Linguistic and Ethnological Relations." *American Philosophical Society Transaction* 14:427–44.

———. 1891. *The American Race: A Linguistic Classification and Ethnographic Description of the Native Tribes of North and South America.* New York: N. D. C. Hodges.

Brochado, José P. 1984. "An Ecological Model of the Spread of Pottery and Agriculture into Eastern South America." Ph.D. diss., University of Illinois at Urbana-Champaign.

Brown, Michael, ed. 1984. *Relaciones Interétnicas y Adaptación Cultural entre Shuar, Achuar, Aguaruna y Canelos Quichua.* Quito: Abya-Yala.

Brown, Michael F., and Eduardo Fernández. 1991. *War of Shadows. The Struggle for Utopia in the Peruvian Amazon.* Berkeley: University of California Press.

———. 1992. "Tribe and State in a Frontier Mosaic: The Asháninka of Eastern Peru." In *War in the Tribal Zone: Expanding States and Indigenous Warfare.* Ed. Brian Ferguson and Neil L. Whitehead. 175–97. Santa Fe, N.Mex.: School of American Research Press.

Brumfiel, Elizabeth M. 1994. Introduction to *Factional Competition and Political Devel-*

opment in the New World. Ed. Elizabeth M. Brumfiel and J. W. Fox. 3–13. Cambridge: Cambridge University Press.

Brüzzi Alves da Silva, Alcionílio. 1977. *A Civilização Indígena do Uaupés*. Rome: Librería Ateneo Salesiano.

Bush, Mark B., Dolores R. Piperno, and Paul A. Colinvaux. 1989. "A 6000-Year History of Amazonian Maize Cultivation." *Nature* 340:303–5.

Butt-Colson, Audrey. 1984a. "A Comparative Study of Contributions." In *Themes in Political Organization: The Caribs and Their Neighbors*. Ed. Audrey Butt-Colson and H. Dieter Heinen. Special issue of *Antropológica* 59–62:9–38.

———. 1984b. "The Spatial Component in the Political Structure of the Carib Speakers of the Guiana Highlands: Kapon and Pemon." In *Themes in Political Organization: The Caribs and Their Neighbors*. Ed. Audrey Butt-Colson and H. Dieter Heinen. Special issue of *Antropológica* 59–62:73–124.

———. 1985. "Routes of Knowledge: An Aspect of Regional Integration in the Circum-Roraima Area of the Guiana Highlands." *Antropológica* 63–64:103–49.

Butt-Colson, Audrey, and H. Dieter Heinen, eds. 1984. *Themes in Political Organization: The Caribs and Their Neighbors*. Special issue of *Antropológica* 59–62.

Cabral, Ana S. 1995. "Contact-Induced Language Change in Western Amazonia: The Non-Genetic Origin of the Kokáma Language." Ph.D. diss., University of Pittsburgh.

Camino, Alejandro. 1977. "Trueque, Correrías e Intercambio entre los Quechuas Andinos y Los Piro y Machiguenga de la Montaña Peruana." *Amazonía Peruana* 1(2):123–40.

Campbell, Lyle. 1988. Review of *Language in the Americas* by Joseph Greenberg. *Language* 64:591–615.

———. 1999. *Historical Linguistics: An Introduction*. Cambridge, Mass.: MIT Press.

Campbell, Lyle, and Ives Goddard. 1990. "Summary Report: American Indian Languages and Principles of Language Change." In *Linguistic Change and Reconstruction Methodology*. Ed. Philip Baldi. 17–32. Berlin: Mouton de Gruyter.

Carneiro, Robert L. 1970. "A Theory of the Origin of the State." *Science* 169:733–38.

———. 1987. "Village Splitting as a Function of Population Size." In *Themes in Ethnology and Culture History: Essays in Honor of David F. Aberle*. Ed. Leland Donald. 94–124. Meerut, India: Archana Publications.

Carranza, Albino. 1894. "Geografía Descriptiva y Estadística Industrial de Chanchamayo." *Boletín de la Sociedad Geográfica de Lima* 4(1–3):18–35.

Carsten, Janet E., and Stephen Hugh-Jones. 1995. Introduction to *About the House: Lévi-Strauss and Beyond*. Ed. Janet Carsten and Stephen Hugh-Jones. 1–46. Cambridge: Cambridge University Press.

Carvajal, Jacinto de. 1892. *Relación del Descubrimiento del Río Apure hasta su Ingreso en el Orinoco*. León, Spain: Diputación Provincial.

Cassani, Joseph. 1967. *Historia de la Provincia de la Compañía de Jesús del Nuevo Reyno de Granada en la América*. Caracas: Biblioteca de la Academia Nacional de la Historia.

Caulín, Antonio. 1841. *Historia Corográfica, Natural y Evangélica de la Nueva Andalucía, Provincia de Cumaná, Nueva Barcelona, Guayana y Vertientes del Orinoco*. Caracas: George Corser.

Cavalli-Sforza, L. L., Paolo Menozzi, and Alberto Piazza. 1996. *The History and Geography of Human Genes*. Princeton, N.J.: Princeton University Press.

Chanca, Diego Alvarez. 1907. *The Letter of Dr. Diego Alvarez Chanca, Dated 1498, Relating to the Second Voyage of Columbus to America. By Augustine Marcus Fernández de Ybarra*. Washington, D.C.: Smithsonian Institution.

Chernela, Janet M. 1988. "Righting History in the Northwest Amazon: Myth, Structure, and History in an Arapaço Narrative." In *Rethinking History and Myth: Indigenous South American Perspectives on the Past*. Ed. Jonathan D. Hill. 35–49. Urbana: University of Illinois Press.

———. 1993. *The Wanano Indians of the Brazilian Amazon: A Sense of Space*. Austin: University of Texas Press.

Chrétien, Jean. 1725. *Lettre inédite sur les Galibis*. Chantilly: Archives des Jésuites des Paris.

Cieza de León, Pedro. 1967. *El Señorío de los Incas* (1553). Lima: Instituto de Estudios Peruanos.

Civrieux, Marc de. 1980. *Watunna: An Orinoco Creation Cycle*. Trans. David Guss. San Francisco: North Point Press.

Clastres, Pierre. 1987. *Society against the State: Essays in Political Anthropology*. New York: Zone Books.

Cohen, Percy. 1969. "Theories of Myth." *Man* 4(3):337–53.

Colinvaux, Paul A., P. E. de Oliveira, and M. B. Bush. 2000. "Amazonian and Neotropical Plant Communities on Glacial Time Scales: The Failure of the Aridity and Refuge Hypotheses." *Quaternary Science Reviews* 19:141–69.

Colón, Fernando. 1947. *Vida del Almirante don Cristóbal Colón*. Mexico City: Fondo de Cultura Económica.

Comaroff, John, and Jean Comaroff. 1992. *Ethnography and the Historical Imagination*. Boulder, Colo.: Westview Press.

Condillac, Etienne Bonnot de. 1793. *Essai sur l'origine des connaissances humaines*. Paris: Chez les Libraires Associés.

Contreras, Fernando. 1906. "Representación de Fernando Contreras a S.M. sobre la Reducción de la Aucaya, Austria-América, Nueva Provincia de los Minarvas" (1651). In *Exposición de la República del Perú . . . en el Juicio de Límites entre el Perú y Bolivia conforme al Tratado de Arbitraje de 30 de Diciembre de 1902*. 15 vols. Ed. Víctor M. Maúrtua. 5:59–79. Barcelona: Imprenta de Henrich y Comp.

Coudreau, Henri. 1893. *Chez nos Indiens: quatre années dans la Guyane Française, 1887–1891*. Paris: Hachette.

Crevaux, Jules, P. Sagot, and L. Adam. 1882. "Arawakisch-Deutsches Wörterbuch." In *Grammaires et vocabulaires roucouyenne, arrouague, piapoco et d'autres langues de la région des Guyanes*. Paris: Maisonneuve.

Crocker, Christopher J. 1979. "Selves and Alters among the Eastern Bororo." In *Dialectical Societies: The Gê and Bororo of Central Brazil*. Ed. David Maybury-Lewis. 249–300. Cambridge, Mass.: Harvard University Press.

Crumley, Carol L. 1987. "A Dialectical Critique of Hierarchy." In *Power Relations and State Formation*. Ed. T. C. Patterson and C. W. Gailey. 155–68. Washington D.C.: American Anthropological Association.

———. 1991. "Historical Ecology: A Multidimensional Ecological Orientation." In *Historical Ecology: Cultural Knowledge and Changing Landscapes*. Ed. Carol L. Crumley. 1–16. Santa Fe, N.Mex.: School of American Research.

Cuervo, Antonio B. 1893–4. *Colección de Documentos Inéditos sobre la Geografía e Historia de Colombia*. Vols. 3–4. Bogotá: Imprenta de Zalamea Hermanos.

Daniel, João. 1916. "Parte Segunda do Thesouro Descoberto no Maximo Rio Amazonas." *Revista do Instituto Historico e Geographico Brasileiro* 2:338–74.

DeBoer, Warren, and J. Scott Raymond. 1987. "Roots Revisited: The Origins of the Shipibo Art Style." *Journal of Latin American Lore* 13(1):115–32.

De la Cruz, Laureano. 1986. "Relación del Descubrimiento del Río de las Amazonas, hoy S. Francisco de Quito, y Declaración del Mapa donde esta Pintado." In *La Aventura del Amazonas*. Ed. Rafael Díaz. 231–52. Madrid: Historia 16.

Denevan, William M. 1976. "The Aboriginal Population of Amazonia." In *The Native Population of the Americas in 1492*. Ed. William M. Denevan. 205–34. Madison: University of Wisconsin Press.

———. 1980. *La Geografía Cultural Aborigen de los Llanos de Mojos*. La Paz: Librería Editorial Juventud.

De Oliveira, Adélia E. 1994. "The Evidence for the Nature of the Process of Indigenous Deculturation and Destabilization in the Brazilian Amazon in the Last Three Hundred Years." In *Amazonian Indians from Prehistory to the Present. Anthropological Perspectives*. Ed. Anna C. Roosevelt. 95–119. Tucson: University of Arizona Press.

De Préfontaine, Jean Antoine Bruletout. 1749. "Notes manuscrites portées sur 'La Carte Géographique de l'Isle de Cayenne.'" In *Atlas de Gabriel Marcel*. Paris: Bibliothèque Nationale.

Derbyshire, Desmond C., and Doris L. Payne. 1990. "Noun Classification Systems in Amazonian Languages." In *Amazonian Linguistics: Studies in Lowland South American Languages*. Ed. Doris L. Payne. 243–71. Austin: University of Texas Press.

Derbyshire, Desmond C., and Geoffrey K. Pullum, eds. 1986. *Handbook of Amazonian Languages*. 4 vols. 1:469–566. Berlin: Mouton de Gruyter.

Descola, Phillipe. 1996. *In the Society of Nature: A Native Ecology in Amazonia*. Cambridge: Cambridge University Press.

Detienne, Marcel. 1980. "Mito/Rito." In *Enciclopedia Einaudi*. Ed. Ruggiero Romano. 16 vols. 9:348–363. Turin: G. Einaudi.

Deyrolle, E. 1916. "Notes d'anthropologie guyanaise: les Indiens marouanes." *Bulletins et Mémoires de la Société d'Anthropologie de Paris* 6(7):153–64.

Dixon, Robert M. W. 1995. "Fusional Development of Gender Marking in Jarawara Possessed Nouns." *International Journal of American Linguistics* 61(3):263–94.

———. 1997. *The Rise and Fall of Languages*. Cambridge: Cambridge University Press.

———. 1999. "Arawá." In *The Amazonian Languages*. Ed. Robert M. W. Dixon and A. Y. Aikhenvald. 292–306. Cambridge: Cambridge University Press.

Dixon, Robert M. W., and Alexandra Y. Aikhenvald. 1999. *The Amazonian Languages*. Cambridge: Cambridge University Press.

Dole, Gertrude E. 1961–62. "A Preliminary Consideration of the Prehistory of the Upper Xingu Basin." *Revista do Museu Paulista* 13:399–423.

———. 2000. "Los Amahuaca." In *Guía Etnográfica de la Alta Amazonía*. 3 vols. Ed.

Fernando Santos and Frederica Barclay. 3:125–273. Quito: Smithsonian Tropical Research Institute/Instituto Francés de Estudios Andinos/Abya-Yala.

Dooley, Robert A., and Harold Green. 1977. "Aspetos Verbais e Categorias Discursivas da Lingua Palikúr." *Série Linguística* 7:7–28.

Dreyfus, Simone. 1980–81. "Notes sur la chefferie Taino d'Aiti: capacités productrices, ressources alimentaries, pouvoirs dans une société précolombienne de forêt tropicale." *Journal de la Société des Americanistes* 67:229–48.

———. 1981. "Le peuple de la rivière du milieu: esquisse pour l'etude de l'espace social Palikur." In *Orients pour Georges Condominas*. 301–13. Paris: Sudestasie Privat.

———. 1983–84. "Historical and Political Anthropological Inter-connections: The Multilinguistic Indigenous Polity of the 'Carib' Islands and Mainland Coast from the 16th to the 18th Century." In *Themes in Political Organization: The Caribs and Their Neighbors*. Ed. Audrey Butt-Colson and H. Dieter Heinen. Special issue of *Antropológica* 59–62:39–55.

———. 1988. "Les Palikur." *Ethnies* 1–2:21–22.

———. 1992. "Les réseaux politiques indigènes en Guyane occidentale et leurs transformations aux XVIIe et XVIIIe siècles." *L'Homme* 122–24(2–4):75–98.

Dumont, Louis. 1970. *Homo Hierarchicus: The Caste System and Its Implications*. Chicago: University of Chicago Press.

Duranti, Alessandro, and Donald L. Brenneis, eds. 1986. *The Audience as Co-author*. Special Issue of *Text* 6(3).

Durbin, Marshall. 1977. "A Survey of the Carib Language Family." In *Carib-Speaking Indians: Culture, Society, and Language*. Ed. Ellen B. Basso. 23–38. Tucson: University of Arizona Press.

Earle, Timothy. 1997. *How Chiefs Come to Power: The Political Economy in Prehistory*. Stanford, Calif.: Stanford University Press.

Echeverri, Juan Alvaro. 1997. "The People of the Center of the World." Ph.D. diss., New School for Social Research.

Eder, Francisco Javier. 1985. *Breve Descripción de las Reducciones de Mojos*. Cochabamba: Historia Boliviana.

Eguiluz, Diego de. 1884. *Historia de la Misión de Mojos* (1696). Lima: Imprenta del Universo.

Ehrenreich, Paul. 1891. "Beitrage zur Völkerkunde Brasiliens." *Veroffentlichungen aus dem Königlichen. Museum für Völkerkunde II*. Berlin.

———. 1948. "Contribuições para a Etnologia do Brasil." *Revista do Museu Paulista* 2:7–132.

Erickson, Clark L. 1980. "Sistemas Agrícolas Prehispánicos en los Llanos de Mojos." *América Indígena* 40:731–55.

———. 2000. "An Artificial Landscape-Scale Fishery in the Bolivian Amazon." *Nature* 408:190–93.

Erikson, Philippe. 1994. "Los Mayoruna." In *Guía Etnográfica de la Alta Amazonía*. 3 vols. Ed. Fernando Santos and Frederica Barclay. 2:1–127. Quito: Facultad Latino Americana de Ciencias Sociales/Instituto Francés de Estudios Andinos.

Fabian, Johannes. 1983. *Time and the Other: How Anthropology Makes Its Object*. New York: Columbia University Press.

Facundes, Sidney da Silva. 2000a. "Internal Relationships in Arawak: Apurinã, Piro, and Iñapari." Ms.

———. 2000b. "The Language of the Apurinã (Arawak) People of Brazil." Ph.D. diss., State University of New York at Buffalo.

Farabee, William C. 1967. *The Central Caribs.* The Netherlands: Oosterhout N.B.

Fauque, Père Elzear. 1839. *Lettres edifiantes et curieuses* (1729–36). Paris.

Federmann, Nicolás. 1916. *Narración del Primer Viaje de Federmann a Venezuela.* Caracas: Litografía Comercio.

Feld, Steven, and Keith H. Basso, eds. 1997. *Senses of Place.* Santa Fe, N.Mex.: School of American Research Press.

Fernandes, Eurico. 1948. "Contribuição ao Estudo Etnográfico do Grupo Aruak." *Acta Americana* 6(3–4):200–221.

Fernández de Bovadilla, Francisco. 1964. "Relación del Viaje que hice desde Guayana al Alto Orinoco, de Orden del Coronel Joaquín Moreno de Mendoza." In *Relaciones Geográficas de Venezuela.* Ed. Antonio Arellano. 387–398. Caracas: Biblioteca de la Academia Nacional de la Historia.

Ferreira, Alexandre Rodríguez. 1885. "Diario da Viagem pela Capitania de São José do Rio-Negro. Parte 1." *Revista Trimensal do Instituto Historico, Geographico e Ethnographico do Brazil* 48:1–234.

———. 1886. "Diario da Viagem pela Capitania de São José do Rio-Negro. Parte 2." *Revista Trimensal do Instituto Historico, Geographico e Ethnographico do Brazil* 49:123–288.

———. 1887. "Diario da Viagem pela Capitania de São José do Rio Negro." *Revista Trimensal do Instituto Historico, Geographico e Ethnographico do Brasil* 50:11–141.

———. 1888. "Diario da Viagem pela Capitania de São José do Rio-Negro." *Revista Trimensal do Instituto Historico, Geographico e Ethnographico do Brasil* 51:5–166.

Firth, Raymond. 1936. *We, the Tikopia.* London: George Allen and Unwin.

Flannery, Kent V. 1994. "Childe the Evolutionist: A Perspective from Nuclear America." In *The Archaeology of V. Gordon Childe.* Ed. David Harris. 101–20. Chicago: University of Chicago Press.

Font, Juan (y Antonio Bivar). 1602. "Entrada . . . a los Andes de Jauja en 1602: Expediente, Auto y Declaraciones." In *Biblioteca de Autores Españoles* 185:257–78.

Ford, James A. 1969. *A Comparison of Formative Cultures in the Americas: Diffusion or the Psychic Unity of Man.* Washington, D.C.: Smithsonian Institution Press.

Forêt, Jesse de. 1914. "Original Account of the Expedition of Jesse de Forêt" (1623–24). In *A Wallon Family in America* by E. Forest. London: British Museum.

Fox, Anthony. 1995. *Linguistic Reconstruction: An Introduction to Theory and Method.* Oxford: Oxford University Press.

Frank, Andre Gunder. 1967. *Capitalism and Underdevelopment in Latin America.* New York: Monthly Review Press.

Frank, Erwin. 1994. "Los Uni." In *Guía Etnográfica de la Alta Amazonía.* 3 vols. Ed. Fernando Santos and Frederica Barclay. 2:129–238. Quito: Facultad Latino Americana de Ciencias Sociales/Instituto Francés de Estudios Andinos.

Freitas, Dona Leopoldina. 1983. "História da Cruz: Enemini (Rouxinol)." *Jornal Informativo* (September):6.

Friedland, Roger, and Deidre Boden, eds. 1994. *NowHere: Space, Time, and Modernity.* Berkeley: University of California Press.

Friedman, Jonathan. 1975. "Dynamique et transformations du système tribal: l'exemple des Katchin." *L'Homme* 15(1):63–98.

Galvão, Eduardo. 1967. "Indigenous Culture Areas of Brazil, 1900–1959." In *Indians of Brazil in the Twentieth Century.* Ed. J. Hopper. 167–207. Washington, D.C.: Institute for Cross-Cultural Research.

———. 1979. *Encontro de Sociedades: Indios e Brancos no Brasil.* Rio de Janeiro: Paz e Terra.

Garcés Dávila, Alicia. 1992. "La Economía Colonial y Su Impacto en las Sociedades Indígenas: El Caso de la Gobernación de Quijos, Siglos XVI–XVII." In *Opresión Colonial y Resistencia Indígena en la Alta Amazonía.* Ed. Fernando Santos-Granero. 49–75. Quito: FLACSO-Sede Ecuador/Abya-Yala/CEDIME.

Geertz, Clifford. 1993. *The Interpretation of Cultures.* London: Fontana Press.

Gil, Juan, and C. Varela, eds. 1984. *Cartas de Particulares a Colón y Relaciones Coetáneas.* Madrid: Alianza Editorial.

Gilij, Felipe Salvador. 1965. *Ensayo de Historia Americana.* 4 vols. Caracas: Biblioteca de la Academia Nacional de la Historia.

Gilij, Filippo Salvatore. 1780–84. *Saggio di Storia Americana, o sia, Storia Naturale, Civile e Sacra de'Regni e delle Provinzia Spagnuole di Terra-Ferma nell'America Meridionale.* Vol. 4. Rome: L. Perego erede Salvioni.

Gillin, John. 1963. "Tribes of the Guianas and the Left Amazon Tributaries." In *Handbook of South American Indians.* 7 vols. Ed. Julian H. Steward. 3:799–860. New York: Cooper Square Publishers.

Goddard, Ives. 1987. Review of *Language in the Americas* by Joseph Greenberg. *Current Anthropology* 28:656–57.

Godelier, Maurice. 1969. "La 'Monnaie de Sel' des Baruya de Nouvelle Guinée." *L'Homme* 9(2):5–37.

Goeje, Claudius Henricus de. 1928. *The Arawak Language of Guiana.* Amsterdam: Verhandelingen der Koninklijke Akademie van Wetenschappen.

———. 1939. "Nouvel Examen des Langues des Antilles." *Journal de la Société des Américanistes* 31:1120.

Goldman, Irving. 1955. "Status Rivalry and Cultural Evolution in Polynesia." *American Anthropologist* 57:680–97.

———. 1963. *The Cubeo Indians of the Northwest Amazon.* Urbana: University of Illinois Press.

Golla, Victor. 1987. Review of *Language in the Americas* by Joseph Greenberg. *Current Anthropology* 64:657–59.

———. 1988. Review of *Language in the Americas* by Joseph Greenberg. *American Anthropologist* 90:434–35.

Gonçalves, Marco Antonio. 1991. *Acre: História e Etnologia.* Rio de Janeiro: UFRJ.

González Ñáñez, Omar. 1980. *Mitología Guarequena.* Caracas: Monte Avila Editores.

Gow, Peter. 1991. *Of Mixed Blood: Kinship and History in the Peruvian Amazon.* Oxford: Clarendon Press.

———. 1993. "Gringos and Wild Indians: Images of History in Western Amazonian Cultures." *L'Homme* 126–28:331–51.

————. 2000. "Helpless: The Affective Preconditions of Piro Social Life." In *The Anthropology of Love and Anger: The Aesthetics of Conviviality in Native Amazonia*. Ed. Joanna Overing and Alan Passes. 46–63. London: Routledge.

————. 2001. *An Amazonian Myth and Its History*. Oxford: Oxford University Press.

Green, Harold. 1960. "Palikur: Formulario dos Vocabulários Padrões para Estudos Comparativos Preliminares nas Línguas Indígenas Brasileiras." Ms. Rio de Janeiro: Museu Nacional, Divisão de Antropologia, Setor Lingüístico.

————. 1988. "The Arrival of the Ceará People (Slave Raiders), as told by Moisés Yapara." Ms.

Green, Harold, and Diana Green. 1972. "Surface Structure of Palikur Grammar." Ms.

Green, Harold, Diana Green, I. Gomes, A. Orlando, T. Ioio, and E. Silva. 1997. *Você Pode Ler e Escrever na Lingua Palikúr: Gramatica Sucinta da Lingúa Palikúr*. Belém, Brazil: Summer Institute of Linguistics.

Greenberg, Joseph H. 1956. "The General Classification of Central and South American Languages." In *Selected Papers of the International Congress of Anthropological and Ethnological Sciences*. Vol. 5. Philadelphia.

————. 1957. *Essays in Linguistics*. New York: Wenner-Gren Foundation for Anthropological Research.

————. 1960. "The General Classification of Central and South American Languages." In *Men and Cultures: Selected Papers of the Fifth International Congress of Anthropological Sciences*. Ed. Anthony F. C. Wallace. 792–94. Philadelphia: University of Pennsylvania Press.

————. 1966. *The Languages of Africa*. Bloomington: Indiana University Research Center in Anthropology, Folklore, and Linguistics.

————. 1987. *Language in the Americas*. Stanford, Calif.: Stanford University Press.

Greenblatt, Stephen J. 1991. *Marvelous Possessions: The Wonder of the New World*. Oxford: Clarendon Press.

Grenand, Françoise. 1982. *Et l'homme devint jaguar: univers imaginaire et quotidien des Indiens Wayapi de Guyane*. Paris: L'Harmattan.

Grenand, Françoise, and Pierre Grenand. 1987. "La Côte d'Amapa, de la bouche de l'Amazone à la baie d'Oyapock à travers la tradition orale palikur." *Boletim do Museu Paraense Emílio Goeldi* (Série Antropologia) 3(1):177.

Grenand, Pierre. 1979. "Histoire des Amérindiens, planche 17." In *Atlas des Départements Français d'Outre-mer*. Vol. 4: *La Guyane*. 3–4. Paris: CNRS/ORSTOM.

————. 1981. "Agriculture sur brûlis et changements culturels: le cas des Indiens Wayapi et Palikur de Guyane." *Journal d'Agriculture Traditionnelle et de Botanique Appliquée* 28(1):23–31.

————. 1987. "Les Palikur: une ethnomédecine dans un contexte de réadaptations permanentes." In *Pharmacopées traditionelles en Guyane: Créoles, Wayapi, Palikur*. Ed. Pierre Grenand, C. Moretti, and H. Jacquemin. 75–85. Paris: ORSTOM.

Grenand, Pierre, and Françoise Grenand. 1988a. "Eléments d'histoire amérindienne." In *La question amérindienne en Guyane Française* (special issue). *Ethnies* 1–2:11–14.

————. 1988b. "Situation actuelle des terres." In *La question amérindienne en Guyane Française. Ethnies* 1–2:27–31.

Gross, Daniel. 1975. "Protein Capture and Cultural Development in the Amazon Basin." *American Anthropologist* 77:526–49.

Gumilla, Padre José. 1963. *El Orinoco Ilustrado y Defendido*. Caracas: Biblioteca de la Academia Nacional de la Historia.

Guss, David. 1986. "Keeping It Oral: A Yekuana Ethnology." *American Ethnologist* 13:413–29.

Haberle, Simon G., and Mark A. Maslin. 1999. "Late Quaternary Vegetation and Climate Change in the Amazon Basin Based on a 50,000-Year Pollen Record from the Amazon Fan, ODP Site 932." *Quaternary Research* 51:27–38.

Haffer, Jürgen. 1987. "Quaternary History of Tropical America." In *Biogeography and Quaternary History in Tropical America*. Ed. Timothy C. Whitmore and Ghillean T. Prance. 1–18. Oxford: Clarendon Press.

Harcourt, Robert. 1906. "A Relation of a Voyage to Guiana" (1613). In *Hakluytus posthumus*. Ed. Samuel Purchas. Vol. 16. 358–403. Glasgow: Hakluyt Society.

Heckenberger, Michael J. 1996. "War and Peace in the Shadow of Empire: Sociopolitical Change in the Upper Xingu of Southeastern Amazonia, A.D. 1400–2000." Ph.D. diss., University of Pittsburgh.

———. 1999. "O Enigma das Grandes Cidades: Corpo Privado e Estado em Amazonia." In *A Outra Margem do Occidente*. Ed. Adauto Novaes. 125–52. São Paulo: Companhia das Letras.

———. 2000. "Estrutura, História, e Transformação: A Cultura Xinguano na *Longue Durée*, 1000 a 2000 D.C." In *Os Povos do Alto Xingu: Historia e Cultura*. Ed. Bruna Franchetto and Michael J. Heckenberger. 21–62. Rio de Janeiro: Editora da Universidade Federal do Rio de Janeiro.

———. 2001. "The Ecology of Power: Historical Anthropology in the Southern Amazon." Ms.

Heckenberger, Michael J., Eduardo G. Neves, and James B. Petersen. 1998. "Onde Surgem os Modelos?: As Origens e Expansões Tupi na Amazônia Central." *Revista de Antropologia* 41:69–96.

Heckenberger, Michael J., James B. Petersen, and Eduardo G. Neves. 1999. "Village Permanence in Amazonia: Two Archaeological Examples from Brazil." *Latin American Antiquity* 10(4):353–76.

Hemming, John. 1978. *Red Gold: The Conquest of the Brazilian Indians, 1500–1760*. Cambridge, Mass.: Harvard University Press.

Hilbert, Peter P. 1968. *Archaeologische Untersuchungen am Mittleren Amazonas*. Berlin: L. D. Reiner Verlag.

Hill, Jonathan D. 1983. "Wakuénai Society: A Processual-Structural Analysis of Indigenous Cultural Life in the Upper Rio Negro Region of Venezuela." Ph.D. diss., Indiana University.

———. 1984. "Social Equality and Ritual Hierarchy: The Arawakan Wakuénai of Venezuela." *American Ethnologist* 11:528–44.

———. 1987. "Wakuénai Ceremonial Exchange in the Northwest Amazon." *Journal of Latin American Lore* 13(2):183–224.

———. 1988. "Introduction: Myth and History." In *Rethinking History and Myth: Indigenous South American Perspectives on the Past*. Ed. Jonathan D. Hill. 1–17. Urbana: University of Illinois Press.

———. 1989. "Ritual Production of Environmental History among the Arawakan Wakuénai of Venezuela." *Human Ecology* 17(1):1–25.

————. 1993. *Keepers of the Sacred Chants: The Poetics of Ritual Power in an Amazonian Society.* Tucson: University of Arizona Press.

————, ed. 1996a. *History, Power, and Identity: Ethnogenesis in the Americas, 1492–1992.* Iowa City: University of Iowa Press.

————. 1996b. "Ethnogenesis in the Northwest Amazon: An Emerging Regional Picture." In *History, Power, and Identity. Ethnogenesis in the Americas, 1492–1992.* Ed. Jonathan D. Hill. 142–60. Iowa City: University of Iowa Press.

————. 1996c. "Introduction: Ethnogenesis in the Americas, 1492–1992." In *History, Power, and Identity: Ethnogenesis in the Americas, 1492–1992.* Ed. Jonathan D. Hill. 1–19. Iowa City: University of Iowa Press.

————. 1999. "Nationalisme, Chamanisme et Histoires Indigènes au Venezuela." *Ethnologie Française XXIX*(3):387–96.

————. 2001. "The Varieties of Fertility Cultism in Amazonia: A Closer Look at Gender Symbolism in Northwestern Amazonia." In *Gender in Amazonia and Melanesia: An Exploration of the Comparative Method.* Ed. Thomas Gregor and Donald Tuzin. 45–68. Berkeley: University of California Press.

Hill, Jonathan D., and Robin Wright. 1988. "Time, Narrative, and Ritual: Historical Interpretations from an Amazonian Society." In *Rethinking History and Myth: Indigenous South American Perspectives on the Past.* Ed. Jonathan D. Hill. 78–105. Urbana: University of Illinois Press.

Hock, Henrich. 1991. *Principles of Historical Linguistics.* Berlin: Mouton de Gruyter.

Hoempler, Armin L. 1953. "Domos de Sal en la Cordillera Oriental." *Boletín de la Sociedad Geográfica de Lima* 70:77–82.

Hoff, Berend. 1995. "Language, Contact, War, and Amerindian Historical Tradition: The Special Case of the Island Carib." In *Wolves from the Sea: Readings in the Archaeology and Anthropology of the Island Carib.* Ed. Neil L. Whitehead. 37–60. Leiden, The Netherlands: KITLV Press.

Honigmann, John J. 1959. *The World of Man.* New York: Harper.

Howard, George D. 1943. *Excavations at Ronquin.* New Haven, Conn.: Yale University Press.

Huerta, Francisco de la. 1983. "Relación . . . de la Entrada y Sucesos a las Santas Conversiones de San Francisco Solano en los Gentiles Conibos hecha por el Padre . . ." (1686). *Amazonía Peruana* 4(8):113–24.

Hugh-Jones, Christine. 1979. *From the Milk River: Spatial and Temporal Processes in Northwest Amazonia.* Cambridge: Cambridge University Press.

Hugh-Jones, Stephen. 1979. *The Palm and the Pleiades: Initiation and Cosmology in Northwest Amazonia.* Cambridge: Cambridge University Press.

————. 1989. "Shamans, Prophets, Priests, and Pastors." Paper presented at the workshop "Shamanism, Colonialism, and the State," King's College. October 3.

————. 1995. "Inside-Out and Back-to-Front: The Androgynous House in Northwest Amazonia." In *About the House: Lévi-Strauss and Beyond.* Ed. Janet Carsten and Stephen Hugh Jones. 226–52. Cambridge: Cambridge University Press.

Hulme, Peter, and Neil L. Whitehead. 1992. *Wild Majesty: Encounters with Caribs from Columbus to the Present Day.* Oxford: Clarendon Press.

Humboldt, Alexander de. 1956. *Viaje a las Regiones Equinocciales del Nuevo Mundo.* Vol. 4. Caracas: Ediciones del Ministerio de Educación.

Hunt, George T. 1960. *The Wars of the Iroquois: A Study in Intertribal Trade Relations.* Madison: University of Wisconsin Press.

Hurault, Jean-Marcel. 1989. *Français et Indiens en Guyane, 1604–1972.* Cayenne: Guyane Presse Diffusion.

Hvalkof, Soren. 1986. "El Drama Actual del Gran Pajonal, Primera Parte: Recursos, Historia, Población y Producción Asháninka." *Amazonía Peruana* 6(12):22–30.

Hymes, Dell H. 1986. "Discourse: Scope without Depth." *International Journal of the Sociology of Language* 57:49–89.

Im Thurn, Everard F. 1883. *Among the Indians of Guiana.* London: Kegan Paul.

Ireland, Emilienne. 1988. "Cerebral Savage: The Whiteman as Symbol of Cleverness and Savagery in Waura Myth." In *Rethinking History and Myth: Indigenous South American Perspectives on the Past.* Ed. Jonathan D. Hill. 157–73. Urbana: University of Illinois Press.

Izaguirre, Bernardino, ed. 1922–29. *Historia de las Misiones Franciscanas y Narración de los Progresos de la Geografía en el Oriente del Perú.* 14 vols. Lima: Talleres Tipográficos de la Penitenciaría.

Jackson, Jean E. 1983. *The Fish People: Linguistic Exogamy and Tukanoan Identity in Northwest Amazonia.* Cambridge: Cambridge University Press.

Jensen, Cheryl. 1999. "Tupí-Guaraní." In *The Amazonian Languages.* Ed. Robert M. W. Dixon and A. Y. Aikhenvald. 125–63. Cambridge: Cambridge University Press.

Jerez, Hipólito. 1960a. "Viaje por el Orinoco y el Río Negro." In *Por la Venezuela Indígena de Ayer y de Hoy.* Ed. Cesáreo de Armellada. 183–88. Caracas: Sociedad de Ciencias Naturales La Salle.

———. 1960b. "Viaje por el Orinoco y el Río Negro, Afluente del Amazonas." In *Por la Venezuela Indígena de Ayer y de Hoy.* Ed. Cesáreo de Armellada. 189–92. Caracas: Sociedad de Ciencias Naturales La Salle.

Johansson, Ella. 1990. "Free Sons of the Forest: Storytelling and the Construction of Identity among Swedish Lumberjacks." In *The Myths We Live By.* Ed. Raphael Samuel and Paul Thompson. 129–42. London: Routledge.

Journet, Nicolas. 1995. *La paix des jardins: structures sociales des Indiens Curripaco du Haut-Rio Negro, Colombie.* Paris: Institut d'Ethnologie, Musée de l'Homme.

Kaufman, Terence. 1990. "Language History in South America: What We Know and How to Know More." In *Amazonian Linguistics: Studies in Lowland South American Languages.* Ed. Doris L. Payne. 13–73. Austin: University of Texas Press.

Keegan, William F. 1992. *The People Who Discovered Columbus: The Prehistory of the Bahamas.* Gainesville: University Press of Florida.

Key, Mary Ritchie. 1979. *The Grouping of South American Languages.* Tübingen: Gunter Narr.

Keymis, Lawrence. 1596. *A Relation of a Second Voyage to Guiana Performed and Written in the Yeare 1596.* London: T. Dawson.

Kidd, Stephen W. 2000. "Knowledge and the Practice of Love and Hate among the Enxet of Paraguay." In *The Anthropology of Love and Anger: The Aesthetics of Conviviality in Native Amazonia.* Ed. Joanna Overing and Alan Passes. 114–32. London: Routledge.

Kirch, Patrick V. 1984. *The Evolution of Polynesian Chiefdoms.* Cambridge: Cambridge University Press.

Kirch, Patrick V., and R. C. Green. 1987. "History, Phylogeny, and Evolution in Polynesia." *Current Anthropology* 28:431–56.

Klein, Harriet E. Manelis. 1994. "Genetic Relatedness and Language Distribution in Amazonia." In *Amazonian Indians from Prehistory to the Present: Anthropological Perspectives*. Ed. Anna C. Roosevelt. 343–61. Tucson: University of Arizona Press.

Knauft, Bruce. 1993. *South Coast New Guinea Cultures: History, Comparison, Dialectic*. New York: Cambridge University Press.

———. 1996. *Genealogies for the Present in Cultural Anthropology*. New York: Routledge.

———. 1999. *From Primitive to Postcolonial in Melanesia and Anthropology*. Ann Arbor: University of Michigan Press.

Koch-Grünberg, Theodor. 1911. "Aruak-Sprachen Nordwestbrasiliens und der Angrenzenden Gebiete." *Mitteilungen der Anthropologischen Gesellschaft in Wien* 41:33–153, 203–82.

———. 1967. *Zwei Jahre unter den Indianern: Reisen in Nordwest Brasilien, 1903–05*. Stuttgart: Strecher und Shroder.

Kopytoff, Igor. 1999. "Permutations in Patrimonialism and Populism: The Aghem Chiefdoms of Western Cameroon." In *Beyond Chiefdoms: Pathways of Complexity in Africa*. Ed. Susan Keech Mcintosh. 88–96. Cambridge: Cambridge University Press.

Kroskrity, Paul V., ed. 2000. *Regimes of Language: Ideologies, Polities, and Identities*. Santa Fe, N.Mex.: School of American Research Press.

Laët, Jean de. 1633. *Novus Orbis*. Leyden.

Lagrou, Elsje. 1998. "Cashinahua Cosmovision: A Perspectival Approach to Identity and Alterity." Ph.D. diss., University of St. Andrews.

Las Casas, Bartolomé de. 1992. *Apologética Historia Sumaria*. Madrid: Alianza.

Lathrap, Donald. 1970a. *The Upper Amazon*. London: Thames and Hudson.

———. 1970b. *The Upper Amazon*. New York: Praeger.

———. 1972. "Alternative Models of Population Movements in the Tropical Lowlands of South America." *Actas y Memorias del 39 Congreso Internacional de Americanistas* 4:13–23.

———. 1975. *O Alto Amazonas*. Lisbon: Editorial Verbo.

———. 1977. "Our Father the Cayman, Our Mother the Gourd: Spinden Revisited; or, A Unitary Model for the Emergence of Agriculture in the New World." In *Origins of Agriculture*. Ed. Charles A. Reed. 713–51. The Hague: Mouton.

———. 1985. "Jaws: The Control of Power in the Early Nuclear American Ceremonial Center." In *Early Ceremonial Architecture in the Andes*. Ed. Christopher Donnan. 241–67. Washington, D.C.: Dumbarton Oaks.

Lathrap, Donald W., Angelika Gebhart-Sayer, and Ann M. Mester. 1985. "Roots of the Shipibo Art Style: Three Waves at Imariacocha; or, There Were 'Incas' Before the 'Inca.'" *Journal of Latin American Lore* 11:31–119.

Lathrap, Donald W., Thomas Myers, Angelika Gebhart-Sayer, and Ann M. Mester. 1987. "Further Discussion of the Roots of the Shipibo Art Style: A Rejoinder to DeBoer and Raymond." *Journal of Latin American Lore* 13:225–72.

Lehmann, Winfred P., ed. 1967. *A Reader in Nineteenth-Century Historical Indo-European Linguistics*. Bloomington: Indiana University Press.

———. 1992. *Historical Linguistics*. London: Routledge.

Leprieur, M. 1843. "Voyage dans la Guyane centrale, 1831." *Bulletin de la Société Géographique* 2(1):200–229.

Lévi-Strauss, Claude. 1943. "Guerre et commerce chez les Indiens de l'Amérique du Sud." *Renaissance* 1:122–39.

———. 1963. *Structural Anthropology.* Trans. Claire Jacobson and Brooke Grundfest Schoepf. New York: Basic Books.

———. 1967. *Race et histoire.* 1952. Paris: Gonthier.

———. 1969. *The Raw and the Cooked.* Trans. John Weightman and Doreen Weightman. New York: Harper and Row.

———. 1974. *The Savage Mind.* London: Weidenfeld and Nicolson.

———. 1976. "Guerra e Comércio entre os Indios da América do Sul" (1942). In *Leituras de Etnologia Brasileira.* Ed. Egon Schaden. 325–39. São Paulo: Companhia Editorial Nacional.

———. 1982. *The Way of the Masks.* Trans. Sylvia Modelski. London: Jonathan Cape.

———. 1986a. *The Raw and the Cooked.* Harmondsworth: Penguin.

———. 1986b. *Structural Anthropology.* Harmondsworth: Penguin.

———. 1987. *Anthropology and Myth: Lectures, 1951–1982.* Oxford: Blackwell.

Llanos, Héctor, and Roberto Pineda. 1982. *Etnohistoria del Gran Caquetá, Siglos XVI–XIX.* Bogotá: Fundación de Investigaciones Arqueológicas Nacionales/Banco de la República.

Locke, John. 1690. *An Essay Concerning Human Understanding.* London: Thomas Basset.

Lombard, Père. 1857. "Lettres à son frère" (1723–33). In *La mission de Cayenne.* Paris: M. F. Montezon.

Lothrop, Samuel K. 1940. "South America as Seen from Middle America." In *The Maya and Their Neighbors.* Ed. Clarence L. Hay and Alfred Tozzer. 417–29. New York: D. Appleton-Century.

Loukotka, Cestmír. 1968. *Classification of South American Indian Languages.* Los Angeles: University of California Press.

Lyon, Patricia, ed. 1974. *Native South Americans: Ethnology of the Least-Known Continent.* Boston: Little, Brown.

Magalhães, Pero de. 1576. *Historia da Provincia Santa Cruz a que Vulgarmente Chamamos Brasil.* Lisbon.

Marbán, P. de, C. Baraze, and J. del Castillo. 1676. "Carta de los Padres que Residen en la Misión de los Mojos." In Vargas Ugarte Colección Papeles varios, mss., t.50 (copia). Archivo de la Curia de la Provincia Peruana de la Compañía de Jesús. Lima.

Markgraf, Vera, T. R. Baumgartner, J. P. Bradbury, H. F. Díaz, R. B. Dunbar, B. H. Luckman, G. O. Seltzer, T. W. Swetnam, and R. Villalba. 2000. "Paleoclimate Reconstruction along the Pole Equator–Pole Transect of the Americas (PEP 1)." *Quaternary Science Reviews* 19:125–40.

Maroni, Pablo. 1988. *Noticias Auténticas del Famoso Río Marañón* (1738). Iquitos, Peru: Instituto de Investigaciones de la Amazonía Peruana/Centro de Estudios Teológicos de la Amazonía.

Mason, John Alden. 1950. "The Languages of South America." In *Handbook of South American Indians.* 7 vols. Ed. Julian H. Steward. 6:157–317. Washington, D.C.: Government Printing Office.

Mason, Ronald J. 1976. "Ethnicity and Archaeology in the Upper Great Lakes." In *Cultural Change and Continuity: Essays in Honor of James Bennet Griffin.* Ed. Charles E. Cleland. 335–61. New York: Academic Press.

Matteson, Esther, ed. 1965. *The Piro (Arawakan) Language.* Berkeley: University of California Press.

———, ed. 1972a. *Comparative Studies in Amerindian Languages.* The Hague: Mouton.

———. 1972b. "Proto-Arawakan." In *Comparative Studies in Amerindian Languages.* Ed. Esther Matteson. 160–242. The Hague: Mouton.

Maúrtua, Víctor M., comp. 1906. *Exposición de la República del Perú . . . en el Juicio de Límites entre el Perú y Bolivia Conforme al Tratado de Arbitraje de 30 de Diciembre de 1902.* 15 vols. Barcelona: Imprenta de Henrich y Comp.

Maybury-Lewis, David, ed. 1979. *Dialectical Societies: The Gê and Bororo of Central Brazil.* Cambridge, Mass.: Harvard University Press.

Meggers, Betty J. 1979. "Climatic Oscillation as a Factor in the Prehistory of Amazonia." *American Antiquity* 44(2):252–66.

———. 1987. "The Early History of Man in Amazonia." In *Biogeography and Quaternary in Tropical America.* Ed. Timothy C. Whitmore and Ghillean T. Prance. 151–74. New York: Clarendon Press.

———. 1996. *Amazonia: Man and Culture in a Counterfeit Paradise.* Washington, D.C.: Smithsonian Institution Press.

Meggers, Betty J., and Clifford Evans. 1957. *Archeological Investigations at the Mouth of the Amazon.* Washington, D.C.: Government Printing Office.

———. 1961. "An Experimental Formulation of Horizon Styles in the Tropical Forest of South America." In *Essays in Precolumbian Art and Archaeology.* Ed. Samuel K. Lothrop. 372–88. Cambridge, Mass.: Harvard University Press.

Mendoça Furtado, Francisco Xavier. 1906. "Viagem que fez i Illm. Sr. Francisco Xavier Mendoça Furtado, do Conselho da Sua Magestade Fidelíssima, Commendador de Santa Marinha de Mattas de Lobos na Ordem de Christo, Governador e Capitão Geral do Maranhão, etc." *Revista do Instituto Historico e Geographico Brasileiro* 1(67):251–337.

Menget, Patrick. 1993. "Les frontières de la chefferie: remarques sur le système politique du Haut Xingu." *L'Homme* 33(2–4):59–76.

Mich, Tadeusz. 1994. "The Yuruparí Complex of the Yucuna Indians. The Yuruparí Rites." *Anthropos* 89(1–3):39–49.

Montout, Emmanuel. 1994. "De Rokawa à Kamuyene: approche de la mutation sociale et magico-réligieuse du peuple Palikur." Paper presented at the Université des Antilles et de la Guyane, Cayenne. November 8.

Moquet, Jean. 1617. *Voyage en Afrique, Asie, Indes Orientales et Occidentales.* Paris: J. de Hauqueville.

Morey, Nancy. 1975. "Ethnohistory of the Colombian and Venezuelan Llanos." Ph.D. diss., University of Utah.

Morin, Françoise. 2000. "The Shipibo-Conibo." In *Guía Etnográfica de la Alta Amazonía.* 3 vols. Ed. Fernando Santos and Frederica Barclay. 3:275–435. Quito: Smithsonian Tropical Research Institute/Instituto Francés de Estudios Andinos/Abya-Yala.

Murdock, George. 1951. "South American Culture Areas." *Southwestern Journal of Anthropology* 7:415–36.

Myers, Thomas P. 1974. "Spanish Contacts and Social Change on the Ucayali River, Peru." *Ethnohistory* 21(2):135–59.

Navarro, Manuel. 1924. *La Tribu Amuesha*. Lima: Escuela Tipográfica Salesiana.

Neto, Carlo de Araújo Moreira. 1988. *Indios da Amazônia, de Maioria a Minoria, 1750–1850*. Petrópolis, Brazil: Vozes.

Neves, Eduardo G., Robert N. Bartone, James B. Petersen, and Michael J. Heckenberger. 2001. "The Timing of Terra Preta Formation in the Central Amazon: New Data from Three Sites Near Manaus." Ms.

Nimuendajú, Curt. 1950. "Reconhecimento dos Rios Içana, Ayarí e Uaupés. Relatório Apresentado ao Serviço de Proteção aos Indios do Amazonas e Acre" (1927). *Journal de la Société des Américanistes* 39:125–82, 44:149–78.

———. 1971. "Die Palikur Indianer und ihre Nachbarn" (1926). Ms. (Unpublished French translation by Claudie Jousse; original in *Göteborgs Kungl. Vet. Vitt. Handligar* 31(2):1–97.

———. 1981. *Mapa Etno-Historico de Curt Nimuendajú*. Rio de Janeiro: Instituto Brasileiro de Geografia e Estatistica.

Nimuendajú, Curt, and Rosario Farani Mansur Guérios. 1948. "Cartas Etno-lingüísticas." *Revista do Museu Paulista* 2:207–41.

Noble, G. Kingsley. 1965. "Proto-Arawakan and Its Descendants." *International Journal of American Linguistics* 31(3):1–129.

Noelli, Francisco. 1996. "As Hipóteses sobre o Centro de Origem e Rotas de Expansão dos Tupi." *Revista de Antropologia* 39(2):7–53.

Nordenskiöld, Erland. 1913. "Urnegrabe und Mounds in Bolivianische Flachlande." *Baessler Archiv* 3:205–55.

———. 1924. *The Ethnography of South America as Seen from the Mojos in Bolivia*. Göteborg: Elanders Boktryckeri Aktiebolag.

Obeyesekere, Gananath. 1992. *The Apotheosis of Captain Cook: European Myth-Making in the Pacific*. Princeton, N.J.: Princeton University Press.

Ocampo Conejeros, B. 1923. "Descripción . . . de la provincia de Vilcabamba" (1611). In *Colección de Libros y Documentos Referentes a la Historia del Perú*. 11 vols. Ed. Horacio H. Urteaga and Carlos A. Romero. 7(2):154–93. Lima: Sammartí.

Ochs, Elinor, Ruth Smith, and Carolyn Taylor. 1988. "Detective Stories at Dinnertime: Problem Solving through Co-narration." Paper presented at the symposium "Narrative Resources for the Creation of Order and Disorder," American Ethnological Society annual meeting, St. Louis. March 25.

Oliva, P. Anello. 1895. *Historia del Perú y Varones Insignes*. Lima: Imprenta y Libreria de San Pedro.

Oliver, José R. 1989. "The Archaeological, Linguistic, and Ethnohistorical Evidence for the Expansion of Arawakan into Northwestern Venezuela and Northeastern Colombia." Ph.D. diss., University of Illinois at Urbana-Champaign.

Ordinaire, Olivier. 1988. *Del Pacífico al Atlántico y Otros Escritos*. Lima: Instituto Francés de Estudios Andinos/Centro de Estudios Teológicos de la Amazonía.

Orellana, Antonio de. 1906. "Carta del Padre Antonio de Orellana sobre el Origen de las Misiones de Mojos" (1687). In *Exposición de la República del Perú . . . en el Juicio de*

Límites entre el Perú y Bolivia Conforme al Tratado de Arbitraje de 30 de Diciembre de 1902. 15 vols. Ed. Víctor M. Maúrtua. 10:1–24. Barcelona: Imprenta de Henrich y Comp.

Oricain, Pablo José. 1906. "Compendio Breve . . . formado por Pablo J. Oricain, Año 1790" (1790). In *Exposición de la República del Perú . . . en el Juicio de Límites entre el Perú y Bolivia Conforme al Tratado de Arbitraje de 30 de Diciembre de 1902.* 15 vols. Ed. Víctor M. Maúrtua. 11:373. Barcelona: Imprenta de Henrich y Comp.

Overing, Joanna. 1995. "O Mito como Historia: Um Problema de Tempo, Realidade e Outras Questões." *Mana* 1(1):107 40.

Overing, Joanna, and Alan Passes. 2000. Introduction to *The Anthropology of Love and Anger: The Aesthetics of Conviviality in Native Amazonia.* Ed. Joanna Overing and Alan Passes. 1–30. New York: Routledge.

Oviedo, González Fernández de. 1535. *Historia General y Natural de las Indias, Islas y Tierra Firme.* Seville: Juan Cromberger.

Pané, Ramón. 1999. *An Account of the Antiquities of the Indians.* (1496). Durham, N.C.: Duke University Press.

Panlon Kumu, Umúsin, and Tolaman Kenhíri. 1980. *Antes o Mundo não Existia.* São Paulo: Livraria Cultura Editora.

Parker, Stephen G. 1995. *Datos de la Lengua Iñapari.* Lima: Ministerio de Educación/Instituto Lingüístico de Verano.

Passes, Alan. 1998. "The Hearer, the Hunter, and the Agouti Head: Aspects of Intercommunication and Conviviality among the Pa'ikwené (Palikur) of French Guiana." Ph.D. diss., University of St. Andrews.

————. 2000a. "The Place of Politics: Powerful Speech and Women Speakers in Everyday Pa'ikwené (Palikur) Life." Paper presented at the Centre for Indigenous American Studies and Exchange, University of St. Andrews. April 18.

————. 2000b. "Hearing and the Emotion of Politics among the Pa'ikwené." Paper presented at a departmental seminar, Department of Social Anthropology, University of St. Andrews. November 16.

————. 2001. "You Are What You Speak, or Are You? Identity and Language in the Context of Sociocultural Change in Indigenous Guyane (French Guyana)." Unpublished ms.

Payne, David L. 1991. "A Classification of Maipuran (Arawakan) Languages Based on Shared Lexical Retentions." In *Handbook of Amazonian Languages.* 4 vols. Ed. Desmond C. Derbyshire and Geoffrey K. Pullum. 3:355–499. The Hague: Mouton de Gruyter.

Pelleprat, Pierre. 1655. *Relation des missions des pères Jésuites.* Paris: Chez S. Cramoisy and G. Cramoisy.

Petersen, James B. 1996. "Chronological and Settlement Data," part 3 of "The Archaeology of Trants, Montserrat." *Annals of the Carnegie Museum* 65:323–61.

————. 1997. "Taino, Island Carib, and Prehistoric Amerindian Economies in the West Indies: Tropical Forest Adaptations to Island Environments." In *The Indigenous People of the Caribbean.* Ed. Samuel M. Wilson. 118–30. Gainesville: University Press of Florida.

Petersen, James B., Michael J. Heckenberger, and Jack A. Wolford. 2001. "Spin, Twist, and Twine: An Ethnoarchaeological Examination of Group Identity in Native Fiber Industries from Greater Amazonia." In *Fleeting Identities: Perishable Material Culture in*

Archaeological Research. Ed. Penelope B. Drooker. 226–53. Carbondale: Southern Illinois University Press.

Petersen, James B., Eduardo G. Neves, and Michael J. Heckenberger. 2001. "Gift from the Past: Terra Preta and Prehistoric Amerindian Occupation in Amazonia." In *The Unknown Amazon.* Ed. Colin McEwan, Cristiana Barreto, and Eduardo G. Neves. 86–105. London: British Museum Press.

Piperno, Dolores R., Anthony J. Ranere, Irene Holst, and Patricia Hansell. 2000. "Starch Grains Reveal Early Root Crop Horticulture in the Panamanian Tropical Forest." *Nature* 407:894–97.

Porro, Antonio. 1993. *As Crônicas do Rio Amazonas: Notas Etno-históricas sobre as Antigas Populações Indígenas da Amazônia.* Petrópolis, Brazil: Vozes.

———. 1996. *Os Povos das Aguas: Ensaios de Etnohistória Amazônicas.* Petrópolis, Brazil: Vozes.

Price, Richard. 1983. *First-Time: The Historical Vision of an Afro-American People.* Baltimore: Johns Hopkins University Press.

Prous, André. 1991. *Arqueologia Brasileira.* Brasilia: Editora Universidade de Brasilia.

Quandt, C. 1807. *Nachricht von Suriname.* Amsterdam: S. Emmering.

Radin, Paul. 1946. *Indians of South America.* Garden City, N.Y.: Doubleday.

Rafinesque, Constantine S. 1836. *The American Nations; or, Outlines of Their General History, Ancient and Modern.* Philadelphia: C. S. Rafinesque.

Ralegh, Walter. 1928. *The Discoverie of the Large, Rich, and Bewtiful Empire of Guiana* (1592–96). London: Hakluyt Society.

Ramos Pérez, Demetrio. 1946. *El Tratado de Límites de 1750 y la Expedición de Iturriaga al Orinoco.* Madrid: Consejo Superior de Investigaciones Científicas.

Rappaport, Joanne. 1989. "Geography and Historical Understanding in Indigenous Colombia." In *Who Needs the Past?: Indigenous Values and Archaeology.* Ed. Robert Layton. 84–94. London: Routledge.

Rapport, Nigel, and Joanna Overing. 2000. *Social and Cultural Anthropology: The Key Concepts.* London: Routledge.

Redmond, Elsa M., ed. 1998. *Chiefdoms and Chieftaincy in the Americas.* Gainesville: University Press of Florida.

Reichel-Dolmatoff, Gerardo. 1985. "Tapir Avoidance in the Colombian Northwest Amazon." In *Animal Myths and Metaphors in South America.* Ed. Gary Urton. 107–44. Salt Lake City: University of Utah Press.

———. 1989. "Biological and Social Aspects of the Yuruparí Complex of the Colombian Vaupés Territory." *Journal of Latin American Lore* 15(1):93–135.

———. 1996. *Yuruparí: Studies of an Amazonian Foundation Myth.* Cambridge, Mass.: Harvard University Press.

Renard-Casevitz, France-Marie. 1972. "Les Matsiguenga." *Journal de la Société des Américanistes* 61:215–53.

———. 1977. "Du proche au loin." *Actes du 42e Congrès International des Américanistes* 2:121–40.

———. 1981. "Las Fronteras de las Conquistas en el Siglo XVI en la Montaña Meridional del Perú." *Bulletin de l'Institut Français d'Etudes Andines* 10(3–4):113–40.

———. 1985. "Guerre, violence, et identité a partir de sociétés du piémont amazonien des Andes centrales." *Cahiers ORSTOM* (Série Sciences Humaines) 21(1):81–98.

———. 1991a. *Le banquet masqué: une mythologie de l'etranger.* Paris: Lierre et Coudrier.

———. 1991b. "Commerce et guerre dans la forêt centrale du Pérou." Document de Recherche du Credal no. 221, Document Ersipal no. 49.

———. 1992a. "Les guerriers du sel: chronique 92." *Cahiers des Amériques Latines* 13:107–18.

———. 1992b. "História Kampa, Memória Ashaninca." In *História dos Indios no Brasil.* Ed. Manuela Carneiro da Cunha. 197–213. São Paulo: Fundação de Amparo à Pesquisa do Estado de São Paulo/Companhia das Letras/Secretaria Municipal de Cultura.

———. 1993. "Guerriers du sel, sauniers de la paix." *L'Homme* 33(2–4):25–44.

———. 1998–99. "Acerca de Algunas Teorías sobre Parentesco y Alianza: El Matrimonio entre la Hija de la Hermana del Padre y el Hijo del Hermano de la Madre." *Revista Antropológica* 16:7–47, 17:21–62.

Renard-Casevitz, France Marie, and Olivier Dollfus. 1988. "Geografía de Algunos Mitos y Creencias: Espacios Simbólicos y Realidades Geográficas de los Machinguenga del Alto Urubamba." *Amazonía Peruana* 8(16):7–40.

Renard-Casevitz, France-Marie, Thierry Saignes, and Anne-Christine Taylor. 1986. *L'Inca, l'Espagnol et les sauvages: rapports entre les sociétés amazoniennes et andines du XVe au XVIIe siècle.* Paris: Editions Recherche sur les Civilisations.

Renfrew, Colin. 1987. *Archaeology and Language: The Puzzle of Indo-European Origins.* London: Jonathan Cape.

Ribeiro, Darcy, and Mary Ruth Wise. 1978. *Los Grupos Etnicos de la Amazonía Peruana.* Lima: Instituto Lingüístico de Verano.

Ribeiro de Sampaio, Francisco Xavier. 1825. *Diario da Viagem que em Visita, e Correição das Povoações da Capitania do S. José do Rio Negro fez o Ouvidor, e Intendente Geral da misma Francisco Xavier Ribeiro de Sampaio no Anno 1774 e 1775.* Lisbon: Typographia da Academia.

Ricardo, Carlos Alberto, ed. 1983. "Palikur." In *Povos Indígenas no Brasil 3, Amapá/Norte do Pará.* Ed. Carlos Alberto Ricardo. 19–39. São Paulo: CEDI.

Ricken, Ulrich. 1994. *Linguistics, Anthropology, and Philosophy in the French Enlightenment.* London: Routledge.

Rivero, Juan. 1883. *Historia de las Misiones de los Llanos de Casanare y los Ríos Orinoco y Meta.* Bogotá: Imprenta de Silvestre y Compañía.

Rivet, Paul. 1924. "Langues de l'Amérique du Sud et des Antilles." In *Les langues du monde.* Ed. Antoine Meillet and Marcel Cohen. 639–712. Paris: La Societé de Linguistique de Paris.

Rivet, Paul, and Pierre Reinburg. 1921. "Les Indiens Marawan." *Journal de la Société des Américanistes* 13:13–118.

Rivet, Paul, and P. C. Tastevin. 1919–24. "Les langues du Purus, Jurua et des régions limitrophes: le groupe pré-andin." *Anthropos* 14–15:857–90, 16–17:298–325, 18–19:106–12.

Rivière, Peter. 1971. "The Political Structure of the Trio Indians as Manifested in a System of Ceremonial Dialogue." In *The Translation of Culture.* Ed. Thomas O. Beidelman. 293–311. London: Tavistock.

Rodrigues, Aryon Dall'Igna. 1986. *Línguas Brasileiras: Para o Conhecimento das Linguas Indígenas.* São Paulo: Edições Loyola.

———. 1999. "Tupí." In *The Amazonian Languages.* Ed. Robert M. W. Dixon and Alexandra Y. Aikhenvald. 107–24. Cambridge: Cambridge University Press.

Rojas, Filintro Antonio. 1994. "La Ciencia Kurripako: Origen del Miyaka o Principio." Ms.

Roosevelt, Anna C. 1980. *Parmana: Prehistoric Maize and Manioc Subsistence along the Amazon and Orinoco.* New York: Academic Press.

———. 1989. "Resource Management in Amazonia before the Conquest: Beyond Ethnographic Projection." In *Resource Management in Amazonia: Indigenous and Folk Strategies.* Ed. Darrell A. Posey and William Balée. 30–62. New York: New York Botanical Garden Press.

———. 1991. *Moundbuilders of the Amazon: Geophysical Archaeology on Marajo Island, Brazil.* New York: Academic Press.

———. 1994. "Introduction: Amazonian Anthropology—Strategy for a New Synthesis." In *Amazonian Indians from Prehistory to the Present: Anthropological Perspectives.* Ed. Anna C. Roosevelt. 1–29. Tucson: University of Arizona Press.

———. 1997. *The Excavations at Corozal, Venezuela: Stratigraphy and Ceramic Seriation.* New Haven, Conn.: Yale University Press.

———. 1999. "The Development of Prehistoric Complex Societies: Amazonia, a Tropical Forest." In *Complex Societies in the Ancient Tropical World.* Ed. Elisabeth A. Bacus and Lisa J. Lucero. 13–34. Washington, D.C.: American Anthropological Association.

Rosengren, Dan. 1987. *In the Eyes of the Beholder: Leadership and the Social Construction of Power and Dominance among the Matsigenka of the Peruvian Amazon.* Göteborg: Göteborgs Etnografiska Museum.

Rostain, Stéphen. 1991. *Les champs surélevés amérindiens de la Guyane.* Cayenne: ORSTOM/IGN/Conseil Général de la Guyane et Centre National d'Etudes Spatiales.

Rouse, Irving. 1948a. "The Arawak." In *Handbook of South American Indians.* 7 vols. Ed. Julian H. Steward. 4:507–46. Washington, D.C.: Government Printing Office.

———. 1948b. "The Carib." In *Handbook of South American Indians.* 7 vols. Ed. Julian H. Steward. 4:547–65. Washington, D.C.: Government Printing Office.

———. 1978. "The La Gruta Sequence and Its Implications." In *Unidad y Variedad: Ensayos en Homenaje a José M. Cruxent.* Ed. Erika Wagner and Alberta Zucchi. 203–29. Caracas: Centro de Estudios Avanzados-IVIC.

———. 1985. "Arawakan Phylogeny, Caribbean Chronology, and Their Implications for the Study of Population Movement." *Antropológica* 63–64:9–21.

———. 1986. *Migrations in Prehistory: Inferring Population Movement from Cultural Remains.* New Haven, Conn.: Yale University Press.

———. 1992. *The Tainos: Rise and Decline of the People Who Greeted Columbus.* New Haven, Conn.: Yale University Press.

Rouse, Irving, and Douglas Taylor. 1956. "Linguistic and Archaeological Time-Depth in the West Indies." *International Journal of American Linguistics* 21:105–15.

Rousseau, Jean-Jacques. 1959. *Discours sur l'origine et les fondements de l'inegalité parmi les hommes.* Paris: Bibliothèque de la Pléiade.

Ruette, Krisna. 1998. "El Caño Aki: Dos Cosmografías y un Territorio." Licentiate thesis,

Escuela de Antropología; Facultad de Ciencias Económicas y Sociales; Universidad Central de Venezuela.

Saake, Wilhelm. 1959–60. "Iniciação de um Pajé entre os Baniwa e a Cura de Marecaimbara." *Sociologia* 6:424–42.

Sahlins, Marshall. 1968. *Tribesmen.* Englewood Cliffs, N.J.: Prentice Hall.

———. 1974. *Stone Age Economics.* London: Tavistock.

———. 1995. *How "Natives" Think about Captain Cook, for Example.* Chicago: University of Chicago Press.

Sala, Gabriel. 1905–9. "Exploración de los Ríos Pichis, Pachitea, Alto Ucayali i de la Región del Gran Pajonal, por el Padre . . ." (1897). In *Colección de Leyes, Decretos, Resoluciones i Otros Documentos Oficiales Referentes al Departamento de Loreto.* 18 vols. Ed. Carlos Larrabure i Correa. 12:5–154. Lima: Imprenta de La Opinión Nacional.

Salgado de Araujo, Andrés. 1986. "Memorial" (1663). *Amazonía Peruana* 7(13):135–59.

Samanez y Ocampo, José B. 1980. *Exploración de los Ríos Peruanos, Apurímac, Eni, Tambo, Ucayali y Urubamba, hecho por Samanez y Ocampo en 1883 y 1884.* Lima: SESATOR.

Samuel, Raphael, and Paul Thompson. 1990. Introduction to *The Myths We Live By.* Ed. Raphael Samuel and Paul Thompson. 1–22. London: Routledge.

San Antonio, Joseph de. 1906. "Memorial de Fray Joseph de San Antonio. . . . Misión de Infieles del Cerro de la Sal" (1750). In *Colección de Documentos que apoyan el Alegato de Bolivia en el Juicio Arbitral con la República del Perú.* 2:331–56. Buenos Aires: Cía. Sud-Americana de Billetes de Banco.

Sanford, Robert L., J. Saldarriaga, K. E. Clark, C. Uhl, and R. Herrera. 1985. "Amazon Rain-Forest Fires." *Science* 227:53–55.

Santos-Granero, Fernando. 1980. "Vientos de un Pueblo: Síntesis Histórica de la Etnía Amuesha, Siglos XVII–XIX." Licentiate thesis, Pontificia Universidad Católica del Perú.

———. 1986a. "The Moral and Social Aspects of Equality amongst the Amuesha of Central Peru." *Journal de la Société des Américanistes* 72:107–31.

———. 1986b. "Power, Ideology, and the Ritual of Production in Lowland South America." *Man* 21(4):657–79.

———. 1987. "Templos y Herrerías: Utopía y Recreación Cultural en la Amazonía Peruana." *Bulletin de l'Institute Français d'Etudes Andines* 17(2):1–22.

———. 1991. *The Power of Love: The Moral Use of Knowledge Amongst the Amuesha of Central Peru.* London: Athlone Press.

———. 1992. "Anticolonialismo, Mesianismo y Utopía en la Sublevación de Juan Santos Atahuallpa, Siglo XVIII." In *Opresión Colonial y Resistencia Indígena en la Alta Amazonía.* Ed. Fernando Santos Granero. 103–34. Quito: Abya-Yala/CEDIME/FLACSO-Ecuador.

———. 1993a. "From 'Prisoner of the Group' to 'Darling of the Gods': An Approach to the Issue of Power in Lowland South America." *L'Homme* 33(2–4):213–30.

———. 1993b. "Templos e Ferrarias: Utopia e Reinvenção Cultural no Oriente Peruano." In *Amazônia: Etnologia e História Indígena.* Ed. Eduardo Viveiros de Castro and Manuela Carneiro da Cunha. 67–93. São Paulo: Núcleo de História Indígena e do Indigenismo da USP: FAPESP.

———. 1995. "¿Historias Etnicas o Historias Interétnicas?: Lecciones del Pasado Amuesha (Selva Central, Perú)." In *Memorias del I Seminario Internacional de Etnohistoria del Norte de Ecuador y Sur de Colombia.* Ed. Guido Barona and Francisco Zuluaga. 351–71. Santiago de Cali, Colombia: Universidad del Valle/Universidad del Cauca.

———. 1998. "Writing History into the Landscape: Space, Myth, and Ritual in Contemporary Amazonia." *American Ethnologist* 25:128–48.

———. 2000. "The Sisyphus Syndrome; or, The Struggle for Conviviality in Native Amazonia." In *The Anthropology of Love and Anger: The Aesthetics of Conviviality in Native Amazonia.* Ed. Joanna Overing and Alan Passes. 268–87. New York: Routledge.

Santos-Granero, Fernando, and Frederica Barclay. 2000. *Tamed Frontiers: Economy, Society, and Civil Rights in Upper Amazonia.* Boulder, Colo.: Westview Press.

Sapir, Edward. 1931. "Language, Race, and Culture" (1921). In *The Making of Man: An Outline of Anthropology.* Ed. V. F. Calverton. 142–54. New York: Modern Library.

———. 1949. "The Status of Linguistics as Science" (1929). In *Selected Writings of Edward Sapir.* Ed. David G. Mandelbaum. 160–66. Berkeley: University of California Press.

Schäfer, Manfred. 1991. "Ayompari, 'El que me da las Cosas': El Intercambio Entre los Ashéninga y Asháninca de la Selva Central Peruana en Perspectiva Histórica." In *Etnohistoria del Amazonas.* Ed. Peter Jorna, Leonor Malaver, and Menno Oostra. 45–62. Quito: Abya-Yala/Movimiento Laicos para América Latina.

Schama, Simon. 1995. *Landscape and Memory.* London: Harper Collins.

Schmidt, Max. 1914. "Die Paressi-Kabishi." *Baessler Archiv* 4(475):167–250.

———. 1917. *Die Aruaken. Ein Beitrag zum Problem de Kulturverbrietung.* Leipzig: Veit and Comp.

Schmidt, Wilhelm. 1977. *Die Sprachfamilien und Sprachenkreise der Erde* (1926). Hamburg: H. Baske.

Schneider, Jane, and Rayna Rapp, eds. 1995. *Articulating Hidden Histories: Exploring the Influence of Eric R. Wolf.* Berkeley: University of California Press.

Seeger, Anthony. 1981. *Nature and Society in Central Brazil: The Suyá Indians of Mato Grosso.* Cambridge, Mass.: Harvard University Press.

———. 1987. *Why Suyá Sing: A Musical Anthropology of an Amazonian People.* Cambridge: Cambridge University Press.

Sherzer, Joel. 1983. *Kuna Ways of Speaking.* Austin: University of Texas Press.

———. 1992. "A Richness of Voices." In *America in 1492.* Ed. Alvin M. Josephy Jr. 251–75. New York: Knopf.

Silverblatt, Irene. 1987. *Moon, Sun, and Witches: Gender Ideologies and Class in Inca and Colonial Peru.* Princeton, N.J.: Princeton University Press.

Simón, Pedro. 1882. *Noticias Historiales de las Conquistas de Tierra Firme en las Indias Occidentales.* 4 vols. Bogotá: Imprenta de Medardo Rivas.

Smith, Richard Chase. 1977. "Deliverance from Chaos for a Song. A Social and Religious Interpretation of the Ritual Performance of Amuesha Music," Ph.D. diss., Department of Anthropology, Cornell University.

———. 1985. "Política Oficial y Realidad Indígena: Conceptos Amuesha de Integración Social y Territorialidad." *Amazonía Indígena* 5(10):11–16.

Sorensen, Arthur P., Jr. 1967. "Multilingualism in the Northwest Amazon." *American Anthropologist* 69:670–82.

———. 1972. "Multilingualism in the Northwest Amazon." In *Sociolinguistics.* Ed. J. Pride and J. Holmes. 78–93. Harmondsworth: Penguin Books.

Southall, Aidan. 1999. "The Segmentary State and the Ritual Phase in Political Economy." In *Beyond Chiefdoms: Pathways to Complexity in Africa.* Ed. Susan Keech-McIntosh. 31–38. Cambridge: Cambridge University Press.

Stæhelin, Fritz. 1913. *Die Mission der Brudergemeine in Suriname und Berbice im achtzehnten Jahrhundert.* Paramaribo, Suriname: Herrnhutt.

Steinen, Karl von den. 1886. *Durch Zentral-Brasilien, Expedition zur Erfoschung des Schingu im 1884.* Leipzig: F. A. Brockhaus.

———. 1894. *Unter den Naturvölkern Central-Brasiliens.* Berlin: Dietrich Reimer

Steward, Julian H., ed. 1946–59. *Handbook of South American Indians.* 7 vols. Washington, D.C.: Government Printing Office.

———. 1949. "South American Cultures: An Interpretive Summary." In *Handbook of South American Indians.* 7 vols. Ed. Julian H. Steward. 5:669–772. Washington, D.C.: Government Printing Office.

Steward, Julian H., and Louis C. Faron. 1959. *Native Peoples of South America.* New York: McGraw-Hill.

Stradelli, Ermanno. 1929. "Das Lendas Indigenas Recolhidas por Max J. Roberto, Transcriptas por Antonio Amorim, Ineditas." *Revista do Instituto Historico e Geographico Brasileiro* 104(158):740–68.

Strathern, Marilyn. 1996. "Closing Comments" at the Wenner-Gren Symposium No. 121, "Amazonia and Melanesia: Gender and Anthropological Comparison," Mijas, Spain. September.

Sturtevant, William C. 1961. "Taino Agriculture." In *The Evolution of Horticulture Systems in Native South America: Causes and Consequences.* Ed. Johannes Wilbert. 69–82. Caracas: Sociedad de Ciencias Naturales La Salle.

Sued Badillo, Jalil. 1978. *Los Caribes: Realidad o Fábula?* Rio Pedras, Puerto Rico: Editorial Antillana.

———. 1995. "The Island Caribs: New Approaches to the Question of Ethnicity in the Early Colonial Caribbean." In *Wolves from the Sea: Readings in the Archaeology and Anthropology of the Island Carib.* Ed. Neil L. Whitehead. 61–89. Leiden, The Netherlands: KITLV Press.

Summer Institute of Linguistics. 2001. Ethnologue 14. at <http://www.ethnologue.com/language_index.asp>.

Swadesh, Morris. 1950. "Salish Internal Relationships." *International Journal of American Linguistics* 16:157–67.

———. 1951. "Diffusional Cumulation and Archaic Residue as Historical Explanations." *Southwestern Journal of Anthropology* 7:1–21.

———. 1952. "Lexicostatistical Dating of Prehistoric Ethnic Contacts." *Proceedings of the American Philosophical Society* 96:452–63.

Sweet, David. 1975. "A Rich Realm of Nature Destroyed: The Middle Amazon Valley, 1640–1750." Ph.D. diss., University of Wisconsin.

Taylor, Anne-Christine. 1996. "The Soul's Body and Its States: An Amazonian Perspective on the Nature of Being Human." *Journal of the Royal Anthropological Institute* 2:201–15.

Taylor, Douglas. 1946. "Kinship and Social Structure of the Island Carib." *Southwestern Journal of Anthropology* 2:180–212.

———. 1954. "Diachronic Note on the Carib Contribution to Island Carib." *International Journal of American Linguistics* 20:28–33.

———. 1961. Review of R. Schaefer, "Algumas Equações Fonéticas em Arawakan, Anthropos 54, 1959." *International Journal of American Linguistics* 27:273–78.

———. 1977. *Languages of the West Indies*. Baltimore: Johns Hopkins University Press.

Taylor, Douglas, and B. Hoff. 1980. "The Linguistic Repertory of the Island-Carib in the Seventeenth Century: The Men's Language—A Carib Pidgin?" *International Journal of American Linguistics* 46:301–12.

Tessmann, Günter. 1930. *Die Indianer Nordost-Peru*. Hamburg: Friederischen, De Gruyter and Cy.

Thomas, David. 1982. *Order without Government: The Society of the Pemon Indians of Venezuela*. Urbana: University of Illinois Press.

Thomas, Rosalind. 1990. "Ancient Greek Family Tradition and Democracy: From Oral History to Myth." In *The Myths We Live By*. Ed. Raphael Samuel and Paul Thompson. 203–15. London: Routledge.

Thomason, Sarah Grey, and Terence Kaufman. 1988. *Language Contact, Creolization, and Genetic Linguistics*. Berkeley: University of California Press.

Tibesar, Antonine S. 1950. "The Salt Trade among the Montaña Indians of the Tarma Area of Eastern Peru." *Primitive Man* 23:103–8.

Tonkin, Elizabeth. 1990. "History and the Myth of Realism." In *The Myths We Live By*. Ed. Raphael Samuel and Paul Thompson. 25–35. London: Routledge.

Tovar, Antonio. 1986. *Las Lenguas Arahuacas: Hacia una Delimitación y Clasificación más Precisa de la Familia Arahuaca*. Bogotá: Instituto Caro y Cuervo.

Tovar, Antonio, and Consuelo Larrueca de Tovar. 1984. *Catálogo de las Lenguas de América del Sur*. Madrid: Editorial Gredos.

Townsley, Graham. 1994. "Los Yaminahua." In *Guía Etnográfica de la Alta Amazonía*. 3 vols. Ed. Fernando Santos and Frederica Barclay. 2:239–358. Quito: Facultad Latino Americana de Ciencias Sociales/Instituto Francés de Estudios Andinos.

Trouillot, Michel-Rolph. 1991. "Anthropology and the Savage Slot: The Poetics and Politics of Otherness." In *Recapturing Anthropology*. Ed. Richard G. Fox. 17–44. Santa Fe, N.Mex.: School of American Research Press.

Turner, Terence. 1988. "Commentary: Ethno-Ethnohistory—Myth and History in Native South American Representations of Contact with Western Society." In *Rethinking History and Myth: Indigenous South American Perspectives on the Past*. Ed. Jonathan D. Hill. 235–81. Urbana: University of Illinois Press.

Urban, Greg. 1991. *A Discourse-Centered Approach to Culture*. Austin: University of Texas Press.

———. 1992. "A História da Cultura Brasileira Segundo as Linguas Nativas." In *História dos Índios do Brasil*. Ed. Manuela Carneiro da Cunha. 87–102. São Paulo: Fundação de Amparo à Pesquisa do Estado de São Paulo/Companhia das Letras/Secretaria Municipal de Cultura.

Urban, Greg, and Joel Sherzer. 1988. "The Linguistic Anthropology of Native South America." *Annual Review of Anthropology* 17:283–307.

Valenti, Donna. 1986. "A Reconstruction of the Proto-Arawakan Consonantal System." Ph.D. diss., New York University.

Valenzuela, Pilar M. 1991. "Comprobación del Lugar de la Lengua Iñapari dentro de la Rama Pre-andina de la Familia Arahuaca." *Revista Latinoamericana de Estudios Etnolingüísticos* 6:209–40.

Vall, Keyla. 1998. "El Caño San Miguel: El Recuerdo de los Comienzos." Licentiate thesis, Escuela de Antropología; Facultad de Ciencias Económicas y Sociales; Universidad Central de Venezuela.

Van der Hammen, María Clara. 1992. *El Manejo del Mundo: Naturaleza y Sociedad entre los Yukuna de la Amazonía Colombiana.* Bogotá: Tropenbos/Estudios de la Amazonía Colombiana.

Van der Hammen, Tomás. 1972. "Changes in Vegetation and Climate in the Amazon Basin and Surrounding Areas during the Pleistocene." *Geologie en Mijnbouw* 51:641–43.

———. 1974. "The Pleistocene Changes in Vegetation and Climate in Tropical South America." *Journal of Biogeography* 1:3–26.

———. 1982. "Paleoecology of Tropical South America." In *Biological Diversification in the Tropics.* Ed. Ghillean T. Prance. 61–67. New York: Columbia University Press.

Vansina, Jan. 1980. "Memory and Oral Tradition." In *The African Past Speaks: Essays on Oral Tradition and History.* Ed. J. Miller. 262–72. Folkestone: Dawson and Archon.

———. 1985. *Oral Tradition and History.* Madison: University of Wisconsin Press.

———. 1990. *Paths in the Rainforest: Towards a History of Political Tradition in Equatorial Africa.* Madison: University of Wisconsin Press.

Varese, Stefano. 1968. *La Sal de los Cerros.* Lima: Universidad Peruana de Ciencias y Tecnología.

Vargas, Iraida. 1981. *Investigaciones Arqueológicas en Parmana.* Caracas: Biblioteca de la Academia Nacional de la Historia.

Vazavil, Rodrigo. 1921. "Información dada . . . la Entrada del Cerro de la Sal . . . (28/02/ 1687)." *Revista del Archivo Nacional* 2:391–410.

Vega, Agustín de. 1974. "Noticia del Principio de las Misiones de Gentiles en el Río Orinoco por la Compañía de Jesús." In *Documentos Jesuíticos Relativos a la Historia de la Compañía de Jesús en Venezuela.* 3 vols. Ed. José del Rey Fajardo. 2:3–149. Caracas: Biblioteca de la Academia Nacional de la Historia.

Vernant, Jean-Pierre. 1974. *Mythe et société en Grèce ancienne.* Paris: François Maspero.

Verdugo, Alonso. 1764. "Informe sobre las misiones de Mojos" (Santa Cruz, carta de 8/01/1764), Archive General de Indias (Sevilla) (AGI), Charcas, 474, fol. 12–16.

Vico, Gianbattista. 1970. *The New Science of Gianbattista Vico.* Ithaca, N.Y.: Cornell University Press.

Vidal, Silvia M. 1987. "El Modelo del Proceso Migratorio Prehispánico de los Piapoco: Hipótesis y Evidencias." Master's thesis, Centro de Estudios Avanzados, Instituto Venezolano de Investigaciones Científicas.

———. 1993. "Reconstrucción de los Procesos de Etnogénesis y de Reproducción Social entre los Baré de Río Negro, Siglos XVI–XVIII." Ph.D. diss., Centro de Estudios Avanzados, Instituto Venezolano de Investigaciones Científicas.

———. 1997. "Liderazgo y Confederaciones Multiétnicas Amerindias en la Amazonía Luso-Hispana del Siglo XVIII." *Antropológica* 87:19–46.

———. 1999. "Amerindian Groups of Northwest Amazon: Their Regional System of Political Religious Hierarchies." *Anthropos* 94:515–28.

———. 2000. "Kuwé Duwákalumi: The Arawak Secret Routes of Migration, Trade, and Resistance." *Ethnohistory* 47(3):221–80.

Vidal, Silvia, and Alberta Zucchi. 1996. "Impacto de la Colonización Hispanolusitana en las Organizaciones Sociopolíticas y Económicas de los Maipures-Arawakos del Alto Orinoco-Río Negro, Siglos XVII–XVIII." *América Negra* 11:107–29.

Vital, Antonio. 1985. "Crónica de la Entrada del Padre . . . a las Zonas Habitadas por los Cunibos y Campas" (1687). *Amazonía Peruana* 6(12):157–64.

Viveiros de Castro, Eduardo. 1984–85. "Proposta para um II Encontro Tupi." *Revista de Antropologia* 27–28:403–7.

———. 1992. *From the Enemy's Point of View: Humanity and Divinity in an Amazonian Society.* Chicago: University of Chicago Press.

———. 1993. "Alguns Aspetos da Afinidade no Dravidianato Amazônico." In *Amazônia: Etnologia e História Indígena.* Ed. Eduardo Viveiros de Castro and Manuela Carneiro da Cunha. 149–210. São Paulo: Núcleo de História Indígena e do Indigenismo da USP/FAPESP.

———. 1996. "Images of Nature and Society in Amazonian Ethnology." *Annual Review of Anthropology* 25:179–200.

———. 1998. "Cosmological Deixis and Amerindian Perspectivism." *Journal of the Royal Anthropological Society* 4(3):469–88.

Vygotsky, Lev S. 1986. *Thought and Language.* Cambridge, Mass.: MIT Press.

———. 1994. *The Vygotsky Reader.* Oxford: Blackwell.

Wallace, Alfred Russell. 1969. *A Narrative of Travels on the Amazon and Rio Negro, with an Account of the Native Tribes.* New York: Greenwood Press.

Wallerstein, Immanuel. 1974. *The Modern World-System: Capitalist Agriculture and the Origins of the European World-Economy in the Sixteenth Century.* New York: Academic Books.

Weiner, James. 1988. "Durkheim and the Papua Male Cult: Whitehead's Views on Social Structure and Ritual in New Guinea." *American Ethnologist* 15:567–73.

Weiss, Gerald. 1973. "Shamanism and Priesthood in Light of the Campa Ayahuasca Ceremony." In *Hallucinogens and Shamanism.* Ed. Michael J. Harner. 40–47. London: Oxford University Press.

———. 1975. *Campa Cosmology: The World of a Forest Tribe in South America.* New York: American Museum of Natural History.

Whitehead, Harriet. 1986. "The Varieties of Fertility Cultism in New Guinea." *American Ethnologist* 13:80–99, 271–289.

Whitehead, Neil L. 1988. *Lords of the Tiger Spirit: A History of the Caribs in Colonial Venezuela and Guyana, 1498–1820.* Dordrecht: Foris Publications.

———. 1990a. "Carib Ethnic Soldiering in Venezuela, the Guianas, and Antilles, 1492–1820." *Ethnohistory* 37(4):357–85.

———. 1990b. "The Snake Warriors—Sons of the Tiger's Teeth: A Descriptive Analysis of Carib Warfare, 1500–1820." In *The Anthropology of War.* Ed. Jonathan Haas. 146–70. Cambridge: Cambridge University Press.

———. 1992. "Tribes Make States and States Make Tribes: Warfare and the Creation of Colonial Tribe and State in Northeastern South America, 1492–1820." In *War and the*

Tribal Zone: Expanding States and Indigenous Warfare. Ed. Brian Ferguson and Neil L. Whitehead. 127–50. Santa Fe, N.Mex.: School of American Research Press.

———. 1993a. "Ethnic Transformation and Historical Discontinuity in Native Amazonia and Guayana, 1500–1900." *L'Homme* 33(2–4):289–309.

———. 1993b. "Native American Cultures along the Atlantic Littoral of South America, 1499–1650." *Proceedings of the British Academy* 81:197–231.

———. 1994. "The Ancient Amerindian Polities of the Amazon, the Orinoco, and the Atlantic Coast: A Preliminary Analysis of Their Passage from Antiquity to Extinction." In *Amazonian Indians from Prehistory to the Present: Anthropological Perspectives.* Ed. Anna C. Roosevelt. 33–53. Tucson: University of Arizona Press.

———. 1995a. "Ethnic Plurality and Cultural Continuity in the Native Caribbean: Remarks and Uncertainties as to Data and Theory." In *Wolves from the Sea: Readings in the Archaeology and Anthropology of the Island Carib.* Ed. Neil L. Whitehead. 91–111. Leiden, The Netherlands: KITLV Press.

———. 1995b. "Introduction: The Island Carib as Anthropological Icon." In *Wolves from the Sea: Readings in the Archaeology and Anthropology of the Island Carib.* Ed. Neil L. Whitehead. 9–22. Leiden, The Netherlands: KITLV Press.

———. 1996a. "Ethnogenesis and Ethnocide in the European Occupation of Native Surinam, 1499–1681." In *History, Power, and Identity: Ethnogenesis in the Americas, 1492–1992.* Ed. Jonathan D. Hill. 20–35. Iowa City: University of Iowa Press.

———. 1996b. "The Mazaruni Dragon: Golden Metals and Elite Exchanges in the Caribbean, Orinoco, and the Amazon." In *Chieftains, Power, and Trade: Regional Interaction in the Intermediate Area of the Americas.* Ed. Carl H. Langebaek and Felipe Cárdenas Arroyo. 107–32. Bogotá: Universidad de los Andes.

———. 1998a. "Colonial Chieftains of the Lower Orinoco and Guayana Coast." In *Chiefdoms and Chieftaincy in the Americas.* Ed. Elsa Redmond. 150–63. Gainesville: University Press of Florida.

———. 1998b. *The Discoverie of the Large, Rich, and Bewtiful Empire of Guiana by Sir Walter Ralegh.* Norman: University of Oklahoma Press.

———. 1999a. "The Crises and Transformations of Invaded Societies, 1492–1580: The Caribbean." In *The Cambridge History of the Native Peoples of the Americas.* 3 vols. Ed. Frank Salomon and S. Schwartz. 3(2):864–903. Cambridge: Cambridge University Press.

———. 1999b. "Native Peoples Confront Colonial Regimes in Northeastern South America, c. 1500–1900." In *The Cambridge History of the Native Peoples of the Americas.* 3 vols. Ed. Frank Salomon and S. Schwartz. 3(2):382–442. Cambridge: Cambridge University Press.

Whorf, Benjamin. 1962. *Language, Thought, and Reality.* Cambridge: Technology Press of Massachusetts Institute of Technology.

Wijmstra, Tiete A., and Thomas Van der Hammen. 1966. "Palynological Data on the History of Tropical Savannas in Northern South America." *Leidse Geologische Mededelingen* 38:71–90.

Williams, Dennis. 1981. "Excavation of the Barabina Shell Mound, North-West District." *Archaeology and Anthropology* 4(1):14–34.

Williams, Raymond. 1976. *Keywords: A Vocabulary of Culture and Society.* London: Fontana.

Wise, Mary Ruth. 1990. "Valence-Changing Affixes in Maipuran Arawakan Languages." In *Amazonian Linguistics: Studies in Lowland South American Languages.* Ed. Doris L. Payne. 90–116. Austin: University of Texas Press.

Wise, Mary Ruth, and Harold Green. 1971. "Compound Propositions and Surface Structure Sentences in Palikur." *Lingua* 26:252–80.

Wissler, Clark. 1917. *The American Indian: An Introduction to the Anthropology of the New World.* New York: Douglas C. McMurtrie.

Wolf, Eric. 1982. *Europe and the People without History.* Berkeley: University of California Press.

Woolard, Kathryn A. 1998. "Introduction: Language Ideology as a Field of Inquiry." In *Language Ideologies: Practice and Theory.* Ed. Bambi Schieffelin, Kathryn A. Woolard, and Paul V. Kroskrity. 3–47. New York: Oxford University Press.

Wright, Robin M. 1981. "The History and Religion of the Baniwa Peoples of the Upper Rio Negro Valley." Ph.D. diss., Stanford University.

———. 1983. "Lucha y Supervivencia en el Noroeste de la Amazonía." *América Indígena* 43(3):537–54.

———. 1987–89. "Uma História de Resistência: Os Heróis Baniwa e Suas Lutas." *Revista de Antropologia* 30–32:355–81.

———. 1990. "Guerras e Alianças nas Histórias dos Baniwa do Alto Rio Negro." In *Anuário de Antropologia, Política e Sociologia.* 217–36. São Paulo: Vertice/ANPOCS.

———. 1991. "Indian Slavery in the Northwest Amazon." *Boletim do Museu Paraense Emílio Goeldi* (Série Antropologia) 7(2):149–79.

———. 1992a. "Guardians of the Cosmos: Baniwa Shamans and Prophets." *History of Religions* 32(1):32–58, 32(2):126–45.

———. 1992b. "Uma Conspiração contra os Civilisados: História, Política e Ideologias dos Movimentos Milenaristas dos Arawak e Tukano do Noroeste da Amazônia." *Anuário Antropológico* 89:191–234.

———. 1992c. "História Indígena do Noroeste da Amazônia: Hipóteses, Questões e Perspectivas." In *História dos Índios no Brasil.* Ed. Manuela Carneiro da Cunha. 253–66. São Paulo: Fundação de Amparo à Pesquisa do Estado de São Paulo/Companhia das Letras/Secretaria Municipal de Cultura.

———. 1993. "Pursuing the Spirit: Semantic Construction in Hohodene Kalidzamai Chants for Initiation." *Amerindia* 18:1–40.

———. 1998. *Cosmos, Self, and History in Baniwa Religion: For Those Unborn.* Austin: University of Texas Press.

Wright, Robin M., and Jonathan D. Hill. 1986. "History, Ritual, and Myth: Nineteenth-Century Millenarian Movements in the Northwest Amazon." *Ethnohistory* 33(1):31–54.

Xerez, Joseph Antonio de. 1954. "Viaje del Padre Fray José Antonio de Xerez á las Misiones del Orinoco." In *Relaciones Geográficas de la Gobernación de Venezuela, 1767–68.* Ed. Angel de Altolaguirre y Duvale. 309–17. Caracas: Ediciones de la Presidencia de la República.

Yoffee, Norman. 1993. "Too Many Chiefs?; or, Safe Texts for the 90s." In *Archaeological Theory: Who Sets the Agenda?* Ed. Norman Yoffee and Andrew Sherratt. 60–78. Cambridge: Cambridge University Press.

Zarzar, Alonso. 1983. "Intercambio con el Enemigo: Etnohistoria de las Relaciones Inter-tribales en el Bajo Urubamba y Alto Ucayali." In *Relaciones Intertribales en el Bajo Urubamba y Alto Ucayali.* Ed. Alonso Zarzar and Luis Román. 11–86. Lima: Centro de Investigación y Promoción Amazónica.

Zucchi, Alberta. 1991a. "Las Migraciones Maipures: Diversas Líneas de Evidencia para la Interpretación Arqueológica." *América Negra* 1:113–38.

———. 1991b. "El Negro–Casiquiare–Alto Orinoco Como Ruta Conectiva entre el Ama-zonas y el Norte de Suramérica." In *Proceedings of the Twelfth Congress of the Interna-tional Association for Caribbean Archaeology.* 1–33. Martinique: International Associa-tion for Caribbean Archaeology.

———. 1991c. "Prehispanic Connections between the Orinoco, the Amazon, and the Caribbean Area." In *Proceedings of the Thirteenth Congress of the International Associ-ation for Caribbean Archaeology.* 202–20. Curaçao: International Association for Carib-bean Archaeology.

———. 1991d. "Procesos de Fisión, Migraciones Permanentes Tempranas y Etnicidad Arqueológica entre Grupos Maipures del Norte." In *Proceedings of the Fourteenth Con-gress of the International Association for Caribbean Archaeology.* 368–379. Barbados: International Association for Caribbean Archaeology.

———. 1992. "Lingüística, Etnografía, Arqueología y Cambios Climáticos: La Dispersión de los Arawako en el Noroeste Amazónico." In *Archaeology and Environment in Latin America.* Ed. Omar R. Ortiz-Troncoso and Thomas Van der Hammen. 223–52. Amster-dam: Instituut voor Pre-en Protohistorische Archeologie Albert Egges Van Giffen, Universiteit van Amsterdam.

———. 1993. "Datos Recientes para un Nuevo Modelo sobre la Expansión de los Gru-pos Maipure del Norte." *América Negra* 6:131–48.

Zucchi, Alberta, Krishna Ruette, and Keyla Vall. 2001. "La Construcción del Paisaje entre Algunos Grupos Arawakos." In *Proceedings of the Eighteenth Congress of the Interna-tional Association for Caribbean Archaeology.* Granada Island: International Association for Caribbean Archaeology.

Zucchi, Alberta, and Kay Tarble. 1984. "Los Cedeñoides: Un Nuevo Grupo Prehispánico del Orinoco Medio." *Acta Científica Venezolana* 35:293–309.

Zucchi, Alberta, Kay Tarble, and J. E. Vaz. 1984. "The Ceramic Sequence and New TL and C-14 Dates from the Aguerito Site of the Middle Orinoco." *Journal of Field Archaeolo-gy* 11(2):155–80.

Contributors

PETER GOW teaches in the Department of Social Anthropology at the London School of Economics and Political Science. He is the author of *Of Mixed Blood: Kinship and History in Peruvian Amazonia* (1991) and has done ethnographic and historical research with the Piro and neighboring indigenous peoples of eastern Peru for the past fifteen years.

MICHAEL J. HECKENBERGER teaches in the Department of Anthropology at the University of Florida and has done ethnographic and archaeological work with Arawakan peoples living in the Upper Xingu region of Brazil. He is the editor of a forthcoming book on the Upper Xingu peoples and is part of a research team doing field excavations at Acutuba along the Lower Rio Negro in Brazil.

JONATHAN D. HILL teaches in the Department of Anthropology at Southern Illinois University at Carbondale and has conducted ethnographic and historical research for the past twenty years in the Upper Rio Negro (Guainía) basin of Venezuela. He is the author of *Keepers of the Sacred Chants: The Poetics of Ritual Power in an Amazonian Society* (1993) and the editor of *Rethinking History and Myth: Indigenous South American Perspectives on the Past* (1988) and *History, Power, and Identity: Ethnogenesis in the Americas, 1492–1992* (1996).

ALAN PASSES is affiliated with the Centre for Indigenous American Studies and Exchange of the School of Philosophical and Anthropological Studies at the University of St. Andrews, Scotland, and has done fieldwork with the

Pai'kwené (Palikur) of northeastern Brazil. He is coeditor (with Joanna Overing) of *The Anthropology of Love and Anger: The Aesthetics of Conviviality in
Native Amazonia* (2000).

FRANCE-MARIE RENARD-CASEVITZ is a staff researcher with the
Equipe de Recherche en Ethnologie Amerindienne at the Centre National de
Recherche Scientifique in Paris, where she specializes in the ethnology and
history of the Machiguenga of eastern Peru. She is the author of *Le Banquet
Masqué: Une Mythologie de l'Etranger* (1991) and coauthor (with Thierry
Saignes and Anne Christine Taylor) of *L'Inca, l'Espagnol, et les Sauvages.
Rapports entre les Sociétés Amazoniennes et Andines du XVe au XVIIe Siècle*
(1986).

FERNANDO SANTOS-GRANERO is a staff researcher at the Smithsonian
Tropical Research Institute, Panama, and has done fieldwork with the Yanesha of eastern Peru. He is author of *The Power of Love: The Moral Use of
Knowledge amongst the Amuesha of Central Peru* (1991) and *Etnohistoria de
la Alta Amazonía, Siglos XV–XVIII* (1992). He is coauthor (with Frederica
Barclay) of *Selva Central: History, Economy and Land Use in Peruvian Amazonia* (1998) and *Tamed Frontiers: Economy, Society, and Civil Rights in Upper Amazonia* (2000). He is also coeditor (with Frederica Barclay) of the three-
volume work *Guía Etnográfica de la Alta Amazonía* (1994, 1994, 2000).

SIDNEY DA SILVA FACUNDES teaches in the Graduate Program of the
Universidade Federal do Pará. He specializes in the comparative linguistics
of the Arawakan family of languages in Lowland South America and has done
field research among the Apurinã of southwestern Brazil.

SILVIA M. VIDAL teaches in the Department of Anthropology at the Instituto Venezolano de Investigaciones Científicas and has done fieldwork
among Arawak-speaking peoples of the Upper Rio Negro in Venezuela for
the past twenty-five years. She is coeditor (with Alberta Zucchi) of *Historia
y Etnicidad en el Noroeste Amazónico* (1998).

NEIL L. WHITEHEAD teaches in the Department of Anthropology at the
University of Wisconsin at Madison and has done historical and ethnographic fieldwork on Arawak-speaking peoples of Guyana and the Caribbean Basin. He is the editor of *Ethnohistory* (journal) and *Wolves from the Sea: Readings in the Archaeology and Anthropology of the Island Carib* (1995), has
annotated a new edition of *The Discoverie of the Large, Rich, and Bewtiful*

Empire of Guiana by Sir Walter Ralegh (1998), and has coedited (with R. Brian Ferguson) *War in the Tribal Zone: Expanding States and Indigenous Warfare* (1993). He is also the author of *Lords of the Tiger Spirit: A History of the Caribs in Colonial Venezuela and Guyana, 1498–1820* (1988).

ROBIN M. WRIGHT teaches in the Department of Anthropology of the Instituto de Filosofia e Ciências Humanas at the Universidade Estadual de Campinas and has done fieldwork among the Baniwa of northwestern Brazil for twenty-five years. He is the author of *Cosmos, Self, and History in Baniwa Religion: For Those Unborn* (1998).

ALBERTA ZUCCHI teaches in the Department of Anthropology at the Instituto Venezolano de Investigaciones Científicas and has done extensive archaeological excavations in the Venezuelan Llanos east of the Andes as well as in the Upper Negro and Orinoco river basins in the Venezuelan Amazon. She is the author of *Caño Caroní: Un Grupo Prehispánico de la Selva de los Llanos de Barinas* (1975), coauthor (with William Denevan) of *Campos Elevados e Historia Cultural Prehispánica en los Llanos Occidentales de Venezuela* (1979), editor of *Simposio: Desarrollos Recientes en la Historia de los Llanos del Orinoco, Colombia y Venezuela* (1991), and coeditor (with Silvia Vidal) of *Historia y Etnicidad en el Noroeste Amazónico* (1998).

Index

Piro language, 85–91, 149, 150–52, 153–55, 157;
  toponymy, 161
plazas, 109, 111, 112, 120
plurilingualism. *See* multilingualism
polyandry, 145n
polygamy, 41, 46, 145n
polygyny, 40, 145n
polylingualism. *See* multilingualism
population: prehistoric levels, 101–2, 219;
  pressure, 116–19
Portuguese, 33–34, 180, 181, 260–62
pottery. *See* ceramics
pre-Andine Arawak, 123–25, 142, 143n, 156,
  158, 159, 167, 176; definition of, 129–30, 149,
  150–52; indigenous perspectives on, 153–
  56; origins of, 125–26. *See also* Campa;
  Matsiguenga
prisoners. *See* captives
prophets and prophetic movements, 270,
  274, 281–84, 285, 286–87, 288–90, 291–92
Protestants and Protestantism, 60, 64, 182. *See
  also* evangelical Christianity; evangelism
Proto-Apurinã-Bauré-Ignaciano, 159
Proto-Apurinã-Piro (P-AP), 87, 90
Proto-Apurinã-Piro-Iñapari (P-API), 74,
  86–87, 89–91, 96
Proto-Arauán (Proto-Arawá), 81, 122n
Proto-Arawak, 74, 80–82, 83, 86, 95, 100, 106,
  112, 113, 122n, 150, 151, 158, 200, 217, 218
Proto-Campa-Matsiguenga, 159
Proto-Carib, 122n
Proto-Indo-European, 77, 94
protolanguages, 20, 26, 81, 86–87, 91, 94–95,
  106, 158
Proto-Lokono-Guajiro, 85
Proto-Maipure (Proto-Maipuran), 81, 159,
  200, 217, 218
Proto-Pano, 122n
Proto-Tupi, 122n
Proto-Xingu, 85
punctuated equilibrium model, 94–95
Puquina, 81, 82, 122n
purity and purification, 269, 275–77, 281, 291

Quechua, 144n, 149, 170n

Radin, Paul, and *Indians of South America*,
  3–4, 15, 28
Rafinesque, Constantine S., 73n
raiding, 17, 29, 32, 37, 39, 41–42; of Pano, 134,
  144n; prohibition of, 130; for women, 47,
  68. *See also* warfare
"rank consciousness," 113–14, 122n

"rank revolution," 100, 119
rebellion: against Europeans, 262; Yekuana,
  243–45
reciprocity, 18, 162–63
reflex, 86–88
regionality (regional social organization),
  100, 102, 110, 111–12, 113–16, 118, 121
Reichel-Dolmatoff, Gerardo, 72
religion, 45, 47
Remo (Pano speakers), 28
Renard-Casevitz, France-Marie, 151–52, 153
residence: patterns, 40, 128–29; rules, 30, 46,
  138, 144n. *See also* patrilocality; uxorilocality; virilocality
Resígaro, 83–84, 220
Ricken, Ulrich, 73n
Rio Branco subfamily, 104
Rio Negro, 32–33, 84, 120, 228, 241, 261, 269–
  72, 290
ritual, 16, 17–19, 21, 31, 47, 72, 111–12, 114–15,
  116, 119, 225, 252, 253–55, 263–65, 266, 293n;
  Baniwa, 274; childbirth, 232–33; curing,
  240, 242, 269, 275, 280, 290; economy, 118;
  funerary, 55, 57, 115, 142; immersion, 143n;
  initiation and puberty, 18, 132, 139, 229,
  233–37, 240, 252, 253–55, 256–57, 264, 272;
  language and discourse, 46, 72, 234, 291; as
  performance, 46, 242; and warfare, 30, 115;
  whipping, 234, 255, 263–64, 265. *See also*
  chants; fertility cultism; Kúwai; landscape; *málikai;* myth; seclusion; shamanic
  discourse; shamans and shamanism
ritual hierarchies, among the Curripaco,
  230–31. *See also* fertility cultism
ritual societies, male, 253–55, 257–58, 266
ritual specialists, 208–9, 222n. *See also* shamans and shamanism
riverine lifeway, 101–2, 104, 106, 110–11, 112–
  13, 117–19
Rivet, Paul, 150–51, 176
Rochefort, Charles Cesar de, 60, 64–65
Rodrigues, Aryon Dall'Igna, 81, 122n
Rojas, Filintro A., 253
Roosevelt, Anna C., 108, 193n
Rouse, Irving, 53, 55, 70–71
Rousseau, Jean-Jacques, 61, 65
rubber boom, 6, 135, 145n, 267, 281; diaspora,
  126, 228
rubber trade, 6, 30, 32, 159, 166, 224, 225

Sabana de los Mojos, 123, 135, 136–37, 139,
  140, 141, 145n
sacred places. *See* landscape

Tukano (Tucano) languages, 12, 35, 49, 94, 271
Tupac Amaru, 129, 144n
Tupi, 18, 115
Tupi-Guaraní, 72, 115, 116, 122n
Tupi languages, 12, 54, 59, 73n, 94–95, 102
Turner, Terence, 191
Turuqueira, 57

umbilical cord, symbolism of, 232–33, 234, 237, 242
Upatarinavo, 49
uplands, 101–2, 103
Upper Xingu, 109, 111, 112, 115; region, 134
Urban, Greg, 27, 122n, 160
uxorilocality, 46, 128, 138, 139, 144n

Varese, Stefano, 130
várzea, 100–101, 122n
Vaupés River basin, 35, 94, 143n, 223–24, 228
vendettas, 17, 30, 40, 130, 144n; Iroquois, 144n; prohibition of, 130
viceroys, Spanish, 124, 127
Vidal, Silvia, 32–33, 37, 202, 273, 292n
Vilcabamba: empire, 124, 127, 130; region, 136
villages, 109, 111, 112–13, 114, 120, 122n; Bauré, 137; interethnic, 144n. *See also malocas*
violence, 17, 29–30, 45. *See also* raiding; warfare
virilocality, 40, 46
Viveiros de Castro, Eduardo, 163, 165
vocabularies, 87; Piro, 151; quantitative study of, 78–80; reconstruction of, 90–91, 95
Vygotsky, Lev S., 65

Wainuma, 220
Wakuénai. *See* Curripaco
Wallerstein, Immanuel, 173
Wanano, 36, 225
Wapishana, 104
Warao, 67
Warekena, 34, 200–201, 205, 218, 220, 228, 248, 270, 272, 292n; myth, 256–58, 273; ritual, 263–65; social organization, 251–53
warfare, 29–34, 36–37, 40, 41–42, 45, 47–48,

67, 261; absence of, 188; against Andean peoples, 144n; Apuriná, 160, 162–63; endo-, 15, 17–18, 29, 32, 36, 38–39, 41–42, 45–46, 47, 115; Pano, 29; prohibition of, 130–31, 142; ritual, 39, 258; shamanic, 182; among "sub-Andine Arawak," 152
Waríperi-dakéenai, 201, 203, 218
Watunna, 230, 244–45
Waurá, 83, 183, 189
weaving. *See* textiles and weaving
Weiss, Gerald, 151
whipping (ritual), 234, 255, 263–64, 265
Whitehead, Neil L., 27, 39, 48, 179, 230–31, 149
Wissler, Clark, 26
witchcraft, 241–42, 276–77, 280, 281, 284, 292n
women: captured in raids, 29, 37, 39, 41, 53, 68; among the Mojos, 137–38; and ritual, 264
Wright, Robin, 35, 36, 201, 267

Xingu, 134, 149, 176
Xinguano, 85, 104, 116

Yabaana, 84
Yaminahua, 155
Yanesha, 29, 30, 129, 143n, 150, 151–52, 158, 159; ironworks, 31; myth, 130; and the Piro, 154–55; province of, 125; salt mines, 145n; self-definition, 133; shamans, 139; social organization, 46–47, 122n
Yanesha language, 104, 149, 157–58
Yao, 42, 67, 178, 179–80, 187
Yavitero, 84, 220, 265
Yekuana (Ye'kuana), 42, 230
Yekuana Uprising, 243–45
Yine. *See* Piro
Yineru, 152
Yukuna, 35, 84, 218, 220, 270, 272
Yumaguaris, 33
Yumana-Passé, 220
Yuruparí myth, 72

Zucchi, Alberta, 33, 104

The University of Illinois Press
is a founding member of the
Association of American University Presses.

————————————————————————

University of Illinois Press
1325 South Oak Street
Champaign, IL 61820-6903
www.press.uillinois.edu

Printed by Printforce, United Kingdom